Amazin' Met Memories

Four Decades of Unforgettable Moments

HOWARD BLATT

with an Introduction
by
Bud Harrelson

ALBION PRESS
Tampa, Florida

Library of Congress Cataloging-in-Publication Data

Blatt, Howard.
    Amazin' Met memories : four decades of unforgettable moments / Howard Blatt; with an introduction by Bud Harrelson.
      p. cm.
    ISBN 0-9709170-2-3
  1. New York Mets (Baseball team)—History. I. Title.
    GV875.N45 B53 2002
    796.357'64'097471—dc21

                          2001007452

Interior design and typesetting by Sue Knopf, Graffolio.

Photos courtesy AP/Wide World Photos.

Published by Albion Press, Tampa, Florida.

Printed in Canada.

To my son, Marc, who taught me how to love
unconditionally and whose birth represents
my all-time most amazing moment;
to my mother, Ruth, for having her most amazing moment
when she gave birth to me;
and to my pop, Irving, who showed me how much it meant
that we would always have Flushing.

Contents

Part 2: Greatest Games in Met History

Part 3: Metscellaneous

Bibliography

Acknowledgments

Much thanks to my lovely and talented crackerjack co-researcher Lee Stowbridge for his invaluable time and feedback. Also much appreciated was the encouragement and the direction provided by Cliff Chanin, still my best man after all these seasons. Thanks, also, to Bud Harrelson for being generous with his time; to Lonnie Herman and David Wilk for seeing the wisdom of this project; to all the dedicated baseball writers whose work, on deadline, provided the basis for the accounts in this book; to the Elias Sports Bureau for their help; to the inimitable Elli Wohlgelernter for applying his compulsiveness to my cause; and finally to my wife, Nina, for breaking me out of the prison that is the newspaper business.

Introduction

Buddy Harrelson

Although I no longer work for the Mets, I will always be a Met. It delights me to be remembered and recognized as a 1969 Met and to see the other guys from that championship team a few times a season for card shows and appearances—because it was a special group of players, unique in that we truly pulled for each other and were united by a lifetime bond. It's still enjoyable for me to hear supporters of that team recall, after so many years, what that World Series victory meant. It meant and continues to mean quite a bit to those who played on that team, too.

Over three decades, from when the Mets signed a skinny shortstop from northern California in 1963 until six years ago, I did almost everything there is to do in the game as part of the Mets organization. I was a Met player in 1,322 games from 1965 through 1977, winning a World Series and an NL pennant and making the All-Star team twice. I was the first-base coach for George Bamberger in 1982, a SportsChannel color man on games in '83, a minor league manager who won a championship with Little Falls of the New York-Penn League in '84, a third-base coach and bench coach for Davey Johnson from 1985 through 1990, a major league manager for part of 1990 and all but the last week of '91 and an American League scout and a roving instructor.

When I came to the Mets to stay in 1966, a veteran pitcher named Jack Fisher told me, "Kid, you are going to be very popular here. Take advantage of it. Move here and make some money in the winters." I did. I moved here from California soon after I was promoted to the majors. I have lived in Long Island for 32 years. Everybody thinks I am from here and I did make my roots here. These days, I am one of the owners and the director of player procurement for the Long Island Ducks of the independent Atlantic League—and I consider my baseball legacy to be bringing affordable, minor league baseball to Suffolk County.

Three decades of being part of the Mets produced a lot of memories, mostly joyous, a few painful.

My happiest recollections come from that 1969 season. Although some players on that team had their differences, we were genuinely committed to each other. We did something that has only become more historical as time has passed, because it hasn't been done that many times in sports. We're still living off that and that is OK, because it really was special.

Over the years, I have kept in touch with some of the guys who remained in the New York area, including Tommie Agee, Sham (Art Shamsky), Ed Charles, Krane (Eddie Kranepool) and Tom Seaver, before he moved back to the West Coast. And when Tommie recently died of a heart attack at 58—he is greatly missed—reality set in for all of us. It was sobering. I celebrated my 57th birthday recently. I was born June 6, 1944, or D-Day, as broadcaster Lindsey Nelson always enjoyed mentioning, because he was there (not at my birth).

We were at least partially aware, while it was unfolding in 1969, that we were part of something special and that there was a quality of our achievement that made it somehow bigger than us. It's still a ride for us. I sign autographs and the father says, "Can you put '69 Mets on it?" I say sure. I was 25. There was so much more ahead. It was impossible to fully appreciate the pure wonder of it at the time, but that doesn't mean we didn't love every minute.

After every victory, we would sort of shrug and say, "Well, we won another one." I remember we swept a doubleheader in Pittsburgh by identical 1-0 scores—and each of our pitchers, Jerry Koosman and Don Cardwell, drove in the only runs (Sept. 12). The Pirates' Bob Moose pitched a no-hitter against us (Sept. 20 at Shea), but it didn't even slow us down. We took it in stride and said, "We can't win without a hit, so let's move on."

It really came together after the front office brought Donn Clendenon into the mix, at the trade deadline. Until then, we didn't have that one guy who could hit a three-run homer, the way that Darryl Strawberry did for the 1986 Mets. With one swing from Clendenon, all of a sudden, we had a three-run lead. And he was a good guy and very happy to be in New York.

He said, "It is wonderful being on a club that has good young pitching. In Pittsburgh, we would lose, 20-2." They called Donn "Clink," but he was outstanding with the glove at first base. I threw balls way high sometimes and he'd just get on his toes, reach up and pull them down. I'd say, "Wow, it's nice having him over there."

The Baltimore Orioles were loaded, with great starting pitching and a lineup featuring Frank and Brooks Robinson and Boog Powell, among others. Man for man, none of us rated an advantage at any position in the newspaper matchups. Maybe Seaver and Jim Palmer were a push, but after that, forget it. You even had to take Mark Belanger over Bud Harrelson at shortstop. But, as I said at the time, you don't win on paper.

We were just happy to be there. We won 100 games and everybody in baseball said, "OK, they beat St. Louis and Chicago and they won the National League East." Then people said, "Well, they are not going to beat the Braves. Look at the hitting on the Braves." When we swept Atlanta in the NLCS, it was, "Now they'll never get by the Orioles." We didn't care what people said. Things were going our way and it felt like the whole nation was rooting for us. We were just moving with the force that was happening around us.

I am certain that a big part of that force was Gil Hodges. Maybe he was the charm. To lose the first game and then never lose again in the World Series was amazing. And, of course, so many strange things happened—the bunt play with J.C. Martin in Game 4 and the hit-by-pitch controversies with Frank Robinson and Cleon Jones in Game 5.

There were questionable things, including that famous shoe polish incident with Cleon, which were ruled in our favor, because Gil was the manager. Hodges would say, "Good teams make their breaks." But there were breaks we got simply because Gil was the manager on our side and Earl Weaver, who had the reputation of arguing all the time, was the manager on the other. Gil was so well-respected by the umpires. They might think Weaver would trick them by applying shoe polish on the ball—but they never thought Gil would do something like that.

Of course, that wouldn't work now, because they don't polish the shoes.

Gil taught me so much. He talked to players individually and made them better individually and he never showed up players in front of other players. I was one of the guys whom he really liked and he would bring me into the office to talk because he wanted to make me smarter. I would ask a question and he would say, "This is what you should be thinking." He taught me how to be more professional, that to err is human, but to make a mental mistake is not professional.

Everyone on that club felt the same way about him: you were afraid of him, you respected him and you loved him. And there were times you didn't like him, because maybe he punched you in the ass. But, to a man, the guy scared the shit out of us. Partly, it was because of his physical size, but it also was because he would be quiet and then just tear up the clubhouse.

There was the famous time when we were getting swept in a double-header by the Astros and Gil walked out to left and pulled Cleon in the middle of a 10-run Houston third inning, because Hodges felt that Cleon hadn't hustled. What Gil did made a statement: If you can't give your all, don't be out there—and that applies to everyone, including the guy who hit .340.

I can remember the day it happened (July 30). He came walking toward the mound and kept walking. He started coming toward me and he said, "No, the other guy," and I walked with him out to left.

Gil said, "Are you OK, Cleon?"

Cleon said, "My leg is bothering me a little bit."

Gil said, "Come with me."

Everyone knew what the actual significance of the substitution was. I don't know if you could get away with that if you were managing now. In fact, when people ask me what Gil would do with some of today's players, I tell them that he probably would have wound up in in prison.

Hodges made tough rules, things like no jeans and mandatory ties on the road, and he stuck with them. They applied to everyone— including Frank Howard, who was about the same age as Gil when Hodges was his manager with the Senators. I carried those dress rules over when I became manager.

Gil communicated a sense of professionalism and he was always ahead of everybody. You would think that it might soon be time for a pitching change and then you would look up and see he already had someone up.

However, Gil did almost nothing his first year of managing the Mets, in 1968, when we finished next to last. He just let us play and watched and evaluated. Then he mixed in some new veteran players in 1969 and went to work.

The first time he addressed us during spring training in '69, Gil appealed to our pride and our good sense.

He said, "You guys lost 37 one-run games last year [the 1968 Mets had a 26-37 record in one-run games]. You are a good defensive team and you have good pitching. You need to think a little more positively in the late innings, instead of thinking, 'Here we go, we're going to lose by one run again.' If you win half of those games you lost, you will be a contending ballclub. If every pitcher on this ballclub wins one more game than last season, we'll be a contender."

Hodges really knew how to get the most out of his players and he was definitely the biggest reason we went from second-to-last to a championship team. If he hadn't died so soon after 1969 (of a heart attack, April 2, 1972), the whole Met franchise might have taken another course. Gil would've been the perfect guy to move into the front office when he had had enough of managing.

As it was, we won another pennant in 1973—the hard way. We were banged up for most of the season, but then we made a September run that pushed us to the top of the East, even though we managed only 82 wins and didn't hit the top until September 21. Tug McGraw always said that the 1969 Mets weren't the Miracle Mets (even though there was a halo around that team), the 1973 Mets were. And he was right.

We had Rusty Staub on the '73 club and he was like Clendenon had been for the '69 team. We'd come back to the clubhouse when he was slumping and the team was losing and Rusty would say, "Come on, guys, what is this? Can't we win without me hitting?" He had the right attitude. We realized he was right, we had jobs to do. In September, Rusty said, "Guys, face it. We can't lose another series all year. It's simple." We were down here and Pittsburgh was way up there. What helped us was that the last month we were playing the people above us so we steadily climbed. We didn't lose many series. We won two of three. We won three of four.

I remember that 13-inning game against the Pirates (Sept. 20) at Shea, when a ball hit by Dave Augustine hit the top of the fence in left field and caromed right back to Cleon, who threw to Wayne Garrett, who was our shortstop that night. Garrett threw out the Pirate runner trying to score from first. He was Richie Zisk, who was slow. I had been surprised they didn't pinch-run for him.

The finish was remarkable—it was the kind of game that fuels "team of destiny" talk. Honestly, those games only truly become magical after you win a pennant—and then you remember the magic that happened along the way. That 1973 team didn't hit its stride until Tug got his season turned around. He struggled for most of '73—and I don't know if it was because of some personal problems or whether it was mechanical.

On the mound, McGraw was a craftsman, a tough cookie with ability. And Tug was always happy. He was always laughing. In fact, since his retirement, Tug has had some heart problems, but he said to me, "It's not like I have been doing anything to avoid it." Back in those

Reds' Pete Rose, left, gets in the face of bantamweight Buddy Harrelson after the short-stop expressed disgust with a cheap-shot slide, triggering a wrestling match and an ugly scene that left the natives restless at Shea.

days, McGraw would say, "All right, guys there is no more Irish whiskey left here. We need to go to another state."

Now he is on the wagon and he has a new child.

The lasting memory for most people from the 1973 post-season—when we beat the Reds for the pennant after they had won 99 games and then extended the Athletics to seven games before losing in the World Series—is my wrestling match with Pete Rose in the fifth inning of NLCS Game 3.

All the fuss began with a casual comment and attempt at humor that I had made to the press after Game 2, in which Jon Matlack shut out and shut down Cincinnati. Matlack had pitched a great game. They had trouble fouling the ball off against him that day—that is the kind of stuff he had. His pitches had moved everywhere. I mean, he had just dismantled the Big Red Machine.

I lockered next to Matlack and the reporters were crowded around him while I sat and sipped my beer. And one of them asked me what I thought of the way Cincinnati had hit in the game. I said, "They all looked like me hitting." That was all I said. I don't think that got back to the Reds exactly as spoken, because, if it was just those words, I think they would have understood. But they were annoyed at what they felt was a major slight from me.

Before Game 3 at Shea, Joe Morgan came out during the warmups and grabbed my uniform shirt just under my neck and said, "If you ever say that about me again . . ."

He was very perturbed. And I knew Joe, who also came from northern California. I said, "What the hell are you talking about?"

Rusty, who had heard what I had said to the writers, came over—he had played with Morgan in Houston—and said, "Joe, he didn't say shit."

Then Joe relaxed and said, one middle infielder to another, "Pete is going to use this to get the club fired up. If he has a chance, he is going to come and get you at second."

With us leading by a 9-2 score in the fifth, Rose slid on a 3-6-3 double-play ball, then got up and hit me with his elbow. I made him slide. He was down and I was watching my relay throw when he nailed me. I had had the warning from Morgan. I had broken my hand covering second earlier in the year, but I never worried about that stuff. I might have been small and frail-looking, but I never was afraid.

I said to Pete, "That was a cheap fucking shot."

He said, "What did you say?"

I repeated it. I got in his face and he grabbed my arms. As he grabbed me and took me down, Garrett clobbered him and I wound up on top of Pete. I had this Red arm choking me, but it was one of their coaches, pulling me out of there. I suffered a bruise over my eye, but it came from my broken sunglasses.

I was shaking. It all happened so fast.

I guess the reason the crowd at Shea was so angry afterwards—Rose and the Reds left the field briefly because of the flying objects thrown from the stands—had to be the David and Goliath thing. I was David. Pete wasn't that much taller than me, but he was 50 pounds bigger.

The famous picture from that incident was taken the next day, when I taped an "X" over the "S" on the Superman T-shirt that I always wore under my uniform. I was trying to make light of things.

Truth is, I had liked Rose before the fight and liked him after it. I wound up playing with him in Philadelphia. I like guys who hustle and scratch and who are overachievers. He would go first to third on any outfielder. And I have seen Pete a lot over the years at shows. We sign boxing gloves and pictures. Pete likes to say that, although he won all those batting titles and championships and set the all-time hit record, that fight is what people remember the most about his playing days.

Pete homered in Game 4 to get Cincinnati even in that series, but Seaver beat the Reds in Game 5. And Tom was a very special teammate for me. As roommates, we became close.

I vividly remember my first look at him. It was in Homestead, Fla. and Tom came walking in during spring training of '66. He had just been plucked out of the hat by the Mets in that drawing after the commissioner had voided his deal with the Braves because it was ruled that

Atlanta had illegally given him a $50,000 bonus. He had all this notoriety, coming out of USC.

My assumption was this big shot, this guy whom all these teams had bid on, would come marching in like he owned the place. I was from California, but I went to San Francisco State for a year. Not USC. We had heard that he was coming and he walked out onto the field with this entourage of reporters. He had his USC Trojan shirt, that reddish thing, under his uniform and, even though it was brutally hot, he had this long-sleeve shirt on.

Seaver got loose as we were working out and then they marched him out to throw batting practice. You would have thought that, with everyone watching, this kid would have made it into pitching practice. Instead, he threw ball after ball nice and easy, to be hit, just like I would throw them as a coach during BP, so guys could get their swings. I said to myself, "I like this guy."

Seaver maintained that pragmatic approach throughout his whole career. He didn't do anything to impress you. Tom just did things to get himself ready. In his first couple of starts in spring training, he would throw fastball after fastball—no matter how the hitters would tee off on them. Then, he would kick it into gear for the season in his last two starts and throw breaking balls. Before that, he was just doing his work.

Both of us were sent to Jacksonville. I was already married and he had Nancy with him. Soon, they were engaged and got married. I came up to the Mets in August 1966, after Roy McMillan had blown out his shoulder for the last time. Then we were together with the Mets in '67, which was Seaver's first full year with the team. When we broke camp, he was asked whom he wanted to room with and he said, "I know only one guy on this team—Harrelson."

That was an eight-year marriage. We got along well. We were both California kids, one northern and one southern. He was a pitcher and I was a regular player. He liked rooming with someone who was not on his schedule and so did I. You didn't see us having breakfast every day together.

The first time we went on the road as roommates, Tom walked into the room, turned on all the lights and the television and went in to brush his teeth. He came out and said, "Will the lights and the TV bother you?" I was out cold already.

To this day, he calls me "roomie." I call him "roomie." And Nancy calls me "roomie."

To me, what set Seaver apart from other pitchers, even great pitchers, was that Tom could throw or he could pitch. That was something that even Dwight Gooden and Nolan Ryan had a tough time doing. Of course, Ryan didn't really have to adjust much—he was a power pitcher every night, throughout his career. Seaver was the best self-analyst among the pitchers I have seen. He would come in from his warmups in the bullpen knowing exactly what he had to work with in that game and adjust accordingly.

Bud Harrelson, with moustache, and Tom Seaver, with sunglasses, watch their kiddies frolic on a sea wall during spring 1974. The bond between roommates was strong and the night of Seaver's exile was nearly as painful for Buddy as for The Franchise.

People used to say that I played better behind him and I did—but it wasn't because I was trying harder. It was because if the pitch was supposed to be a fastball away, it was a fastball away. If it was supposed to be a fastball in, it was a fastball in. You could always anticipate where to play and in which direction to cheat. When he didn't have his good fastball, he would throw his slow stuff more often and hit spots. Sometimes, he would come back after throwing a fastball, pick up the rosin bag and gesture to me to move back in a step.

Was Seaver that much better than Jerry Koosman or Gary Gentry? Well, Gentry had nasty stuff and was the guy a lot of teams didn't want to face—but he could lose it in the first inning. Koosman would get screwed up sometimes and it might take him a while to get right, but for nine innings, he was as strong as anybody. But Tom always controlled his game. He would say to me, "I only have to make five pitches [at critical moments] to win." And I would look at him funny, but, if you thought about it, he was right.

Seaver always knew just what he was doing, right from the start of his career. In that way, Seaver was like Johnny Bench, who, as a young catcher when he first came up with the Reds, controlled those major league pitchers from the start. Bench and Seaver knew what they were doing—and that is just a gift. You said, "Jesus, this guy is only 21 years old—look at him. He is playing like he has been around for five or six years." Very few guys come up and do that as rookies.

When Tom was dealt away, on June 15, 1977, it was like losing my brother. In fact, I had spent more time with him than I had with my brother. He said, "They are going to do it. They will trade me." I didn't believe him, because even at that point we felt he was going to be a Hall of Famer. It has become common for future Hall of Famers to be traded now, but back then it was a little different. I just couldn't believe they were doing this based on what the difference was in money between what he wanted and what they were willing to pay him.

The night before it happened, he said to me, Koosman and Jerry Grote, who all hung out together, "Come on, we're going out tonight.

I will be gone tomorrow." We were in Atlanta and we went out to dinner, kind of like the Four Musketeers. Then later, sometime during the game, they called him to the clubhouse and I went in and he said to me, "They traded me to Cincinnati." And I cried. I came back out and we still had a game to play and I still had to play in it. The guys said, "You will get over this."

But it was not that easy for me.

And, by the end of that season, I knew that I was in trouble and my Met days were numbered, too, because Doug Flynn was one of the four players who came over in the Seaver trade. Flynn's best position was second base, but manager Joe Torre decided he would play more at shortstop. I understood the pressure on Torre to go with younger players.

By the age of 30, a middle infielder is already old, and I had gone through some knee surgeries by the time I was 33. In the spring of 1978, I was traded to the Phillies. By that point, it was a relief to me, because I knew that I wouldn't be playing much if I stayed with the Mets.

I just didn't understand the way the Mets handled my departure.

In the winter, the Mets got Tim Foli from the Giants and announced he would be their regular shortstop—and the way I heard about that was on the television news.

I called (GM) Joe McDonald and I said to him, "I just saw you got Foli and he'll be the regular shortstop. Out of respect for me, you could have at least called and told me."

He said, "Well, we don't really need your services anymore."

When I came to spring training, I said to Torre every day, "Please trade me. You have to help me out." And I went to the writers and said, "Do me a favor and ask them what they are going to do with me?"

The Mets wanted me to be a backup and work with a couple of other guys at shortstop.

Piggy (coach Joe Pignatano) said to me, "Stay. You can be here as a backup."

I said to him, "Piggy, I am hurt. I can't stay here."

I always felt, when you play regularly for so long with one team, it is much easier to be a backup on some other team.

I am a guy who didn't even have an agent and I had given them everything I had for a lot of years. I had played hurt—never with broken bones, but I played with a lot of stuff.

When I broke my sternum, I played the game the next night. I walked into the clubhouse that night and I said to Seaver, "I'm hurt." And he said, "Get back to your locker. You are playing tonight. I am pitching." Then they sent me for an X-ray and they found the break after that. That stuff counts with players—but not necessarily with management.

I felt a bit burned by the way I exited.

By the time I decided I had enough of playing, things had changed in the organization and Frank Cashen was in charge. I hit .272 for the Rangers in 1980, my last year, and I could have continued my playing career. I had said when the Phillies released me that I wanted to walk away from the game on my own terms and I did. Now, I was ready to move on.

I came back to the majors to stay in 1985, as a third-base coach for Davey Johnson in the middle of the season, when Bobby Valentine left to take the Texas managerial job. I had Wally Backman in my house in New York and I had to evict him, because I was coming back. And, honestly, I had mixed emotions, because I liked it down in Columbia, S.C., where I was managing. I had never really decided that I had wanted to manage. It just sort of happened. But, in the minors, it was a great experience. You are working with raw talent and you aren't working with guys making 30 times what you are.

Anyway, in 1985, Dwight Gooden was in his second season with the Mets—the best season of his career—and he was so young and very talented and Davey made sure he didn't lose. Lots of times, he would pull Doc out of games early after he had done a good job. Davey nurtured Gooden—and that treatment was very different than the one accorded Darryl Strawberry when he first arrived in 1983. Darryl came up as King Kong.

Gooden was one of the most amazing young arms I had ever seen, because Doc could throw you a 3-and-2 hook and get you. He was like Ryan in that he could walk the bases loaded and then strike out the side. You could steal second and then steal third on him and Doc would just leave you standing there.

I remember during one of the Mets' Old-Timers games early in Doc's career, the team had Gooden walk in alongside Willie Mays from center field. And I said to myself: Yikes, what a thing to do to such a young kid so early in his career. He was a kid who, at a young age, pitched like a veteran. But to clearly place those Hall of Fame expectations on him cannot have helped him.

As for Straw, almost everyone who played with him, coached him or managed him liked him. They worry about what will become of him now that he is no longer in the game, because they know he was his own worst enemy and he was always best when he was on the field. You can't do all the stuff that he did and be functional at baseball. He always seemed to get back and then self-destruct again—and now, of course, he is sick and that is very sad.

What struck me most about Darryl was the way he was with kids: unbelievably warm and caring. He is so much more outgoing than Doc, who was sort of reserved and shy. I'd say, "Straw, I got this kid. He is in the hospital and he is dying." And he would say, "Sure." I would leave and then come back and he would still be on the phone. I hung around and hung around and he was still on the phone. He was talking to this kid for 20 minutes and most players would just say, "Feel better."

Straw simply related to kids. He would come in after batting practice, take off his batting gloves and hand them to some kid. He would make these kids' lives and he was always doing things like that. Darryl was really giving, but the sad reality is he simply couldn't control himself. But even half of the player that he might have been was awfully good.

When I replaced Davey as the manager in 1990, my first meeting was with Straw and my third meeting was with Straw and my fifth meeting was with Straw. I just told him that he needed to be a leader on the ballclub. He said, "Yeah, yeah."

I said, "No, not a cheerleader, a leader by example on the field. When other players see you standing around the outfield before games and you don't want to take flyballs or outfield practice or you are not really into batting practice, it sucks us down. Sometimes in baseball, you have to be the 'Great Pretender.' No matter how you feel, no matter what you did the night before, you have to be the Great Pretender and bust your ass. Then, it is all right to go 0-for-4."

Actually, the one season in which I managed him, Straw played hard and he was actually a better outfielder, so I think he heard me. I thought he had a marvelous year in 1990. But he hurt his back late in '90 and he didn't play when we needed him at the end. I don't know if he should have or could have played through it. I was shocked he didn't play at the time. But I don't know if it was the result of a bad turn in his contract negotiations. His deal was up at the end of that year and, of course, he did eventually leave for Los Angeles as a free agent.

The following year, 1991, was a difficult one. The media got on my case, right from spring training, because now this was my team. Jeff Torborg, who came in to manage after me, said, "I know New York. I was a coach here [with the Yankees]." Of course, the media ate him up, too.

However, I admit that I didn't handle a lot of things well. I am a pretty sensitive guy. I went through my playing career trying hard and everybody loved me. Suddenly, I was the boss and I was making mistakes. It was hard for me. I was less experienced than my own bench coach, Doc Edwards.

In 1990, I made $140,000 as manager because they doubled my coaching salary. In 1991, I made $200,000 and WFAN Radio paid me about $35,000 to do a call-in show with Howie Rose. It was done just before the game and it was all about yesterday's game. It was Bernie from Brooklyn and Stan from Staten Island—the same guys all the time—and Howie was trying to get answers for these guys about strategy from me. Eventually, I had enough of explaining myself to them and I quit it. It was a big negative. And I could have used the $35,000. But, the way it was working, I figured that nobody pays me enough to abuse me, so take back the money.

It was the way the Mets fired me that hurt the most—with five games left in the season. I had no contract for 1992 anyway. So there was no reason to announce it then—other than that Cashen was leaving and Al Harazin was taking over as GM and they wanted him to have a clean slate. They could have just left it alone, then announced we are not exercising Buddy's option, that he will be a scout, and we're hiring Torborg.

Instead, when I took my kid to the bus stop on Monday morning, after they had fired me on the previous Saturday night, every kid on the bus was booing me and my kids didn't want to get on the bus. I was Bud Harrelson, long-time New Yorker. I wasn't going home to Iowa. I was staying right here. That hurt.

I felt they should have tried to do right by the guy who had always done right by them.

But time heals all wounds.

I worked for the Mets in community relations and visited schools during the strike year, when, understandably, nobody from the organization wanted to talk to the public. I always represented the team with enthusiasm and with pride.

And I feel honored to have been asked to be the player writing this introduction to this book of Amazin' Met Memories—because I am a Met and always will be a Met at heart.

PART 1

Greatest Post-Season Games

One Strike from Winter of Regret, Mets Shock Themselves, Red Sox

METS 6, RED SOX 5

1986 World Series Game 6
October 25, 1986 in New York

The closing curtain was creeping down on the Mets in Game 6 of the 1986 World Series. The Red Sox had taken a 5-3 lead with two runs in the 10th inning and 20 cases of borrowed champagne were on ice in the visitors' locker room at Shea.

Long-suffering fans in New England and even some Boston players had begun celebrating a championship so long in coming—the franchise's last one occurred in 1918 and was followed by the heartbreak of World Series Game 7 defeats in 1946, 1967 and 1975—that the inability to wait any longer was understandable. Even the message board at Shea Stadium oozed resignation as it briefly, graciously and prematurely flashed "Congratulations, Red Sox."

The television cameras panned the dugouts, recording the high drama of the moment: the faces of the Red Sox, filled with the joy of overcoming the burden of franchise history at last, and the faces of the

Mets, pained and empty to be staring at a bottom line of defeat. After 108 regular-season victories and then a heart-stopping, Mike Scott-defying NLCS triumph over Houston, the 1986 Mets were about to be relegated to the status of historical footnote: a wire-to-wire team that never did cross the final wire.

Losing the first two games of this World Series at home, the first by a 1-0 score on an unearned run, was going to haunt the Mets, after all. Dave Henderson's leadoff homer on a sinker, Wade Boggs' double and Marty Barrett's RBI single off Rick Aguilera in the 10th inning of Game 6 were now looming as the final memories that these Mets would carry into a winter of being asked, "Hey, what happened to you guys in the World Series, anyway?"

And, after so much swagger, so many fights and so many comebacks from the brink, the Mets were feeling humility and desperation as they saw their three remaining outs become one.

After ex-Met reliever Calvin Schiraldi retired virus-weakened Wally Backman on a weak fly to left and then got Keith Hernandez on a long shot to center for the second out, Hernandez flung his helmet to the turf, returned to the dugout long enough to grab his glove and his cap, stalked off to the clubhouse and finally plopped himself down in a director's chair in manager Davey Johnson's office and lit up a cigarette. Hernandez felt the final out would be easier to bear here, inhaling, than watching from the losing dugout.

If you think hope still burned brightly in the Mets' dugout, that players were shouting encouragement to each other and the Mets, to a man, believed that things would turn out fine, think again.

"I was going to go out and get drunk and stay up all night," said Hernandez. "I was thinking about eating a hamburger at 7 a.m."

Hope was indeed dead, or at least mortally wounded, and the morose Met faces screamed it was the end of the line.

Meanwhile, Oil Can Boyd, the Red Sox' scheduled Game 7 starter, was dancing in the Boston dugout. His teammates were only slightly more restrained, lining the top step.

Aguilera, one out away from being the losing pitcher in the final game of the 1986 Series, sat quietly in the dugout.

"My heart was breaking. Just a terrible feeling I had, as well as we played all game . . ." he said. "Down two runs and two outs . . ."

The hitter was Gary Carter.

"I was *not*, so help me, going to make the last out of the World Series," Carter wrote in his book. "I felt certain of that. It would have been unacceptable, impossible; I would have lived with it all winter and probably beyond. It might have stalked me for the rest of my career."

Carter lashed a fastball into left field for a single. The potential tying run was stepping to the plate now—in the form of late-arriving rookie Kevin Mitchell. Mitch had to be fetched from the clubhouse for this pinch-hit at-bat, because he also thought the season was over.

Manager Davey Johnson, having been spotted by the cameras banging his head against the dugout's back wall, was tortured and living in his own doghouse. The media was circling in the sky in vulture fashion now—and the case to convict was a good one. As Johnson would later admit, with the refreshing candor that only a winner can afford, "It was not one of my better ones."

At the start of the ninth inning, Davey, running out of quality relievers, had removed Darryl Strawberry from a 3-3 game and sent Lee Mazzilli, limited by a weak arm and certainly not a power threat like Strawberry, to replace Straw in the outfield. This double switch was designed to get an extra inning out of Aguilera, an excellent hitting pitcher whom Johnson nevertheless didn't want to hit for himself as the fourth scheduled hitter in the ninth. Davey also didn't want to hit for Aggie and be forced to rely on either Randy Niemann or Doug Sisk if the game went to extra innings.

So, Johnson left Mazzilli in the game in the ninth hole and Aguilera was inserted into the fifth slot. Johnson had had the chance to double-switch Mookie Wilson out of the game when Davey brought in Orosco to get the final out of the eighth, but the manager chose to keep Wilson's bat around at that time.

Now, it was the 10th, with the tying run at the plate and a right-hander on the mound—and, in what had been the spot once occupied by Straw, Davey instead had to turn to the right-handed Mitchell. Mitchell singled—and neither player nor manager was inclined to take credit for the successful outcome.

"My grandparents at home must've been doing a lot of praying," Mitchell said.

Schiraldi still seemed in command at this point. Calvin appeared re-focused after a visit from pitching coach Bill Fischer and even managed to get an 0-and-2 count on Ray Knight. The Red Sox were now in the exact position that the California Angels had been against them in Game 5 of the ALCS—a strike away from a clinching—before Henderson rescued Boston with a homer and began his campaign for New England icon status.

Knight, meanwhile, was harboring feelings of self-loathing for throwing away Jim Rice's grounder—the error that led to the run which left the Mets trailing, 3-2, in the seventh. When the Mets returned to their dugout in the 10th, Knight grabbed a bat and prepared to hit, even though he was scheduled fifth in the inning.

"I didn't want to be the goat who lost the last game of the World Series," said Knight. "I said a prayer and I thought, if there were redemptive factors in this game, then I'd get another at-bat. So, I was so happy to be up in that situation."

Knight, whose bat caught fire after he had been stung by a Game 2 benching, looped a hit into center, scoring Carter to make it 5-4 and sending Mitchell to third with the tying run.

"I didn't hit the ball as well as I'd hit some of the others, but then some of the others didn't fall for base hits, either," said Knight. "Sometimes, I try to swing too hard, but with an 0-and-2 count, I just wanted to be sure I didn't panic. I think I am a better hitter with two strikes."

It was at this point that the superstitious Hernandez rejected an impulse to grab his hat and glove and return to the dugout—"I was going to go back out and then I said, 'Uh-uh, this seat has got hits in it,'" said Keith—but a once-reeling Shea was rocking and Boston manager John McNamara felt the need to make a move.

He pulled Schiraldi for sinkerballing Bob Stanley.

"I made the pitches I wanted to—except to Mitchell," said Schiraldi. "But I'm not going to make excuses. I've got no excuses . . . The guys were counting on me to do the job and I didn't do it. We had a chance to be drinking champagne now."

"It was a dream for me to be in there," said Stanley. "It's every pitcher's dream to be on the mound for the last out of the World Series. But it didn't come out the right way."

Stanley was ruined by one fastball that went awry and a physically diminished first baseman's inability to bend down and field a roller. By all rights, the sore-ankled Bill Buckner should never have still been out there wearing a glove at first base—but it is Buckner who will never be allowed to forget an error that should have been charged to McNamara.

Of course, none of the need for blame placing would have ensued if not for the stubborn resistance of Wilson.

Wilson—an awfully tough out, although he was inclined, in his words, to "swing at balls over my head and in the dirt"—fouled off the first pitch from Stanley, took two balls and then fouled off another for a 2-and-2 count. Wilson fouled off two more pitches, then somehow extricated himself from the path of an inside pitch that was menacing his ribs.

It involved gymnastics, not strategy or presence of mind.

"As intelligent as I am, my instincts took over—my instinct for self-preservation," said Wilson, who had thrown out Jim Rice at the plate for the final out of the seventh inning to keep the Red Sox from making it 4-2. "I didn't want to get hit."

Rich Gedman might have been able to catch the pitch or stop it, but the Boston catcher didn't. Mitchell, alerted to the possibility of such an occasion, was waved home without delay by third-base coach Bud Harrelson. Mitchell still didn't break immediately, but he crossed, anyway, on the most famous wild pitch in history and the score was tied at 5.

"I hesitated. I couldn't see it at first, because Gedman blocked my view," said Mitchell, who scored standing without a throw when the ball sailed all the way to the backstop. "Once I saw the ball go by, I ran."

"I tried to get it inside, but over the corner," said Stanley. "It didn't do what it was supposed to do and went too far inside . . . Usually, the ball runs back over the plate, but this one went the other way."

Now Knight was on second and the count was full to Wilson. Mookie fouled off two more pitches, got a new bat and awaited a 10th delivery from Stanley. Wilson sent a slow roller toward Buckner, who was playing 30 feet behind the bag at first, and it appeared like the race to the bag between the pitcher and Wilson might be a photo finish.

"I figured if I could beat him to the bag, the worst that would happen is we would have runners at first and third," said Wilson, who went down the line the way he always did, in bust-ass fashion.

Wilson still loomed as the would-be loser in this race, but there would be no throw to Stanley, of course. Buckner, gimpy from those two sore ankles, decided he wouldn't go to one knee in order to get more on the throw and the grounder went right under his glove, between his legs and into right field. It stopped dead on the grass as Knight crossed the plate with the game-winning run, jumping up and down and clinging to his helmet as jubilant, disbelieving Mets leaped into the air.

"I did concentrate on the ball. I saw it well. It bounced and bounced and then it didn't bounce. It just skipped," said Buckner. "The ball missed my glove . . . I can't remember the last time I missed a ground ball. I'll remember that one."

No kidding.

"Usually, he makes that play with no problem," said Stanley. "I thought we were out of the inning. I made a mistake. Bill made a mistake."

McNamara made a mistake. In fact, he made two. First, he declined to pinch-hit for Buckner with the right-handed Don Baylor, his unemployed designated hitter, against the lefty Jesse Orosco in the eighth.

Buckner popped up the first pitch to leave the bases loaded. And then McNamara departed from his custom of having Dave Stapleton replace the gimpy Buckner in the late innings when the Red Sox had a lead.

"Normally, with Buckner, we pinch-run for him, but we didn't have to tonight. He has very good hands and he was moving pretty well," said the manager, in an attempt to defend the indefensible.

"This is a very tricky infield," said Mets first-base coach Bill Robinson. "It's a good infield, but it hasn't been the same since the fans came out on the field and destroyed it."

"I don't remember holding my head," said Knight. "I was almost numb. It was unbelievable. Like it really wasn't happening. Like I was dreaming it."

"I'm not an emotional guy. I never run on the field," said Davey Johnson, "but when I saw the ball get by Buckner, I was out on the field."

Met fans will remember that the Red Sox starter in this game was none other than Roger Clemens, who was a little less macho back in his pre-pinstriped days. At the start of the eighth inning, Clemens left on the long end of a 3-2 score with a nasty booboo on the middle finger of his right hand—a blister that he said was caused by throwing his slider so effectively. Clemens allowed only four hits and one earned run and struck out eight Mets before asking out—following a nifty escape of a first-and-third, one-out predicament in the sixth and an easy 1-2-3 seventh.

"Roger just said he had enough," said McNamara.

"My blister was at a point where I couldn't finish off my slider. I didn't want to hang my slider and jeopardize the team," explained Clemens, who could have abandoned the pitch and gone after the last six outs with his fastball and saved his team from its own suspect bullpen. "But I thought I did my job."

The Red Sox scored single runs off an ineffective but game Bobby Ojeda in the first inning (Dwight Evans' RBI double) and the second inning (singles by Spike Owen, Wade Boggs and the Met-killing Barrett).

That advantage was erased in the fifth, when Strawberry drew his second walk, stole second for a second time and scored on a single by Knight, the Mets' first hit. Wilson singled through the right side and, when Evans bobbled the ball for an error, Knight raced to third. Davey Johnson, playing it aggressively, used Danny Heep as a pinch-hitter for No. 8 hitter Rafael Santana and Heep hit into the double play that tied the game at 2.

It stayed that way until the seventh, when, with one out, Barrett on second and Roger McDowell on the mound, Rice hit a routine bouncer to Knight, whose high and wide throw to first put runners at the corners. The Red Sox took a 3-2 lead when the Mets just missed turning the double play on Evans.

"I was down," said Knight of his misplay. "I thought, this is going to cost us the World Series . . . Then I thought, if someone has to make the error, it may as well be me. I have so many positives in my life. I can stand it."

Knight didn't know, of course, that Clemens would tell his manager "no mas" just six outs from a World Series clinching, leaving McNamara at the mercy of his relief corps—chiefly the shaky ex-Met, Schiraldi.

In the eighth, with Schiraldi on the mound, Mazzilli, pinch-hitting for Orosco, pulled a single through the right side. Soon, there were Mets at first and second with none out thanks to a fielder's (regrettable) choice, as Schiraldi tried to force Maz at second on Len Dykstra's bunt and threw too low for shortstop Owen to handle it.

After a sac bunt by Backman, Hernandez was walked intentionally to get to Carter. The Kid ran the count to 3-and-0 and then made his green light count with a line drive to deep left for the sac fly that scored Mazzilli and made it a 3-3 game. Needing a hit to plate the go-ahead run here, Strawberry popped to center for the final out, dropping his World Series average to .200 (with 18 Ks in 42 post-season at-bats).

Then Darryl was removed by Johnson in the double switch.

After the Mets had pulled their great escape, a sullen, already dressed Strawberry stood apart in the blissful clubhouse, smack in the center of a world that revolved around him, vowing to never forgive his manager for disgracing him.

"I'm disturbed. I'm embarrassed. It made me look bad and it showed the manager doesn't have confidence in me," said Straw. "At this point, he can't say anything to me [to make things better]. I don't even want to sit down with him. I don't want to talk with him."

Strawberry called the move "a terrible mistake." His sulk was so pronounced that it seemed like he hadn't even noticed the Mets had survived and forced a Game 7.

"At this particular time, I lost a lot of respect for him [Johnson] . . . That's just the way it is," he said. "It's a hurting feeling inside . . . I'll never forget it in my career. Down the line, I'll think about getting snatched out of a game in the World Series."

"After Darryl gets a few more years in, maybe he'll be managerial material," said Johnson, making light of his infant right fielder's fuming. "But right now, I wouldn't classify him as that."

Thanks to the double switch, Davey pointed out, Mazzilli was in the ideal spot to win the game with his ninth-inning flyout and likely would have done just that—if both Davey and Howard Johnson hadn't screwed up in tandem. With Mets at first and second and none out in the ninth, Davey hit for Elster—a rookie whose bunting skills he said he did not trust—with HoJo. Then Davey switched away from the sac strategy, after Howard had displayed a weak approach to the pitch on his first attempt.

"It scared me," said Davey. "I thought if that was the best he was going to do, we might end up in a double play—so I let him swing away."

HoJo struck out and Mazzilli's subsequent flyball was therefore not a game-ending blow.

Then, Henderson went yard as Aguilera wasted no time digging the Mets a deep, 10th-inning grave. They bounced out of it, one shovel short of being six feet under, and, somehow, the misery went home with Buckner and Stanley and McNamara.

Sore-ankled Red Sox first baseman Bill Buckner hobbles off to a lifetime sentence of being asked how he let Mookie Wilson's grounder go through him for an unforgettable error that scored Ray Knight and capped a three-run, down-to-their-final-strike rally.

"I feel lousy the way things happened—but if God had meant it to be, I would have caught it," said Buckner, who left 27 men on in the first six games. "It was a great game. It was exciting and it was a lot of fun—except for the last inning. I look at it this way: I have never played in a Game 7 of a World Series—and now I will."

Stanley was more realistic about the deflating effects of what had transpired, recalling the Red Sox' freshest nightmare: Bucky Dent taking Mike Torrez over the wall in that one-game playoff eight years earlier.

"So close, yet so far," said Stanley. "Seventy-eight was bad, but this is the worst."

"It's baseball and we've got to live with it," said Henderson.

"It's hard to believe," said Aguilera. "It's something you sit back and say, 'How did we do it?'"

With a little grit and with a lot of help. And maybe by being on the opposite side from seriously bad karma.

"I don't know nothing about history," McNamara said when the word jinx was used for the millionth time. "And I don't want to hear anything about choking or any of that junk . . . We needed just one out and didn't do it."

"I'm stunned," said Hernandez. "It was a gift."

BOSTON	ab	r	h	bl	METS	ab	r	h	bl
Boggs 3b	5	2	3	0	Dykstra cf	4	0	0	0
Barrett 2b	4	1	3	2	Backman 2b	4	0	1	0
Buckner 1b	5	0	0	0	Hernandez 1b	4	0	1	0
Rice lf	5	0	0	0	Carter c	4	1	1	1
Evans rf	4	0	1	2	Strawberry rf	2	1	0	0
Gedman c	5	0	1	0	Aguilera p	0	0	0	0
Henderson cf	5	1	2	1	Mitchell ph	1	1	1	0
Owens ss	4	1	3	0	Knight 3b	4	2	2	2
Clemens p	3	0	0	0	Wilson lf	5	0	1	0
Greenwell ph	1	0	0	0	Santana ss	1	0	0	0
Schiraldi p	1	0	0	0	Heep ph	1	0	0	0
Stanley p	0	0	0	0	Elster ss	1	0	0	0
					Johnson ss	1	0	0	0
					Ojeda p	2	0	0	0
					McDowell p	0	0	0	0
					Orosco p	0	0	0	0
					Mazzilli rf	2	1	1	0
Totals	42	5	13	5	Totals	36	6	8	3

Boston	110	000	100	2 — 5
Mets	000	020	010	3 — 6

Game Winning RBI-none. E-Evans, Knight, Elster, Gedman, Buckner. DP-Boston 1, Mets 1. LOB-Boston 14, Mets 8. 2B-Evans, Boggs. HR-Henderson (2). SB-Strawberry 2 (3). S-Owen, Dykstra, Backman. SF-Carter.

Boston	IP	H	R	ER	BB	SO
Clemens	7	4	2	1	2	8
Schiraldi (L, 0-1)	2²/₃	4	4	3	2	1
Stanley	0	0	0	0	0	0
Mets						
Ojeda	6	8	2	2	2	3
McDowell	1²/₃	2	1	0	3	1
Orosco	¹/₃	0	0	0	0	0
Aguilera (W, 1-0)	2	3	2	2	0	3

Two outs when winning run scored.

Stanley pitched to 1 batter in the 10th. HBP-Buckner (by Aguilera). WP-Stanley.

Umpires: Home-Ford (AL); First-Kibler (NL); Second-Evans (AL); Third-Wendelstedt (NL); Left-Brinkman (AL); Right-Montague (NL).

T-4:02. A-55,078.

Mets Rise from Dead, Survive 16-Round Fight To Finish Astros

METS 7, ASTROS 6

1986 NLCS Game 6
October 15, 1986 in Houston

The greatest Met moment of all—until Game 6 of the World Series 10 nights later—lasted a torturous four hours and 42 minutes. It was 16 delicious, painful innings of knockdown punches and counter punches, blown leads and dramatic comebacks, challenges to the heart and to the mind, and, finally, unbridled joy.

Or was it simply relief?

Game 6 of the 1986 NLCS against the Astros in Houston was essentially a Game 7 for both teams, even though the Mets carried a three-games-to-two advantage. Houston was staring at immediate elimination, its Domesday, but the Mets faced something even more horrifying. In the wings was the specter of having to beat unhittable Astros ace Mike Scott (two complete-game wins, 19 strikeouts, 16⅔ consecutive scoreless innings) in a finale.

14

As manager Davey Johnson said, from beneath his champagne bath in the wild minutes following the Mets' far wilder 7-6 victory, in the aftermath of the franchise's first pennant-clinching in 13 years, "I feel like I am on parole. Like I have been pardoned . . . We didn't want to face him again. That is why we played this game like it was the last."

"We could have beaten him, but I am sure glad we don't have to try," said Ray Knight of Great Scott, the ex-Met split-finger (or scuff-ball) maestro who cast such a large shadow over this Series that he was named NLCS MVP, *even though his team lost.* "I've never been involved in something so emotional or been under such mental strain."

"If there was a Game 7, I don't know that I would have slept very well," said Wally Backman. "Scott made us look like high school kids out there. There were times we were looking for a pitch and got it and still couldn't do anything with it. You know you are in trouble when that happens."

"He manhandled us and we knew he would again," said Lenny Dykstra.

"I know Scott could have beaten them three games," said Houston manager Hal Lanier.

"Now he can't scuff the ball again until next year," said Darryl Strawberry.

The Mets, a first-place team from April 23 to the wire, 108-game winners in the regular season and potent beyond any team in club history, hit .189 for the NLCS. They scored 20 earned runs and generated 43 hits in 64 innings. Their cleanup hitter Gary Carter hit a sad .148 and they struck out a record 57 times.

"Either that was the greatest pitching I have ever seen or I'm horrible," said Mookie Wilson, a .115 hitter in the NLCS. "I don't drink and I don't like the taste of champagne. But, after this, I will drink some."

It was bottoms up for Mookie because the Mets found a way—with three last at-bat victories—to cut the hearts out of the Astros, despite that collective offensive nightmare. And the Houdini act in Game 6 was the topper.

"Maybe I had a heart attack. I don't know. I am not sure," said Backman. "I think I aged 10 years in the last two days I am so numb. This was the greatest game I ever played or ever saw."

The contest seemed numbingly routine entering the ninth, as the Mets were deep in a two-hit coma against their other tormentor, Bob Knepper, and on the wrong end of an immediate 3-0 hole that felt more like 300-0.

"The whole game he had been mowing us down like babies," said Dykstra. "They were going through us like swiss cheese."

The Astros had put together four hits for three first-inning runs against Bobby Ojeda, Game 2 winner. Before Bobby O settled down and pitched four scoreless innings, Denny Walling's RBI double and scoring hits by Glenn Davis and Jose Cruz put the Mets in peril—and more damage was averted thanks to a busted suicide squeeze bunt.

Knepper had beaten the Mets three times without losing during the '86 season. He had shackled them again for five innings in NLCS Game 3, until an error and a gopher ball in the sixth led to his undoing. On this day, the finesse lefty retired his first seven Mets and, after Rafael Santana's single and a walk to Wilson in the third, recorded 14 more consecutive outs prior to Tim Teufel's single in the eighth.

"I didn't think we had a chance to win this," said Ron Darling, Yale product and man of reason. "Not a chance at all."

Leading off the ninth, Dykstra, moored on the bench in Davey Johnson's world of platoons, was the pinch-hitter for Rick Aguilera. It was lefty vs. lefty. When Knepper pushed the count to 0-and-2, Dykstra looked like a first out waiting to happen.

"I was just looking for a hit," said Dykstra, who finished the NLCS with a .304 average and a team-leading 13 total bases. "If I don't get on, we lose."

Dykstra drove a too-good-for-0-and-2 pitch just beyond the reach of Billy Hatcher in center and didn't break stride until he hit third base.

"I was close to it, but it was crazy," said Hatcher. "He doesn't play against left-handers. I knew he was trying to make contact with two strikes. So I cheated toward left field and he ends up hitting a live ball that carried [to right center]."

"Dykstra started it for us," said Davey Johnson. "I should've started him in the game."

"When Lenny hit the triple, you could see guys saying to themselves, 'Hey, we can hit this guy,'" said Carter.

"We were playing him in, because he never hit a ball that hard off us all year. He never showed that kind of power against us," said Lanier, having blocked the memory of Dykstra's decisive, ninth-inning homer off Dave Smith in Game 3.

Kevin Bass, angry at the Mets' accusations that Scott must be cheating and supremely frustrated after this Series was finally over, concluded that the only way that Dykstra could juice a ball like that was to have already juiced his bat.

"Check that bat," said Bass. "You don't think he's corking? How does a guy flying off the top hand hit the ball that far?"

"I can hit left-handers. I have hit them before. All I need is the chance," said Dykstra, whom some suspected of having a corked head.

Wilson followed with a liner that touched down in short right for an RBI single—because second baseman Bill Doran mistimed his leap and the ball deflected off his glove instead of settling in it for the first out. Game of inches and all that . . . and soon, a tie game of inches.

Wilson moved up a base on Kevin Mitchell's groundout to third and then Hernandez outwilled Knepper. The clutchest of RBI men sent a 2-and-1 pitch to the wall in center for the double that made the score 3-2.

Now, Lanier felt he had no choice but to go to the pen. Charlie Kerfeld had thrown 2⅓ innings in Game 5 and Lanier was determined to not use his idle No. 4 starter Jim Deshaies in an unaccustomed role. So the Houston manager's best remaining option was the befuddled, frustrated Smith.

This veteran 33-save man had been a Met whipping boy all year. When Smith was done in this game, he had a combined 1-3 mark with a 12.60 ERA against the Mets, season plus post-season. They had gotten into his head and one indication of it came before Game 6, when Smith had told a Houston reporter, "We've got to beat these guys, because I can't stand them."

Smith should've been licking his lips at the sight of Carter and his 2-for-25 miseries at the plate. Instead, Gary extended him to a 3-and-2 count, fouled off two pitches then walked after the right-hander thought he had him struck out. Strawberry, twice a K victim in Game 6, also went to a full count. Then he hit a curving bomb into the upper deck that was foul. Then he walked.

The bases were loaded now, with one out.

"When you take a three-run lead into the ninth inning, you should win," said Lanier. "When you walk two men in a row in the ninth inning, you are just asking for trouble."

"Smitty had a great season, but he lost his control and his composure at the wrong time," said Backman. "It can happen to anybody."

The next hitter was Knight, the Astro castoff. On a 1-and-2 count, Ray took a fastball that was, well, very close. Smith and catcher Alan Ashby were already seething about home-plate umpire Fred Brocklander's shifting strike zone and this ball call triggered more verbal fire. This time, Ashby's groan angered the intense Knight, who screamed at the catcher, "That was not a strike. You don't know what a strike is."

"If that pitch was not a strike, then I am a pitcher's ass," said Smith, who stomped his foot. "It wasn't even close. It wasn't on the black."

Knight's sac fly on a 2-and-2 fastball—"He hit it far enough for me to score and I didn't have the energy to dash home on a medium fly," noted Hernandez—meant the game was tied and the real fun was just starting. It remained 3-3 through the 13th inning. Roger McDowell gave the Mets five spectacular shutout relief innings. Meanwhile, Smith managed a scoreless 10th inning and then Larry Andersen posted three zeroes for the Astros.

Then, in the 14th, it appeared the Mets had grabbed this game around the throat. Backman's single off Aurelio Lopez drove in Dykstra with the go-ahead run and left the visitors on the doorstep to a World Series date with the Red Sox.

However, with the Mets two outs away from nirvana, Hatcher crushed one fastball for a long, foul home run and then lofted another from Jesse Orosco right down the left-field line. It sailed into the screen attached to the foul pole, six inches fair.

Home run.

A 4-4 game.

"I told myself, it's not over—not yet," said Orosco, who came into the game with five scoreless innings under his belt and who would finish it with his third win of the NLCS.

Hernandez said to Orosco, "Hold them, Jesse. Don't give in. We will score."

Sure enough, they did, in the 16th. Remarkably, Hatcher went from hero to goat, as the center fielder broke the wrong way on Strawberry's high pop fly and gave the Mets a gift double. Knight, whose post-season heroics represented a personal vindication, followed with a single to right off Lopez to plate Straw and the score was now 5-4.

"I know the Astros thought I was through, but they made a gross misjudgment," said Knight.

"I knew he could still play," said Davey Johnson. "I knew because Ray told me he could. Ray Knight epitomizes the competitive spirit on this ballclub."

When Knight's hit was followed by a walk, a sacrifice, a wild pitch and Dykstra's RBI single off Jeff Calhoun, it looked like nothing more than icing. The score was 7-4. It was definitely all over now, right?

Wrong.

In the bottom of the 16th, a weary Orosco was on the ropes and running on fumes. After striking out Craig Reynolds, Jesse walked Davey Lopes and gave up singles to Doran and Hatcher that made it 7-5 and put the tying runs on base.

Hernandez made a critical defensive play on Walling's grounder wide of first, getting a force play at second. If Mex had made the play at first, Davis' subsequent soft single to center would have made it 7-7, not 7-6.

Now the hitter was Bass.

Then came a famous disputed meeting on the mound.

Hernandez later said that he had told Carter, if the catcher called for one more fastball instead of sticking entirely with Orosco's bread-and-butter slider, "We're going to have a fight."

Carter said that exchange never happened, that Hernandez wouldn't tell him how to do his job any more than he would tell Keith how to play first base.

No matter, the point was made by someone.

"I told Jesse I would call for other pitches, but just keep shaking me off to confuse them," said Carter. "Just throw the slider."

"I was scared," said Backman. "We all were. But I'll say this for Jesse, a lot of guys would have folded up and said, 'I don't want to be here.' Not him."

"I'd blown one lead," said Orosco. "I wasn't about to blow another one ... I was a little tired, but I knew what had to be done ... I told myself, 'You have the ball. You have the power. Don't let these guys down.'"

A hit would tie it. An extra-base hit would mean defeat. Scott was around the bend. The true believers among the 45,718 in attendance, the ones who stayed, were screaming again.

A banner spotted in the stands at the Astrodome said it all: Does anyone know CPR?

Orosco ran the count full to Bass and threw a sixth consecutive slider. Probably ball four. Swing and a miss.

The Mets won the pennant, the Mets won the pennant.

"I'm very teed off," said Bass. "I had a vision of getting the hit. His big pitch is the breaking ball and it's a tough pitch to hit. I was gearing for just one fastball, but I never saw one. I saw nothing but breaking balls. He beat me."

Having already squandered one extra-inning lead and all but one run of another, a relieved Jesse Orosco leaps into the air after striking out the Astros' Kevin Bass to finally end the 16th inning of Game 6. The lefty's third win of the NLCS sealed the pennant.

"I felt we should have beaten them. I feel we should be in the Series, not them," said Knepper.

Hernandez didn't really care what Knepper or Lanier or Bass thought.

"The whole National League wanted us to lose but right now I don't give a bleep what they think. They have to respect us now," he said. "Without this, 108 wins wouldn't have meant anything."

METS

	ab	r	h	bl
Wilson cf	7	1	1	1
Mitchell lf	4	0	0	0
Elster ss	3	0	0	0
Hernandez 1b	7	1	1	1
Carter c	5	0	2	0
Strawberry rf	5	2	1	0
Knight 3b	6	1	1	2
Teufel 2b	3	0	1	0
Backman 2b	2	1	1	1
Santana ss	3	0	1	0
Heep ph	1	0	0	0
McDowell p	1	0	0	0
Johnson ph	1	0	0	0
Orosco p	0	0	0	0
Ojeda p	1	0	0	0
Mazzilli ph	1	0	0	0
Aguilera p	0	0	0	0
Dykstra cf	4	1	2	1
Totals	**54**	**7**	**11**	**6**

HOUSTON

	ab	r	h	bl
Doran 2b	7	1	2	0
Hatcher cf	7	2	3	2
Garner 3b	3	1	1	1
Walling 3b	4	0	0	0
Davis 1b	7	1	3	2
Bass rf	6	0	1	0
Cruz lf	6	0	1	1
Ashby c	6	0	0	0
Thon ss	3	0	0	0
Reynolds ss	3	0	0	0
Knepper p	2	0	0	0
Smith p	0	0	0	0
Puhl ph	1	0	0	0
Andersen p	0	0	0	0
Pankovits ph	1	0	0	0
Lopez p	0	0	0	0
Calhoun p	0	0	0	0
Lopes ph	0	1	0	0
Totals	**56**	**6**	**11**	**6**

Mets	000	000	003	000	010 3	—	7
Houston	300	000	000	000	010 2	—	6

Game Winning RBI-Knight (1). E-Bass. DP-Houston 2. LOB-Mets 9, Houston 5. 2B-Garner, Davis, Hernandez, Strawberry. 3B-Dykstra. HR-Hatcher (1). SB-Doran (2). S-Orosco. SF-Knight.

Mets	IP	H	R	ER	BB	SO
Ojeda	5	5	3	3	2	1
Aguilera	3	1	0	0	0	1
McDowell	5	1	0	0	0	2
Orosco (W, 3-0)	3	4	3	3	1	5
Houston						
Knepper	8⅓	5	3	3	1	6
Smith	1⅔	0	0	0	3	2
Andersen	3	0	0	0	1	1
Lopez (L, 0-1)	2	5	3	3	2	2
Calhoun	1	1	1	1	1	0

Wild pitch-Calhoun 2.

Umpires: Home-Brocklander; First-Harvey; Second-Weyer; Third-Pulli; Left-Rennert; Right-West.

T-4:42. A-45,718.

It's Seventh Heaven at Last, after One Final Comeback

1986 World Series Game 7
October 27, 1986 in New York

Having already performed the incredible and still in need of an encore for a championship, the Mets encountered one final, large roadblock in the 1986 World Series. Because of a rainout that pushed Game 7 back one night, they had to beat Bruce Hurst. The postponement loomed as a huge break for the reeling Red Sox and it meant the Mets would not see Oil Can Boyd, but rather the formidable left-hander Hurst on three days' rest.

Hurst, about to be named the World Series MVP before the Red Sox' world melted in Game 6, had already beaten the Mets twice and had permitted them two earned runs over 17 innings. When he held them to one single over the first five innings of Game 7 while his teammates punished and banished an ineffective Ron Darling to grab a 3-0 lead, Hurst appeared a good bet to become the fifth pitcher in history to win three games in a seven-game World Series.

Of course, in reality, the Mets had the Red Sox exactly where they wanted them. With Sid Fernandez coming out of the bullpen to keep them within hailing distance, the Mets found themselves in a familiar spot—on the comeback trail, salivating at the prospect of facing the Boston bullpen. They made a dramatic comeback to tie the game in the sixth against a suddenly weary Hurst, then got five more runs in the seventh and eighth innings. The revival was remarkable—though not as sudden as the one that won Game 6 after two were out and nobody was on base in the 10th inning.

The Game 7 climb to a championship reached its peak as Jesse Orosco retired Marty Barrett for the final out in the ninth inning and threw his glove 30 feet into the air to celebrate the 8-5 victory that gave New York its second world championship and first in 17 years, in front of 55,032 witnesses at Shea.

"This club has come back so often this year that 3-0 didn't mean a thing," said Mookie Wilson. "I know what it is like to be in the cellar, to be at home watching the World Series with a pizza and beer . . . I can remember the way it used to be and, believe me, this is better than it used to be."

Better than it used to be for Ray Knight.

The 33-year-old Knight was named the World Series MVP after hitting the go-ahead homer off Calvin Schiraldi in the seventh inning. But he began the 1986 season feeling fear and worry about his rumored impending release.

"I went into spring training hearing things like they were going to eat my contract," said the ex-Red and ex-Astro, who hit .391 with five RBI and four runs in the Series. "I've lived with pressure all season, so this didn't seem like all that much pressure to me. I was dealing with the fact that my career may be over.

"I don't have any speed and I've had three shoulder operations, but I have always prided myself on being a winner. What hurt me most the last couple of years was that people lost faith in me . . . I proved I am not [just] Ray Lopez [LPGA standout Nancy Lopez' husband]."

Better than it used to be for Gary Carter.

Carter's most productive years were spent winning nothing in Montreal. His only real previous shot at a championship was ruined by the Dodgers' victory in the 1981 playoffs. Carter, who caught all 13 post-season contests on the road to this world championship, insisted he knew all along this crowning moment was ahead for the '86 Mets, even when times were the darkest.

"I knew we would do it," said Carter, The Kid who was no longer a kid. "I never doubted it. I didn't doubt it in Houston. I didn't doubt it with two outs and two [runs] down in the sixth game. I didn't doubt it early, when we fell behind by three runs. I knew we would find a way. We did the inevitable."

Better than it used to be for Keith Hernandez.

Hernandez had partied his way into Cardinal manager Whitey Herzog's doghouse and out of St. Louis. He came to the last-place Mets with deep reluctance in 1983, only to become the club's leader and tour guide to winning.

"I will never forget this, even if we win the next five world championships," said Hernandez, whose two-run, bases-loaded single off Hurst keyed the critical three-run, game-tying rally in the sixth. "My last thoughts on my deathbed will be this world championship.

"This club was down after Game 2, as down as I had ever seen it. It was the first time since I'd been here that I wasn't sure we would bounce back . . . But the ability to come back from adversity marks this club."

Better than it used to be for Tim Teufel.

Teufel was about to be the guy remembered only for making the decisive error in the Mets' 1-0 Game 1 defeat. That was before the burden of a blunder that no one will ever forget had landed on the shoulders of Boston's Bill Buckner, the poor 102-RBI man who didn't get his glove down far enough in Game 6.

"I took a lot of criticism for one play and, if we had lost, everyone would have looked at me," said Teufel. "They would have viewed me on that one error and not the whole season. Now maybe Bill Buckner will have to live with it. That's too bad. He is a good player."

Better than it used to be for Darling—especially in the early stages of the biggest start of his life, in which he was battered for six hits and three runs in just 3⅔ innings.

"I had nothing," said Darling, who was bailed out by Fernandez' four strikeouts and scoreless 2⅓ relief innings. "We didn't even play well and we won. We may not even have deserved to win—and we did . . . We were destined to win after finishing second the last two years. Somehow, some way, we got it done."

Better than it had ever been for Mets manager Davey Johnson.

"This is as good as it gets," said Johnson, who tasted champagne as an Oriole player, but was on the wrong end of a miracle in '69. "I'm just happy the bad guys won. I'm proud of these guys. It couldn't be any sweeter than it is."

The Red Sox took a 3-0 lead in the third, on back-to-back homers from Dwight Evans and Rich Gedman, then a walk, a sacrifice and Wade Boggs' RBI single. Johnson's hook found Darling's neck in the fourth inning, after Dave Henderson had walked and reached second on a sacrifice. Davey brought in the left-handed Fernandez to face the lefty Boggs, telling his pitcher to "just hold them and we will win this thing."

"I don't like to take one of my starting pitchers out early," explained Johnson. "But he wasn't throwing very well and I wanted to get Sid Fernandez in the game, because he pitched very well in Fenway. And I didn't feel we could afford to give up any more runs . . . Sid was the hero. He shut them down and got the crowd back on our side."

Fernandez, never one to do things the easy way, walked Boggs. But he wound up getting the Met killer Barrett (13 hits in the World Series) on a fly for the final out of the inning. Passed over as a starter in the Series, the 24-year-old Fernandez added two more blanks—he put down seven straight hitters—and Boston was done scoring until the eighth.

"We hit Darling hard and it could have been worse [than just three runs of damage]," said Buckner. "But Sid got us out. He slowed us down."

"He [Fernandez] kept them in the game," said Gedman. "If he doesn't do the job, we win."

"Sid is the one who got them going," said Schiraldi.

"When Sid was in there, we began to feel like we might win this game, after all," said Hernandez.

Through the first five innings, Hurst looked unhittable, again. At least to most folks. Darryl Strawberry said he and his friends were expecting a feast.

"We were sitting in the dugout, telling ourselves, 'We can get this guy. He's not sharp.' No one on this team thought he was going to beat us again," said Straw.

"I said on the bench that if we can tie this game, we will beat them," said Hernandez.

The gas gauge hit E without warning on Hurst in the sixth, as the Mets suddenly tied the game after the pitcher had retired 16 of the first 17 batters he faced.

After Hurst got Rafael Santana to begin the sixth inning, pinch-hitter Lee Mazzilli singled between third and short, Wilson slapped a single to left and Teufel walked. Now the hitter was Hernandez, who was overdue to find a hole with a .208 average and one RBI in the World Series.

"In Game 1, he threw me 90 percent fastballs and in Game 5 he threw me 95 percent curves. Today, I had a hunch he would go fastball in a tight spot," said Hernandez. "He threw me a curveball on the first pitch and there was no way I was going to swing at his hook. So I waited for his fastball and he threw it. He was trying to come up and in, but he got it out over the plate."

Hernandez deposited it into left center, scoring two and sending the tying run to third.

"I felt like I was throwing the ball well," said Hurst. "I wanted to throw a fastball down to Keith Hernandez. It was up. I missed. He didn't. He's one of the best hitters ever. He broke my back."

Carter hit a looper to right that fell in front of a diving Evans and pinch-runner Wally Backman crossed with the tying run as the Red Sox completed a force play on Hernandez at second.

"I just wasn't conditioned to pitch on three days' rest," said Hurst, who had thrown 74 pitches going into the sixth. "I hadn't done it all season. I knew I couldn't go the whole way. But I wanted to hold the lead."

Hurst was lifted for a hitter in the seventh, leaving Boston manager John McNamara at the mercy of his putrid bullpen (13 earned runs allowed in 15⅓ World Series innings) once again. He opted for Schiraldi, his shaky closer, in the seventh inning of this tie game, figuring that Game 6 starter Roger Clemens would get the last outs of this one if Boston took the lead.

"Once we got into the Sox' bullpen, I knew we were in pretty good shape," said Knight. "They didn't have any left-handers. They were playing right into our strength . . . and they all throw hard."

Some Mets felt certain that Schiraldi, the Game 6 losing pitcher, would come apart again from what they had observed when the right-hander was still a Met prospect.

"We knew he didn't have any guts," said one Met, who retained his anonymity if not his sensitivity. "Believe me. Guys don't change overnight."

Schiraldi, who went from the Mets to the Red Sox in the Bobby Ojeda deal, saw his World Series ERA swell to 13.50 before the Mets were done burying him. His first hitter in the seventh was Knight, who went boom with a 2-and-1 fastball that he was fully expecting.

"I knew I hit it well enough to go out," said Knight, who had two singles and a homer. "I didn't know if it was high enough. I've hit many balls off the wall that were hit hard enough to go out."

It landed over the left-field wall and the Mets had the lead for good, 4-3. And now Schiraldi appeared to be shaken by the homer and the chant of "Caalll-vinnnnn . . . Caallll-vinnn." Pinch-hitter Lenny Dykstra singled and was wild-pitched to second. Santana slapped an RBI single to make it 5-3. After a sac bunt—the only out that Schiraldi managed to get—he was replaced by Joe Sambito. When Hernandez managed a sac fly later in the inning, Schiraldi was charged with a third run.

"I wasn't nervous. I was pretty calm, but things didn't go right . . . We should've won this thing," said Schiraldi. "I couldn't hold the lead the other night [in Game 6] and I couldn't do nothing tonight."

The Red Sox gave the Mets a giant scare in the eighth, when they cut the margin to a single run against Roger McDowell. Singles by Buckner and Jim Rice and a two-run double to right center by Evans made it 6-5 with none out, but Orosco came riding to the rescue.

"I wasn't thinking about baseball when I came in, I was looking for a bathroom. I was pretty nervous," said Orosco, who had two saves in the Series and was unscored upon by Boston. "I just told myself, 'Stay within yourself. This is no time to fold.'"

Orosco found and gave relief. He got the lefty Gedman on a liner to second, struck out the righty Henderson on four consecutive sliders and turned back right-handed pinch-hitter Don Baylor, the designated hitter who became a World Series reserve in the games played at the NL park, on a grounder to short.

"What is unique about Jesse is that he came of age in the post-season. He became a man," said Hernandez. "There was talk of trading him, but right now he is an untouchable Met."

The Mets restored their lead to three with two in the bottom of the eighth. Strawberry—still seething over that double switch that removed him from Game 6—homered off Al Nipper to make it 7-5. Then Orosco managed an RBI single on a swinging bunt through a charging infield that pushed the margin to 8-5.

Three more outs and the Mets would have their 116th victory of the season. The last out—Orosco's 13th consecutive hitter retired—came on a 2-and-2 slider thrown past a swinging Barrett. Jesse then set the Olympic record in the glove toss and weathered a frightening pile of berserk Met humanity on the mound.

"I saw the guys coming and I went to the ground, so they could hit their heads," said Orosco. "They didn't get me. I got down quick."

The Red Sox, who had led Game 7 of their previous World Series appearance by three runs and lost to the Cincinnati Reds in 1975, were also down—way down.

"We lost it Saturday," said Barrett, who hit .433 in the post-season. "They won it today, but we didn't make them earn it . . . A guy gets on base, a wild pitch . . . That's a one-in-a-million comeback for them and they pulled it off."

"I'm beginning to wonder [about a jinx]," said Evans, who hit .308 with two homers and nine RBI in the Series. "Sixty-nine years is a long time. You see the way things go the other night [in Game 6] and you wonder what is going on."

"We just couldn't put them away when we really had to," said Baylor.

"It seemed the closer they [the Red Sox] came [to winning], the farther away they got," said Mets' GM Frank Cashen.

Ray Knight, left, whose homer off Calvin Schiraldi broke a 3-3 tie during the seventh inning of Game 7, shares the ecstasy of being a World Series MVP with Gary Carter. Knight could never have guessed at the time he wouldn't ever wear a Met uniform again.

"No one can take the world championship away from us now, regardless of envy, hatred or jealousy," said Carter.

"We had to win four of five going into Boston and we did it," said Hernandez. "I think you can say this is the greatest Mets team of all time, even better than the '69 Mets."

BOSTON

	ab	r	h	bl
Boggs 3b	4	0	1	1
Barrett 2b	5	0	1	0
Buckner 1b	4	1	2	0
Rice lf	4	1	2	0
Evans rf	4	1	2	3
Gedman c	4	1	1	1
Henderson cf	2	1	0	0
Owen ss	3	0	0	0
Baylor ph	1	0	0	0
Nipper p	0	0	0	0
Crawford p	0	0	0	0
Hurst p	0	0	0	0
Armas ph	1	0	0	0
Schiraldi p	0	0	0	0
Sambito p	0	0	0	0
Stanley p	0	0	0	0
Romero ss	1	0	0	0
Totals	**33**	**5**	**9**	**5**

METS

	ab	r	h	bl
Wilson cf	3	1	1	0
Teufel 2b	2	0	0	0
Backman 2b	1	1	0	0
Hernandez 1b	4	0	1	3
Carter c	4	0	0	1
Strawberry rf	4	1	1	1
Knight 3b	4	2	3	1
Mitchell lf	2	0	0	0
Dykstra cf	2	1	1	0
Santana ss	3	1	1	1
Darling p	1	0	0	0
Fernandez p	0	0	0	0
Mazzilli ph	1	1	1	0
McDowell p	0	0	0	0
Orosco p	1	0	1	1
Totals	**32**	**8**	**10**	**8**

Boston	030	000	020 — 5
Mets	000	003	32x — 8

Game Winning RBI-Knight (1). LOB-Boston 6, Mets 7. 2B-Evans. HR-Evans (2), Gedman (1), Knight (1), Strawberry (1). S-Hurst 2, McDowell. SF-Hernandez.

Boston	IP	H	R	ER	BB	SO
Hurst	6	4	3	3	1	3
Schiraldi (L, 0-2)	1/3	3	3	3	0	0
Sambito	1/3	0	0	0	2	0
Stanley	1/3	0	0	0	0	0
Nipper	1/3	3	2	2	1	0
Crawford	2/3	0	0	0	0	0
Mets						
Darling	3 2/3	6	3	3	1	0
Fernandez	2 1/3	0	0	0	1	4
McDowell (W, 1-0)	1	3	2	2	0	1
Orosco (S,2)	2	0	0	0	0	2

McDowell pitched to 3 batters in the 8th. HBP-Henderson (by Darling), Wilson (by Crawford). Wild pitch-Schiraldi.

Umpires: Home-Kibler (NL); First-Evans (AL); Second-Wendelstedt (NL); Third-Brinkman (AL); Left-Montague (NL); Right-Ford (NL).

T-3:11. A-55,032.

Shoe Enough, Weis Crack Completes The Miracle

METS 5, ORIOLES 3

1969 World Series Game 5
October 16, 1969 in New York

In the end, maybe, there was as much relief as there was joy. Coming up with a daily miracle on an illogical joy ride seemingly without end was emotionally taxing, most of all for the man with the heart condition who presided over all of it.

"It's been a year of miracles and I'm just thanking God that it's over," said the maestro, Gil Hodges, 13 months removed from a heart attack.

"Someone was good to us," said Cleon Jones of New York City's first world championship baseball team since 1962—thanks to a 16-2 season-closing run that included seven wins in eight post-season games.

At 3:17 p.m., on a cool, sunny afternoon, Jones dropped to one knee as he caught Davey Johnson's fly to the warning track in left field for the final out of a 5-3 come-from-behind Game 5 victory that crowned the Mets as world champions.

Then Cleon genuflected, hugged his buddy Tommie Agee and ran for his life.

32

Just like that, the ride was over.

And the 1969 Mets, 100-to-1 shots, finished it as the only team still standing.

"Some people still might not believe in us," said Jones from the midst of the Mets' third clinching celebration at Shea in 22 days. "But then, some people still think the world is flat."

"It was a colossal thing they did," said Hodges. "These young men showed you can realize the most impossible dream of all . . . As a player and as a manager, it's different. It's hard to explain. In a way, this means more [than his 1955 and 1959 World Series titles as a Dodger player]. I'm so proud of them all."

"I never saw anything like it," said Joe DiMaggio, his pinstriped heart apparently moved by the Met mystique.

"This will give heart to every loser in America . . . We are the saints of lost causes," said Ron Swoboda, a .242 career hitter who drove in the winning run with a double off a right-handed pitcher in the eighth inning and finished the Series at .400. "This season has been one high after another. We have gone higher and higher until you can't go any higher. We did it all."

Swoboda had joined the Mets in 1965, when Casey Stengel was still managing and the club finished last for the fourth straight time with 112 losses. Now, he and his teammates were something else: *lovable winners.*

"This is the first time," said Swoboda. "Nothing can ever be as sweet again."

Swoboda was right, of course.

No championship in Met history—including that back-from-the-brink dance with death that the 1986 version performed as the world witnessed again what it means to be the Boston Red Sox—can approach the sheer wonder of this 1969 team's defiance of expectation and reason. Three decades later, it still doesn't feel possible that it happened, especially the way it happened.

"It was the greatest collective victory by any team in sports," said Tom Seaver, Game 4 winner.

Game 5, the clincher, is best remembered for Al Weis hitting a game-tying homer in his first show of power since the July series in Chicago when the infielder went deep in back-to-back games at Wrigley to ruin the Cubs. Not one of the 212 homers that had been hit at Shea Stadium since Weis had come to the Mets from the Chicago White Sox came from him—before this one.

Over the course of his 10-year career, regular season and post-season, Weis hit eight. Strangely, this was the second time he victimized McNally.

"I knew I hit it good, but I didn't know how far it would go," said Weis, a non-rippled 160 pounds of banjo hitter. "I don't have enough experience in judging those things."

"It was a dream to see my boy in a World Series," said Al Weis, Sr., age 58. "But to see him be the batting hero is too much."

Too much to believe, in fact.

First, the Mets—who had never trailed in their previous three World Series wins—dug themselves a little hole that suggested they just might have to win this World Series back in Baltimore. In fact, they didn't sport the look of destiny's darlings at all in the early going and Jerry Koosman didn't look like the guy who threw six no-hit innings in Game 2.

In the third inning, following Mark Belanger's single, Dave McNally, a good-hitting pitcher who had three homers during the '68 season, clubbed a two-run homer. It was Baltimore's first extra-base hit in 35 innings. Then, Frank Robinson—who had two singles and no RBI to show for his first 16 at-bats and who would finish this Series with an average of .187—also hit a homer. Robby's lone extra-base hit of this Series made it 3-0.

In addition to Weis' flexing, Game 5 is also remembered for the symmetry of an umpire's rulings on two pitches that did or did not hit batters.

In the sixth, Frank Robinson was left fuming when he was not awarded first base after being hit by a pitch from Koosman.

The Oriole slugger was nailed by an 0-and-1 delivery and had the bruise high on his left leg to prove it. Robinson started for first base— but was called back by home-plate umpire Lou DiMuro, who insisted the ball had ticked off his bat before hitting Robinson in the leg, which made it a foul ball.

An angry Robinson registered his complaint, asked DiMuro to get help from the first-base umpire, then went to the dugout in mid at-bat, took down his uniform pants and had ethyl chloride applied to the spot for about six minutes while the fans waited and booed and Koosman threw to stay warm.

"It would have been a good idea for him to look at it [the welt on Robinson's right thigh]," said Frank. "But if he's not going to ask another umpire about the pitch, I am sure he isn't going to come down and look at my leg."

DiMuro never did wander over to the dugout for a look, but he did visit.

"DiMuro came to our dugout and told Frank to hurry up or he would force me to take him out of the game and send up a pinch-hitter," said Earl Weaver.

"DiMuro saw what they were doing and I think he was wrong trying to hustle us at that time," said Robinson. "There was no pinch-hitter going up for me, though. I'd have gone back to the plate with my shirt out and my trousers hanging down if that was what he wanted."

Robinson returned to a sea of waving handkerchiefs in the stands and struck out.

"If he had awarded Frank first base, things might have been a lot different," reasoned Weaver. "Boog [Powell] followed with a single and we would have had first and third with one out and might have been able to increase our three-run lead."

Then, in the bottom of the sixth inning, a curve sailed in and low to Jones, who tried to skip out of its way. It appeared it might have nailed Cleon on his right instep, although Jones strangely never moved toward first base at first.

DiMuro insisted that Jones had dodged it.

"I knew the ball hit me," said Jones. "I started for first base, but he said no."

The ball rolled into the Met dugout, between home and first, and was picked up by some Met player—allegedly Jerry Grote—who allegedly saw a smudge on it, an inch-long mark of black shoe polish. It ended up in the massive hands of Hodges.

"There was a big polish mark across the ball," said Gil, who said he didn't retain the sphere in question as a souvenir so that the media would just have to take his word for it. "I'm just happy our clubhouse man keeps our shoes nice and polished."

Now, it was not just a baseball, but rather Exhibit A. A calm Hodges took a deliberate walk to the plate and handed it to DiMuro, saying

Home-plate umpire Lou DiMuro waves Cleon Jones (far left) to first base after being handed scuffed ball by Gil Hodges (right). Donn Clendenon, observing here, followed with a two-run homer and, shoe enough, the Mets were on their way to a clinching.

simply, "Lou, the ball hit him." DiMuro inspected, was instantly convinced and pointed Jones to first base.

Ask yourself, how often does an umpire change his own ruling?

Easy.

Never.

"If the ball goes into their dugout instead of ours," said Hodges, "we never see it again."

Now, out of the Baltimore dugout came Weaver, the Game 4 ejectee, for yet another stimulating discussion with the arbiters. The topic was the chain of evidence and Earl respectfully wondered how DiMuro knew this ball was the same ball.

"The ball hit him," said Weaver. "Everybody in the park knew it. But he didn't call it until they showed him the ball with the shoe polish on it. I just wanted to ask him if he knew the ball went into their dugout. He said he did."

"I watched it all the way," said DiMuro, who incidentally thought the ballboy picked it up and gave it to the manager.

"We have worked on that play since spring training," deadpanned Art Shamsky. "Gil has had that ball with the shoe polish in his jacket all year."

Twenty-four years later, Koosman told an interviewer from *Sport Magazine* another account—which was either a funny practical joke implicating himself and Hodges or the real truth.

"Gil Hodges told me to hit it on my shoe . . . I did and I handed it to him," said Koosman. "Hodges took it right out to the umpire."

The reversal of the call had a lot to do with Hodges' reputation for honesty in the minds of all the umpires, but if there was shoe polish hanky panky, it wouldn't have been the first time. In fact, Casey Stengel was fond of saying it is always wise to keep a few balls with shoe polish handy in the dugout. In the '57 World Series, while playing Stengel's Yankees, a Milwaukee Brave named Nippy Jones was awarded first base on a hit by pitch by umpire Augie Donatelli thanks to shoe polish evidence and it led to a game-winning homer by Eddie Mathews in the inning.

"We Joneses have to stick together," said Cleon.

"They got that one right and Frank's wrong," said Weaver.

Donn Clendenon, about to be named Series MVP, followed by hitting a huge homer, his third of the Series and second against McNally, off the auxiliary scoreboard adorning the second deck down the left-field line.

The Mets, no longer lifeless, were down only 3-2.

"We were kind of dead," reflected Clendenon. "We needed a pickup."

The next pickup came from Weis, who hit a flyball to left in the seventh. Then it just kept carrying.

As Weis stepped into the box, Karl Ehrhardt, the famous sign man in the stands, had held up, "Do you believe in miracles?" When the ball cleared the wall at the 370-foot sign in left center to tie the game, the sign was replaced by another: "We believe."

"I was shocked as hell," said Weis. "I was just trying to hit a single."

"My roomie [Weis] rises to the occasion," said J.C. Martin. "He has muscles that he hasn't used yet."

Weis contributed four singles, four walks and this homer to the Mets' World Series cause.

"I thought we had them when Weis hit it out to tie it," said Bud Harrelson. "You could almost see them collapse and go 'whoosh.' They were saying to themselves, 'Here come these guys again.' . . . Al's homer gave us the momentum. Heck, Clendenon is getting paid to hit. Al isn't . . . In my mind, Weis was the MVP of this Series."

"I was just praying for him to get on some way, because then Gil would have let me hit and I could have bunted him over," said on-deck hitter Koosman, who retired 19 of 21 hitters and gave up one hit over the last six innings to finish with a five-hitter for his second Series victory.

"When he hit it out of the park, I must've jumped as high as the homer went . . . I knew we'd get more runs and I knew I wasn't going to give up any more. I don't lose games in the late innings."

"Their .200 hitters became .400 hitters," said Davey Johnson. "It was a Series for the little men."

Jerry Koosman, the epitome of class and cool, didn't have the overpowering stuff that he had enjoyed in Game 2, but had enough to finish off the extremely blue Birds with a complete game for his second World Series victory.

The final blows came in the eighth, against Baltimore right-hander Eddie Watt.

Jones led off the inning with a double off the center field wall and stayed there as Clendenon, after failing to bunt Cleon to third, grounded out. The hitter was Swoboda, who was not removed in favor of the lefty-swinging Shamsky. Hodges later explained he didn't pinch-hit, because he figured if he had, Shamsky would have been walked intentionally so Watt could face the right-handed-hitting Charles. Then, Gil figured, if he pinch-hit the lefty Wayne Garrett for The Glider, Weaver would have gone to a lefty.

"I decided to stick with Swoboda instead, because I knew what he could do," wrote Hodges in his column the next day. "I knew he has come through before against a right-hander."

Swoboda sent a hump-backed liner into left which Don Buford came very close to backhanding before trapping it on a bounce.

"Their bloops fell in," said Buford. "And we didn't hit any."

It was a double, scoring Jones, and the Mets led, 4-3. The stadium had never rocked like this before, as 57,397 achieved the equivalent of a simultaneous orgasm. It got louder when a pair of errors by first baseman Powell and Watt on the same grounder hit by Grote permitted Swoboda to cross with the run that made it 5-3.

Koosman walked Frank Robinson leading off the ninth, bringing the tying run to the plate.

"It would have broken my heart if we would have lost it after that two-run lead," said Koosman.

But Powell tapped to second and Brooks Robinson hit a long fly to right. Then Johnson hit his ball to left field and for a second it seemed hit well enough to be a threat to the party that was about to break out all over. Instead, it landed in Jones' glove and the field was suddenly inundated with base-stealing, turf-pulling, firecracker-throwing lunatics.

The 1969 Mets were champions.

When you begin a season as a 100-to-1 shot to accomplish a championship, when you read about angels in the outfield and teams of destiny, you eventually get defensive about not getting the proper credit for winning. So, amid the celebration, the Mets revealed their secrets: great pitching, timely hitting, multiple contributors, indomitable confidence, gritty determination.

"There is nothing miraculous about us," said Hodges.

"Don't give me that destiny stuff," said Swoboda, with a beer in the hand that robbed the Orioles of their sanity in Game 4. "Destiny brings you just so far, but destiny doesn't win you 100 games. Destiny doesn't win you a playoff. And destiny doesn't win four games for you in a best-of-seven series.

"We executed. We made the plays. We hit the ball. We got the pitching and they didn't . . . We lost the first game and we came back. We were down three runs and we came back. We were great in late innings and that is why we feel like champions and are champions."

"It boiled down to this: when it had to be done, we did it and they didn't," said shortstop Harrelson, who kept getting in the way of batted balls, to the tune of 17 assists in five games.

"No matter what they did, it was good enough," said Johnson. "No matter what we did, it wasn't good enough . . . The Mets were one of the few clubs we played this year that, when they went on the field, thought they could beat us."

Consider the telling numbers. Frank Robinson, Powell and Paul Blair hit a combined .163 with one homer, one RBI. Pitchers McNally and Mike Cuellar collected three of the Orioles' 23 hits, one of their four extra-base hits and three of their nine RBI. The Mets' pitchers had a collective 1.80 ERA.

"No other pitching staff has contained us this well over the course of a year," said Weaver. "The only thing that surprised me in the Series was that we didn't get more runs."

"I know the whole thing seems like a dream, but if it is, I don't want to wake up," said Clendenon.

BALTIMORE	ab	r	h	bl	METS	ab	r	h	bl
Buford lf	4	0	0	0	Agee cf	3	0	1	0
Blair cf	4	0	0	0	Harrelson ss	4	0	0	0
FRobinson rf	3	1	1	1	Jones lf	3	2	1	0
Powell 1b	4	0	1	0	Clendenon 1b	3	1	1	2
Salmon pr	0	0	0	0	Swoboda rf	4	1	2	1
BRobinson 3b	4	0	0	0	Charles 3b	4	0	0	0
Johnson 2b	4	0	1	0	Grote c	4	0	0	0
Belanger ss	3	1	1	0	Weis 2b	4	1	1	1
Etchebarren c	3	0	0	0	Koosman p	3	0	1	0
McNally p	2	1	1	2					
Motton ph	1	0	0	0					
Watt p	0	0	0	0					
Totals	**32**	**3**	**5**	**3**	**Totals**	**32**	**5**	**7**	**4**

Baltimore	003	000	000	— 3
Mets	000	002	12x	— 5

E-Powell, Watt. LOB-Baltimore 3, Mets 6. 2B-Koosman, Jones, Swoboda. HR-McNally (1), FRobinson (1), Clendenon (3), Weis (1). SB-Agee.

	IP	H	R	ER	BB	SO
Baltimore						
McNally	7	5	3	3	2	6
Watt (L, 0-1)	1	2	2	1	0	1
Mets						
Koosman (W, 2-0)	9	5	3	3	1	5

Hit by pitch-Jones (by McNally).

T-2:14. A-57,397.

Agee's Two Catches Stop Birds from Taking Flight

1969 World Series Game 3
October 14, 1969 in New York

The remarkable story of Game 3 of the 1969 World Series begins and ends with Tommie Agee, who turned in as dominant a performance as any non-pitcher in any post-season game. It begins with Agee's bat (a first-inning homer) and it ends with his glove—two unforgettable snatches of apparent extra-base hits headed for two different alleys. The twin larcenies robbed the Orioles of five runs, maybe six, in a 5-0 Met victory.

"I always felt Tommie Agee can beat you as many ways as Willie Mays can and now he is proving it," wrote Gil Hodges, guest newspaper columnist in his moonlighting job.

"That man has ability," said Baltimore manager Earl Weaver. Nothing he does surprises me . . . If you want to pick a most valuable player on their club, I'll take Agee.

"You have to figure that if Agee has a sore leg or an ingrown toenail that hurts or if he pulls a muscle in the first game, we have five runs in this one. And five runs isn't bad."

Agee's leather work began with the shot which Elrod Hendricks, the Orioles' lefty pull-hitting catcher, smashed the other way to left center with two on and two out in the fourth and the Mets leading, 3-0. Agee, in right center, came so far for that one that it appeared he might have started out in another borough.

Left fielder Cleon Jones shouted "plenty of room" to his old buddy from Mobile, Ala., as Agee neared the wall. And Jones later explained, "For him, two yards is plenty of room."

Actually, Agee had just enough room, but he had to reach as far as he could across his body to backhand the ball in the webbing of his glove before slamming into the wall.

"I haven't hit a ball that well to left-center in two years," said Hendricks. "I didn't think it would be caught. He was shading me to right center. He ran a hell of a long ways . . . I didn't see him catch it. I was just thinking about going for three. I was a short way from second and I figured I had a stand-up triple."

"I was shading him a little toward right field," said Agee. "I saw the ball well, because the sky was cloudy, not as bright as usual. But I wasn't sure if I could reach it. I figured if I touch the ball, I can hold it. I knew it would be tough, because it was away from my glove side —and it almost went through my webbing."

Hendricks couldn't believe his eyes when he glanced to the outfield to enjoy the damage he had wrought.

"I look up and see the white of the ball in his glove, so I figure he might still drop it," said Hendricks. "Then he holds his glove up and I just said, 'Damn.' I was thinking, sooner or later, this stuff has got to stop."

As the Shea crowd of 56,335, including Jackie Onassis, John Kennedy Jr. and his sister Caroline, went berserk, Agee trotted in with that strange, shoulder-swinging gait and displayed his prize—the ball lodged tightly high in the leather webbing—to umpire Shag Crawford on his way to the dugout.

"That ball shouldn't get through that far—not if my glove is right," said Agee. "Tom Seaver always checks my gloves for me. I will have to get after him about that. He's pitching tomorrow. I am sure he will check it this time."

Agee's second catch came during the seventh inning, with the score 4-0. Gary Gentry, the 23-year-old rookie starting pitcher, had just left the bases loaded with two outs and given way to an even younger reliever named Nolan Ryan. Perhaps you have heard of Ryan. He achieved some baseball notoriety for his strikeouts and no-hitters after his first team had given up on him.

But this was the eventual Hall of Famer's crowning moment of his blister-filled, pickle-brine-soaking days as a Met—and Agee made it possible.

Ryan jumped ahead of Paul Blair with an 0-and-2 count, and, like the 22-year-old he was, threw him a fastball that was too good.

"The pitch I gave Blair to hit was better than it should have been on two strikes," said Ryan. "At first, I thought it would drop in, but as soon as I saw Agee tap his glove, I knew he had it."

All it required was for the center fielder to leave his feet and make a tumbling catch.

"He taps his glove and then makes a diving catch," said Frank Robinson. "Where do you see a man tap his glove and then make a diving catch?"

"I thought I had it all the way. I didn't think I would have to dive," explained Agee, who muddied his knee and scraped an arm and elbow on the play. "I thought it would be a pretty easy catch, but the last 30 feet or so the wind picked it up and kept carrying it away from me and I had to hit the dirt."

"If the ball drops, I might've had an inside-the-park home run," said Blair. "I was just a step away from second base when he caught it."

"It was the greatest catch I have ever seen in a World Series," said Hodges. "The first one [ranked by Agee as higher in degree of difficulty, because it wasn't hit to his glove side and he had farther to go] was good, but not in the other one's class . . . The bases were loaded and he had to dive for the ball."

Met coach Yogi Berra has a vivid recollection of Sandy Amoros' amazing catch in the 1955 World Series, possibly because Berra was the robbed party.

"Amoros' catch wasn't as good as Agee's," said Berra. "I didn't hit the ball as well as Blair did . . . Like Gil says, neither of those other guys [Al Gionfriddo, who robbed Joe DiMaggio in 1947, or Amoros] got their uniforms dirty."

The first catch reminded Weaver of other plays made by Agee, including one when Earl was a bush-league boss and Tommie was a minor leaguer in the Chicago White Sox organization.

"It was 1963, in Charleston, West Virginia and I was managing Elmira," said Weaver. "We were playing for first place, Frankie Bertaina hit a shot to center field and he went back to the wall just like he did on the shot today and beat us. He could always play center field."

The only one who sounded unimpressed by Agee's second catch was Blair, a Gold Glove genius in center in his own right. "I didn't hit it hard and it didn't go up a power alley," he said.

Weaver preferred to praise Agee rather than to consider the fact that his powerful team was now hitting .133 for the Series, with 12 hits (10 of them singles) and five runs to show for three games.

"The Mets have the good arms and today they had the good legs— Agee's," said Earl.

Indeed, Agee came a long way on those legs—from the personal depths of a horrid 1968 season. As a first-year Met, Tommie was nailed in the head by a Bob Gibson fastball in his first exhibition game, then went on to hit a scintillating .217 (including an 0-for-10 in one game and an 0-for-34 in one stretch).

The 1969 season was much different for Agee as he became that rare threat: a leadoff man with home-run pop. In the bottom of the first inning of Game 3, he took Jim Palmer's 2-and-1 pitch over the wall in center for his first hit in nine World Series at-bats. It was the fifth time that Agee had led off a game with a homer in '69 and it was no coincidence that the Mets won four of the five.

But the big offensive blow in this game wasn't the Agee homer. It was delivered by, of all people, Gentry.

With two out in the second, Jerry Grote walked and Bud Harrelson singled. The hitter—a term used loosely here—was Gentry, on an 0-for-28 roll since his last hit Aug. 3, with one double and one RBI during the season. Even the picture of Raquel Welch that had been hanging over Gentry's locker since August for good luck—"That is as close as I'll ever get to her," he said—didn't figure to produce results in this mismatch.

"You know the scouting report said that Gentry swings the bat, but that was about all," said Palmer.

"I am not a cheap out," Gentry insisted. "I might not hit the ball but I will swing the bat. I like to hit."

Opponents liked it even more when he hit, because Gentry batted .081 in 1969.

So, naturally, Gentry ripped Palmer's first-pitch batting-practice fastball to the warning track in right center, beyond the grasp of Blair (who was positioned closer to second base than the wall) and right fielder Robinson, who was sore-legged. Two runners crossed the plate on the double and the Mets led, 3-0.

"Palmer wasn't himself today," decided Weaver.

"You know what took the starch out of Baltimore?" said second baseman Ken Boswell, who had an infield hit and scored the Mets' fourth run on Grote's double in the sixth. "It was Gentry's hit. They were dead after that."

Gentry retired 10 of the first 11 Oriole hitters and gave up three hits over 6⅔ innings. Agee bailed him out of that fourth-inning unpleasantness, after Frank Robinson and Boog Powell had singled. Gentry remained in command until he brought about Hodges' hook by issuing three of his five walks in the seventh. The Arizona State product left a big impression.

"He looked faster than Seaver or [Jerry] Koosman to me," said Frank Robinson.

From faster to fastest. Hodges called for Ryan, inconsistent but overpowering as a baby flame thrower.

"I never let it touch my hand," said Grote, sharing the secret of catching the Ryan Express. "I catch it in the webbing of my glove. Of course, I have had to restring my mitt 10 times this year."

Agee saved Ryan's save with his catch on Blair, then Nolan allowed only one hit the rest of the way: an infield single. Ed Kranepool's eighth-inning homer off reliever Dave Leonhard made it 5-0 before Ryan allowed the Birds to load the bases in the ninth. The hitter was Blair, again.

"When I am in relief, I usually just throw fastballs," said Ryan after finishing a combined four-hit shutout with his third strikeout in 2⅓ innings. "I threw Blair two fastballs and then I got him on my curve. He definitely wasn't looking for that."

The truth is, the Orioles—impotent and down two-games-to-one in a Series they had figured to dominate—didn't have a clue about what was hitting them. However, they still insisted that it wasn't divine intervention or a magic spell.

"The man upstairs likes me as much as he likes them," insisted Weaver, who added when asked if he thought the Mets were a team of destiny, "No, I think they are a team with good defensive outfielders."

"Everybody is trying to put a divinity aspect on the Mets," said Don Buford. "But we have as many religious guys on our club as they do."

Perhaps, but who were the chosen people?

"The writers want to make it like someone is looking over them, but there is nothing to that," said F. Robby. "They are making the plays. They probably made them all season . . . The Mets aren't pulling any strings . . . They played better than we did, so they won."

"They are not Supermen. They are just flesh and blood . . . I'll believe it's magic when I see them flying around. The next thing they will be talking about angels in the Mets' outfield."

Did Agee have wings? No, he did not. Just the wind beneath them, according to Davey Johnson, who recognized which way this World Series was blowing.

"The wind was changing in Agee's favor all day," said the cerebral infielder whom Weaver liked to call Little Dummy. "When he hit the homer it was blowing with the ball [out]. When Hendricks hit his, it was blowing the other way, against the ball. When Blair hit his, the wind was blowing back the other way [from right toward center] . . . We are in an unfavorable chance deviation. The chances aren't going with us."

"We're not spooked," said Brooks Robinson. "We're not spooked."

"The Orioles are a perfect team," reasoned Gentry, "but we're lucky—and that's better."

"We certainly picked up some non-believers with this one," said Hodges.

The only holdouts left were in the Baltimore dugout . . . and they were starting to sound unconvincing, with Seaver, due for a big game, and Koosman on tap for Games 4 and 5.

"If they do it two more times, I might start believing it," insisted Palmer.

Meanwhile, on the night that capped his glorious day in Game 3, Agee went home and couldn't sleep.

"I kept dreaming about the catches and I'd wake up screaming," he said. "In my dreams, I kept missing them."

BALTIMORE				METS				
	ab	r	h	bl		ab	r	h	bl
Buford lf	3	0	0	0	Agee cf	3	1	1	1
Blair cf	5	0	0	0	Garrett 3b	1	0	0	0
FRobinson rf	2	0	1	0	Jones lf	4	0	0	0
Powell 1b	4	0	2	0	Shamsky rf	4	0	0	0
BRobinson 3b	4	0	0	0	Weis 2b	0	0	0	0
Hendricks c	4	0	0	0	Boswell 2b	3	1	1	0
Johnson 2b	4	0	0	0	Gaspar rf	1	0	0	0
Belanger ss	2	0	0	0	Kranepool 1b	4	1	1	1
Palmer p	2	0	0	0	Grote c	3	1	1	1
May ph	0	0	0	0	Harrelson ss	3	1	1	0
Leonhard p	0	0	0	0	Gentry p	3	0	1	2
Dalrymple ph	1	0	1	0	Ryan p	0	0	0	0
Salmon pr	0	0	0	0					
Totals	**31**	**0**	**4**	**0**	**Totals**	**29**	**5**	**6**	**5**

Baltimore	000	000	000	— 0
Mets	120	001	01x	— 5

E-Palmer. LOB-Baltimore 11, Mets 6. 2B-Gentry, Grote. HR-Agee, Kranepool. S-Garrett.

	IP	H	R	ER	BB	SO
Baltimore						
Palmer (L, 0-1)	6	5	4	4	4	5
Leonhard	2	1	1	1	1	1
Mets						
Gentry (W, 1-0)	6⅔	3	0	0	5	4
Ryan (S, 1)	2⅓	1	0	0	2	3

T-2:23. A-56,335.

6

Ventura's Slam of a Single Makes for a Sweet 15th

METS 4, BRAVES 3

1999 NLCS Game 5
October 17, 1999 in New York

It was the ultimate finish to the ultimate dance—five hours and 46 minutes' worth of tension, the longest tango in post-season history, as the on-the-brink Mets fought to remain breathing with the Braves' hands around their throats for 15 innings.

It was the drive that assured an NLCS Game 6, that sent the Mets back to Atlanta still dreaming of becoming the first baseball team ever to escape an 0-and-3 post-season series hole.

It was the checkmate in a managerial chess marathon between Bobby V and Bobby C. The two men moved and counter-moved until a playoff-record 44 players, including a record 15 pitchers, had been used, no switches were left unpulled and Valentine and his team were somehow still standing while Cox was explaining.

It assured Melvin Mora's peg to cutoff man Edgardo Alfonzo, which led to the erasing of Keith Lockhart at the plate in the 13th inning— yet another memorable, impactful play by the Forrest Gump of this October—wouldn't wind up being a game-prolonging footnote.

It meant that 12 innings of one-run relief work by the Mets' pen would be rewarded and that the Braves would be haunted by an LCS record 19 runners left on base (18 of them against the relievers) just one game after having stranded no runners at all.

It was so long in coming that Masato Yoshii, who had been knocked out in the fourth inning, insisted that he had completely forgotten that he started the game by the time it was over.

It was set up by the persistence of Shawon Dunston, whose strength of character allowed him to atone for not catching what seemed to be the game-costing triple in the 15th with a remarkable, rally-igniting, 12-pitch war of an at-bat in the bottom half.

It was a triumph for Robin Ventura, who refused to use torn cartilage in his left knee or pain in a right shoulder that would require surgery as an alibi for his NLCS futility, which had reached 0-for-16 prior to an 11th-inning single. It represented personal vindication for the clutch veteran whose ineffectiveness was such that Valentine actually pinch-hit for him with Todd Pratt against John Rocker in Game 3.

It was a 2-and-1 fastball from an overmatched kid named Kevin McGlinchy that Ventura sent soaring through the hard rain, far enough to clear the wall at the 371-foot sign in right center with the bases loaded. It was the blow that snapped a 3-3 tie and sent 55,723 delirious fans to the exits, finally, with the scoreboard flashing "Ya Gotta Believe" and the song "New York State of Mind" blaring.

It was a lot of things.

What it wasn't was a grand slam.

That is because Pratt, the runner on first, perhaps even more excited than when he hit the extra-inning homer that finished Arizona in Game 4 of the Division Series, picked up Ventura like a doll before Robin could reach second base.

So history will always tell us that Ventura's game-winner in a 4-3 Met triumph was the longest of singles, long enough to score pinch-runner Roger Cedeño from third base under the watchful eye of the home-plate umpire Jerry Layne. If Pratt had swallowed Ventura just a little sooner—before he reached first—Robin would have been the second out and if the runners hadn't tagged up properly (which they did to guarantee the run would count), the Mets and Braves might still be playing.

"Maybe tonight, when you guys [the media] go home, I might run the bases," said Ventura, who joked that he was too drained to run them and later teased Pratt about wanting to be the only guy who gets to do a home-run trot on a walk-off homer.

"I was yelling, 'Run, Robin, you gotta run. You hit a grand slam!'" said Dunston. "But he didn't seem to care."

"I'll take the blame. I put him over my head," said Pratt, a 14th-inning sub for Mike Piazza who earned a five-pitch walk that forced in the tying run. "Robin said he had it all planned. He said he was going to pull a Kirk Gibson [in the 1988 World Series Game 1]."

Clutch Robin Ventura, right arm raised in the center of a tornado of Met jubilation, felled the Braves with a 15th-inning grand slam that, thanks to the intervention of a practically berserk Todd Pratt, became the game-winning single that kept the Mets alive.

"No big deal," said Ventura, who had three grand slams during the regular season to boost his career total to 13. "As long as I touched first base, we won. So that's fine with me . . . I'll use it against Todd Pratt, but I won't care."

"They should give it to him," said Orel Hershiser. "Anybody hits it over the fence in that situation, especially in New York, there should be an asterisk."

In his previous at-bat, in the 14th inning, Ventura had just missed hitting a homer off birthday boy Rocker, flying out to the warning track in center.

"He had a great swing at that fastball, but you could tell he had hardly anything left," said Valentine. "But there was something big left."

Ventura fouled a 1-and-0 fastball from McGlinchy straight back—he just missed it—and then watched a nearly wild pitch. Then he pounced.

"I was just looking for a pitch I could hit in the air," said Ventura. "It just seemed like my swing got smoother there, all of a sudden."

"It was just classic of him to come through," said Pratt.

Like in the movies.

"It's almost like that *Field of Dreams* thing, where the ball hits the lights and everything explodes and it starts pouring," said Hershiser, whose 3⅓ innings of one-hit, five-strikeout shutout relief were more unerring than his grasp of film history (it was *The Natural*). "This one was surreal."

"We have been winning some games really freaky-like," said Al Leiter, the Game 6 starter who was throwing for possible insertion in the 14th. "If there is a 1-800-psychic line, they're definitely rallying around us."

The Mets, so accustomed to walking the ledge without a net they almost seemed to insist upon it, hadn't scored from the second through the 14th. But they had returned from the brink. Again.

"All of us went to the edge and looked over," said Hershiser. "Fortunately, all of us got scared and came back to land."

"It was getting crazy," noted Darryl Hamilton. "It was getting to the point where your stomach was coming out of your guts."

"I am sure it was a fun game from the fans' perspective . . . sort of like watching a scary movie," decided Rocker.

"I'm kind of getting used to it. It seems like we have been doing this for a couple of weeks now," said Valentine.

It all started well enough for the Mets.

John Olerud took Greg Maddux deep to right in the first inning, with Rickey Henderson on board via an infield single, giving the Mets a 2-0 lead. Thing is, that was the end of their offense against Maddux, who got Rey Ordoñez to ground into a double play to escape a one-out, bases-loaded fix that resulted from shoddy fielding by first baseman Ryan Klesko in the sixth.

Many hours after throwing his gopher ball to Olerud for the first baseman's third homer of the 1999 post-season, Maddux was lamenting the start to his seven strong innings.

"I'm just upset I gave up those two runs in the first," said Maddux, whose work left the Atlanta starters at 3-0 with a 1.77 ERA over the first five games. "You can lose games in the first."

Not the way Yoshii was going. He gave up the lead in the fourth, when Bret Boone and Chipper Jones doubled and Brian Jordan singled. With the score tied, Klesko walked, putting Braves at first and second with none out. Valentine couldn't stand to watch any more, so he said sayonara to Masato and summoned the 41-year-old Hershiser, who pitched like the calendar said 1988.

Hershiser struck out Andruw Jones and Eddie Perez swinging, then got Walt Weiss on a roller to first. Orel struck out Jordan with two on in the fifth and then he escaped another jam, not of his making, in the sixth. Klesko reached on Olerud's uncharacteristic error. A sacrifice, an intentional walk to Perez and an unintentional one to Weiss meant the bases were loaded for Maddux with one out and a two-strike count.

Cox called for the suicide squeeze and Maddux, who can help

himself with bat and glove and almost always does, made no contact for strike three. Klesko became one dead Brave in the rundown for the third out.

"The ball was right down the middle. He [Maddux] has never missed one of those," said Cox, whose team came into the game with a .198 average for the NLCS and went 1-for-13 with runners in scoring position vs. the Met relievers in Game 5. "I don't know what happened. He didn't either. We would have been home about 3½ hours ago if we got that down. But he missed it."

"It was a critical point of the game, but by the end it was just a footnote," said Hershiser.

The Braves loaded the bases again in the seventh inning as a desperate Valentine overmanaged his bullpen right down to the bone. He removed Hershiser, brought in Turk Wendell, Dennis Cook (for an intentional pass) and Pat Mahomes, who got Andruw Jones on a flyball for the final out. John Franco came on to strand two more Braves in the eighth and stayed for the ninth. After Armando Benitez threw his inning in the 10th, Valentine was left with Kenny Rogers (two blanks) and rookie Octavio Dotel.

"If I ever made more moves than this in a game, I can't remember them," said Valentine, who used nine pitchers and called for five intentional walks.

All that shuffling appeared to be for naught in the 13th, when, with two out, Lockhart singled to right center and Chipper Jones crushed a double to right off Dotel. The go-ahead run was being waved homeward and Mora came charging after the ball.

Magnificent Melvin ignored the slick grass and hit Alfonzo with an off-balance, short-hop throw and the second baseman turned and sent a perfect one-hop peg to Piazza that arrived with Lockhart still 10 feet from paydirt. The catcher absorbed a nasty hit that wound up sending him out of the game, one swinging strikeout later, with a bruised right forearm. But Piazza held onto the ball.

"It was a perfect throw from both of us, but I thought he was going to score easy," said Mora. "I was surprised . . . I thought he was faster than that. I definitely score on that ball."

"They were playing with a watermelon," marvelled Hershiser. "That ball could have skidded. It could have done anything. Not too many defensive plays bring out a whole dugout to greet the three fielders who put it together."

In the 15th, Weiss singled to left and stole second. Weiss scored for a 3-2 Atlanta lead when Dunston, a former infielder playing center in his baseball old age, misjudged a shot off Lockhart's bat and turned the third out into a triple.

"The bench had moved me in . . . I just couldn't get it," Dunston said. "Probably Andruw Jones could catch it. Maybe Kenny Lofton and the rest of the great center fielders. But I gave it my best effort and I don't make any excuses."

Soon, it was Cox' turn to explain. Starting the 15th, the Braves skipper went to the unproven McGlinchy, instead of either starter John Smoltz (whom he had already used as his closer in Game 2 of this series) or Kevin Millwood (his Game 6 starter, if necessary, who had also relieved in the Division Series).

"I wasn't going to use Millwood tonight . . . I'd rather [that he] be given the opportunity to be on our field with a good [not wet] mound," said Cox. "And he [McGlinchy] is a big leaguer."

The first hitter was Dunston, who insisted he "wasn't down" and proved it by fouling off six full-count pitches before slapping a ground single to center to end a 12-pitch duel.

"I would be lying if I said I was spoiling, I was just hacking," said Dunston. "I'm a hacker, not a walker . . . I had two walks this year and maybe 150 in my career. I just said, 'Put the ball in play.' I was up there to swing the bat."

"The biggest part of that inning was Shawon's at-bat," said John Franco.

"I was trying to keep a season alive," said Dunston.

With pinch-hitter Matt Franco at the plate, Dunston took advantage of McGlinchy's high leg kick and stole second. Franco walked. Then Alfonzo reminded everyone that even an RBI man needs to be able to sacrifice when he gave himself up to put runners at second and third with one out. After an intentional pass to Olerud, Pratt worked out the walk that made it 3-3.

Then it was time for Ventura to send everyone home with his, er, single.

"I looked out there, but I didn't see no ball," said Dunston.

"I didn't know it was over the fence," insisted Valentine. "There were a lot of bodies running out on the field.

"I just wanted to hit it in the air and get the run home," said Ventura.

"I am disgusted with myself," said McGlinchy. "I was the last guy out there standing. We had no one left. I hated to be a guy who had to walk off the field at the end."

"I feel so good for Robin," said Hamilton. "Everyone has been ripping him, but nobody realizes he has been going out there on one leg. He has been in terrible pain, but he goes out there every day and never complains. He is a gamer."

A gamer with another game to play.

"We just play another day," said Ventura. "It seems like we've been saying that for a month and a half now."

"It seems like we have had one foot in the grave and one on a banana peel," said Piazza.

So, was this destiny, the hand of fate?

"Maybe a little, but that doesn't mean we haven't worked for it," said Piazza.

"No," said Pratt. "You make your fate. This is a very good team."

ATLANTA

	ab	r	h	rbi	bb	so	lob	avg
Williams lf	7	0	1	0	1	1	3	.268
Boone 2b	3	1	1	0	0	1	1	.351
Nixon pr	0	0	0	0	0	0	0	1.000
Lockhart 2b	4	0	2	1	0	1	2	.333
CJones 3b	6	1	3	1	2	2	1	.241
Jordan rf	7	0	2	1	1	3	5	.316
Klesko 1b	2	0	0	0	1	0	0	.250
Hunter ph-1b	3	0	0	0	1	0	2	.000
AJones cf	5	0	0	0	1	2	6	.194
Perez c	4	0	2	0	1	1	2	.364
Battle pr	0	0	0	0	0	0	0	.000
Myers c	1	0	0	0	1	1	1	.000
Weiss ss	6	1	2	0	1	1	5	.292
Maddux p	3	0	0	0	0	3	4	.000
Hernandez ph	1	0	0	0	0	1	1	.083
Mulholland p	0	0	0	0	0	0	0	.000
Guillen ph	1	0	0	0	0	0	1	.000
Remlinger p	0	0	0	0	0	0	0	.000
Springer p	0	0	0	0	0	0	0	.000
Fabregas ph	1	0	0	0	0	1	0	.000
Rocker p	0	0	0	0	0	0	0	.000
McGlinchy p	1	0	0	0	0	1	1	.000
Totals	**55**	**3**	**13**	**3**	**10**	**19**	**35**	

BATTING: 2B-Perez (2, Yoshii); Boone (2, Yoshii); CJones 2 (2, Yoshii, Dotel); Williams (2, Hershiser); Weiss (2, Mahomes). 3B-Lockhart (1, Dotel). S-AJones. RBI-CJones (2), Jordan (11), Lockhart (1). 2-out RBI-Lockhart. Runners left in scoring position, 2 out-Williams 2, Weiss 1, Jordan 2, AJones 2, Lockhart 1. GIDP-Weiss. Team LOB-19

BASERUNNING: SB-Nixon (2, 2nd base off Wendell/Piazza); Battle (1, 2nd base off Benitez/Piazza); Weiss (2, 2nd base off Dotel/Pratt). CS-Klesko (1, home by Hershiser/Piazza).

FIELDING: E-Klesko 2 (2, ground ball, throw). DP-2 (Weiss-Klesko, Lockhart-Weiss-Hunter).

METS

	ab	r	h	rbi	bb	so	lob	avg
Henderson lf	5	1	1	0	0	1	1	.242
Rogers p	0	0	0	0	0	0	0	.000
Bonilla ph	1	0	0	0	0	1	1	.000
Dotel p	0	0	0	0	0	0	0	.000
MFranco ph	0	0	0	0	1	0	0	.000
Cedeño pr	0	1	0	0	0	0	0	.471
Alfonzo 2b	6	0	1	0	0	2	1	.237
Olerud 1b	6	1	2	2	1	0	1	.351
Piazza c	6	0	1	0	0	3	1	.172
Pratt c	0	0	0	1	1	0	0	.200
Ventura 3b	7	0	2	1	0	1	3	.152
Mora rf	6	0	1	0	0	2	2	.308
Hamilton cf	3	0	2	0	0	0	2	.200
Agbayani ph-if	1	0	0	0	2	0	0	.188
Ordoñez ss	6	0	0	0	0	0	6	.147
Yoshii p	1	0	0	0	0	1	1	.000
Hershiser p	1	0	0	0	0	0	0	.000
Wendell p	0	0	0	0	0	0	0	.000
Cook p	0	0	0	0	0	0	0	.000
Mahomes p	1	0	0	0	0	1	0	.000
JFranco p	0	0	0	0	0	0	0	.000
Benitez p	0	0	0	0	0	0	0	.000
Dunston ph-cf	3	1	1	0	0	1	1	.167
Totals	**53**	**4**	**11**	**4**	**5**	**13**	**20**	

BATTING: 2B-Hamilton (1, Maddux). HR-Olerud (3, 1st inning off Maddux 1 on, 1 out). S-Alfonzo. RBI-Olerud 2 (11), Pratt (3), Ventura (2). Runners left in scoring position, 2 out-Henderson 1, Ordoñez 1. GIDP-Ordoñez, Ventura. Team LOB-12.

BASERUNNING: SB-Agbayani (1, 2nd base off McGlinchy/Myers); Dunston (1, 2nd base off McGlinchy/Myers).

FIELDING: E-Olerud (2, ground ball). Outfield assists-Mora (Lockhart at home). DP-2 (Piazza-Ventura-Hershiser, Ventura-Alfonzo-Olerud).

One out when winning run scored.

IBB-CJones 2 (by Hershiser, by Dotel); Perez (by Hershiser); Jordan (by Cook); Williams (by Mahomes); Olerud (by McGlinchy). HBP-Boone (by Hershiser). Pitches-strikes: Yoshii 51-34; Hershiser 56-35; Wendell 5-3; Cook 2-0; Mahomes 27-14; Franco 15-11; Benitez 12-9; Rogers 24-16; Dotel 69-44; Maddux 91-67; Mulholland 24-20; Remlinger 28-17; Springer 15-9; Rocker 14-10; McGlinchy 47-20. Ground/flyballs: Yoshii 3-3; Hershiser 3-1; Wendell 0-0; Cook 0-0; Mahomes 1-1; Franco 1-1; Benitez 1-1; Rogers 4-1; Dotel 1-2; Maddux 12-4; Mulholland 4-0; Remlinger 1-3; Springer 0-2; Rocker 0-2; McGlinchy 2-0. Batters faced: Yoshii 14; Hershiser 15; Wendell 2; Cook 0; Mahomes 6; Franco 5; Benitez 4; Rogers 7; Dotel 14; Maddux 29; Mulholland 6; Remlinger 7; Springer 4; Rocker 4; McGlinchy 9.

Umpires: Home-Layne; First-Crawford; Second-Montague; Third-Kellogg; Left-Reliford; Right-Rapuano.

T-5:46. A-55,723.

Atlanta	000	200	000	000	001	— 3
Mets	200	000	000	000	002	— 4

Atlanta	IP	H	R	ER	BB	SO	HR	ERA
Maddux	7	7	2	2	0	5	1	2.14
Mulholland	2	1	0	0	0	2	0	6.75
Remlinger	2	1	0	0	0	2	0	5.87
Springer	1	0	0	0	1	1	0	0.00
Rocker	1⅓	0	0	0	0	2	0	0.00
McGlinchy (L, 0-1)	1	2	2	2	4	1	0	13.50
Mets								
Yoshii	3	4	2	2	1	3	0	5.54
Hershiser	3⅓	1	0	0	3	5	0	0.00
Wendell	⅓	0	0	0	1	1	0	1.50
Cook	0	0	0	0	0	0	0	0.00
Mahomes	1	1	0	0	2	1	0	4.50
JFranco	1⅓	1	0	0	0	2	0	0.00
Benitez	1	1	0	0	1	0	0	0.00
Rogers	2	1	0	0	1	1	0	6.17
Dotel (W, 1-0)	3	4	1	1	2	5	0	8.10

Mets Push Birds to Brink on Rocky's Dive, J.C.'s Bunt

METS 2, ORIOLES 1

1969 World Series Game 4
October 15, 1969 in New York

The difference between winning and losing a baseball game and a championship is so small it's frightening.

It is one well-timed defensive play made and another costly play botched. It is a fearless, diving, game-saving catch from the most clumsy of outfielders and a broken-bat gift double on a catchable fly lost in the glare by a usually reliable fielder.

It is a remarkable pitcher performing remarkably in protecting a stake of one run through eight innings and willing himself to make 150 pitches in pursuit of a boyhood dream.

It is an extra-inning bunt that failed at the eventual cost of a go-ahead run and another that became a shocking, game-winning, lucky success because of a rushed throw, the deafening din of a crowd and an umpire's non-call.

Submitted for your immense approval, Game 4 of the 1969 World Series: a 2-1, 10-inning Met victory, fit for the time capsule. It is remembered joyously by 57,367 barely believing witnesses at Shea as the day that Ron Swoboda left his feet for an out-of-body experience that is still a mystery even to him. It is recalled painfully by the deflated Orioles as the day they grudgingly abandoned their hopes that October '69 might yet belong to them.

Swoboda—whose defensive capacity in right field had improved from tragi-comic to simply awkward by 1969, but who would never be confused with Tommie Agee—made a catch twice as miraculous as the two that Agee had made to save five runs in Game 3.

And it came in the ninth inning of a one-run game that might otherwise have ended in a Met loss right then.

To set the stage, the Orioles had run their scoreless streak to 19 straight innings by the ninth inning of this game, which found a tiring Tom Seaver still clinging to a 1-0 lead afforded by Donn Clendenon's second-inning homer off Mike Cuellar.

There was one out and Orioles at first and third on singles by Frank Robinson (now 1-for-12 in the Series) and Boog Powell. Gil Hodges told his pitcher, on a comebacker, to throw home to cut down the tying run rather than take any chance on getting a game-ending double play. However, Brooks Robinson made the instruction moot by driving Seaver's first pitch on a screaming line toward the gap in right center.

As the opposite-field outfielder, Swoboda—known as "Rocky" in recognition of the contents of his head or perhaps just the bumps in his game—was positioned shallow enough to possibly make a play on a tagged-up Frank Robinson at the plate if there was a medium-length fly.

Swoboda broke with the crack of the bat. However, this ball was tagged. Suddenly, the tying run was the least of the Mets' worries. It looked like a double for Brooks, maybe two RBI, and it seemed certain to change the course of this Series.

However, Swoboda launched himself into a dive, caught the ball with glove outstretched across his body, hit the ground hard, skidded on his face, rolled completely over, bounced to his feet and came up throwing. The most stunning sacrifice fly in history had tied the game at 1. The Mets' appeal on Frank Robinson leaving third too soon with Baltimore's second run in 27 innings was denied. No matter—the frustrated and confused Orioles were finished.

More Big Bird than swan in the outfield, Ron Swoboda employs a fearless, fully extended belly flop to rob Brooks Robinson and turn an extra-base hit into a sac fly, then rolls over. The unconventional, irrepressible Rocky was a symbol of the 1969 overachievers.

"Last year, that ball goes to the fence," said Clay Dalrymple, "Swoboda picks it up, drops it, then misses the cutoff man with the throw."

"No, last year that ball hits him in the head," said eventual losing pitcher Dick Hall.

"If he tries to make that play all of next year, they will finish ninth," offered Merv Rettenmund.

Davey Johnson wondered how a play so foolhardy could turn out so well.

"It was an unbelievable catch, but a bad play," said Davey. "If he misses the ball, we take the lead and win the game. He has to try to hold it to a single."

The view from the mound, in the eyes of a grateful pitcher, was less incredulous. Perhaps Seaver would have been more astonished if his expectations for his teammates had not been expanded exponentially by a season of envelope-pushing excellence and embarrassingly good fortune.

"A couple of years ago, I would've thought there was no chance it would be caught," said Seaver. "But the way we have been playing the last four months, I don't consider anything a hit until I see it hit the ground."

It never hit the ground. But Swoboda did, as he put it, "like two bags of cement."

But he held onto the ball.

The way he saw it, he couldn't have cut that ball off if he had decided to play it cautiously. Besides what fun would that have been?

"I didn't think of anything. Me see ball . . . Me go for ball . . . Me catch ball," said Swoboda, who also made a nice play on a deep Elrod Hendricks shot for the final out of the inning. "I want to thank the Rawlings people for making such a fine glove. Didn't [legendary law-breaker John] Dillinger thank the Ford people for making such fast [getaway] cars?"

All there was riding on this dive was a World Series. Lighten up, man. It wasn't life or death. Just do or die.

"You know that if you catch the ball, you aren't going to throw anybody out [tagging], but you have to try," he explained. "If it gets by you, OK, there is nothing you can do . . . It's not a gamble. You either try to catch it or watch it roll to the fence. If you can't [reach it], it's going through anyway, because there is no way to get behind it and cut it off.

"If there is even one chance in a thousand to catch it, I am going to try."

Swoboda was asked if this catch was better than the one he made on Bob Gibson with the bases loaded during the '69 season. He admitted that it was.

Apparently, the impossible just takes a little longer to explain.

"That one I dove with my glove wide open [the pocket and web upwards]," said Swoboda. "On this one, I had to turn my hand backwards to get it. And I just did get it. A backhand dive closes the glove."

Agee noticed that his friend, the extra-base-hit robber in right, picked the perfect time to leave folks with their mouths open in shock.

"What makes a great catch is when you make it," said the center fielder. "It's only great if it matters. It's easy to make a great catch in July. In October, you have to be nervous diving like that."

Swoboda and these Mets didn't know enough about post-season stakes to be nervous. And they did know—as the rest of the public was finding out—The Force was truly with them. And, on this day, so was the Seaver whom they were accustomed to riding.

After the Mets had stranded two runners in the ninth, Johnson reached on Wayne Garrett's error to start the Baltimore 10th. However, Mark Belanger, usually adept at handling the bat though not feared for swinging it, failed to get the runner over, popping up a bunt attempt to Jerry Grote. Thus, no run could score when Dalrymple followed with a single to left center. Seaver got Don Buford on a long fly to right and then threw a 1-and-2 curve to Paul Blair that the center fielder waved at.

Hodges decided that Seaver's workday was finally done with his sixth strikeout, after 150 tension-filled pitches, and that it would be time for Tug McGraw in the 11th, if there was an 11th.

Seaver's day began with the pitcher angry at the sight of his picture on the cover of a leaflet protesting the war in Vietnam with a newspaper quote saying he planned to buy an ad in *The New York Times* that would read, "If the Mets can win the World Series, we can get out of Vietnam." Seaver said any war protest he would make wouldn't come during a World Series and it would be registered in his role as a citizen, not a Cy Young winner.

Seaver didn't need any distractions because this already had been a difficult post-season for him. The 25-game winner was coming off a shelling by the Atlanta Braves in the NLCS and a 4-1 humbling by the Orioles in Game 1 of this Series. However, in Game 4, he was up to the challenge of being his masterful self. In fact, he retired 17 of 18 hitters going into the ninth and allowed only three hits through eight innings.

Seaver's heady handling of Blair's popped bunt attempt—following a nifty play on a one-bouncer that forced Clendenon to extend every inch of his 6-foot-4 frame—were the keys to escaping a two-on, none-out jam in the third. Then Tom was cut behind his left ankle and his toe was bruised when he was spiked by Hendricks while the pitcher covered first in the fourth.

"I took two steps and swore, so I knew I'd be able to pitch," said Seaver, aware that World Series victories are found at the intersection of immense talent and true grit. "I was 100 percent confident the entire time that I could shut them out. I really felt I could, but I made a couple of mistakes."

Seaver's mistake pitches paled next to the two gigantic blunders the Orioles' fielders made in the bottom of the 10th.

Grote, leading off, was nailed on the fists and broke his bat with a big swing on a 3-and-2 count against Hall. The catcher's flare to left became a leadoff double—thanks to one of the world's worst jumps, by Buford.

"I thought the ball was hit harder than it was," testified the guilty party. "My first step was back. Then when I started in, I didn't pick up the ball right away because of the glare."

"I looked at Buford and he wasn't even coming," said Belanger, the shortstop. "He didn't break at all. So I just kept going. I never touched it though."

Al Weis was intentionally walked to set up a force at third base and get to the pitcher's spot. Hodges pinch-hit with J.C. (Joseph Clifton) Martin. Orioles manager-for-a-day Billy Hunter, filling in for the ejected Earl Weaver, replaced the righty Hall with lefty Pete Richert. Hodges flashed the bunt sign, with Agee on deck.

Martin laid down a beauty on Richert's first and only pitch, toward the first-base side. It dropped dead perfectly on the grass 10 feet toward first, equidistant between the Orioles' fourth pitcher of the game and Hendricks. It was going to be close at first. The catcher had the better throwing angle to make a play there, but apparently not enough lung power for his screams to be heard by Richert.

"I just went for the ball," said Richert. "He might have yelled. 'First base' or he might have yelled, 'I got it.' But, with all those people yelling, if I stop to listen, I don't make the play."

"I was yelling, 'I got it, I got it.' But I guess the damned crowd drowned me out," said Elrod. "I didn't think it was that good a bunt. It should have been a routine play."

Richert fielded the bunt, wheeled and threw toward Davey Johnson, covering at first, but the ball never reached Johnson's glove. It hit the elbow of Martin—taking an inside path down the line that would prove controversial when it was too late to matter—and rolled toward no-man's land, second base.

"I knew it was a good bunt," said Martin, wearing what he called a happy knob where the throw had hit him. "As I was going to first, I knew it was going to be a close play. Davey Johnson was getting down real low to take the throw, so I came in high, hoping the ball would hit me and I tried to swell up. When it hit me on the left wrist, it was the greatest feeling in the world."

"He was pumping his arms," said Richert. "If his hand was an inch higher, the ball doesn't hit him."

"A Met bounce," said Belanger, catching on to the trends.

"If the throw had been good," said Johnson, "I would probably have caught it. But I would have been trampled and would have laid there with the ball in my hand while the run scored."

Though the ball was rolling around unattended, pinch-runner Rod Gaspar—providing the answer to the Orioles' taunting, pre-World Series question "Who is Ron Gaspar?"—stopped at third briefly before coach Eddie Yost, waving wildly, screamed at him to go home with the winning run.

"It looked like a Chinese fire drill out there," said Swoboda.

"What a beautiful bunt," said club owner Mrs. Joan Payson, wearing a gold No. 1 on her wool suit and waving one finger in the air as she was escorted through the crowd.

Seaver was even more thrilled than Payson and most of his jubilant teammates about the three-games-to-one Series lead, because the Game 4 victory belonged to him.

"I saw him hit the plate and I said to myself, 'I have won a World Series game. My God, I have won,'" said Seaver. "This is the most exciting moment of my life. When the run scored, I was a kid again and my entire life flashed before my eyes . . . I have wanted this since I was nine years old."

Seaver's first reaction had been to whisper into the ear of his friend, Game 5 starter Jerry Koosman: "Get 'em tomorrow. Stuff it down their throats. One more."

It was only after the umpires had left the field that the controversy about Martin's location surfaced. Photographs showed that, according to the rules, J.C. should have been declared out for interference and the Met runners sent back.

"I'd like to see the replays, because he [Martin] seemed to be right in Davey's line when I threw the ball," insisted Richert.

Unsurprisingly, Weaver placed the blame on NL arbiter Shag Crawford, who had made Earl the first World Series manager to be ejected since Charlie Grimm in 1935. Weaver's sin was coming out of the dugout to argue balls and strikes in the third.

"It's the plate umpire's call," said Weaver. "It takes a lot of guts to call it, but Martin appeared out of the box."

"Martin was running on the line," said Crawford. "His foot was touching it. He was perfectly legitimate."

"My last words to him [Crawford] were, 'Why the hell are there rules then?'" said Hendricks.

"The game is official and that is that," said commissioner Bowie Kuhn. "This is a judgment play. There is no appeal [possible]."

Truth is these Orioles had no appeal whatsoever now—and Seaver was brazen enough to counter their pre-Series arrogance with the truth.

"They overestimated themselves and underestimated the Mets. One more game will really prove it," he said.

At least the humbled, stunned Birds weren't underestimating the NL champions any more.

"If you make the plays, you win," said Weaver. "If you don't, you lose. The Mets made the plays. Swoboda made the play. Agee did yesterday. We haven't made the plays."

"Seaver might be right about what he said the other day when he was talking with [NBC correspondent Sandy] Koufax," said Richert in a concession speech. "Sandy asked Seaver if God is a Met and Seaver said, 'No, but he might have an apartment in New York.'"

"We can't afford to lose until next spring," noticed Brooks Robinson.

Hodges, asked how he liked his team's chances now, said, "I'd say they are better than they were yesterday."

"Remember, I predicted we would win it in four straight," said Koosman, the Nostradamus of southpaws. "I didn't say the first four. I said four straight."

More than two decades later, Swoboda still couldn't fathom the play that he made to make it happen.

"This became the ultimate of my ability at the perfect time," said Ron. "I had no time for conscious thought or judgment. The ball was out there too fast. I took off with the crack of the bat and dove. My body was stretched full out and I felt as if I was disappearing into another world.

"When I see it on film now, I am still amazed by it. When they slow it down, it seems impossible that I could reach the ball. It was just hit too hard. Somehow, it happened. Somehow, I got it."

BALTIMORE

	ab	r	h	bl
Buford lf	5	0	0	0
Blair cf	4	0	1	0
FRobinson rf	4	1	1	0
Powell 1b	4	0	1	0
BRobinson 3b	3	0	0	1
Hendricks c	3	0	0	0
Johnson 2b	4	0	0	0
Belanger ss	4	0	1	0
Cuellar p	2	0	1	0
May ph	1	0	0	0
Watt p	0	0	0	0
Dalrymple ph	1	0	1	0
Hall p	0	0	0	0
Richert p	0	0	0	0
Totals	**35**	**1**	**6**	**1**

METS

	ab	r	h	bl
Agee cf	4	0	1	0
Harrelson ss	4	0	1	0
Jones lf	4	0	1	0
Clendenon 1b	4	1	1	1
Swoboda rf	4	0	3	0
Charles 3b	3	0	0	0
Shamsky ph	1	0	0	0
Garrett 3b	0	0	0	0
Grote c	4	0	1	0
Gaspar pr	0	1	0	0
Weis 2b	3	0	2	0
Seaver p	3	0	0	0
Martin ph	0	0	0	0
Totals	**34**	**2**	**10**	**1**

Baltimore	000	000	001	0 — 1
Mets	010	000	000	1 — 2

E-Garrett, Richert. DP-Baltimore 3. LOB-Baltimore 7, Mets 7. 2B-Grote. HR-Clendenon (2). S-Martin. SF-BRobinson.

None out when winning run scored.

	IP	H	R	ER	BB	SO
Baltimore						
Cuellar	7	7	1	1	0	5
Watt	2	2	0	0	0	2
Hall (L, 0-1)	0	1	1	0	1	0
Richert	0	0	0	0	0	0
Mets						
Seaver (W, 1-1)	10	6	1	1	2	6

T-2:33. A-57,367.

8

Pratt's Homer in 10th Breaks Diamondbacks

1999 NLDS Game 4
October 9, 1999 in New York

Life as the backup to the greatest catcher who ever lived is leisurely, though hardly easy. There is, of course, a good living in it. And Todd Pratt, having been rescued from career oblivion by the Mets and later talked back off the ledge while contemplating the renewal of a career managing a pizza parlor, had the sense to be grateful he was the man behind the mask, behind Mike Piazza.

But inactivity dulls any player's skills and Pratt did more sitting than almost every other backup catcher—until calamity struck Piazza . . . usually on the meat of his hand or under his shin guards. Then the Mets shivered, crossed their fingers and expected Pratt to dust himself off and fill one large pair of cleats.

Which brings us to that memorable day when the Mets eliminated the Diamondbacks, 4-3, in 10 innings to win the NL Division Series in four games in 1999—because it will forever remembered as the afternoon that Pratt did his Piazza impersonation.

With Piazza nursing a swollen and immobile left thumb that made playing impossible for a second straight game, Pratt was afforded a place on the post-season stage. A savage fastball hitter who never gets cheated on a swing, Pratt grounded out twice with runners in scoring position and stranded six runners over the first nine innings, as the Mets left 10 on. However, in the 10th, Todd turned around a heater from Arizona closer Matt Mantei and it defied gravity long enough to dodge Steve Finley's mistimed leap and clear the wall in straightaway center.

This dramatic if not terribly well-played struggle was over, improbably and at precisely 4:33 p.m., as the Pratt shot allowed 56,177 fans in the ballpark to start breathing again. This long shot's long shot over Shea's most distant wall, 410 feet from the plate, wielded as massive an impact as any home run in club history.

It cancelled a Game 5 showdown against Randy Johnson in Phoenix.

It propelled the grateful-for-the-wild-card Mets past the West champions, winners of 100 games, and into the NLCS against the Braves.

And it spelled the beginning of the end of Buck Showalter's managerial tenure in Arizona.

And the moment that Pratt's grandchildren will hear about until they will wish it never happened seemed to last as long in its unfolding as in its re-telling. Like Piazza, who can stop to admire many of his launchings, Todd stopped about a third of the way to second base to watch.

But this pause was not to relish the moment, but to offer a prayer. Please make it go out. Please.

He watched Finley soar, then drop his head and slap his empty glove.

"I wanted to cry," said Pratt, whose 1999 output included three homers (37 fewer than Piazza) in 140 at-bats and who had 16 regular-season homers on his seven-season big league résumé.

"As soon as I saw Steve running back and then start to plant [his feet to make a leap], my heart dropped, because I've seen him so many times go up over the wall and make a catch. As soon as I saw him come

Todd Pratt, his whipsaw of a swing complete, follows the flight of his flyball toward the distant, promised land beyond the center field wall. The backup catcher got to be like Mike with his 10th-inning death blow to the Diamondbacks.

down, I thought he had it and I was bummed out. And it was like a bad fall. First, I thought he was deking me."

"Probably the longest second of the season," said reliever John Franco, who knows from hold-your-breath moments.

"It should have been an easy catch," said Finley. "I didn't jump high enough and the ball hit off the top of my glove . . . I thought I had it. I felt it in my glove. It took me a second to realize I didn't catch it. I still don't believe it."

"I thought he caught it and then I saw him hit the wall with his fist," said Mantei, whom Showalter inexplicably failed to get into Game 1 and then milked for a risky third inning in Game 4. "He crushed that pitch."

Rey Ordoñez ran onto the field and Pratt began a trot around the bases that featured several leaps and ended with a greeting from a mob of delirious Mets at the plate. The souvenir was eventually retrieved by Charlie Rappa, a fireworks technician, and returned to Pratt. The catcher became one of only a few players to hit a walk-off homer in the clinching game of a post-season series, joining Bill Mazeroski (1960 World Series), Chris Chambliss (1976 ALCS) and Joe Carter (1993 World Series).

The homer also made folks forget Pratt's first at-bat against Mantei in the eighth. The Mets had tied the game and had runners at first and third with one out when Pratt hit a grounder back to the Arizona closer, who threw out John Olerud, in no-man's land off third, for the second out.

"I could've easily been the goat today," said Pratt.

But he got a second shot at Mantei and made it count.

"I told myself, 'I am not choking up this time,'" said Pratt. "The first pitch was a curve that wasn't even close and I thought if it's a fastball anywhere I can touch it, I am swinging. He actually threw it just where I like it, a little up and out over the plate."

"Piazza doesn't play and who hits the homer?" asked Arizona owner Jerry Colangelo. "It's like a script. That is baseball in all its glory."

Piazza was so delighted for his backup that he joked about being Wally Pipp-ified by the new Lou Gehrig.

"I don't know if I will be able to break into the lineup now," said Piazza. "I don't know if they will want me after that. And, if that's the case, then, hey, it's fine with me."

Of course, Pratt never lost sight of the fact that he was just keeping the catcher's gear warm for Piazza.

"I'm not going to try to be Mike," said Pratt, who did hit .321 and had an eight-game hitting streak when Piazza went on the DL in April. "I'm not going to do anything different. I'm not Mike. No one in this league is . . . I'm not an offensive power like Mike, but I can handle the bat."

Strangely, there are parallels between Pratt's story of perseverance and the odds-beating tale of Piazza, the only 62nd-round draft pick in history with a date for Cooperstown induction five years after he puts the bat down for a final time.

At the start of the 1998 season, after an atrocious spring, the 31-year-old Pratt was farmed out again—despite the Mets' aching need for a catcher to fill the shoes of the recovering Todd Hundley. Norfolk manager Rick Dempsey had to talk Pratt out of reaching for the mozzarella instead of another chance.

"I hated baseball at that time, because I knew I was too good a player and was just getting a bad rap," said Pratt. "They just didn't think I was good enough. Every time I got sent down, I didn't deserve it."

"He deserves this moment," said Piazza. "He has worked hard all year. That is what this team is all about."

Plenty of Mets shared in the glory of this day—a point definitely not lost on Pratt. "Without that throw from Melvin Mora and that pitching performance Al Leiter gave us, I wouldn't have had the chance to do what I did," he said.

Leiter allowed a measly three hits over 7⅔ innings. He hadn't allowed a hit until Greg Colbrunn hit a homer in the fifth. That snapped Leiter's string at 17 straight scoreless innings and offset Edgardo Alfonzo's third homer of the series, off Brian Anderson in the fourth. When Leiter left—following a walk to Turner Ward and an infield hit by Tony Womack in the eighth—the Mets still clung to the 2-1 lead which they had seized in the sixth, on singles by Rickey Henderson and Olerud and an RBI double by Benny Agbayani.

"What can you say about him?" said Bobby Valentine about Leiter. "He's a money guy, a money pitcher . . . He never lets us down when we really need him."

When Armando Benitez realized the calendar said October and faltered, he needed help from Mora—a late-inning defensive replacement for Henderson in left field—and the 27-year-old rookie from Venezuela saved the closer's large behind.

In the eighth, Benitez surrendered a two-run double to Jay Bell that put the Mets behind, 3-2. Arizona would've scored more—but Mora gunned down Bell at the plate with a two-hop throw after fielding Matt Williams' single to left. The throw was a bit up the first-base line, but Pratt dove back to slap the tag on Bell for the third out.

"I have said a couple of times that Mora is our best defensive outfielder and people snickered at me," said Valentine. "He is in there, just like a reliever is in there, to save a game and that was what he did. He saved a game with an excellent throw."

"I was saying, 'Please hit it to me,'" said Mora. "Then, when the ball came, I knew I had to throw it right away and throw it perfect . . . I knew we could come back from one run down. But two runs? That is difficult."

As it was, it took plenty of luck, lots of assistance—and no hits—for the Mets to come up with the one run they needed to tie in the bottom of the eighth. Greg Swindell walked Alfonzo and the sun-impaired, wind-burned Womack (who had just been moved from second to right field) let Olerud's flyball drop out of his glove for a two-base error.

"I just dropped it. The wind was not a factor. I got there in plenty of time. I should've caught it," said Womack.

Arizona's acrobatic center fielder Steve Finley leaps in pursuit of Todd Pratt's bid for the game-winner and Shea Stadium holds its collective breath . . . until it is clear that Finley returned to earth empty-handed.

"I got lucky," said Olerud. "Sometimes, that is the kind of stuff you need to win."

After Roger Cedeño made it 3-3 with a sac fly and Pratt failed to get the go-ahead run in from third, Darryl Hamilton lined a ball down the left-field line that could've been a tie-breaking hit—if only umpire Charlie Williams hadn't ruled it foul and set off an ejection-earning fit by third-base coach Cookie Rojas. Rojas, beefier than in his middle-infield-playing days, needed Valentine, coaches Mookie Wilson and Bruce Benedict and Robin Ventura to restrain him—but they didn't prevent 60-year-old Cookie from shoving Williams with two hands to the chest.

"I was thinking both of my hamstrings are being pulled and I need reinforcement," said Valentine. "I was thinking Cookie is older than me, but he's manhandling me."

"He [Williams] called me an SOB," said Rojas. "I'm not going to take that from him, from any umpire, from any man alive."

On the topic of SOBs, arguably the Mets' toughest of all, Franco, followed Benitez to the mound at the start of the 10th and threw—of all things—a 1-2-3 inning. The long-in-the-tooth, Brooklyn-born, title-starved lefty, coming back from an injured tendon in his middle finger, even turned a defensive gem. He robbed the former and future Met Lenny Harris on a high bouncer over the mound, turning his back to the plate to make the play.

"Sure, I was scared," said Franco. "Being from here, I never would have heard the end of it if I blew it. It would have been a long winter. I was just thinking, 'Keep the ball down. Don't mess up, don't mess up.' . . . And when I came off the mound, my heart was pumping so fast I thought it would explode."

Not to worry. Soon, Pratt had affixed the W next to Franco's name in the boxscore, the lefty's first victory since Sept. 13, 1997, 10 losses earlier.

"This is the greatest moment in my career," said Franco, eyes red with semi-sweet memories of his late father, a truck driver for the sanitation department. "It's unbelievable to get the win in this game and do it in front of the home crowd. Two champagne celebrations in a week after waiting my whole career for one."

"You know it's going to take a good effort to stop us," said Valentine. "The next team we play is going to be playing against some ghosts, because they said we were dead. I don't know if they have ever played against people who have come back from the grave before."

ARIZONA

	ab	r	h	rbi	bb	so	lob	avg
Womack ss-rf	5	1	1	0	0	2	0	.111
Bell 2b	2	0	1	2	1	0	0	.286
Gonzalez lf	3	0	0	0	1	0	1	.200
Williams 3b	4	0	1	0	0	0	0	.375
Mantei p	0	0	0	0	0	0	0	.000
Colbrunn 1b	3	1	1	1	1	1	0	.400
Finley cf	4	0	1	0	0	0	1	.385
Gilkey rf	3	0	0	0	0	0	1	.000
Frias ss	1	0	0	0	0	1	0	.000
Stinnett c	4	0	0	0	0	3	1	.143
Anderson p	2	0	0	0	0	0	0	.000
Ward ph	0	1	0	0	1	0	0	.500
Olson p	0	0	0	0	0	0	0	.000
Swindell p	0	0	0	0	0	0	0	.000
Harris 3b	1	0	0	0	0	0	0	.000
Totals	**32**	**3**	**5**	**3**	**4**	**7**	**4**	

METS

	ab	r	h	rbi	bb	so	lob	avg
Henderson lf	4	1	1	0	0	0	1	.400
Mora lf	0	0	0	0	0	0	0	.000
Alfonzo 2b	4	2	1	1	1	1	2	.250
Olerud 1b	4	0	2	0	1	0	1	.438
Agbayani rf	3	0	1	1	0	0	1	.300
Cedeño rf	1	0	0	1	0	0	2	.286
Ventura 3b	4	0	1	0	1	0	2	.214
Pratt c	5	1	1	1	0	0	4	.125
Hamilton cf	3	0	0	0	1	0	0	.125
Ordoñez ss	4	0	1	0	0	2	3	.286
Leiter p	3	0	0	0	0	2	1	.000
Benitez p	0	0	0	0	0	0	0	.000
MFranco ph	0	0	0	0	1	0	0	.000
Dunston pr	0	0	0	0	0	0	0	.167
JFranco p	0	0	0	0	0	0	0	.000
Totals	**35**	**4**	**8**	**4**	**5**	**5**	**17**	

BATTING: 2B-Bell (1, Benitez). HR-Colbrunn (1, 5th inning off Leiter 0 on, 1 out). RBI-Colbrunn (2), Bell 2 (3). 2-out RBI-Bell 2. GIDP-Finley. Team LOB-4.

BASERUNNING: CS-Bell (1, 2nd base by Leiter/ Pratt).

FIELDING: E-Womack (2, fly ball).

One out when winning run scored.

BATTING: 2B-Ventura (2, Anderson); Agbayani (1, Anderson). HR-Alfonzo (3, 4th inning off Anderson 0 on, 0 out); Pratt (1, 10th inning off Mantei 0 on, 1 out). S-Mora. SF-Cedeño. RBI-Alfonzo (6), Agbayani (1), Cedeño (2), Pratt (1). Runners left in scoring position, 2 out-Pratt 3, Ordoñez 2, Cedeño 1. Team LOB-10.

FIELDING: Outfield assists-Mora (Bell at home). DP-1 (Alfonzo-Ordoñez-Olerud).

Arizona	000	010	020	0 — 3
Mets	000	101	010	1 — 4

Arizona	IP	H	R	ER	BB	SO	HR	ERA
Anderson	7	7	2	2	0	4	1	2.57
Olson (H,2)	0	0	1	0	1	0	0	0.00
Swindell (BS, 1)	1/3	0	0	0	1	0	0	0.00
Mantei (L, 0-1)	2	1	1	1	3	1	1	4.50
Mets								
Leiter	7²/₃	3	3	3	3	4	1	3.52
Benitez (BS, 1)	1¹/₃	2	0	0	1	2	0	0.00
JFranco (W, 1-2)	1	0	0	0	0	1	0	0.00

IBB-Gonzalez (by Benitez); Ventura (by Swindell); Olerud (by Mantei). HBP-Bell (by Leiter). Pitches-strikes: Leiter 108-67; Benitez 28-16; Franco 17-10; Anderson 107-76; Olson 6-2; Swindell 19-10; Mantei 38-22. Ground balls-flyballs: Leiter 7-11; Benitez 0-1; Franco 2-0; Anderson 5-12; Olson 0-0; Swindell 0-1; Mantei 3-2. Batters faced: Leiter 28; Benitez 6; Franco 3; Anderson 28; Olson 1; Swindell 3; Mantei 10.

Umpires: Home-Davis; First-Froemming; Second-Meals; Third-Winters; Left-Williams; Right-Rieker.

T-3:23. A-56,177.

A Small Miracle:
Nails Hammers Smith

1986 NLCS Game 3
October 11, 1986 in New York

Lenny Dykstra, like many diminutive top-of-the-lineup pests, longed to be like Babe Ruth—a long-ball rainmaker, not a pesky table-setter. To the chagrin of manager Davey Johnson, who wanted Dykstra to maximize his speed by abandoning his uppercut for a butcher-boy approach, Lenny enjoyed going for the jack. He lifted weights and the rumors he was steroid-enhanced began when his muscles suddenly seemed like they had muscles of their own.

In Game 3 of the 1986 NLCS, Dykstra had the Ruthian moment of his dreams. Looking for a hit to bring home the tying run from second in the bottom of the ninth, he turned on a forkball from Astros relief ace Dave Smith and launched it for the two-run homer that gave the Mets a pulsating 6-5 victory and a two-games-to-one lead in the Series.

Dykstra—who began the game on the bench because lefty Bob Knepper was the starter—had hit only eight homers in 431 at-bats during the 1986 season. When asked whether he had ever hit a game-winning homer in as dramatic a situation before, Lenny was ready with an answer as memorable as the homer itself.

"The last time I hit a homer to win a game in the bottom of the ninth was in Strat-O-Matic, that game you play with dice. It was against my brother Kevin," said Dykstra. "I rolled some real good numbers that day."

Dykstra did a real good number on Smith's too-fat 0-and-1 forkball to guarantee that Darryl Strawberry's three-run, game-tying homer in the sixth would have meaning and inspire 55,052 fans to rock the Shea house. Before this remarkable six-game NLCS struggle was over, the Mets would have three victories in their final at-bat, so Dykstra's heroics set a tone.

Wally Backman, Dykstra's partner in grime, had an excellent vantage point from second base. He and Lenny were both leaping madmen on their way around the bases after the ball cleared the fence in right. Backman felt certain his buddy would knock him in to tie the game somehow.

"I've got confidence in Lenny, no matter what the situation," said Backman.

However, there was no predicting this finish.

"I was numb when Lenny hit it," said Ray Knight, whose throwing error had set up the Astros' go-ahead run. "All the blood was draining out of my body."

The crowd of jubilant Mets greeting Dykstra as he neared the plate was so thick that the hero felt like "it was fourth-and-goal" on his final steps to the dish.

"It's something you can cherish as long as you live," said the 25-year-old Dykstra, a pinch-hitter in the seventh who stayed in the game because Johnson was anticipating the arrival of Houston's right-handed relievers. "It's something that doesn't happen to too many people, something you can only dream about. It's a great high, something you can only float through."

And this no-need-to-get-the-uniform-filthy moment couldn't have happened to a grittier little guy.

"Gene Tenace told me in 1982 that, in every playoff or World Series, it is someone not prominently known, who is not expected to be the difference, who comes through," said Keith Hernandez.

"I get on Lenny a lot," said Johnson. "He does like swinging for the fences, but I will forgive him today. But he does hit too many balls in the air. If he would hit the ball on the ground and hit line drives, he would hit .330 every year. I'm sure he will be upper-cutting big time now."

Smith, meanwhile, absorbed this nasty uppercut, which came out of nowhere, with class. "He has got pop in his bat and anyone in a big league lineup can hit the ball out of the park if he guesses right on a pitch," Smith said.

The ninth inning began with the Astros sitting on a 5-4 lead and with a pitching change. Houston manager Hal Lanier replaced over-powering setup man Charlie Kerfeld, who had pitched a 1-2-3 eighth, with Smith, his closer, who had a 2.73 ERA overall and 33 saves but a 15.00 ERA against the Mets in '86. It was standard operating bullpen procedure for Lanier, but it struck some as unwise—at least after Dykstra's homer.

"Kerfeld disposed of us easily in the eighth," wrote Gary Carter in his book. "Why not leave him in there, at least until he got into some trouble? We were surprised but not at all sorry to be rid of Kerfeld."

"You go with your best. When you have a pitcher with 33 saves, you use him . . . I'd make the same move tomorrow and the same move the next day," said Lanier. "You can second-guess me all you want, but he [Smith] is one of the reasons we are here . . . I had it planned just the way it went—seven innings from Knepper, Charlie for the eighth and Dave for the ninth . . . It didn't work out today. But you will see a lot more of Dave, hopefully."

The Mets' ninth was kicked off with a bunt single from Backman, a drag beauty that forced Houston first baseman Glenn Davis to stray from the base to field it. J.C. Martin's creative baserunning on the thrown-away bunt that wound up giving the 1969 Mets a Game 4

World Series victory was called to mind when Backman took a cir-cuitous path around Davis to get to the bag. Neither Martin nor Backman was called out for straying out of the basepaths. The reason Backman got away with his flight plan was that, in the umpire's judg-ment, Davis couldn't reach him anyway, because Wally had already passed the fielder when he slid head-first and grabbed the bag with his hand.

"When I bunt, I always try to dive and throw my body to the out-side, to avoid the tag," said Backman.

"Wally took about what you are allowed to take to avoid a tag," said Johnson. "It wasn't flagrant. It was borderline . . . We've had plays where the guy almost came into the dugout to get away from the tag."

"I was surprised they didn't call him out of the baseline, because I saw him run on the grass," said Smith.

"I contended he went two or three feet out of the way and Glenn couldn't touch him," said Lanier. "I thought he had a chance to tag him, but the umpires said he didn't and they were right."

First-base umpire Dutch Rennert explained, "The runner establishes his own baseline, because Davis doesn't have a play on him. I was con-scious of the three feet [basepath] all the time . . . There was no doubt in my mind."

Backman moved to second on a passed ball by Alan Ashby—so Johnson no longer felt obligated to bunt—but Danny Heep, pinch-hitting for Rafael Santana, flied out. Now the hitter was Dykstra.

Both he and Smith recalled a fastball from the right-hander that Lenny had crushed for a game-winning RBI double July 4.

"I knew he would start me off with the fastball [which Smith did], but I couldn't get around on it and I fouled it off," said Dykstra. "He likes to come back with his forkball. So, on the next pitch, I had a real gut feeling he would throw one and he did. I was waiting for it. I got a pitch I saw real well and I hit it real well."

"I knew it was gone immediately," said Smith.

The ball wound up in the Mets' bullpen.

"I wanted him to hit it into the ground, but he was sitting on it. If I had thrown a fastball, he wouldn't have hit a homer," said Smith. "It was a bad pitch selection . . . This is as bad as I have ever felt . . . Well, it is done. I can't take the pitch back."

"When Wally got on, I thought we would tie the game," said Hernandez. "I knew he'd score somehow, but who would have thought he would score the way he did?"

In fact, who would have envisioned that there would be a happy ending of any kind after Ron Darling's shaky beginning? Darling walked two batters, hit one and threw a wild pitch in his five innings. The Astros punished him for four runs—first-inning RBI singles by Denny Walling and Jose Cruz and Bill Doran's two-run homer in the second —and those four seemed to be more than enough, in the hands of the sharp Knepper.

With his partner in grime Wally Backman representing the tying run at second in the ninth inning, Lenny Dykstra puts his best uppercut swing on a pitch from Dave Smith and strikes a game-ending blow for buffed-up little guys everywhere.

The margin was safe through five innings worth of zeroes, but an error by Houston shortstop Craig Reynolds opened the door in the sixth and Strawberry's exorcism of the frustration from being Knepper's pet for so long tied the game at 4-4.

Kevin Mitchell hit a high bounding single over Walling's leap at third and Hernandez followed with a single, too, to center. The struggling Carter slapped a slow grounder to shortstop that had 6-4-3 written all over it. But it went under Reynolds' glove to bring in a run and Strawberry to the plate as the tying run.

Strawberry—who had made a run-saving sparkler of a catch on Kevin Bass in the fifth—stepped into the box bearing an 0-for-10 cross of non-production against the wily Knepper in '86 and, of course, that was a big reason that the lefty had beaten the Mets three times. Straw, a .209 hitter with just five homers off lefties during the year, was 2-for-9 with five strikeouts for the NLCS and had a strikeout and a 12-foot single to show for his day so far.

However, this time, the right fielder said, he was under orders from Dykstra: go deep and tie the game. So, always a man in need of nothing more than firm direction, Strawberry got all of a first-pitch fastball and launched it to right field, far longer than it needed to be, into the loge, 360 feet from the plate. It was hard to believe that Darryl was 2-for-20 against Knepper for his career before this swing.

"Lenny's homer will get the headlines, but Darryl's was just as big," noted Hernandez. "It got us back in the game. It was a very big hit for him, especially off a left-hander."

"Until then, it looked like Knepper might shut us down the whole way," said Darling.

"He had lost a little that inning as far as spotting the ball," said Straw.

"I've been getting him out all year," said Knepper. "We didn't play well in that inning . . . But I can't let that bother me. My job was to forget about what happened and get the guy at the plate out . . . I was trying to pitch him inside and I didn't get the ball in enough. The way I feel about this game is we didn't get beat—we lost it."

They lost it after they came so close to winning.

In the seventh, reliever Rick Aguilera walked Doran on four pitches, then Knight bobbled and foolishly threw away Billy Hatcher's intended sac bunt to put Astros at the corners. Doran wound up scoring to make it 5-4 on a force-play grounder as Johnson kept his infield back.

"I didn't have a proper grip and I shouldn't have thrown it," said Knight. "The most devastating feeling is to make an error that leads to the winning run . . . The onus is entirely on you."

Not to worry, Ray. Dykstra made sure he wiped the slate clean with his magic wand.

"If I had to do it over again, it would be a fastball," said Smith.

"Don't get used to this," said Dykstra. "You're not going to see too many game-winning homers from me."

Then again, one was quite enough.

"Down to the last two outs, ballgame over," said Hernandez. "I'll be on my death bed, dying, delirious and I will be saying, 'Lenny, Lenny.'"

HOUSTON	ab	r	h	bl	METS	ab	r	h	bl
Doran 2b	4	2	2	2	MWilson cf	4	0	0	0
Hatcher cf	3	1	2	0	Mitchell lf	4	1	2	0
Walling 3b	5	1	1	2	Orosco p	0	0	0	0
Davis 1b	3	0	1	0	Hernandez 1b	4	1	2	0
Bass rf	3	0	0	0	Carter c	4	1	0	0
Cruz lf	3	0	1	1	Strawberry rf	4	1	2	3
Ashby c	4	0	0	0	Knight 3b	4	0	1	0
Reynolds ss	2	1	1	0	Teufel 2b	3	0	0	0
Lopes ph	1	0	0	0	Backman 2b	1	1	1	0
Kerfeld p	0	0	0	0	Santana ss	3	0	0	0
Smith p	0	0	0	0	Heep ph	1	0	0	0
Knepper p	3	0	0	0	Darling p	1	0	0	0
Thon ss	1	0	0	0	Mazzilli ph	1	0	1	0
					Aguilera p	0	0	0	0
					Dykstra cf	2	1	1	2
Totals	32	5	8	5	Totals	36	6	10	5

Houston	220	000	100	— 5
Mets	000	004	002	— 6

One out when winning run scored.

GWRBI-Dykstra (1). E-Reynolds, Knight. DP-Mets 1. LOB-Houston 7, Mets 5. HR-Doran (1), Strawberry (1), Dykstra (1). SB-Hatcher 2 (3), Bass (2). S-Hatcher.

Houston	IP	H	R	ER	BB	SO
Knepper	7	8	4	3	0	3
Kerfeld	1	0	0	0	0	1
Smith (L, 0-1)	1/3	2	2	2	0	0
Mets						
Darling	5	6	4	4	2	5
Aguilera	2	1	1	0	2	1
Orosco (W, 1-0)	2	1	0	0	1	2

HBP-Davis (by Darling). WP-Darling. PB- Ashby 2.

Umpires: Home-Pulli; First-Rennert; Second-West; Third-Brocklander; Left-Harvey; Right-Weyer.

T-2:55. A-55,052.

10

Payton, Franco Rescue Mets from Snow Blow

2000 NLDS Game 2
October 5, 2000 in San Francisco

It was enough to make a Met fan miss Candlestick.
Almost.

The Mets appeared destined to not win a game at Pac Bell ballpark in its inaugural season, after a four-game, regular-season humiliation there in May and a Game 1 Division Series loss in which ace Mike Hampton came unglued and the Mets' peek-a-boo offense looked peaked.

It took Al Leiter's brilliant tightrope act for two measly Met runs to hold up over eight innings of Game 2. Even after Edgardo Alfonzo's two-run, two-out home run in the ninth made it 4-1, there were still three massive outs to get.

Leiter blanked the Giants after Ellis Burks' RBI double in the second and held them hitless for 4⅔ innings from the fourth until the eighth, but the gas tank needle hit "E" and he gave up a leadoff double to Barry Bonds. Al's first post-season win since 1993 was put in the hands of Armando Benitez, who has the disturbing habit of making opposition hitters into Mr. Octobers.

Anything but unhittable in the fall glare, both as an Oriole and as a 1999 Met, the closer came on to confront the demons of his sordid past. Benitez gave up an infield hit that was Jeff Kent's reward for diving head first into the first-base bag, but retired Burks, Hampton's Game 1 nemesis, on a short fly for the first out. Then, Armando was visited by his ghosts. He threw a fit-to-be-pulled 2-and-1 fastball that pinch-hitter J.T. Snow turned into a game-tying, just-fair, just-far-enough, three-run homer.

The ball landed over the 25-foot-wall down the right-field line, just above the "Old Navy Splash Landing" sign, hit a fan's cupped hands and dropped downward. The scoreboard flashed "Snowball" to commemorate this dagger from a hitter who had been benched against a lefty starter and is only the second-best athlete in his own family (his father Jack was an NFL All-Pro).

Suddenly, Giants were leaping and pounding each other, the Coast was East, not West; the park was the Polo Grounds, not Pac Bell; the opponent was the Dodgers, not the Mets. The hitter was Thomson, not Snow, and the pitcher was Branca, not Benitez.

As Snow rounded the bases with right arm raised, jumped on third and received a plate welcome commensurate with his sense of the dramatic, Benitez wandered around and looked like the victim of a building collapse.

"I give him my hat . . . I thought it would go foul. Obviously, I didn't want it to be a home run. But I can't lose my mind over it," said Benitez, referring to the seventh gopher ball of his career in post-season play, *the most of any pitcher in big-league history.* "I have been in a lot of hard situations. I am not scared of nothing."

If this high-strung tough guy wasn't just whistling in the graveyard, then Benitez was alone among the Mets in remaining fearless after this home run. The prospects of avoiding a second defeat suddenly didn't look good.

"I wouldn't say we would have thrown in the chips and given up, but certainly being down 0-2 to a very, very good team like the Giants . . . " said Darryl Hamilton. "I certainly wouldn't have liked our chances. And that would have been one of the toughest losses I have ever been involved in."

"It would have taken a lot out of us if we had lost," said Todd Zeile.

Packed Bell, the Mets' little slice of Hell by the Bay, was rocking with 40,430 delirious Giants fans certain of the imminence of a play-off kill, the Giants' 57th win against 26 defeats at home.

"You could feel the momentum switching," said Snow, who had no homers and no RBI in 22 career at-bats as a pinch-hitter. "Usually, I am a pretty even-keel guy. But these games are big. You get caught up in the emotion."

"My [jammed left] ankle began to feel a lot better after J.T. hit his home run," said Giant starting pitcher Shawn Estes, whose pain from an awkward slide in the third had been sufficient to cause him to desert the bag and get tagged out.

"It appeared we were going to win the game," said Dusty Baker, whose trademark toothpick seemed firmly imbedded in a Mets team about to be gobbled up as an appetizer for his Giants.

"It was awesome," said Rich Aurilia, the Giant shortstop. "I was on deck and I watched that ball sail out of here. It was such an emotional boost. You almost feel as if you won the game."

Indeed, to the Mets, Snow's shot felt like, looked like, smelled like a crawl-off homer.

Except for one small detail: the score was still tied at 4.

"You don't want to know my reaction," said Mike Piazza. "We were fortunate that it just tied the game."

Still, the finishing touch to a horrific end felt imminent. Most teams react to having their hearts torn out without anesthesia by completing a lemmings-into-the-water march. The Mets should have been reeling sufficiently to accept the inevitability of a silent ultra-red-eye flight home on which to contemplate a best-of-five series being two-thirds down the toilet.

But the Mets weren't discouraged.

"Some might have thought we were down after the homer," understated Bobby Valentine. "I thought it just fired us up."

"The road to being amazing isn't easy," noted wise man Lenny Harris, a utility man since the day they discovered fire.

When his numb teammates got back to the dugout after the ninth, Robin Ventura sounded a charge call that you wouldn't be reading about if it hadn't been heeded.

"Let's stay focused," said Ventura. "We can still do this thing."

"Even after we lost the lead, we knew we would have another chance to swing the bats," said Jay Payton, who would make the most of his chance—thanks to a major assist from the usually canny Baker.

The Giants manager left his setup man Felix Rodriguez, his fourth pitcher, out there for the 10th—even though Alfonzo had hit that two-run, ninth-inning dinger off him and the Giants' all-but-automatic closer Robb Nen (41 saves in 2000) was available. There would be an off day the next day. With the game tied, with Benitez still in a funk and still around, this was an opportunity for Baker to go for the Mets' jugular.

"I don't know if surprised is the word," said Valentine when asked about his reaction to Baker's choice of Rodriguez. "We expected him to [go to Nen]. Kind of glad he didn't."

Still, Rodriguez can throw the ball through a wall and had a 1.73 ERA after July 4. In fact, he retired Zeile and Ventura, the first two hitters in the 10th.

But, then, Hamilton pinch-hit for Joe McEwing. Hamilton stepped to the plate thinking about his at-bat against Rodriguez, in Game 1 the night before. The pitcher had performed a little jig to punctuate his strikeout of Hamilton with the bases loaded in the eighth inning of San Francisco's 5-1 win.

"I didn't think it [the dance] was cool at all, especially for the fact that no one on our team showed up anyone on their club. I took offense to that," said Hamilton, a long-time Giant. "I was thinking about Wednesday's at-bat, when Rodriguez struck me out and did that little dance. I really wanted a hit in this at-bat. It was the most intense I've ever been going to the plate."

Hamilton had been passed over by Valentine as a possible lineup replacement for Derek Bell (a comatose bat and a Met-career-ending sprained ankle), in favor of September sparkplug Timo Perez, Hiroshima Carp's contribution to the Mets' cause. Perez, with three hits, one run and two RBI on a two-out single in the second inning of Game 2, quickly became the Melvin Mora of the 2000 post-season . . . until the Yanks exposed Timo as clueless vs. the curveball.

Anyway, now Hamilton—a shadow of the contributor he had been in 1999, because of an arthritic toe that limited him to 105 at-bats—was getting his chance to do a little dance on Rodriguez. The right-hander left a changeup up and Hamilton's eyes grew large. He pounced and crushed a gapper into right center that he legged into a double.

"I remember at the end of May a lot of people didn't think he [Hamilton] would play this year at all," said Valentine. "And, after a third, a fourth and a fifth consultation with some doctors, he came into the office he said, 'I will be back. I will help this team win this year.' . . . It still hurts me to watch him run, so I am sure it hurts him."

That brought Payton to the plate. With first base open and Mike Bordick scheduled to hit next, Baker had Rodriguez face Payton because he anticipated Valentine would hit for Bordick with the left-handed Harris. Of course, Dusty could have gone to Nen. However, the pitcher's spot was due up first for San Francisco in the 10th and Baker said he was loathe to pull right fielder Burks to make a double switch.

"I certainly didn't want to waste Robb for one out," said Baker, who said he was banking on two pieces of information: Payton "struggled against right-handers" and had a poor record with runners in scoring position and two outs.

Payton had been 0-for-7 in the Division Series, but the center fielder insisted he was beyond worry. After traversing a painfully slow, injury-riddled path to the majors that made him a 27-year-old rookie, Payton wasn't prone to indulging in self-doubt any longer.

"I have been at the point in my career where I didn't think I would ever play baseball again," he explained. "Right now, I am on Cloud Nine. I don't worry about each at-bat."

There was no time to worry, anyway. Payton, a hacker, slapped the first pitch—"a pretty hard slider that got too much of the plate"—for a line-drive single to center.

"I was just worried that he hit it too hard," said Hamilton, who scored easily to make it 5-4.

All five Met runs had scored with two outs.

"I felt great," insisted Rodriguez. "When you have a good hitter at the plate and make a mistake, you pay. I made three mistakes tonight and I paid all three times."

Of course, there was still the sticky matter of surviving the October follies of Benitez. To start the 10th, Valentine stuck with the closer who brought him—a finger-crossed show of faith in recognition of Armando's career-high 41 saves during 2000.

Armando had yet another lead, this time only one run. Benitez later insisted he was not thinking about Snow's homer.

Or the grand slam Albert Belle hit off him in the 1996 Division Series.

Or the famous homer that Derek Jeter hit off him at Yankee Stadium that some juvenile named Jeffrey Maier caught in the ALCS that season.

Or those three game-deciding hits that he allowed the Indians in the 1997 ALCS—including a three-run long ball by Marquis Grissom in Game 2 and a homer by Tony Fernandez in the 11th inning of a score-less game in that Series finale.

"That is all in the past," he said.

In his present was Armando Rios, a pinch-hitter who greeted him with a single.

Now Valentine had seen enough.

Fortunately, Bobby V could turn to a 420-save man with the stones to bail out the big fella.

He summoned John Franco, a cool customer in the face of this kind of heat since his big league debut in 1984 and the longest-tenured Met on the club, having come back to his hometown in 1990. This 40-year-old artifact—now a setup man coming off an ailing finger on his pitching hand that helped cost him his closer's job in 1999—was handed the ball and told to nail down his first post-season save.

"There is no one I trust as much as John," was the way Valentine spun it later.

Pinch-hitter Marvin Benard sacrificed.

Then Rios made the base-running mistake of the century, inexplicably attempting to cross to third on Bill Mueller's grounder to short-stop Bordick. Now there were two outs and the Giants had lost a runner in scoring position.

"You have to stay strong in your mind and I made a huge mental mistake," said Rios.

"Great for us," decided Franco, who still had to contend with Bonds, a future Hall of Famer always in scoring position whenever he is in the batter's box.

The lefty threw two balls to Bonds, then got him to swing and miss for strike one. The next pitch was low and outside. But Franco threw a fastball that Bonds took for strike two. Bonds fouled another back.

Piazza signalled for yet another fastball. Franco shook off his catcher. He wanted to throw the pitch that has kept him in the majors—the changeup.

"I've been facing Barry so many years now. He wins some. I win some," said Franco, who froze Bonds with his trademark pitch, exactly where the pitcher had wanted it. "I had gotten him out with that pitch a few times this year.

"I've been making my living for 17 years getting people out on my changeup. What better time to throw it? . . . I knew it was over the

METS

	ab	r	h	rbi	bb	so	lob	avg
Perez rf	5	1	3	2	0	1	0	.429
Alfonzo 2b	5	1	1	2	0	1	3	.222
Piazza c	4	0	2	0	1	0	0	.286
Zeile 1b	5	0	0	0	0	1	3	.125
Ventura 3b	3	0	0	0	1	0	1	.000
Agbayani lf	2	0	1	0	2	0	1	.400
McEwing pr-lf	0	0	0	0	0	0	0	.000
a-Hamilton ph-lf	1	1	1	0	0	0	0	.333
Payton cf	5	1	1	1	0	0	5	.125
Bordick ss	4	1	1	0	1	2	1	.286
Leiter p	4	0	0	0	0	2	4	.000
Benitez p	0	0	0	0	0	0	0	.000
JFranco p	0	0	0	0	0	0	0	.000
Totals	**38**	**5**	**10**	**5**	**5**	**7**	**18**	

SAN FRANCISCO

	ab	r	h	rbi	bb	so	lob	avg
Murray cf	4	0	1	0	0	2	2	.250
d-Benard p	0	0	0	0	0	0	0	.000
Mueller 3b	5	0	1	0	0	2	1	.300
Bonds lf	5	1	1	0	0	1	2	.375
Kent 1b-2b	4	2	2	0	0	0	0	.429
Burks rf	3	0	1	1	1	1	2	.333
Martinez 2b	3	0	0	0	0	1	2	.000
b-Snow ph-1b	1	1	1	3	0	0	0	.500
Aurilia ss	4	0	0	0	0	0	2	.250
Estalella c	4	0	0	0	0	0	2	.000
Estes p	0	0	0	0	1	0	0	.000
Rueter p	0	0	0	0	1	0	0	.000
Henry p	0	0	0	0	0	0	0	.000
a-Crespo ph	1	0	0	0	0	0	0	.500
Rodriguez p	0	0	0	0	0	0	0	.000
c-Rios ph	1	0	1	0	0	0	0	1.000
Totals	**35**	**4**	**8**	**4**	**3**	**7**	**13**	

a-doubled for McEwing in the 10th.

BATTING: 2B-Piazza (1, Rueter); Hamilton (1, Rodriguez). HR- Alfonzo (1, 9th inning off Rodriguez, 1 on, 2 out). RBI-Perez 2, Alfonzo 2 (2), Payton 2. 2-out RBI-Perez 2, Alfonzo 2, Payton. Runners left in scoring position, 2-out-Alfonzo 1, Payton 1, Zeile 1. GIDP-Leiter, Payton. Team LOB-9.

FIELDING: DP-1 (Bordick-Zeile).

a-fouled to 3rd for Henry in the 8th; b-homered for Martinez in the 9th; c-singled for Rodriguez in the 10th; d-sacrificed for Murray in the 10th.

BATTING: 2B-Burks (1, Leiter); Bonds (1, Leiter). HR-Snow (1, 9th inning off Benitez 2 on, 1 out). S-Benard. RBI-Burks (4), Snow 3 (3). Runners left in scoring position, 2 out-Estalella 1. GIDP- Mueller. Team LOB-5.

BASERUNNING: SB-Kent (1, 2nd base off Leiter/Piazza)

FIELDING: DP- 2 (Estalella-Aurilia-Martinez, Martinez-Aurilla-Kent).

Leiter pitched to 1 batter in the 9th, Benitez pitched to 1 batter in the 10th.

HBP-Ventura (by Estes). Pitches-strikes: Estes 44-26; Rueter 71-40; Henry 9-4; Rodriguez 39-27; Leiter 123-76; Benitez 23-16; Franco 10-6. Ground balls-flyballs: Estes 5-1; Rueter 7-5; Henry 2-0; Rodriguez 1-2; Leiter 5-12; Benitez 1-2; Franco 2-0. Batters faced: Estes 16; Rueter 16; Henry 2; Rodriguez 10; Leiter 30; Benitez 6; Franco 3.

Umpires: Home-Cederstrom; First-Montague; Second-Morrison; Third-Young; Left-Barrett; Right-Kellogg.

T-3:41. A-40,430.

Mets	020	000	002	1 — 5
San Francisco	010	000	003	0 — 4

Mets	IP	H	R	ER	BB	SO	HR	ERA
Leiter	8	5	2	2	3	6	0	2.25
Benitez (W,1-0;BS-1)	1	3	2	2	0	0	1	18.00
Franco (S,1)	1	0	0	0	0	1	0	0.00
San Francisco								
Estes	3	3	2	2	3	3	0	6.00
Rueter	4⅓	3	0	0	1	0	0	0.00
Henry	⅔	0	0	0	1	0	0	0.00
Rodriguez (L,0-1)	2	4	3	3	0	3	1	11.57

plate, but it was just a matter of whether the umpire would call it a strike. He was a little delayed in the call. I just had to wait a little bit."

Eventually, plate umpire Gary Cederstrom rang up Bonds, who threw away his bat in disgust and left the locker room without meeting with reporters. Bonds, who has a few things to share with Benitez in a group therapy session concerning post-season failure, was well on the way to an invisible Division Series.

"This is the biggest moment of my career," said Franco.

The Mets were going home with their much-coveted, absurdly hard-earned split, after all.

"The home run doesn't mean anything now. We lost the game," said Snow.

"It was a heck of a turnaround in a short period of time," said Baker.

"We could have rolled over, but we took a good punch and we came back," said Piazza.

"This team never does cease to amaze me," said Valentine.

"Coming back to win in the 10th shows we are strong enough mentally not to ever give up," said Leiter. "We won—that's all that matters, but this wasn't good for my heart."

"That was heart—heart and courage," said Mets GM Steve Phillips. "God, that game was hard to watch."

"Stuff like this seems to happen to the Mets," said Hamilton. "Last year, you always wondered what crazy thing would happen next. It's hard on the fans and it's hard on us. But it's great when we win."

11

After Buddy Sees Red, Fans Make Life Thorny for Rose

METS 9, REDS 2

1973 NLCS Game 3
October 8, 1973 in New York

The Mets were kicking the butts of the heavily favored Reds the old-fashioned way, on the scoreboard, in the fifth inning of a 9-2 Met rout in NLCS Game 3—and then it got ugly.

"I was trying to knock him into left field," said Pete Rose, 200 chiseled pounds of Charlie Hustle muscle, concerning his elbowing of Buddy Harrelson. "I don't think it was my obligation to apologize to anybody over this, because I think I did the right thing. I play hard, not dirty . . . I might even slide harder tomorrow, if it's possible."

"Hell, I am not a fighter. I'm a lover," said a calm Harrelson, 146 pounds soaking wet while holding a bat donut but not about to silently swallow a malicious hit from Rose. "He came into me after I threw the ball . . . I thought he hit me with his elbow on the left side of my head intentionally . . . I didn't like what he did and he didn't like what I said."

And the explosive wrestling match that ensued between Rose and Harrelson escalated into a benches-clearing, bullpens-emptying brawl when Wayne Garrett became the third man in. Garrett said he wasn't about to watch the bigger Rose abuse a teammate whom Garrett later referred to as "a midget"—which might've wounded the Mets' mighty mite even more than Rose's elbow.

There was even a comical undercard, featuring Pedro Borbon, who punched Met pitcher Buzz Capra (sucker-punched, according to Capra). After the fracas had been defused and order restored, Bourbon had an even better fit. The Reds reliever, being held back by teammates, freaked when he was told that he had accidentally stuffed a blue Met cap on his head, instead of a Red one.

What's a madman to do?

Borbon chewed a chunk out of the cap and threw the pieces to the ground.

"I see something blue," said Borbon. "I was a little angry."

Now, that is angry. Or maybe just very hungry.

The Met fans in the left-field stands among a total crowd of 53,967 could relate to the anger. They weren't about to forgive Rose for picking on their skinny shortstop. In the bottom of the fifth inning, they aimed a steady shower of objects at Rose's head that lacked only a kitchen sink. The rain of refuse brought to mind a similar treatment afforded by Detroit fans to the Cardinals' Joe "Ducky" Medwick in the 1934 World Series.

Soon, ugly had given way to surreal at Shea.

What other word would describe the Reds abandoning the field in mid-inning? What word could better characterize the sight of Willie Mays, Tom Seaver, Rusty Staub, Cleon Jones and manager Yogi Berra pleading with Met fans in the left-field seats to cease and desist—a mission designed by NL president Chub Feeney to spare Rose from execution by projectile and the Mets from a possible forfeit?

"Pete Rose has contributed too much to baseball to die in left field at Shea Stadium," said Reds' manager Sparky Anderson, explaining why he instructed all his players to take clubhouse refuge for 20 minutes.

Feeney left his seat to confer with commissioner Bowie Kuhn, Mets GM Bob Scheffing and the six umpires before making his peacemaking request. Later, Feeney explained the game would not have been forfeited, but rather suspended and resumed the next day if order had not been restored.

Feeney said he figured that the fans "would recognize Willie, but if I went out there, they would probably throw things at me."

You don't get to be league president without being smart. In fact, the fans welcomed their visit from the doves in Met clothing.

"They were cheering when we walked out," said Jones. "They hadn't seen [the injured] Willie in quite awhile and they were happy to see him."

Why not peace talks?

Earlier, organist Jane Jarvis had played her own composition, inspired by the Vietnam war, entitled "Prayer for Peace."

Mays—making his first appearance since he announced his impending retirement—took time out on his way to Cooperstown to be Henry Kissinger.

Not surreal enough for your tastes, yet?

How about the umpires—who decided to eject no one after the brawl—actually suggesting to Anderson that Rose be put out of the fans' hurling range, in center field?

"Why should I play a man out of position?" asked Sparky.

Who knows if center field would have been safe, anyway?

A half-full beer can struck Reds pitcher Gary Nolan in the bullpen and Nolan said, "I was lucky that I saw it coming and I got my hand up just in time to deflect it and it just grazed my eye."

Rose proved too quick a target to absorb a beaning. But Pete did want to know why, in order to play the game that he loved, he should have to duck an empty bottle hurled by a ticket-holder with a head as empty as his ammunition.

"It [a liquor bottle] zoomed right past my head," said Rose, who just kept going to the dugout after it sailed past, shortly after he caught a fly for the second out of the fifth. "I didn't mind the booing and some of the other things, like the cups and the programs, but when the whiskey bottles start coming, I don't like that. I mean, a Jack Daniels bottle?"

Someone told Pete that Anderson had said it was Johnnie Walker—presumably, Johnnie Walker Red.

"I don't know. I don't drink, but it looked heavy," said Rose, who returned fire with some of the garbage. "I want to play tomorrow. I don't want my eye put out by a whiskey bottle."

It didn't help that the Reds were craving full bottles thanks to the definitive way the Mets—last-place residents in late August—had taken a two-games-to-one lead in this best-of-five. This Series was supposed to be a tuneup for potent Cincinnati, before meeting the Athletics in the World Series. But, through three games, the Mets had outscored the Reds, 15-4, and outhit them, 21-16.

"Maybe they thought they had easy pickings," wondered Berra.

If not for the fisticuffs, this game would have been remembered for Staub's two homers and four RBI in his first two at-bats. The first one, off loser Ross Grimsley, gave Jerry Koosman—who gave up eight hits and struck out nine in posting the Mets' third straight complete game—a 1-0 lead in the first. It was a huge shot to right center.

"I thought it was gone when I hit it," said Staub. "I hit it about as hard as I could."

Two batters later, a high inside fastball nearly creased John Milner's skull. "I told the guys, 'Forget it, don't retaliate, just win the game,'" said Staub.

Rusty's words were heeded only briefly, because of a five-run second that broke the game open and guaranteed an escalation of hostilities. Jerry Grote walked, Don Hahn singled and Grimsley fell on his butt fielding Koosman's attempt at a sacrifice, turning it into a hit. Bases loaded, none out. Garrett made it 2-0 with a sac fly, Felix Millan made it 3-0 with a single to right and Anderson yanked Grimsley.

The manager had seen what Staub had done to the 21-year-old lefty's high fastball the last time and was convinced. Anderson brought in lefty Tom Hall. Staub took Hall's second pitch—a hanging slider, according to catcher Johnny Bench—over the auxiliary scoreboard down the right-field line, above the 341-foot sign, for his third homer of the NLCS and a 6-0 lead.

"He is a money player who comes through when they need it the most," said Bench.

"I can't really express how good this feels," said Staub of his first post-season exposure. "I'm just so very pleased to be here. For 10 years, I had to go home when the [regular] season was over, when I still wanted to play ball."

The Met margin reached 9-2 following two more Met runs in the fourth. Now Koosman—working easily with "a fastball that I haven't seen since 1969" and an equally effective changeup—was riding enough of a bulge to make the Reds note that Milner's knockdown had a price tag.

In the fifth, Koosman sent his first pitch to Rose whistling past his helmet. Keep in mind, too, Rose was already irked at Harrelson, because the Met shortstop had said something to the reporters about how totally the Reds' hitters were tamed by Jon Matlack in Game 2— "They looked like me, hitting"—and Rose took it as a knock at his manhood.

Rose singled, then Joe Morgan hit a grounder to first and Milner threw to Harrelson. Rose came into the bag hard, but had to hit the dirt to avoid being nailed by the relay that assured the completion of a slick 3-6-3 double play. As he bounced back to his feet, Rose gave Buddy a present—a shot from his elbow.

"He said, 'You blank, blank, you tried to elbow me,'" said Rose. "I said, 'What are you talking about?' And I pushed him."

"If he did it out of spite, I just wanted to tell him that I'm not a punching bag," said Buddy.

"It's a peaceful game," said Morgan, "but not at second base."

Bantamweight Buddy Harrelson enjoys a laugh at his own expense the day after he fought with Pete Rose, showing off a shirt beneath his uniform that declared him the anti-Superman.

When push quickly became a wrestling match, Rose assumed the missionary position. Pete said it was strategic, because of all the Mets around him, rather than the result of blows from Garrett.

"I wanted him to get on top of me," said Rose. "I was the only one in a grey uniform out there and I wanted to get on the bottom where the other Mets couldn't get at me."

"He [Garrett] should have left it one on one," said Anderson. "That is just a good little scrimmage."

"That is pretty cheap of Pete, picking on a guy that size," said Garrett. "I'm not going to back off a thing like that . . . If I tangled with a midget, I could do anything, too."

"Garrett did the right thing, trying to protect his shortstop," said Rose. "He is a helluva shortstop."

Harrelson wore a scrape over his left eye as a souvenir after the game and he wanted the world to know this new bruise didn't come from Rose's fists or elbow.

"When we were rolling around, my sunglasses broke. I think that is how I got it," he said.

Now there were players everywhere. And Borbon, professed peacemaker, suspected troublemaker and confirmed hat gourmand, punched Capra.

"He cheap-shotted me," said Capra, whose honor was defended by catcher Duffy Dyer. "He blindsided me on the right side of my face. But it wasn't much of a punch. I've been hit harder when I was pitching."

Harrelson later told reporters it wasn't personal. He said he had liked Rose since 1966, when the perennial NL batting champ had suggested that the rookie shortstop use a smaller glove.

"I like the way Pete Rose plays," said Harrelson. "I just didn't like the way he came into second."

Bench was able to see the big picture of a Series that was tilting heavily toward the underdogs.

"It was a small battle," said Bench, "but we are losing the war."

CINCINNATI	ab	r	h	bl	METS	ab	r	h	bl
Rose lf	4	0	2	0	Garrett 3b	4	0	0	1
Morgan 2b	4	0	1	1	Millan 2b	3	2	1	1
Perez 1b	4	0	0	0	Staub rf	5	2	2	4
Bench c	4	0	1	0	Jones lf	3	1	2	0
Kosco rf	4	0	0	0	Milner 1b	4	0	1	1
Armbrister cf	4	0	1	0	Grote c	3	2	1	0
Menke 3b	4	1	1	1	Hahn cf	4	1	2	0
Chaney ss	3	0	0	0	Harrelson ss	4	0	0	0
Gagliano ph	1	0	0	0	Koosman p	4	1	2	1
Grimsley p	0	0	0	0					
Hall p	0	0	0	0					
Stahl ph	1	1	1	0					
Tomlin p	0	0	0	0					
Nelson p	1	0	0	0					
King ph	1	0	1	0					
Borbon p	0	0	0	0					
Totals	35	2	8	2	Totals	34	9	11	8

Cincinnati		002	000	000	—2
Mets		151	200	00x	—9

E-Kosco, Garrett. DP-Mets 1. LOB-Cincinnati 6, Mets 6. 2B-Jones, Bench. HR-Staub 2 (3), Menke (1). SF-Garrett.

	IP	H	R	ER	BB	SO
Cincinnati						
Grimsley (L, 0-1)	1²/₃	5	5	5	1	2
Hall	¹/₃	1	1	1	1	1
Tomlin	1²/₃	5	3	3	1	1
Nelson	2¹/₃	0	0	0	1	0
Borbon	2	0	0	0	0	2
Mets						
Koosman (W, 1-0)	9	8	2	2	0	9

T-2:48. A-53,967.

Benny's HR in 13th Leaves Giant Mark

1999 NLDS Game 3
October 7, 2000 in New York

B enny Agbayani was a natural fan favorite because of his everyman demeanor. His cherubic face, world-class set of cheeks, exotic heritage and slob-next-door appeal made him lovable. And his affability made it easy to root for him and to forgive his sins.

On Aug. 12, 2000, Agbayani miscounted the number of outs in an inning and donated a live ball to a Shea patron while a Giant runner scored. Benny didn't hide in the players-only room from the glare of New York's interrogation light as some responsibility-shy players might have. Agbayani stood up to the cameras and microphones and notebooks and said simply, "Mea culpa."

Or whatever the equivalent is in Hawaiian.

About 100,000 times.

And then Agbayani graciously accepted the fans in left field reminding him how many outs there were for the rest of the season.

Although he had hit 10 homers in his first 73 at-bats in the majors in 1999, Benny began the season with one foot in Norfolk. Agbayani gained a reprieve from demotion with a game-winning, pinch-hit grand slam in Tokyo plus well-timed injuries in the Met outfield. So, all in all, some good-natured abuse from the left-field patrons in Queens seemed like a light cross to bear.

In Game 3 of the NL Division Series, after a day of frustration, Benny made certain he "won't be remembered just for that [discarding a live ball] any more." Now, at least in New York, Agbayani will be known forever as the clutch performer whose game-winning homer sent the Mets to an unforgettable 3-2, 13-inning victory in the pivotal game of a fabulous showdown vs. the Giants.

With one swing, Benny achieved redemption for an 0-for-5 performance that included an extra-inning failure to bunt two runners over. When the ball carried over the Office Depot sign and touched down several rows deep into the bleachers in left center, Agbayani was more than just a favorite son to the delighted 56,270 at Shea. He was a walk-off home-run-hitting October sensation.

"I don't know where we would be without him," said manager Bobby Valentine, always a Benny believer.

Agbayani had been a 30th-round pick in the 1993 draft, out of Hawaii Pacific University, who didn't have an agent and was projected as a career minor leaguer. In fact, he was 27 years old when he got his first prolonged major league shot in '99. That chance came only because Bobby Bonilla was even more poorly conditioned and more immobile than the too-big Ben.

"There have been a lot more down times for me than good times," reflected Agbayani. "I've been through a lot in this organization . . . I am like that lone survivor on the *Survivor* series, except that I don't get the million dollars. I even live on an island."

The reference was to Hawaii, but, on this day, he could have meant Fantasy Island.

By taking rookie left-hander Aaron Fultz' fastball out of the park, Benny rewarded an amazing show of depth and resilience by the Mets' pen and ended a five-hour, 22-minute saga. Agbayani also reminded folks once again: Forget the squat body and the humongous cheeks, I am one tough out.

"It's a great feeling to be The Man," he said. "It's like a tingling feeling. Nothing could compare to this. Nothing.

"To be running around the bases and everyone is starting to cheer . . . It's like a silence. You can hear the crowd, but it was like everything was blocked out. When I was coming around third, I saw all of my teammates. I said, 'Uh-oh, there they are.'"

As Agbayani rounded first, he gave the Hawaiian shaka sign—extending his right thumb and his last finger while shaking his hand—for the first time in 2000 since the slam against the Cubs that shook Tokyo. It means "aloha."

When he reached the plate, the Mets jumped up and down in unison and pounded on Agbayani's helmet hard enough to give him a post-game headache. Eventually, coach John Stearns, the former linebacker, risked a hernia and took on the massive task of lifting Agbayani skyward. "Who Let the Dogs Out?" blared over the speakers as the crowd chanted, "Ben-ny, Ben-ny."

Jay Payton was among the most delighted of Mets, because he and Benny are close friends going back to their prolonged imprisonment in the minors.

"I gave him a big hug and I told him, 'Great job. You deserve it. It was awesome.' There is nobody happier for him than I am right now," said Payton.

Earlier, Payton had noticed the wind was blowing hard, out to left, and urged Benny to try to get something to pull.

"I kept it in my head," said Agbayani. "I felt like I could do it. But I've seen a lot of balls hit pretty hard here at Shea and they never went out."

"There was a definite jetstream," said J.T. Snow.

During the regular season, Fultz had struck out Agbayani on a fastball. The lefty threw one on 1-and-0, with 91-mile-per-hour velocity, but, according to Agbayani, it was "up in the zone where I could get good wood on it."

And all that was left for him to do, other than trot, was to enlist a higher power.

"I was praying, 'God, please, please make it go out,'" said Benny.

Before his prayer was finally answered, there was a long afternoon of baseball—the second-longest, in terms of time, in post-season history. Among the happenings were: the Shea fans' first-inning, impromptu, mocking, tomahawk-chop celebration of the KO suffered by the hated, feared Braves at the hands of the NLCS-bound Cardinals, five innings of no-hit pitching by Giants starter Russ Ortiz, a game-tying, eighth-inning hit by Edgardo Alfonzo off closer Robb Nen that would get lost in the shuffle, plus inning after inning of escape acts by Met relievers.

The Giants broke on top in the fourth with two runs against Rick Reed (0-2 with a 6.08 ERA in his two starts against San Francisco during the regular season). Singles by Ellis Burks and J.T. Snow set up an RBI single by Bobby Estalella and another run-scoring hit by Marvin Benard.

The Mets broke through against Ortiz (4-0, 2.83 against the Mets in his career coming in) in the sixth, but even that inning ended in frustration for them. Mike Bordick walked and went to third on Darryl Hamilton's pinch single. Timo Perez singled to shallow left to cut the Giant margin to 2-1 and put runners at first and second with none out. However, Alfonzo's groundout and an intentional pass to Mike Piazza set up Robin Ventura's bases-loaded, double-play grounder off lefty reliever Alan Embree.

Giant manager Dusty Baker decided to start the eighth with Doug Henry, who had pitched a 1-2-3 seventh—and the decision proved costly. The ex-Met nailed Bordick with an 0-and-2 pitch that simply slipped out of Henry's hand. Then Lenny Harris, pinch-hitting for Turk Wendell, slapped a force-play grounder to second baseman Jeff Kent on which Harris hustled down the line to beat shortstop Rich Aurilia's relay.

After Henry got Perez on a popout, Baker made an earlier-than-usual call to Nen, the ace whom he had never played in Game 2, the remarkably consistent reliever who was riding a string of 28 straight save conversions and had 41 in 46 chances overall. Nen works a single inning, not more, and it's usually the ninth. He had worked more than one inning in only three of his 68 appearances.

"When he comes into a game, we're pretty confident he is going to get the job done," said Snow.

On Nen's first pitch, Harris broke for second—"I was going from the moment I got off the bench," he said—knowing that keeping runners from running is an Achilles' heel for the Giant closer. The steal put Harris in scoring position and now the stage was set for Alfonzo's specialty: a two-out hit to provide the Mets with a desperately needed run. Sure enough, Edgardo hit a line-drive double to left and the game was tied.

"Fonzie's entire career it seems like he does the big thing that gets us to the point we have a chance to win and then somebody else does something right at the end," said Valentine.

"It doesn't matter when he [Baker] calls me," said Nen. "It doesn't matter if it's the first inning, the eighth inning or the ninth inning. This is the post-season . . . I made a mistake. I left a slider up and he did what he had to do with it."

"It's damned if you do, damned if you don't," said Baker. "If I bring in Nen, I am wrong. If I don't bring in Nen [as he didn't in the 10th inning of a tied Game 2], I am wrong. I can't be wrong both days. You know what I mean? . . . I go with what I think is right."

John Franco reprised his Game 2-ending 10th-inning strikeout of Barry Bonds by punching out Bonds again, swinging this time on an 84-mile-per-hour fastball, for the final out in the ninth. Even when he is head-strung and worried about home-plate ump Jerry Crawford's strike zone, Bonds looms as such a threat that Franco pumped his left fist repeatedly during his return to the dugout

"It's not like I have got his number," said Franco, who combined with Dennis Cook, Wendell, Armando Benitez and winning pitcher Rick White for a total of seven blanks.

Meanwhile, the Mets repeatedly knocked on a closed door. In the

Benny Agbayani finally delivered the Hawaiian punch to Aaron Fultz and the Giants in the 13th inning—but it is brave, strong Met third-base coach John Stearns who is doing the heaviest lifting at the center of this party.

11th, when Piazza singled and Ventura singled with none out against Felix Rodriguez, the end appeared near. But Agbayani couldn't get the bunt down two times and wound up flying out to center, Payton struck out and, after Todd Zeile walked, pinch-hitter Todd Pratt flied out to right center. Benny returned to left field, feeling like a goat.

"He [Agbayani] really felt like he let the team down," said Valentine. "He was pacing in the dugout, hoping to get another chance."

"When Felix got out of that jam, we felt we were going to win," said Snow. "We kept telling ourselves it was our game."

White pitched himself into a mess in the 13th. Singles by Ramon Martinez and Bill Mueller left two Giants on base for Bonds with two out. In the 12th, White had walked Bonds and wound up getting Doug Mirabella to strand two. This time, Barry went after the first pitch, a two-seam fastball away . . . and hit a towering drive.

To the second baseman.

"He was getting ahead of everybody 0-and-2. He made a good pitch. I just tried to hit a line drive, but it went straight up in the air," said Bonds.

"If you read his track record, he hasn't done very good in the post-season," noticed White, who struck out four in his two innings. "So that is all I was thinking about: just don't make a mistake here."

Bonds was now 1-for-his-last-11 in this NLDS after starting it with two hits. The left fielder's 0-for-5 in this game left him with the following career post-season stats: a .204 batting average, with six RBI in 93 at-bats.

"Rick White getting Bonds at the end there, throwing those strikes low and away, getting his breaking ball over, you'd think he has been in a playoff situation for the last 10 years," said Valentine.

After Fultz got the first out in the bottom of the 13th, Agbayani landed his haymaker. The Mets had triumphed in their final at-bat in their last five post-season wins.

"I don't know what inning it was," said Baker. "It was long."

"These [marathon post-season thrillers] are nerve-wracking," said Piazza. "A lot of guys really couldn't swallow out there."

Especially Bonds.

"We just need to go to bed and let it go," said Bonds. "Today is over with."

"Both bullpens did an outstanding job," said Nen. "It's got to end sometime. They came out on top."

"Brilliant finish," decided Valentine.

SAN FRANCISCO

	ab	r	h	rbi	bb	so	lob	avg
Benard cf-rf	6	0	1	1	1	4	2	.100
Mueller 3b	6	0	2	0	0	1	3	.313
Bonds lf	5	0	0	0	2	1	3	.231
Kent 2b	6	0	2	0	0	3	4	.385
Burks rf	4	1	1	0	2	1	2	.300
Fultz p	0	0	0	0	0	0	0	.000
Snow 1b	4	0	2	0	2	1	2	.500
Aurilia ss	4	0	0	0	0	2	5	.167
Nen p	0	0	0	0	0	0	0	.000
a-Rios ph	1	0	0	0	0	0	1	.500
Mirabella c	1	0	0	0	0	0	2	.000
Estalella c	4	1	1	1	0	1	3	.083
b-Crespo ph	1	0	0	0	0	0	2	.333
Rodriguez p	0	0	0	0	0	0	0	.000
Murray cf	1	0	0	0	0	1	0	.200
RuOrtiz p	3	0	0	0	0	1	2	.000
Embree p	0	0	0	0	0	0	0	.000
Henry p	0	0	0	0	0	0	0	.000
Martinez ss	3	0	2	0	0	1	0	.333
Totals	**49**	**2**	**11**	**2**	**7**	**17**	**31**	

a-flied to right for Nen in the 10th; b-flied to center for Estalella in the 10th.

BATTING: 2B-Mueller (2, Reed). S-Mueller. RBI-Estalella (1), Benard (1). 2-out RBI-Benard. Runners left in scoring position, 2 out-Estalella 1, Kent 2, Mueller 1, Crespo 1, Mirabelli 1, Bonds 1. Team LOB-16.

FIELDING: DP-2 (Estalella-Aurilia, Kent-Aurilia-Snow).

METS

	ab	r	h	rbi	bb	so	lob	avg
Perez rf	6	0	1	1	0	0	1	.308
Alfonzo 2b	5	0	2	1	1	0	0	.286
Piazza c	4	0	1	0	1	3	2	.273
McEwing pr-3b	1	0	1	0	0	0	0	1.000
Ventura 3b-1b	5	0	0	0	1	1	3	.083
Agbayani lf	6	1	1	1	0	1	3	.273
Payton cf	5	0	1	0	0	2	3	.154
Zeile 1b	3	0	0	0	2	1	1	.091
White p	0	0	0	0	0	0	0	.000
Bordick ss	2	1	0	0	1	1	2	.222
Benitez p	0	0	0	0	0	0	0	.000
c-Pratt ph-c	1	0	0	0	0	0	3	.000
Reed p	1	0	0	0	0	0	0	.000
a-Hamilton ph	1	0	1	0	0	0	0	.500
Cook p	0	0	0	0	0	0	0	.000
Wendell p	0	0	0	0	0	0	0	.000
b-Harris ph	1	1	0	0	0	0	1	.000
JFranco p	0	0	0	0	0	0	0	.000
Abbott ss	2	0	0	0	0	1	0	.000
Totals	**43**	**3**	**9**	**3**	**6**	**10**	**19**	

a-singled for Reed in the 6th, b-hit into fielder's choice for Wendell in the 8th, c-Flied to center for Benitez in the 11th.

BATTING: 2B-Alfonzo (1, Nen). HR-Agbayani (1, 13th inning off Fultz, 0 on, 1 out). RBI-Perez (3), Alfonzo (3), Agbayani (1). 2-out RBI-Alfonzo. Runners left in scoring position, 2 out-Piazza 1, Bordick 1, Pratt 2. GIDP-Ventura. Team LOB-10.

BASERUNNING: SB-Harris (1, 2nd base off Nen/Estalella), Payton (1, 2nd base off Nen/Estalella), CS-Alfonzo (1, 2nd base by RuOrtiz/Estalella).

San Francisco	000	200	000	000	0—2	
Mets	000	001	010	000	1—3	

One out when winning run scored.

San Francisco	IP	H	R	ER	BB	SO	HR	ERA
RuOrtiz	5⅓	2	1	1	4	4	0	1.89
Embree (H,1)	⅔	0	0	0	0	0	0	0.00
Henry (H,1)	1⅔	0	1	1	0	1	0	3.86
Nen (BS, 1)	1⅓	2	0	0	1	3	0	0.00
Rodriguez	2	2	0	0	1	2	0	6.29
Fultz (L,0-1)	1⅓	3	1	1	0	0	1	6.75
Mets								
Reed	6	7	2	2	2	6	0	3.00
Cook	⅔	0	0	0	1	0	0	0.00
Wendell	1⅓	0	0	0	1	3	0	0.00
Franco	1	1	0	0	0	1	0	0.00
Benitez	2	1	0	0	1	3	0	6.00
White (W, 1-0)	2	2	0	0	2	4	0	0.00

IBB-Bonds (by Reed); Piazza (by RuOrtiz); Snow (by Benitez). HBP-Bordick (by Henry). Pitches-strikes: Reed 105-67; Cook 12-5; Wendell 24-18; Franco 16-9; Benitez 40-20; White 40-24; RuOrtiz 95-48; Embree 2-1; Henry 18-13; Nen 28-18; Rodriguez 47-31; Fultz 19-8. Ground balls-flyballs: Reed 3-9, Cook 2-0, Wendell 1-0, Franco1-1, Benitez 1-2, White 0-2, RuOrtiz 3-8, Embree 2-0, Henry 3-1, Nen 0-1, Rodriguez 0-4, Fultz 3-0. Batters faced: Reed 27, Cook 3, Wendell 5, Franco 4, Benitez 8, White 10, RuOrtiz 21, Embree 1, Henry 6, Nen 7, Rodriguez 9, Fultz 6.

Umpires: Home-Crawford; First-Gorman; Second-Roe; Third-Dimuro; Left-Rieker; Right-Craft.

T-5:22. A-56,270.

13

Revenge vs. Rocker in the Face of Sweep

METS 3, BRAVES 2

1999 NLCS Game 4
October 16, 1999 in New York

This was before the philosopher-sociologist-closer-cracker John Rocker shared his personal expertise and spewed that barrel of racist, sexist, anti-Semitic garbage about New York and the riders of the No. 7 train, before he became a most-wanted hombre and full-fledged villain in the city. At this point, all the venom that had come out of the Atlanta reliever's prodigious mouth was that he hated New York City and wondered how many times the Braves would have to beat the Mets before the fans would "shut up."

And, before Game 4 of the 1999 NLCS, when Rocker was asked if he would change his attitude toward Shea and the Mets' fans, he said simply, "The only thing I am changing is my clothes, after I get champagne all over them tonight."

Mostly, to the Mets and their fans, Rocker was still more annoying reminder than anti-hero, sort of a human brick wall that wore their head imprints. If the Brave lefty with the sharp arm and dull mind was detested in Queens, it was simply for being on the mound for too many final-out celebrations against the local heroes.

On this night, the Mets went face-to-face with the prospect that Rocker and Co. were about to have another party, at their season-ending expense, in front of the Shea fans. The eternally first-place Braves, their tormentors, were four outs away from closing out the Mets in the minimum four games. The Mets had already flushed a 1-0 lead just six outs from the finish line and were feeling the kind of despair that suggests a godless universe.

John Olerud broke a string of 15 Met scoreless innings with a sixth-inning homer off a flat cutter from John Smoltz and it seemed like it might be enough for Rick Reed, who was all but perfect through seven. Reed retired the first 10 Braves and permitted only one runner and one hit—a fourth-inning single by Bret Boone, who was thrown out stealing.

"I don't think it gets any better than that," said Reed, who showed a command he considered superior to what he enjoyed in his must-win, three-hit, no-walk, 12-strikeout game vs. the Pirates Oct. 2. "My pitches went wherever I wanted, until the eighth inning."

That was when the gutsy Reed—or Greg Maddux Lite, as Met fans thought of him—lost his corner mastery in a horrible instant, even though his pitch count was a ridiculously thrifty 70. Brian Jordan homered to left center on the first pitch of the inning. Ryan Klesko followed with another homer, off the base of the scoreboard, in right.

Back to back. Thank you and drive into the off-season safely.

Atlanta led, 2-1, to go with a three-games-to-none advantage in the Series, and Smoltz' 13th career post-season victory seemed imminent. The smell of winter was in the air in Flushing as the 55,872 fans suddenly wished their seats had been furnished with barf bags.

"If I could've crawled under the mound, I would have . . . If there was a tunnel from the mound to the dugout, I would've taken it," said Reed, who was replaced by Turk Wendell. "To be honest, walking off, I thought the season was over."

Not yet.

In the bottom of the eighth, Roger Cedeño singled to center, his third hit of the night, but Rey Ordoñez popped up another in a series of futile bunt attempts, fouling out to first. Mike Remlinger—a quality lefty inexplicably sold by the Mets to a Japanese League team in a brainless cash transaction in 1995—was brought in to relieve Smoltz, so Benny Agbayani pinch-hit for pinch-hitter Matt Franco. Cedeño stole second—the Mets' first steal of the series—as Agbayani struck out. But Melvin Mora, a defensive replacement for Rickey Henderson, walked.

So Braves manager Bobby Cox made a double switch, bringing in ancient Ozzie Guillen at shortstop for slick-fielding Walt Weiss and asking his closer, Rocker, to beam down to Planet Earth long enough to get Olerud and the three additional outs needed for a sweep.

Rocker had saved five games against the Mets during the regular season and two more in the NLCS. No wonder he was the embodiment of eagerness as he came sprinting in from the visitors' bullpen in left, avoiding a water bottle and other smaller aerial tributes from his fellow fools in the stands.

As Rocker warmed up, Mora took a stroll to second for a conference with Cedeño. According to Mora, it went sort of like this: Psst, Roger, I think Rocker is a tad high-strung, like Roseanne with PMS, so let's pull on Superman's cape and see if he unravels.

"I said we have to put a runner on third base, because I know with a man on third base, Rocker gets nervous. He doesn't want to throw the curveball in the dirt," said Mora. "I saw it in Atlanta. I made a fake like I was going to home plate and he was nervous."

Cedeño—who had stopped trying to swipe bases after the All-Star break for reasons unknown and still wound up with a career-high 66 steals—was reluctant to run. However, Mora—the 27-year-old rookie who spent most of that season at Triple-A Norfolk—prevailed and turned Roger rabbit.

"I said, 'Hey, let's steal,'" said Mora. "You have to play the game like that. We're not hitting. We're struggling. We have to do something . . . [Cedeño] said, 'No, I don't want to be the third out.' I said, 'No, go. He is not going to pay any attention to you. He's going to pay attention to Johnny.'"

"He [Mora] has baseball written all over him," said Bobby Valentine, the control freak who strangely felt no need to weigh in with a managerial plan while his two outfielders conducted this strategy Yalta on the field.

Later on, Cedeño insisted the idea to run was his.

"The manager [Cox] pointed at me and said [to Rocker], 'Don't worry about the runner, just get the hitter.' I was watching, trying to see what they were talking about and that's what I thought he was saying . . . I told Melvin to be ready to go in case I go. I went on my own."

Later on, Cedeño shared the credit with Mora.

In any event, Rocker didn't even check the Met runners and they stole third and second respectively on a 1-and-1 curve down and away, without a throw from Eddie Perez. Now the winning run was in scoring position, along with the tying one, and the Mets needed only one hit to get them both across the plate.

"I knew they were going to double steal there. That was automatic," said Cox. "But I think he [Rocker] was intent on getting the hitter out."

"I wasn't thinking about the runners at all. I was concentrating on the hitter and I really couldn't tell you who was on first," said Rocker. "I have a terrible pickoff move and if you make a mistake on Olerud and he hits one in the gap, they score two runs anyway."

Olerud is a lefty hitter who hangs in against lefty pitchers about as well as Keith Hernandez once did. But his career log was 0-for-9 vs. Rocker, including five strikeouts.

Not too encouraging.

"I have tried a bunch of different approaches off him and haven't had a whole lot of success," said Olerud. "He's got a great fastball, good slider, good breaking pitch. He can throw them all for strikes, so you can't really rule out one particular pitch and that makes it rough."

Unleashing that gorgeous swing, John Olerud launches a home run in the sixth inning. It was just an appetizer, because the main course was Olerud's dinky, game-winning infield hit off John Rocker in the eighth that put the Braves' brooms away.

Olerud hit a 2-and-2 pitch, sending a modest bouncer up the middle.

"It was a fastball, down and away, and I was over the top of it a little bit," he said. "I didn't know if it was going to get through or not."

The ball got through because it went off the glove of the creaky Guillen, kicking toward right field, as Cedeño and Mora scored. It was a single, sort of.

"If I catch it, he is going to be out, because he is a slow runner," said Guillen.

"I don't think any of our shortstops catch that ball," said Cox. "We're shaded too much the other way [toward third]."

"Two, three inches to the left, Guillen makes the play," said Reed. "Who knows? Maybe that was the break we needed. We'll find out."

"It was one of the cheaper hits I have ever given up," decided Rocker. "It was an infield hit. It wasn't like it was a double off the wall."

The man had a point, for a change. It wasn't pretty, this smallest of blows. But it was effective. It established a Game 5—even though the Mets had managed only eight runs in the series and lost 21 of their last 28 games against Atlanta.

"To come back and get the win and get a couple of runs off Rocker, whom we really haven't done much against . . . It is a big win for us," said Olerud.

"He has been a thorn in our side," said Darryl Hamilton. "That is what you call getting over the hump. That was huge."

The fact that Rocker had raised the stakes with his Olympic-sized mouth certainly didn't contribute to his defeat. It just made it more sweet for the Mets and, of course, the riffraff who ride the No. 7 train.

"It was very pleasurable," said winning pitcher Wendell. "I think he [Rocker] got what was coming to him . . . You can talk all the smack you want if you can back it up and up till now he has been able to. But nobody's perfect."

"He [Rocker] has had plenty of these situations," said Smoltz. "And he has been successful nine out of 10 times."

"My confidence didn't get shaken," testified Rocker. "I don't feel the least bit bad about my performance . . . A routine ground ball found a favorable spot. It was an infield hit. We still have a comfortable lead [in the Series] . . . The fans think they are in my head, but I'm really in their head."

There is no telling, really, what, if anything, is in Rocker's head. In fact, when he strode off to the dugout at the end of the eighth with the

Mets ahead, 3-2, he flashed three fingers and an OK sign at fans, presumably reminded them of the Series status.

Then again, maybe Rocker was just showing them he could count that high.

After Armando Benitez survived a scary foul home run by Guillen in the ninth and nailed down the triumph by extending his season-plus-post-season mastery of Atlanta hitters to 0-for-24, the Mets had a different appreciation of still breathing.

"What was really gratifying was to see Guillen's ball miss the foul pole, because those things haven't been going our way," said Valentine. "It allows us to win and play tomorrow, so that makes it a breakthrough . . . We won one game and we did it the hard way."

The Braves weren't exactly panicked.

"It seems like we got the breaks early in the series," said Chipper Jones. "They just got the big hit when they needed it. Realistically, we came here just wanting to win one game [they got that one, 1-0, in Game 3]."

"They've got to beat us three more times and they've only beat us four times all year—I'm pretty confident," said Rocker.

"I'm not going to say this is a huge life-changing event, but at least it's a start," said Mike Piazza, with sore knees and a painful thumb. "It's not the Magna Carta [then again, what is?], but at least it's something to build on."

ATLANTA

	ab	r	h	rbi	bb	so	lob	avg
Williams lf	4	0	0	0	0	0	0	.294
Boone 2b	3	0	1	0	0	1	0	.353
Lockhart ph	1	0	0	0	0	1	0	.000
CJones 3b	3	0	0	0	0	2	0	.174
Jordan rf	3	1	1	1	0	0	0	.323
Klesko 1b	3	1	1	1	0	1	0	.278
Hunter 1b	0	0	0	0	0	0	0	.000
AJones cf	3	0	0	0	0	0	0	.226
Perez c	3	0	0	0	0	0	0	.345
Weiss ss	3	0	0	0	0	1	0	.278
Rocker p	0	0	0	0	0	0	0	.000
Smoltz p	2	0	0	0	0	0	0	.400
Remlinger p	0	0	0	0	0	0	0	.000
Guillen ss	1	0	0	0	0	0	0	.000
Totals	29	2	3	2	0	6	0	

BATTING: HR-Jordan (3, 8th inning off Reed 0 on, 0 out); Klesko (1, 8th inning off Reed 0 on, 0 out). RBI-Jordan (10), Klesko (2). Team LOB-0

BASERUNNING: CS-Boone (1, 2nd base by Reed/Piazza).

METS

	ab	r	h	rbi	bb	so	lob	avg
Henderson lf	3	0	0	0	0	1	1	.250
Mora lf	0	1	0	0	1	0	0	.429
Olerud 1b	4	1	2	3	0	0	0	.355
Alfonzo 2b	4	0	0	0	0	3	1	.250
Piazza c	3	0	0	0	0	2	0	.174
Ventura 3b	3	0	0	0	0	0	0	.115
Hamilton cf	3	0	0	0	0	2	0	.118
Cedeño rf	3	1	3	0	0	0	0	.471
Ordoñez ss	3	0	0	0	0	0	2	.179
Reed p	2	0	0	0	0	0	1	.000
Wendell p	0	0	0	0	0	0	0	.000
MFranco ph	0	0	0	0	0	0	0	.000
Agbayani ph	1	0	0	0	0	1	1	.200
Benitez p	0	0	0	0	0	0	0	.000
Totals	29	3	5	3	1	9	6	

BATTING: HR-Olerud (2, 6th inning off Smoltz 0 on, 2 out). RBI-Olerud 3 (9). 2-out RBI-Olerud 3. Runners left in scoring position, 2 out-Henderson 1. Team LOB-3.

BASERUNNING: SB-Cedeño 2 (3, 2nd base off Remlinger/Perez, 3rd base off Rocker/Perez); Mora (1, 2nd base off Rocker/Perez).

Atlanta			000	000	020	— 2
Mets			000	001	02X	— 3

Atlanta	IP	H	R	ER	BB	SO	HR	ERA
Smoltz	7⅓	4	2	2	0	7	1	3.52
Remlinger (L, 0-1)	⅓	0	1	1	1	1	0	7.94
Rocker (BS, 1)	⅓	1	0	0	0	0	1	0.00
Mets								
Reed	7	3	2	2	0	5	2	2.77
Wendell (W, 2-0)	1	0	0	0	0	0	0	1.59
Benitez (S, 1)	1	0	0	0	0	1	0	0.00

Pitches-strikes: Reed 73-53; Wendell 8-7; Benitez 12-7; Smoltz 100-68; Remlinger 10-4; Rocker 8-6. Ground balls-flyballs: Reed 8-7; Wendell 2-1; Benitez 0-2; Smoltz 5-10; Remlinger 0-0; Rocker 0-0. Batters faced: Reed 23, Wendell 3, Benitez 3, Smoltz 26, Remlinger 2, Rocker 2.

Umpires: Home-Rapuano; First-Layne; Second-Crawford; Third-Montague; Left-Kellogg; Right-Reliford.

T-2:20. A-55,872.

14

Koosman, Weis Show O's Mets Are Full of Life

METS 2, ORIOLES 1

1969 World Series Game 2
October 12, 1969 in Baltimore

After Game 1 of the 1969 World Series, the Baltimore Orioles were feeling understandably underwhelmed by the Mets and their allegedly magical ways. The O's—an experienced group of base-ball assassins who had won 109 games in the regular season and had clinched their title on Sept. 13—knocked around the Mets' 25-game winner, Tom Seaver, while 23-game-winner Mike Cuellar hardly broke a sweat during a 4-1 knockout of a Series opener at Memorial Stadium.

No rabbits. No hats. Not much suspense.

And, according to the opinion expressed to the media by the Orioles' fiery vocal team leader Frank Robinson, not even much life in the Mets' dugout when they loaded the bases in the seventh inning.

"Well, we weren't scoring very much and we don't often cheer when the other team is scoring," said Jerry Koosman, his sarcasm as crackling as his curve would be during his two-hit pitching in Game 2.

"I'm glad to see Frank is watching our bench, but I am not concerned about what he says," said manager Gil Hodges.

When that last remark was brought back to F. Robby by the messengers who use pens and microphones to stir the fecal matter, Frank said, "Tell Hodges he should manage his ballclub and I will play right field."

"We are out to prove there is no Santa Claus," said Brooks Robinson, half Grinch and half vacuum cleaner at third base.

Fair enough.

And there really was no smoke and no mirrors in the way the Mets won Game 2 to send the series back to New York even instead of half over. This 2-1 victory was fashioned in the Mets' manner, however: gritty pitching backed by one timely hit from somebody, anybody. It was built on Koosman's mastery of a loaded, righty-dominated Baltimore batting order—and a ninth-inning, two-out, game-winning single by Al Weis, a .215 hitter during the season.

OK, maybe a wisp of smoke and one mirror.

"If he had decided to hit for me, I wouldn't have been the least bit disappointed," said Weis, platoon second baseman and hero without ego. "I have been a utility man long enough to understand these things."

Leading up to the Weis guy and his moment of glory was plenty of tension—and only one run scored by each team in an old-fashioned duel to the finish (or close to it) between two elegant, ballsy lefties: Koosman (17-9, 2.28 in 1969) and Dave McNally (20-7, 3.22).

The Mets broke on top in the fourth inning, when they ended McNally's string of 23 straight scoreless post-season innings (12 of them in the World Series) that extended back to the 1966 World Series.

On a 1-and-1 count, Donn Clendenon—the June 15 trade addition whom Tug McGraw called "our pressure exorcist"—lifted a curving, slicing drive over the 370-foot mark and into the right-field seats. It was the first of three home runs that the 34-year-old platoon first baseman would hit in his four starts en route to being named the MVP of the Series.

"I'm too old to pull," joked Clendenon, who had a pulled muscle in his thigh, tendinitis in his shoulder and thunder still left in that menacing swing that he had come close to prematurely retiring in the spring.

The rest of the first six innings belonged to Koosman. Although he didn't expect his command to be sharp because of a longer-than-usual layoff between starts, Koosman gave the Orioles nothing, not even a hit —thanks to two fine plays by shortstop Buddy Harrelson to rob Don Buford.

Buford was the Bird who had said to Harrelson while trotting out during a first-inning Game 1 homer off Seaver, "You guys ain't seen nothing yet."

"That sort of aroused us," said Buddy.

In the third, Harrelson dove to his right and backhanded Buford's liner. In the sixth, Buddy charged Buford's grounder, reacted quickly to a sudden, erratic hop, gloved it over his head and nailed the speedy Oriole at first.

Not until Paul Blair lined a 1-and-0 off-speed pitch through the left side for a leadoff single in the seventh did Koosman have to let go of a goal set back in his boyhood in Appleton, Minn.

"When I was 16, I made myself a goal to pitch a no-hitter in the World Series and get a hit every time at bat," said Koosman, who went 0-for-4 and stranded two runners in the seventh. "I knew I was going to make it to pro ball and I wanted to make it a difficult goal so it wouldn't come easy."

Koosman admitted that the Blair hit and the fact that it concluded his chase of Don Larsen (whose 1956 perfect game remains the only no-hitter in World Series history) brought more relief than disappointment "because the pressure was off."

Of course, Koosman wasn't feeling relaxed when the Orioles got even in that inning. With two outs, Blair narrowly beat Jerry Grote's throw and stole second. When Brooks Robinson grounded a single through the middle, the score was 1-1. Ed Charles' great stab of Davey Johnson's bullet one-hopper bailed the Mets out of the inning.

In the eighth inning, four mini-skirted Met wives—Ruth Ryan, Lynn Dyer, Nancy Seaver and Melanie Pfeil—walked the lower-deck aisle among the 50,850 fans present in Baltimore that day, holding aloft a bedsheet that read "Let's go Mets." They were pelted with peanuts for their show of support for the visitors and perhaps for ruining the Sheraton's linen.

Then again, these Mets needed all the assistance they could get. This was a team that never had a clue where its next run was coming from and now it needed another. It looked like it might be awhile as McNally—who had permitted three hits through eight—began the ninth by striking out Clendenon and getting Ron Swoboda on a grounder. The bottom of the Mets' order was next.

But Charles, the platoon third baseman who already had a double in this game, grounded a hit between B. Robby and peerless shortstop Mark Belanger (a task, given their range, as difficult as threading a needle during an earthquake).

For his next trick, Charles, 36 years old, was off and running. Hodges knew for magic to occur with a lineup like his, sometimes a manager needed to wave a wand or two.

"Yes, at his age," repeated Hodges. "Charles had a steal sign on the pitch before and didn't get a good jump. Then, on 2-and-2 to Grote, he went. Strictly speaking, it's not a hit-and-run play. It's a run-and-hit play. The runner goes and takes his chances."

Charles ran and Grote hit—a line single to left that sent The Glider into third, sans cap.

First and third, two outs. Base open, at second. No. 8 hitter, Weis, due. Koosman on deck. Decision time.

Orioles manager Earl Weaver decided to go after Weis, though he offered two versions as to his reasoning. And his pitching coach George Bamberger—who visited with McNally at this critical juncture—offered a third avenue of thought.

First, Bamberger.

Bambi insisted that he and McNally never talked about intentionally passing Weis, but rather discussed how to play a double steal and decided, if Grote took second, they would walk Weis to get to Koosman.

"If Koosman hits for himself, we have an excellent chance of getting him out. If they hit for him, we get him out of the game," said Bamberger, presenting a win-win proposition.

Now, Weaver, from the first side of his mouth.

"I wanted to pitch to him," testified Weaver to some of the writers. "If I walk Weis, they hit for Koosman. After eight innings I would rather face Koosman than a fresh arm. I thought we were getting to him."

Then the probably more honest version from Weaver, to another set of writers: "I didn't want to walk Weis, because I felt they would pinch-hit for Koosman with a better hitter than Weis."

After all, Weis wasn't exactly The Bambino. Although the Cubs would beg to differ, off their 1969 humiliations at his hand, Weis was a Judy hitter (Punch and Judy, minus Punch). McNally had made him look foolish with breaking balls while striking him out in the fifth after making the mistake of serving him a fastball that Weis turned into a single in the third.

So what if McNally was on a short list entitled "Pitchers Who Have Thrown Gopher Balls to Al Weis" some time in his eight major league seasons?

"Yeah, he is one of the six," said Al, who had taken McNally deep when Weis was a member of the White Sox.

The first pitch was a poorly located high slider that Weis—expecting a breaking ball—saw well and turned into his version of a tape-measure blast. He lined it over shortstop and into left, scoring Charles. If Charles hadn't been running on the Grote hit, he might have scored from second on this single. Maybe not.

"I bet McNally would like to have that pitch back," said Weis, who cannot tell a lie. "I didn't see myself winning a game with my bat. I saw myself winning a game with my glove. It just so happens I've made the only error in the Series so far.

"I am a quiet guy . . . but in my own way I play the game hard . . . The players call me Mr. Cool. I show no emotion."

Except post-game gratitude.

"Had it been any other manager, I believe I would have been taken out. Gil has stayed with me and I am thankful," said Weis, back at .215 for the post-season after his two hits.

Three more outs to get. And a couple of more moves from Hodges, one of them unorthodox.

Koosman got Buford to fly out and Blair to ground out. Now there were two outs and the hitter was Frank Robinson. Hodges, following a strategy he had employed against big boppers with his team a run ahead and the bases empty, instructed Weis to leave second base unmanned and position himself near the left-field foul line, so Cleon Jones could park in left center. In 1969, Hodges had gone with the extra outfielder in the pull field against Willie McCovey, Willie Stargell, Richie Allen and Hank Aaron— only in situations where he thought it imperative to take away the extra-base hit. It never backfired on Hodges.

Hodges was willing to give Robinson an opposite-field single if Robby was willing to forego a home-run swing.

"We were trying to shut off the extra-base alleys," explained Hodges. "We are not trying to tempt the hitter or taunt him. We are trying simply to keep the man from getting a double or a triple.

"If a hitter of this caliber wants to settle for a single by going for the wide open hole on the right side of the infield, let him. We'll give it to him. It still takes two more singles to get the run in. If he gets a double, it only takes one more hit."

The strategy made perfect sense—and no difference whatsoever in this case. Frank Robinson walked. So did Boog Powell. After walking one over the first eight innings, Koosman had passed two in a row. So Hodges walked—to the mound to fetch the baseball.

"Koosman had thrown 100 pitches, 22 of them in the ninth inning alone," said Met pitching coach Rube Walker. "He wasn't tired, but he was cutting it a little too fine. You can start aiming the ball too much at that stage."

"I would've liked to stay, but nobody questions Gil," said Koosman. "He has made all the right moves. He came out and asked me for the ball and said I had done a real fine job. But then he says that if you have just given up 10 runs. He always comes out with a word of confidence."

Gil also had some words of confidence for relief ace Ron Taylor, the only Met with previous World Series experience. Hodges said to Taylor, who had already worked two scoreless innings and had struck out three Orioles in Game 1, "You have to get one man."

Later, the manager explained, "I didn't want him to think he was going to have to be out there for three days."

"I knew I had to get Brooks out or we might go back to New York two games down," said the cerebral right-hander. "This was the toughest one-on-one test I ever had . . . Don't get behind him, that was all I was thinking about."

Taylor, determined to throw sliders and sinkers down and away, almost hit Brooks Robinson with the first pitch, fell behind him 3-and-1 and got a foul ball to work the count full. Now the runners were going to be in motion and a lefty pinch-hitter loomed if Taylor walked Brooks.

"I was praying he would pop it up or strike out or hit a grounder, so we could go on to New York and take the rest of them," said Koosman.

Taylor's money pitch was the sinker and Brooks hit one on the ground to Charles while Met fans held their collective breath. When he had an in-between hop under control, wide of third, Ed made a move toward the bag, thinking he might get the force on pinch-runner Merv Rettenmund there.

"I figured I could save the throw," said Charles. "Why take a chance on throwing the ball away when you don't have to?"

But when Charles felt Rettenmund go past him, Ed knew he was going to get to the bag a step too late. Now, he *had* to throw.

"I was playing deep because I know Brooks is slow," said Charles.

"So, even when I got to third base and found the runner there, I knew I could still get him at first."

"Brooks is not the fastest thing on foot," said Clendenon.

And Charles' soft, deliberate toss to first sailed into the dirt, but was rescued by Clendenon to nip Brooks.

"Two steps short. Two steps. That's the story of my life," said Brooks.

Exhale. Tied Series. Now a relieved Hodges could abandon Desperation Plan B, which was to start Seaver in place of Gary Gentry in a must-win Game 3.

"I think I was lucky," said Taylor, who was then asked if he is always so modest and responded, "Not when I talk to Mr. Johnny Murphy [GM and contract negotiator]."

"If I can't maintain my cool now, who can on this club?" said Charles. "If I told you I was tight these two games, I would be lying.

Donn Clendenon, who got the slumbering Met bats started with a homer off Dave McNally in Game 2, receives a hero's welcome from his teammates and delighted, doddering club owner Joan Payson, in the stands at the corner of the visitors' dugout.

The more experienced you are, the more relaxed you should be in situations like this. I'm not a tense guy."

The Orioles were neither tense nor all that impressed. But they were getting the idea of how these Mets operated.

"Seaver is faster than Koosman," said Brooks Robinson. "But they have a good club and, with guys like that in there, they stay close and can beat you 1-0 and 2-1. They don't run you out of the park, but they don't have to with pitchers like that."

Johnson said Koosman reminded him of the "quick and fast" Jim Kaat for the smoothness of his motion and suggested that Koosman wanted hitters "to hit the curve." Powell said Koosman was a little like Sam McDowell, "but McDowell was quicker."

"That's the best game I've ever seen Koosman pitch," said Clay Dalrymple, the catcher and former National Leaguer. "I think the Mets are a helluva club now. When I knew them, they were a ninth-place club."

Frank Robinson, who hit a drive in the first inning that the wind held up for Swoboda to catch about 390 feet away from the plate, was unsold on the Mets' left-hander.

"He didn't exactly dazzle us with his stuff," said Frank. "We hit the ball well 10 or 12 times against him, but they went right to somebody. If they fell in, we could have scored three or four runs."

But they didn't. And the Mets found a way. Or maybe they made one.

"I'm tired of everyone telling me how great the Baltimore Orioles are," said Clendenon. "We're great, too. We are the champions of the National League. They're a great ballclub, but we're going to find some way to beat them . . . If I have any grandchildren, this is the year I can tell them about."

Even Frank Robinson had to admit these Mets didn't bear any resemblance to the punchline, punch-drunk Mets of old, the ones he had abused as a member of the Cincinnati Reds.

"The Mets I used to see wouldn't be here," said Frank. "These are the new Mets. The old Mets are retired . . . The old Mets expected to make mistakes and made them. These Mets have strong feelings for themselves. They win and they expect to win. Success does that to a team."

METS	ab	r	h	bl	BALTIMORE	ab	r	h	bl
Agee cf	4	0	0	0	Buford lf	4	0	0	0
Harrelson ss	3	0	0	0	Blair cf	4	1	1	0
Jones lf	4	0	0	0	FRobinson rf	3	0	0	0
Clendenon 1b	3	1	1	1	Rettenmund pr	0	0	0	0
Swoboda rf	4	0	0	0	Powell 1b	3	0	0	0
Charles 3b	4	1	2	0	BRobinson 3b	4	0	1	1
Grote c	4	0	1	0	Johnson 2b	2	0	0	0
Weis 2b	3	0	2	1	Etchebarren c	3	0	0	0
Koosman p	4	0	0	0	Belanger ss	3	0	0	0
Taylor p	0	0	0	0	McNally p	3	0	0	0
Totals	33	2	6	2	Totals	29	1	2	1

Mets	000	100	001	— 2
Baltimore	000	000	100	— 1

LOB-Mets 7, Baltimore 4. 2B-Charles. HR-Clendenon. SB-Blair.

	IP	H	R	ER	BB	SO
Mets						
Koosman (W, 1-0)	8²/₃	2	1	1	3	4
Taylor	¹/₃	0	0	0	0	0
Baltimore						
McNally (L, 0-1)	9	6	2	2	3	7

Wild pitch-McNally.

T-2:20. A-50,850.

15

Ya Gotta Take Cover as Seaver Finishes Reds

METS 7, REDS 2

1973 NLCS Game 5
October 10, 1973 in New York

T he sheer delicious improbability of it all was what made the 1973 Mets' rise from a notch below mediocrity to an upset pennant victory over the powerhouse Reds so special. This remains the king of the from-the-ashes baseball ascent stories. These Mets, crippled for much of the summer, had been 12 games off the pace in July and 13 games under .500 as late as August. They went into first place and reached .500 on the same night, Sept. 21.

Somehow, they managed to win the sad NL East with a month of title-worthy ball—20 wins in 28 September games—and an 82-79 record overall. And when Yogi Berra's team chopped down the mighty Reds, winners of 99 games, in five emotional contests, the feat was complete.

However, in the insane, joyous moments following the Mets' 7-2 Game 5 NLCS victory, their accomplishment was at least temporarily overshadowed by the scary manner in which the clinching was celebrated by some in the crowd of 50,323.

Over-enthusiastic Met fans or a destructive mob of New York's all-time lowlifes—depending on whose locker room you happened to be taking cover in—burst loose from the barriers, wrestled players for their caps, stole home plate and the other three bases, ripped off hunks of Shea Stadium sod and parts of the outfield fence and made NLCS villain Pete Rose run like a man with a bounty on his life.

The heavily favored Reds were feeling pretty raw. They had just been beaten by an improvising Tom Seaver, working on three days' rest and without the customary oomph on his heater, plus Ed Kranepool and Willie Mays, replacements for an injured Rusty Staub. Then, they were hunted like game by the marauding fans.

So you can excuse that, when it was over, they pounded on lockers with their bats in anger and sounded like tourists who had been stripped clean of their valuables in Times Square, reacting with genuine if somewhat excessive horror to the trampling of the good old middle American value of peace on turf.

"New York doesn't deserve a pennant," said Rose, who had the misfortune of being a runner between first and second when the final out was made, but made it to safety anyway. "They let the fans out of the zoo for the game and take them back when it's over."

Before the final outs were in the books, Seaver begged the fans to return to their seats and the game was delayed 10 minutes during the ninth inning. Rose, meanwhile, appreciated but didn't exactly require the well-meaning suggestions from umpire Ed Sudol and Met catcher Jerry Grote that, in Grote's words, "he better get the hell out of here in a hurry" when this game was over.

"I'm still thinking, we can still win this game, and they are scaring me to death," said Rose.

Rose knew that there were better times to be stranded on base than the end of this Series. He realized it would be inadvisable for him to linger and greet the mouth-breathers, presuming they might make this future Hall of Famer the first human collectible.

"I had 15 guys [teammates] with bats ready to protect me, but nobody touched me. I got out of there fast," said Rose, whose Game 3 fight with Bud Harrelson and game-winning, extra-inning homer in Game 4 had made him Public Enemy No. 1.

"I don't understand these people. The other day, the umpires wanted me to play center field so the fans couldn't throw things at me. I couldn't play left field because of the fans and, on the last out, I couldn't finish running to second base because of the fans . . . I was an open field runner and I had to make it to the goal line."

"Our first concern was Pete's safety," said Reds catcher Johnny Bench. "I thought someone might try to kill him. If the cops weren't going to stop these maniacs, then we would."

"I was thinking when all the trouble was going on, I hope Pete decks a dozen of those SOBs," said Harrelson. "We are professionals."

The wild bunch really wasn't bloodthirsty. Mostly, they whooped and hollered and yelled, "We're No. 1."

However, even deliriously happy mobs will be mobs. Sue Ballou, wife of the Reds' team doctor George Ballou, was knocked down and had her hair pulled, leaving her frightened and crying. And buying a ticket to a baseball game to determine a pennant winner shouldn't involve the risk of limb.

"It's unbelievable to me," said Reds manager Sparky Anderson. "I just can't believe they don't have better control over the people. It makes me ashamed I am in this country. But I am not too sure New York is in this country. Not after this week . . . Normal fans wouldn't act that way. They must be on dope or something."

No, Sparky, they just *were* dopes.

"I saw two little kids, they couldn't have been more than two or three years old, get pushed down face first in the dirt . . . It was a disgrace," said Bench. "If that is what police protection is like here, hell,

I am going to rob some banks in New York . . . What you needed were a few billy clubs over a few heads."

Although Seaver was as horrified as some of the Reds about the poor behavior of the fans, some Met players saw it as benign.

Grote even took teammate Jim Beauchamp back out onto the field about an hour after the game ended and delightedly surveyed the damage. The catcher told him that it wasn't nearly as bad as it was in 1969.

"It only happens in New York because the people feel they have to be a part of it," said Cleon Jones. "It got out of hand, but it stems from their strong feeling for us. I can't be mad at them for that."

They were simply flushed with success, which is what happens to fans of teams with the great pitching necessary to stop great hitting. The Reds, boasting a deep lineup featuring many more dangerous hitters than the Staub-dependent Mets, were outscored, 23-8, in the NLCS. In no game did Cincinnati score more than two runs. Yet, nothing came easy for the Mets—not even a five-run victory in Game 5.

The Seaver who fanned 13 in a 2-1 loss to Jack Billingham in Game 1 was nowhere to be found. Struggling instead to find a way to compensate for a fastball that was obeying the speed limit, Tom Terrific struck out only four. Each pitcher faced a first-inning crisis, but Seaver wriggled out of his unscathed, and the Mets scored twice off Billingham.

With one out, Seaver walked Joe Morgan, surrendered a single to Dan Driessen and wild-pitched the runners to second and third. Then came the key out of the inning, as Seaver got Tony Perez swinging on a foul tip held onto by Grote. An intentional pass to Bench led to Ken Griffey's final-out flyball to center.

"I had to strike out Perez, so I would have a base to put Johnny Bench on," said Seaver, who scattered seven hits in 8⅓ innings that were more gutsy than dominant. "I got Perez with a sinker, a good pitch. And God bless Grote, he made a hell of a play in the first inning that might have changed the whole game.

"In a game you have to win, it's important not to give up that first run. I didn't want us to have to play catch-up today. We'd been fighting uphill all year long."

"We had Seaver on the ropes in the first inning," lamented Bench. "With the bases loaded, another hit and, bingo, maybe he is out of there. But we didn't get that hit."

In the bottom of the inning, Felix Millan singled up the middle, Jones crushed the first of his three hits into left and then John Milner walked. Bases loaded, one out. The next hitter was Mr. Original Met, Kranepool, making his first start since Sept. 15, in left field, because the shoulder that Staub injured making a sensational, fence-crashing, game-prolonging catch in Game 4 was too stiff for him to be able to swing.

On Billingham's first pitch, Steady Eddie lashed a single to left for two runs—his first RBI in 36 days—and the Mets had a lead that didn't last through the Cincinnati fifth. In the third, Morgan's double, an error by right fielder Jones and Driessen's sac fly made it 2-1. In the fifth, Rose doubled to left and eventually scored on Perez' two-out single to right center.

Yes, the game was tied. However, Seaver—nursed carefully by Grote with more than the usual number of changeups against Rose and Bench —had toughed it out long enough to buy time for the Mets to assemble a four-run fifth.

The rally began with a leadoff double by Wayne Garrett, who had been 0-for-19 since a Game 1 single in his first NLCS at-bat. All in all, not a bad time to remember how to hit.

Then came the play the Reds—particularly Driessen, a rookie and a converted third baseman—will never forget. Millan bunted. Billingham fielded it and, properly instructed by Bench, the pitcher threw to third in plenty of time to get Garrett.

There was just one catch: Driessen, a first baseman in the minors, received the throw with his foot on the base and forgot that it was a tag play, not a force. No tag meant no out. Garrett was safe and there were Mets at first and third, none out, instead of just Millan at first with one out.

"That's inexperience," said a protective Anderson.

"I don't want that as a crutch. I just goofed," said Driessen of his brainlock. "Usually, when they throw to third on that play, there are runners at first and second and it's a force play. I forgot there was only a man on second. It was just one of those things. I know I messed up."

It was one of those things teams like the Mets need to go boom.

Jones was next and the heat was on Billingham to keep the game tied.

"I felt I had to strike out Cleon then," said the right-hander. "My first pitch was a curveball. I still feel it was a pretty good pitch."

Jones certainly liked it, crushing it off the fence in left center for a double to give the Mets a 3-2 lead and finish off Billingham. Anderson summoned lefty Don Gullett to face the left-handed Milner—and Gullett came awfully chose to getting the strikeout Sparky wanted on a 2-and-2 fastball that was probably too close for The Hammer to have taken. It was called a ball and Gullett eventually walked him to load the bases.

The next scheduled hitter was the lefty Kranepool, but Berra told Willie Mays to grab a bat. Mays hadn't had a base hit since Aug. 29 and was hitting for the first time since cracking three ribs in Montreal Sept. 9. Even though Mays was a few steps from retirement, Anderson switched from the overpowering Gullett to righty Clay Carroll. After all, at 42 years old, Willie Mays was still Willie Mays—and he wasn't going to let a pitching change keep him from rising to the moment.

"I was glad [the harder thrower] Gullett went out," said Mays. "Just because he is a left-hander don't mean I am going to hit him. With the right-hander, I felt confident I was going to hit the ball somewhere."

He hit it somewhere where they weren't. Mays chopped the first pitch about 20 feet in the air toward the third-base side of the mound. Carroll's throw home wasn't close to in time to get Millan and the score was 4-2 on a large, short, infield single by an old, wonderful, baseball God.

"The Big Guy upstairs took care of Willie with that chop hit," reasoned Staub. "It evens up some of the ropes they have caught off him in the last 10 years."

"I wanted to do something for this team," said Mays. "They have taken care of me all year. I mean they didn't bother me about playing. You always want to play, but when you get older . . ."

The Mets' fifth run scored one out later when Don Hahn lofted a fly to short center that fell untouched. Grote was thrown out at second, but Milner crossed to make it 5-2. Then Harrelson pushed a single past third and the bulge was four runs. In the sixth, a double by Seaver and a single by Jones pushed the score to 7-2.

Seaver tired in the ninth and, with one out, Larry Stahl singled and Hal King walked. Then Seaver walked Rose after he thought he had Pete struck out looking on an 0-and-2 pitch. The bases were loaded and it was time for Tug McGraw, the human symbol of this Met team's resurgence. The lefty recorded the last two outs of this NLCS—Morgan on a pop to short and Driessen on a roller to first baseman Milner.

The riot began on the field and a riotous celebration started in the Met clubhouse.

Seaver doused Mayor John Lindsay with champagne.

"Once again," said Lindsay, referring to 1969 vintage bubbly he had worn in the same spot.

"Once again," said Seaver.

Lindsay wanted to shake hands with Mays, who said to him, "Mr. Mayor, you don't know how good I feel" and

CINCINNATI	ab	r	h	bl	METS	ab	r	h	bl
Rose lf	4	1	2	0	Garrett 3b	5	1	1	0
Morgan 2b	4	1	1	0	Millan 2b	4	2	2	0
Driessen 3b	4	0	1	1	Jones rf	5	1	3	2
Perez 1b	4	0	1	1	Milner 1b	3	1	1	0
Bench c	3	0	0	0	Kranepool lf	2	0	1	2
Griffey rf	4	0	1	0	Mays cf	3	1	1	1
Geronimo cf	4	0	0	0	Grote c	4	0	1	0
Chaney ss	2	0	0	0	Hahn rf	4	0	0	1
Stahl ph	1	0	1	0	Harrelson ss	4	0	2	1
Billingham p	2	0	0	0	Seaver p	3	1	1	0
Gullett p	0	0	0	0	McGraw p	0	0	0	0
Carroll p	0	0	0	0					
Crosby ph	1	0	0	0					
Grimsley p	0	0	0	0					
King ph	0	0	0	0					
Totals	33	2	7	2	Totals	37	7	13	7

Cincinnati	001	010	000 — 2
Mets	200	041	00X — 7

E-Jones, Driessen. LOB-Cincinnati 10, Mets 10. 2B-Morgan, Griffey, Rose, Garrett, Jones, Seaver. S-Millan. SF-Driessen.

	IP	H	R	ER	BB	SO
Cincinnati						
Billingham (L, 0-1)	4	6	4	4	1	3
Gullett	0	0	1	1	1	0
Carroll	2	5	2	2	0	0
Grimsley	2	2	0	0	1	1
Mets						
Seaver (W, 1-1)	8⅓	7	2	1	5	4
McGraw	⅔	0	0	0	0	0

Save-McGraw. Wild pitch-Seaver.

T-2:40. A-50,323.

then added as the mayor walked away, "I came in a winner and I am going out a winner."

"Who ever figured we would win it and wind up in the World Series?" said Berra, the philosopher-button pusher. "They really played ball since we got them all together again."

"I'd have loved to have been out there," said Staub, whose three homers had powered the Mets' other two NLCS wins.

"I'm so stunned I could scream," said Mrs. Joan Payson, owner of the club.

"Ya Gotta Believe," said McGraw.

Months earlier, McGraw said, "We might be the first team in last place on August 20 to ever win a pennant."

And damned if he wasn't right.

Carter's Vindication Ends Battle of the Ages: Gooden vs. Ryan

METS 2, ASTROS 1

1986 NLCS Game 5
October 14, 1986 in New York

Gary Carter had every right to feel the weight of the world on his shoulders in the 12th inning of Game 5 of the 1986 NLCS. Once again, the opposing manager was daring him to be a true cleanup hitter instead of the overmatched automatic out that he had seemed to become during a 1-for-21 playoffs.

Another in a series of intentional walks to Keith Hernandez to get at the hopelessly lost Carter was sound and obvious strategy, setting up an inning-ending DP possibility. Houston's Hal Lanier had done this twice, both with successful outcomes, in the late innings of Game 2. But that didn't make all these invitations to inflict damage any less insulting to a perennial All-Star performer, who felt the Astros' reliever Charlie Kerfeld had deliberately shown him up earlier in the Series.

Even a player with the extraordinary track record enjoyed by Carter feels doubt and frustration in the throes of this kind of a slide: 0-for-15 with five strikeouts.

How could Carter be immune from wondering?

If he had produced, would this 1-1 pitching duel between 39-year-old mound genius Nolan Ryan and 21-year-old pitching prodigy Dwight Gooden have been tipped in the Mets' favor?

Would the Mets have been in better shape in the Series and not in their current desperate need of a victory to take a three-games-to-two edge back to Houston?

Now Wally Backman was on second after collecting the Mets' third hit of a long, tense afternoon, there was one out and it would take another hit to score him. Kerfeld, tough on the Mets in general and on Carter in particular all season, was going to come at him with fastballs, lots of very fast fastballs. Once upon a time, The Kid ate hard throwers for breakfast. Now, too often, one of the greatest-hitting catchers of all time waved at the hard stuff with a bat slowed by the weight of too many years of crouching.

"I wasn't thinking about bringing in Dave Smith to pitch to Carter in that situation," said Lanier. "In Carter and Kerfeld, we had the matchup we wanted."

Carter stepped in, trying to lay down the mental burden outside the box. He thought this time would be different—the damning numbers be damned.

"It's not a lot of hits that count," he said. "It's the key hits. When I went up there, I kept telling myself, 'I'm going to come though here.' . . . The only thing you can do is keep your head up, try to maintain your confidence. I felt it was just a matter of time. I am not an .050 hitter."

Actually, Carter was an .048 hitter (with two RBI and nine runners stranded) in the NLCS. His teammates tried to tell him that they expected him to succeed, to lighten Carter's load.

"I knew that he was going to come through," said Hernandez. "Athletes have strong egos. They are strong mentally . . . He was the

Carter of old on his previous at-bat. He was on every pitch. I had a feeling he would break out of it. He hit the ball hard to third [a 10th-inning bid for a double off Kerfeld], but right at [Denny] Walling. When Kid came back to the dugout, I told him, 'You are back.'"

During the intentional walk, Darryl Strawberry, standing in the on-deck circle next to Carter, went on a searching expedition for Gary's sense of pride. "Don't let them do this to you, Kid," he told him. "All you need is a little base hit. Don't worry about it."

The Astros' Bill Doran engaged Backman in conversation at second, observing, "I don't like this. I don't like [facing] Carter when he is 1-for-21."

Of course, the only opinion that mattered was Carter's—born, as it had to be, in the confidence of a true believer, in himself and his abilities.

"One thing I'm never going to lose is my enthusiasm. I am not going to curl up and die," said Carter. "Yes, 1-for-21 is frustrating. but you can't let it get you down."

When Kerfeld fell behind him 3-and-0, Carter was flashed the take sign. Later, he said his reaction was relief. Yes, folks, if you prick an All-Star catcher, he doth bleed. Yes, he doth.

"I thought about the walk, thought about settling for it," Carter wrote in his book. "I wanted to get the big hit, but I couldn't help thinking that I am 1-for-21 and, God knows, if I hit this ball, it might go right at somebody."

Carter fouled off a nasty fastball on 3-and-1. Now, manager Davey Johnson had a tough choice: should he put the runners in motion or not? On the first full-count pitch, Backman and Hernandez were held. Carter fought off a fastball, fouling it off. And then Johnson switched off and put them in motion as Carter managed another foul ball off the fastball.

"I had the runners going, because I wanted to stay out of the double play," said Davey of his internal dialogue. "But I don't like to run in a situation like that, because if he strikes out and the runners are safe, then they walk Strawberry."

And Carter admitted he might've been tempted to take that second 3-and-2 pitch—which was a borderline strike if it caught the plate at all—if he hadn't known they would be running. "In that situation, there was no way I was going to be called out on strikes," he reasoned.

On the next pitch, the runners held and Carter reached down for yet another fastball and smashed it through the middle, past Kerfeld and into center. When the ball was slowed by Shea's wet grass—rain kept the crowd that watched this wrenching struggle at 33,377, although 21,609 more tickets had been sold—a charging Billy Hatcher lost any chance to throw out Backman at the plate.

Backman slid anyway, just in case.

Mets 2, Astros 1. The Mets were just one more victory away from their first pennant since 1973.

Carter called it the most memorable game of his 12 major league seasons, saying, "There is definitely justice in the world. My dream is still to get to a World Series . . . I want to thank the good Lord for being with me on that hit . . . Winning this means so much to me. I guess I have been trying too hard."

"I have faced Carter a lot this year and it's the first time he has gotten a hit off me," said Kerfeld, among he Astros who had received telephone death threats during his team's stay in New York. "But give him credit. The guy does have 100 RBI. This time, he got his hit at the right time.

"I challenged him and he beat me. He won the bet . . . He is a great player. That is why he bats fourth on a team that won 108 games."

"We were really lucky to still be in the game, with only two hits in 11 innings," figured Davey Johnson.

The reason the Mets were still in the game was clearly twofold: 10 amazingly gritty, now-you-got-me-now-you-don't innings of pitching by Gooden in response to an even more brilliant effort by Ryan and a possible blown call by first-base umpire Fred Brocklander that cost the Astros a run in the second.

Ryan, in his 20th major league campaign, had pitched through elbow problems during a 1986 season in which he went only 12-8 and finished only one of his 30 starts. In the Mets' 5-1 Game 2 victory at the Astrodome, Nolan was knocked around in the fourth and fifth innings after breezing through the early going, leading Lenny Dykstra, Backman and Ray Knight to speculate about his stamina.

In this game, Ryan retired his first 13 Mets, eight of them on strike-outs, before Darryl Strawberry hit a liner just hard enough and just fair enough to make it out of the park down the right field line and create a 1-1 tie in the fifth.

Strawberry, who finished this game at 4-for-17 with 10 Ks in this NLCS, said of his second game-tying shot in the last three games, "I knew it was going out of the park, but it started to swing back toward the stands and I thought the ball was going to go foul. I think I battled him real well . . . I figured he would come inside on that pitch, because he had come in on the previous pitch for a strike."

"In that case, if I am going to get beat, I'm going to get beat with my best pitch," said Ryan, who threw mostly fastballs and just a few change-ups among his 134 pitches when he realized early on that he didn't have a curve. "The count was 3-and-2 and I threw him a fastball. It was down and in and he went down and got it. He hit a good pitch."

Ryan gave the Mets next to nothing to hit before exiting for a pinch-hitter in the 10th inning. The Hall of Famer Who Got Away finished his nine innings having allowed just two hits. Nolan retired his last seven hitters after Hernandez had singled in the seventh and wound up with 12 strikeouts and just one walk. Facing only three more than the minimum 27 hitters, Ryan struck out the pesky table-setters in the Mets' lineup, Dykstra and Backman, five times as if to say to his detractors, "Stick that in your radar guns, my tiny friends."

"He was like he was five years ago," said Knight, a former teammate of Ryan with the Astros. "His recent problems are due to his running out of gas in the middle innings. But this time he got stronger, just like the old days."

"It was the best-pitched game I have ever seen under the circumstances," marvelled Mike Scott. "He pitched half of it with a foot that could be broken [injured on a slide]. He just wasn't going to be beaten."

"I don't think I ever had a game when I felt it was more important where I pitched better," said Nolan. "In the end, I was just throwing my fastball. I don't know what the velocity was [it was in the 90s], but I was throwing hard . . . It was as good a performance as I've had all year. But what good is it? We didn't win."

They didn't win, because Gooden proved so adept at bending but not breaking.

Pitching into the 10th inning for the first time in his three-season career, much to his surprise, Gooden gave up nine hits and two walks. The Astros had at least one man on base in seven of his 10 innings. Gooden even pitched his way out of trouble in his final inning, getting Hatcher on a flyball to right after pinch-hitter Terry Puhl had singled and stole second and Doran had walked.

The only run off The Doctor came in the fifth, after Alan Ashby doubled to right and Craig Reynolds singled to left. With one out, Backman double-clutched while fielding Doran's grounder and that enabled the speedy Astro leadoff man to barely beat Rafael Santana's relay in search of an inning-ending 4-6-3 double play while Ashby scored.

A 1-0 loser to Scott in Game 1, Gooden had pitched 17 NLCS innings and allowed two runs without a win to show for it. Still, he was proud of his standout work in this standoff with the old master, Ryan.

"I kept us in the game against a great pitcher and we won," said Gooden, who got a boost when center fielder Mookie Wilson's made a superb snatch of Walling's liner and doubled Doran off second base in the eighth. "Maybe, I will get a win in the World Series."

The controversial call the Astros felt denied them an early run came when Brocklander ruled the Mets completed an inning-ending double play on Reynolds by a hair in the second. Singles by Kevin Bass and Jose Cruz had put Astros at the corners with none out, but Gooden fanned Ashby. Then, Reynolds hit a grounder to Backman, who flipped to

Santana for the force at second. On the final out, at first, Ryan and Reynolds both were certain that Santana's relay throw to Hernandez arrived late.

"I'm not going to second-guess the umpire because I wasn't involved in the play but if the right call is made, we are gone [with a 2-1 victory] in nine," said Ryan. "I don't need any TV replay. I saw it myself."

Reynolds was so enraged that first-base coach Matt Galante had to do yeoman work to keep the shortstop from getting ejected for ump bumping.

"I just lost it," said an embarrassed, no longer angry Reynolds after the game. "I don't think I have ever lost it like that before. I don't get mad too often. More than anything, I was surprised . . . In my mind, there was no question that I was safe.

"These guys have a lot of pressure on them and I am sure Fred was doing his best. But they can't do anything right. Uh, let's clarify that —they can't do everything right."

"It was a hell of a close play, as close a play as you can get," said Brocklander. "Therein lies the difficulty . . . There is no depth perception from the camera angle because it is from high up. And I thought from the replay that it looked dead even [a tie goes to the runner]. But I saw daylight between Reynolds' foot and the base when Hernandez caught the ball. The runner was definitely out. There was no hesitation."

"I could tear up the clubhouse and rant and rave, but it wouldn't do me any good," said Lanier.

Kerfeld had thrown two hitless shutout innings, with three strikeouts, entering the 12th. However, Jesse Orosco—deposed as the Mets' No. 1 reliever by Roger McDowell during the course of the season—countered by pitching two 1-2-3 innings of his own. For his trouble, Orosco got his second victory of the Series.

"I feel pretty good. Mike Scott is also 2-and-0 and he is killing us," joked Orosco.

"Jesse was a man," said Hernandez, paying the lefty the ultimate Mex compliment. "He came in and went after them and shut them down. There are no more questions about Jesse . . . I wouldn't trade him for anything."

"He has pitched good all year, but he had great stuff today," said Davey Johnson. "Even from where I was sitting, he seemed to be hitting the corners with all of his pitches. I really like to use a left-hander against the Astros, especially following a right-handed pitcher."

Kerfeld pushed his string of consecutive Mets retired in this post-season to 12 by getting Dykstra to start the 12th. But Backman hit a ball off third baseman Walling for a single. Hernandez was the hitter and the count was 1-and-1 when Kerfeld threw away an attempted pickoff throw, sending Backman to second and leaving the rawboned right-hander with so many regrets.

"I should have lobbed the ball to first," said Kerfeld. "As soon as I threw it, I said, 'Oh, bleep.' It slipped out of my hand and tailed away from Glenn (Davis). I was just trying to keep Backman close. It was a mistake. That was stupidity on my part. That was a total screw-up on my part. It was nobody's fault but mine."

As Carter stepped in, following the obvious intentional pass to Hernandez, Kerfeld was thinking about a double play.

Carter was thinking about that one-bounce comebacker which he had hit off this reliever in the eighth inning of Game 3. The bullet was grabbed on a backhanded stab by Kerfeld, who then took the ball and waved it in the direction of home plate, where Carter was still standing, before getting the out at first.

Not cool.

"We all saw what Kerfeld did—that Little League stuff," said Gooden.

Kerfeld insisted he was merely waving it at his catcher, like a child who had discovered unexpected candy, not taunting Carter. But The Kid, already feeling picked on, was in no mood to give Charlie the benefit of this doubt.

"The other day he pointed at me and that really fired me up," said Carter. "He did show me the ball and I felt that was trying to show me up."

Appropriately, the game-winning blow was sent back through the originator again—but this shot left Kerfeld watching, not gloating. For the second time in three games, the Astros had to swallow a walk-off defeat.

"I don't think he was going to try to play that one behind his back," said The Kid. "Let's just say it felt good to get that hit."

Although Carter felt the glory finally belonged to him, some of the Met reserves—whose wearing of their Met hats in strange positions in hope of inspiring their team to score some runs became a 1986 legend —figured it must have been the hats.

"We had been through a lot of hats," said Tim Teufel, Rally Cap-tain. "We tried the Napoleon Bonaparte hat, but that had a bad day. We knew we had to go for the big one."

Under orders from Hernandez, in the 12th, Howard Johnson, Teufel and Kevin Mitchell went to "The Claw" —towel over their heads, towel over their arms like a waiter and hands pointing out.

"I knew that would win the game," said HoJo. "Gary's hit was incidental."

"The big thing that people forget about baseball is the intangibles," said Teufel. "The Rally Hats do it for us in close games. That is about as intangible as you can get."

HOUSTON	ab	r	h	bl	METS	ab	r	h	bl
Doran 2b	4	0	1	1	Dykstra cf	5	0	0	0
Hatcher cf	3	0	1	0	Backman 2b	5	1	1	0
Walling 3b	5	0	1	0	Hernandez 1b	4	0	1	0
Davis 1b	5	0	0	0	Carter c	5	0	1	1
Bass rf	5	0	2	0	Strawberry rf	3	1	1	1
Cruz lf	5	0	1	0	MWilson cf	4	0	0	0
Ashby c	5	1	1	0	Orosco p	0	0	0	0
Reynolds ss	4	0	1	0	Knight 3b	4	0	0	0
Thon ss	1	0	0	0	Santana ss	3	0	0	0
Ryan p	3	0	0	0	Mazzilli ph	1	0	0	0
Puhl ph	1	0	1	0	Elster ss	0	0	0	0
Kerfeld p	0	0	0	0	Gooden p	3	0	0	0
					Heep lf	1	0	0	0
Totals	41	1	9	1	Totals	38	2	4	2

Houston	000	010	000	000	— 1	
Mets	000	010	000	001	— 2	

One out when winning run scored.

GWRBI-Carter (2). E-Kerfeld. DP-Mets 2. LOB-Houston 7, Mets 4. 2B-Ashby. HR-Strawberry (2). SB-Doran (1), Puhl (1). S-Hatcher.

Houston	IP	H	R	ER	BB	SO
Ryan	9	2	1	1	1	12
Kerfeld (L, 0-1)	2⅓	2	1	1	1	3
Mets						
Gooden	10	9	1	1	2	4
Orosco (W, 2-0)	2	0	0	0	0	2

Umpires: Home-West; First-Brocklander; Second-Harvey; Third-Weyer; Left-Pulli; Right-Rennert.

T-3:45. A-54,986.

Clutch Benny Makes
El Duque, Yanks Bleed

2000 World Series Game 3
October 24, 2000 in Flushing, N.Y.

In Game 1 of the 2000 Subway Series, Timo Perez and Todd Zeile inexcusably felt no need to run out batted balls, Todd Pratt spectated when he should've been scoring and Armando Benitez let yet another October one get away. In Game 2, the Mets failed to show a pulse against Roger Clemens, future Hall of Famer in the world-class, low-life division, and managed to dig a hole large enough that five ninth-inning runs amounted to too little, too late, too painful to contemplate.

All in all, not a lot of jollies for Met fans who don't regard waking up in a cold sweat, screaming, as an amusement.

Game 3, the first in the friendly confines of Shea, presented new hope for the Met faithful that the ticket holders from the Bronx would be left agape at the magic that somehow delivers post-season Mets teams—but only when all seems lost.

After all, this Series was not over yet. All the Mets had to do to be back in the picture was end the Yanks' 14-game World Series winning streak by beating Orlando Hernandez, who entered the night with an 8-0 record and a 1.90 ERA in post-season play. Piece of cake. Compared to an arch villain like Clemens, whom the Mets had wanted to batter so badly that it contributed to their impotence, El Duque was just another opposing pitcher.

"I mean El Duque was 8-0 and they were 14-0—something had to happen," reasoned John Franco.

"If you look at the odds, they were bound to lose," was the assessment of part-time actuary, full-time flake Turk Wendell.

"That was all we heard about El Duque—that he had never lost in the post-season," said Benny Agbayani. "But anything can happen in a World Series. So there is always a first for everyone."

Thanks to Agbayani's habit of coming up big in the clutch, Game 3 was an epic victory that was a first and an only—the Mets' only moment to savor in this baseball Armageddon.

The Yankees won the Subway Series by a little, again and again and again and again. The lesson? A string of narrow victories doesn't necessarily prove that two teams are evenly matched, but can illustrate that one repeatedly finds a way to be better while the other does not. Close defeats while playing for a championship are not necessarily about coincidence or fortune.

Ironically, the Yanks' admirable championship bearing and whatever-it-takes comportment might be the best reason the Mets should be proud of their hard-won 4-2 Game 3 victory, which momentarily kept faith alive. Those stone-cold-killer Yankee world championship teams usually didn't permit their World Series opponents even a single victory in which to revel. Perhaps avoiding a sweep was a modest miracle in itself.

It was a brilliant duel between Rick Reed and Hernandez through six taut innings.

Robin Ventura watched Hernandez strike out three Mets ahead of him. So the Met third baseman jumped on a first-pitch, 90-miles-per-hour, four-seam fastball for a homer to right center that gave the Mets a 1-0 lead in the second inning—then sat back down and watched Hernandez strike out the three hitters after him.

"You are watching other guys and he is throwing hard and jumping ahead," said Ventura. "It's just something you have to take a shot at . . . You don't want him to jump ahead of you, because you are fending for yourself after that."

Reed, working on seven days' rest, struck out six of his first nine hitters. However, the Yanks rallied to tie it at 1-1 with two out in the third on a single by Derek Jeter and David Justice's double, on the ground past a diving Zeile and into the right-field corner. With a clever slide, Jeter narrowly beat the relay of second baseman Edgardo Alfonzo, who hesitated one costly beat before firing, slightly high, to Mike Piazza.

The Yanks took a 2-1 lead in the following inning. Paul O'Neill crossed up the Met defense—which had been shaded toward his opposite field, left field—by turning on an outside fastball and crushing a one-out triple to right center that scored Tino Martinez (leadoff single).

Hernandez was on a huge roll, meanwhile, until he hit a real divot in the sixth. The threat began with a double down the left-field line by Piazza, who readily admitted that El Duque had made him "look foolish" in his first two at-bats.

"He's got great control," marvelled Piazza. "He knows how to pitch and is very poised on the mound. He is able to win when he doesn't have his best stuff. But if that wasn't his best stuff, I'd hate to see it."

Ventura walked and the Mets had the tying and go-ahead runners on base with none out for No. 5 hitter Zeile. The Met first baseman was given the bunt sign, squared and took a strike. He stared at third-base coach Cookie Rojas and saw it again. Zeile stepped out, looked into the Met dugout and pleaded his case with manager Bobby Valentine.

"I looked into the dugout and almost begged to swing away," said Zeile, who didn't have a sacrifice all season and who finished the night with a .462 World Series average. "I said, 'Let me swing the bat. We're here in the middle of the lineup for a reason.'"

Valentine apparently couldn't resist the sight of a grown man begging because he gave Zeile his much-desired green light. And Todd lined Hernandez' pitch into the left-field corner.

"Todd is an RBI guy and he doesn't get the kind of RBI that, in a 10-3 game, make it 11-3," said Mets GM Steve Phillips of the veteran hitter whom he imported to never quite fill the shoes of the departed John Olerud. "When the game gets closer and later, his at-bats get better."

The game was tied at 2-2, with Mets at second and third and none out. Agbayani, 0-for-2, earned a walk with a very tough at-bat and now the bases were loaded and the stands were rocking in anticipation of this being the inning in which the Yankees and Hernandez would break.

Of course, you don't become an October icon by surrendering to moments like this and El Duque simply lifted his game and went to work. Brutal on right-handed hitters (who hit .210 against him), Hernandez struck out the too-tense Jay Payton (2-for-21 with the bases loaded during the season) with a nasty full-count slider and dispatched overmatched, sore-thumbed No. 8 hitter Mike Bordick (4-for-30 in the post-season to this point) with another K on a full-count fastball.

Perhaps, you wondered when you saw Bordick—half-expecting to be yanked—step to the plate, what better time for Lenny Harris or Matt Franco or Darryl Hamilton, Valentine's eventual choice to pinch-hit for Reed? Valentine had hit for Bordick in the seventh inning of Game 1 and the eighth inning of Game 2. But, in the sixth inning of this one, Bobby V, asleep at the switch, fed Bordick to the shark. And, now, with two outs and the bags still loaded and the game still tied, Valentine had no choice but to pinch-hit for Reed, who had allowed only two runs and six hits through six innings.

"I did my job. I kept us close against El Duque," said Reed in consoling himself.

Reed's last chance for a victory disappeared when Hamilton

grounded to Jeter for a force at second. Three outs. The Houdini act was complete. The usually impassive El Duque shouted and raised both fists, pumping them three times, on his way back to the visitors' dugout.

"It was typical El Duque," said Yankee manager Joe Torre, whom no one called a genius while he presided over the Met teams of the late '70s and early '80s. "He is up on the high wire and you don't think that he is going to come down from there . . . He has the heart of a lion."

"That could have been a big letdown for this team," said Pratt. "But the players stayed up."

Valentine went to Wendell at the start of the seventh and Turk punched out Hernandez and Game 1 nemesis Jose Vizcaino before walking Jeter and feeling Valentine's rapid hook. Dennis Cook hit Justice with a pitch—so much for Bobby V's coveted lefty-vs.-lefty matchup—and that brought Bernie Williams to the plate with a runner in scoring position. Williams, who finished the night 0-for-11 in this Series, struck out swinging.

The Mets went in order in the seventh, then Cook walked Martinez to start the eighth. Valentine felt he could wait no longer, summoning Franco, who induced a 5-4-3 double play from Jorge Posada. Good thing, too, because O'Neill smashed a single to center and then Torre pinch-hit the dangerous Glenallen Hill for Scott Brosius.

Hill's history against Franco was impressive: 6-for-12 with three homers. This time, Johnny B. Good was Johnny B. Careful. Franco kept the ball away from Hill and finally got him on fly to right.

"I was sure I was going to see him at some point in the Series. He has had a lot of hits against me, but tonight I won the battle," said Franco.

"I can't do it every time," said Hill. "He has his own style. He throws that screwball and sometimes he can leave it up. He just got me."

In the eighth inning, Hernandez showed he had solved even Ventura, claiming Robin as his 12th strikeout victim of the night. However Zeile sent a shot just past the diving shortstop Jeter and into left center for a single—"I thought I had it," said Derek—and the next hitter was Agbayani.

Benny, struck out only once by Hernandez but hitless, was thinking he needed to find a pitch he could shoot into a gap.

"He is a tough pitcher, he comes at you at different angles and he has that big sweeping curve, so you have to be patient," said Agbayani. "That was a slider outside on the first pitch and I was just looking for something I could drive to the outfield."

Agbayani hit a rocket between left fielder Justice and center fielder Williams. Zeile, who runs exactly as well as Olerud does, was on the move and thinking, "You have to score."

"We were screaming, 'Legs don't fail him now,' " said Wendell.

Zeile scored. Agbayani stood at second base, hands on massive hips. He now had a 13-game post-season hitting streak that included all 11 in 2000 and the Mets were back on top, 3-2. Shea was a madhouse.

Payton beat out an infield single before Torre finally pulled his exhausted starter. The manager all but admitted the decision to stay with El Duque was made as much with his heart as with his head.

"His getting out of the bases-loaded jam the way he did, he deserved the right to get a decision in this one," said Torre about heeding Hernandez' insistence he still felt strong in the eighth. "It was really tough to deny him what he wanted . . . He probably just made a mistake to Agbayani."

"The number of pitches [134 overall] aren't important," insisted El Duque through El Interpreter. "It is how you feel. I'm not going to be happy to come out of a game. Would you want to lose your job? Baseball is a challenge. You have to fight to get outs. I didn't get Agbayani out."

Clearly, getting Agbayani out is not easy.

"Benny can just flat-out hit," said Payton, his buddy and personal publicist. "He hasn't elevated his game. He has been hitting all year. He is just a great hitter."

"I was baffled by people who followed our team all season thinking he shouldn't play today," said Valentine. "I never considered him not playing and I never considered pinch-hitting for him. And I'm glad about that."

John Franco, never one to hide his feelings, reacts after retiring nemesis Glenallen Hill to end the eighth inning. The ancient lefty preserved a tie and became the second-oldest pitcher ever to win a World Series game.

After pinch-hitter Bubba Trammell's sac fly to center scored pinch-runner Joe McEwing from third with an insurance run, Valentine could have sent Franco out to the mound for a second inning. Instead, he made a show of faith by pinch-hitting for Franco, sticking with the season-long plan and summoning the troubled Benitez.

Pinch-hitter Chuck Knoblauch led off with a single to center and everyone in a Met uniform or state of mind, including Armando, was thinking, "This can't be happening again."

Edgardo Alfonzo visited the mound. He told Benitez—who had already blown save chances in Division Series Game 2 and World Series Game 1—he must remain strong mentally and focused on the task at hand, presumably in Spanish and perhaps in a threatening tone.

Benitez got pinch-hitter Luis Polonia on a fly to center, struck out Jeter looking and got Justice to pop up to Alfonzo with a 94-mph heater for his second save of this post-season.

"Was I excited? I don't know," said Benitez. "After the game is the time to be excited. When I am out there, I know I'm just in to do my job."

"It's like I have been telling him all year long, 'There is nobody better than him,'" said Franco, who, at 40, after 17 years of waiting to get a World Series stage, became the second-oldest pitcher to win a Series game.

"Johnny did his thing and Armando did his," said Valentine.

The Yankees were losers in a World Series game for the first time since dropping Game 2 to the Atlanta Braves on Oct. 21, 1996 at Yankee Stadium. And they were beaten for the first time since 1981 in a road World Series game, by a Met team that was now 60-26 at Shea for the season plus post-season. The Yanks hurt themselves instead of their opponent for a change, too, going 2-for-16 with men on base in Game 3 and leaving 10 men on. That made 37 Yanks stranded in the first three games.

"We feel we let something slip away by having so many opportunities," said Torre.

"It seems like a light-year's difference between 3-0 and 2-1," said Valentine. "I thought we were in those first two games, but you could only go so long saying they were close games. If we didn't get a victory tonight . . . "

"I don't want to go back home yet," said Agbayani, which is saying something since home is Hawaii.

"We all knew what was on the line," said Franco. "Nobody had to say anything. Nobody had to say anything. Nobody had to yell. We all knew."

YANKEES

	ab	r	h	rbi	bb	so	lob	avg
Vizcaino 2b	4	0	0	0	0	2	2	.286
c-Polonia ph	1	0	0	0	0	0	1	.500
Jeter ss	4	1	2	0	1	2	1	.462
Justice lf	3	0	1	1	1	0	2	.200
Williams cf	4	0	0	0	0	2	4	.000
Martinez 1b	3	1	1	0	1	1	1	.429
Posada c	4	0	0	0	0	2	2	.250
O'Neill rf	4	0	3	1	0	0	0	.583
Brosius 3b	2	0	0	0	0	1	1	.250
a-Hill ph	1	0	0	0	0	0	1	.000
Sojo 3b	0	0	0	0	0	0	0	.000
Hernandez p	2	0	0	0	0	2	1	.000
Stanton p	0	0	0	0	0	0	0	.000
b-Knoblauch ph	1	0	1	0	0	0	0	.111
Totals	**33**	**2**	**8**	**2**	**3**	**12**	**16**	

a-flied to right for Brosius in the 8th; b-singled for Stanton in the 9th; c-flied to center for Vizcaino in the 9th.

BATTING: 2B-O'Neill (2, Reed); Justice (2, Reed). 3B-O'Neill (1, Reed). S-Hernandez. RBI-Justice (3), O'Neill (2). 2-out RBI-Justice. Runners left in scoring position, 2 out-Brosius 1, Williams 2, Vizcaino 2, Martinez 1, Justice 1. GIDP-Posada. Team LOB-10.

METS

	ab	r	h	rbi	bb	so	lob	avg
Perez rf	3	0	0	0	1	1	1	.077
Alfonzo 2b	4	0	0	0	0	2	3	.154
Piazza c	4	1	1	0	0	2	0	.231
Ventura 3b	3	1	2	1	1	1	0	.250
Zeile 1b	4	1	2	1	0	2	1	.462
Agbayani lf	3	0	1	1	1	1	1	.364
McEwing pr-lf	0	1	0	0	0	0	0	.000
Payton cf	4	0	1	0	0	2	3	.231
Bordick ss	3	0	1	0	0	1	3	.167
b-Harris ph	0	0	0	0	0	0	0	.000
c-Trammell ph	0	0	0	1	0	0	1	1.000
Benitez p	0	0	0	0	0	0	0	.000
Reed p	1	0	1	0	0	0	0	1.000
a-Hamilton ph	1	0	0	0	0	0	3	.000
Wendell p	0	0	0	0	0	0	0	.000
Cook p	0	0	0	0	0	0	0	.000
JFranco p	0	0	0	0	0	0	0	.000
d-Abbott ph-ss	1	0	0	0	0	1	1	.250
Totals	**31**	**4**	**9**	**4**	**3**	**13**	**17**	

a-hit into fielder's choice for Reed in the 6th; b-pinch-hit for Bordick in the 8th; c-hit sacrifice fly to center for Harris in the 8th; d-struck out for JFranco in the 8th.

BATTING: 2B-Ventura (1, Hernandez); Piazza (1, Hernandez); Zeile (2, Hernandez); Agbayani (2, Hernandez). HR-Ventura (1, 2nd inning off Hernandez 0 on, 0 out). S-Reed. SF-Trammell. RBI-Ventura (1), Zeile (1), Agbayani (1), Trammell (3). Runners left in scoring position, 2-out: Agbayani 1, Alfonzo 1, Hamilton 2. Team LOB-8.

FIELDING: DP: 1 (Ventura-Alfonzo-Zeile).

HBP-Brosius (by Reed); Justice (by Cook). Pitches-strikes: Reed 102-70. Wendell 13-8, Cook 11-3, Franco 9-8, Benitez 14-10, Hernandez 134-91, Stanton 7-6. Ground balls-flyballs: Reed 5-5, Wendell 0-0, Cook 0-0, Franco2-1, Benitez 0-2, Hernandez 3-7, Stanton 0-1. Batters faced: Reed 26, Wendell 3, Cook 3, Franco 3, Benitez 4, Hernandez 34, Stanton 2.

Umpires: Home-Kellogg; First-Welke; Second-McClelland; Third-Crawford; Left-Montague; Right-Reliford.

T-3:39. A-55,299.

Yankees	001	100	000	— 2
Mets	010	001	02x	— 4

Yankees	IP	H	R	ER	BB	SO	HR	ERA
Hernandez (L, 0-1)	7 1/3	9	4	4	3	12	1	4.91
Stanton	2/3	0	0	0	0	1	0	0.00
Mets								
Reed	6	6	2	2	1	8	0	3.00
Wendell	2/3	0	0	0	1	2	0	5.40
Cook	1/3	0	0	0	1	1	0	0.00
Franco (W, 1-0)	1	1	0	0	0	0	0	0.00
Benitez (S, 1)	1	1	0	0	0	1	0	4.50

Cook pitched to 1 batter in the 8th.

18

Payton's Clutch Hit Fells House of Cards

2000 NLCS Game 2
October 12, 2000 in St. Louis

It was only Game 2 of the NLCS and the pressure clearly was on the Cardinals, already down one game and struggling to keep their heads above water, at home. However, after St. Louis overcame Rick Ankiel's strange and exotic self-destruction and matched two Met runs in the eighth inning to tie the game at 5-5 in the bottom half, 52,250 delirious fans in Busch Stadium were rocking.

And the Mets should have been rolling.

Now, it was the Mets who faced a moment of truth—as it turned out, their only one in the 2000 NLCS. Would the Series go back to Shea with the best-of-seven tied at a game apiece and the Cardinals riding the rush that comes from punishing a bullpen and dodging a bullet?

Not bloody likely.

The Mets don't often lose this kind of measure-of-the-will-and-depth-of-the-bullpen struggle in the post-season. This was the longest nine-inning NLCS game in history, at a minute less than four hours. They weren't even behind in this one. They were just tied and ready to improvise en route to a fifth straight post-season win—three of them achieved in their final at-bat.

It often begins with help from above, or sometimes the Mets depend on the kindness of an opposing fielder (paging Bill Buckner, for one final thank you). In this case, it was the usually sure-handed first baseman Will Clark, so important to the Cardinals after they lost Mark McGwire to injury, who provided the wrong team with a large assist. The Thrill made a ninth-inning error on Robin Ventura's two-hop grounder, a screamer on a 3-and-1 count. Clark's glove bounced a little higher than the hop and it skittered beneath his mitt and off his right foot.

"You go out there and take ground balls every day. You try to get every hop possible. I just flat-out booted that one," said Clark, a career .992 fielder whose error was one of three by the Cardinals in the game. "I was expecting it to come up and it didn't. It was one of those balls that had top spin on it. It hit me in the shoe. Basically, it was your routine boot . . . It was a shame. I misplayed a ball and it caused us to lose the game."

Yes, Clark opened the door. However, the Mets were shoved through it—and into a commanding hold on a pennant by Jay Payton, who saved a very big hit for when the Mets needed it most.

Payton, the hitting hero of Game 2 of the NL Division Series with a game-winning RBI in the 10th, was nevertheless just a .179 hitter in the 2000 post-season when he stepped in the batter's box against Mike Timlin in the ninth. Joe McEwing, pinch-running for Ventura, was on second base, thanks to Benny Agbayani's first sacrifice bunt of 2000.

"I don't care if I am 0-for-20," noted Payton. "In my 21st at-bat, I'm going to be confident and try to get a hit . . . There is nothing I can go through on the field that can compare to what I have gone through off the field [with injuries that threatened to end his career and resulted in his rookie season coming at age 27]."

"There is no one on this team—maybe no one in the league—who has as much confidence in himself as Jay Payton," said manager Bobby Valentine. "He didn't have any hits going into that at-bat, but I know he believed deep down in his heart, right down to his toes, that he was the best man in that situation."

Working his way out of an 0-and-2 hole, Payton hit the sixth pitch to him on a line up the middle and St. Louis' brilliant center fielder Jim Edmonds decided to stay back on the ball, so he might have a chance to nail McEwing at home on the hit. Instead, the liner short-hopped Edmonds and bounded off his glove for a two-base error as the Mets scored the winning run in their 6-5 triumph.

"I feel like I just lost this game all by myself," said Edmonds, a .571 hitter in the Cards' Division Series sweep of the Braves who went 0-for-4 with two strikeouts in this game, but was walked by Armando Benitez in the ninth.

"I just got caught in a bad situation. I didn't think the ball was going to travel that far and I probably should have caught it. I tried to take it on one nice hop and throw the guy [McEwing] out. But looking back, maybe I should've taken a chance on that ball. I probably would have caught it. I just missed it."

Game 2 started out in a bizarre fashion that was comical if you were not named Rick Ankiel.

The 21-year-old left-hander had followed up an 11-7 season with an amazingly inept surprise start against Atlanta in Game 1 of the Division Series. In that game, working with a six-run lead, Ankiel walked six and gave up four hits and four runs. He threw five wild pitches in the third inning alone before his manager, Tony LaRussa, mercifully came and got him, remarkably before anyone was hurt. The wild ones, mostly really wild ones, marked the first time in any big league game since 1890 that a pitcher uncorked that many in one inning.

Ankiel picked up where he left off, against the Mets, as LaRussa discovered that having his pitcher throw to a new catcher wasn't going to fix whatever ailed him. The first pitch to Timo Perez went to the backstop. Even though Perez somehow managed to strike out looking, Ankiel walked three, allowed one hit and threw two wild pitches in two-thirds of an inning. Three other balls went to the backstop—five among his first 20 pitches—but weren't wild pitches because nobody was on base.

"It was scary," said Edgardo Alfonzo, a survivor.

"It's a mystery. Obviously, he has got something on his mind," said Todd Zeile, the Sigmund Freud of the double-knit set.

Ankiel didn't quite make it through his seventh hitter, getting rescued after falling behind Payton 1-and-0. Ankiel, biting his lip, walked off to sympathetic applause. That is how bad it was.

"He said something about not feeling the baseball," said LaRussa. What Ankiel felt was terrible.

"It was the exact same thing as last time," he said. "It's unfortunate. I feel like I let this team down . . . It's the worst feeling you can have."

During this mockery, Clark visited the mound—it was the fourth company to call on Ankiel during the inning—and tried levity as a cure for panic wildness.

"Stop using the backstop as a pitch-back [a taut net that enables kids to play catch with themselves]," said the first baseman.

But Ankiel was too confused to be amused and too laughable to be laughing at himself.

"I wasn't finishing my pitches and I'm not keeping my shoulder in," said Ankiel, clinging to a mechanical explanation for a failure with mental roots. "They told me what I am doing; I just didn't fix it."

"His last 10 starts were pretty dominating," said Clark. "To all of a sudden lose it, I can't explain it—not to the point that our catcher needs springs in his shoes . . . What Rick has been going through these last two starts has been really tough to watch. We were really trying to pull him through it."

LaRussa, without the injured Garrett Stephenson and loathe to depend on any starter other than Darryl Kile now that Ankiel was a write-off, offered his broad shoulders to the rookie.

"The manager's responsibility is to put guys in the right position [which might not have been as the Game 1 starter against the Braves]," said LaRussa. "I don't blame Rick. Before kicking him around, I hope somebody puts the blame on me for putting him there."

OK, Tony, arrogant self-crowned genius, you are to blame.

By the time that Ankiel was finally given the hook in favor of Britt Reames, Zeile had a sacrifice fly and Agbayani had an RBI double and the Mets led, 2-0.

But Al Leiter, who would finish the World Series with his streak of post-season starts without a victory at 11, wasted no time giving back his gift stake. He permitted a second-inning double by ex-Met Shawon Dunston and a single to left by Ray Lankford that Agbayani surrounded like he was a one-man wagon train under siege or perhaps just a pitiful outfielder. Eli Marrero got the first run in with a grounder.

Mike Piazza's homer off Reames made it 3-1 before Leiter came undone in the fifth. A bunt single by Fernando Vina, yet another ex-Met, and RBI doubles by Edgar Renteria (three hits, three steals) and Fernando Tatis knotted the score at 3-3. By now, Ankiel's outing was forgotten by everyone but him.

Leiter could have gotten the W in this one, if the Mets had held onto the 5-3 lead they took in the eighth, when the lefty was removed for a pinch-hitter. With two out and nobody on, Perez, the 23-year-old wonder boy from the Dominican Republic by way of Japan, Class A and a pit stop at Norfolk, singled to left off Matt Morris. When Alfonzo singled to right center, Perez—in motion on a full-count pitch—came all the way around to score ahead of a throw from Edmonds that sailed up the third-base line. When it comes to clutch hits, Alfonzo—with RBI in his last five post-season games—is an old hand. However, the base-running play by Timo was a staggering anomaly on a team that usually goes station to station, even on a triple.

"I got a little surprised," admitted Alfonzo, who took second on the throw.

After an intentional pass to Piazza, LaRussa summoned his bullpen ace, Dave Veres, probably a too-early call. Zeile wasn't impressed by the sense of urgency shown by LaRussa as he singled to left off Veres to make it 5-3.

John Franco, unscored upon in the Division Series against the Giants, issued a one-out walk, a sharp single to right by Clark and a run-scoring wild pitch. After Dunston grounded out, LaRussa—with the hobbled McGwire on the bench with helmet in hand—sent up Placido Polanco to hit for the lefty, Lankford. Valentine brought in the righty, Wendell, whose bread-and-butter slider is a hittable pitch for lefties. LaRussa pinch-hit with lefty J.D. Drew.

Advantage, LaRussa.

Drew lashed a double to tie the game at 5-5, but he didn't hear LaRussa yelling at him to stop at first. If he had taken just one base it would've meant the Mets would have had to pitch to McGwire, whom LaRussa pinch-hit with next, for Veres. The Cards' manager didn't want to burn his only other remaining position player, his last catcher, Rick Wilkins, a one-time Met for a minute.

However, first base was open and why should the Mets face McGwire?

"Obviously, just throw four pitches to him, walk him and go after the next guy," said Wendell.

The next hitter was another ex-Met, Craig Paquette, who went down swinging. McGwire, baseball's all-time single-season homer champion until 2001, was unavailable to hit in the ninth when a long one would have tied or won the game.

Disadvantage, LaRussa.

"What it came down to is [by pinch-hitting with McGwire for the pitcher], we had a chance to win the game with a position player [Paquette] at bat," reasoned LaRussa. "So, it came down to Paquette with a chance to put us ahead and it's a shame."

A shame on LaRussa for overmanaging himself into a corner and tying an NLCS record by using 20 players in the game.

LaRussa handed the ball to Timlin in the ninth and, thanks to Clark's

METS

	ab	r	h	rbi	bb	so	lob	avg
Perez rf	5	1	1	0	0	2	1	.259
Alfonzo 2b	3	2	2	1	2	1	1	.333
Piazza c	2	2	1	1	3	0	1	.300
Zeile 1b	3	0	2	2	1	0	1	.190
JFranco p	0	0	0	0	0	0	0	.000
Wendell p	0	0	0	0	0	0	0	.000
Benitez p	0	0	0	0	0	0	0	.000
Ventura 3b	4	0	1	0	1	0	3	.150
McEwing pr-3b	0	1	0	0	0	0	0	1.000
Agbayani lf	4	0	1	1	0	0	2	.304
Payton cf	4	0	1	1	1	2	3	.200
Abbott ss	3	0	0	0	0	2	2	.000
a-MFranco ph-1b	2	0	0	0	0	0	1	.000
Leiter p	3	0	0	0	0	2	0	.000
b-Hamilton ph	1	0	0	0	0	0	0	.400
Bordick ss	1	0	0	0	0	0	1	.125
Totals	**35**	**6**	**9**	**6**	**8**	**9**	**16**	

ST. LOUIS

	ab	r	h	rbi	bb	so	lob	avg
Vina 2b	5	1	1	0	0	1	0	.273
Renteria ss	5	1	3	1	0	0	0	.333
Edmonds cf	4	0	0	0	1	2	3	.435
Tatis 3b	3	0	1	1	0	1	2	.200
Morris p	0	0	0	0	0	0	0	.000
Hernandez c	1	1	0	0	1	1	1	.250
Clark 1b	4	1	2	0	0	0	1	.316
Dunston rf-lf	3	1	1	0	0	0	1	.400
Lankford lf	3	0	1	0	0	2	1	.286
b-Polanco ph	0	0	0	0	0	0	0	.308
c-Drew ph-rf	1	0	1	1	0	0	0	.200
Marrero c	3	0	0	1	0	1	1	.000
Veres p	0	0	0	0	0	0	0	.000
d-McGwire ph	0	0	0	0	1	0	0	.500
Kile pr	0	0	0	0	0	0	0	.000
Timlin p	0	0	0	0	0	0	0	.000
Ankiel p	0	0	0	0	0	0	0	.000
Reames p	1	0	0	0	0	1	1	.000
a-Davis ph	1	0	0	0	0	0	0	.100
Paquette 3b	2	0	0	0	0	2	2	.000
Totals	**36**	**5**	**10**	**4**	**3**	**11**	**13**	

a-grounded to 2nd for Abbott in the 8th; b-flied to left for Leiter in the 8th.

BATTING: 2B-Agbayani (2, Ankiel); Zeile (2, Morris). 3B-Alfonzo (1, Reames). HR-Piazza (1, 3rd inning off Reames 0 on, 0 out). S-Agbayani. SF-Zeile. RBI-Zeile 2 (3), Agbayani (2), Piazza (2), Alfonzo (7), Payton (5). 2-out RBI-Agbayani, Alfonzo, Zeile. Runners left in scoring position, 2-out-Payton 3, Abbott 1, Ventura 2, Bordick 1. Team LOB-12.

a-fouled to first for Reames in the 5th; b-pinch-hit for Lankford in the 8th; c-doubled for Polanco in the 8th; d-intentionally walked for Veres in the 8th.

BATTING: 2B-Dunston (1, Leifer); Clark (2, Leiter); Renteria (1, Leiter); Tatis (1, Leiter); Drew (1, Wendell). S-Dunston. RBI-Marrero (1), Renteria (1), Tatis (1), Drew (1). 2-out RBI-Tatis, Drew. Runners left in scoring position, 2 out-Tatis 2, Reames 1, Marrero 1, Clark 1, Paquette 1. Team LOB- 8.

BASERUNNING: SB-Renteria 3 (5, 2nd base off Leiter/Piazza 2, 3rd base off Leiter/Piazza).

FIELDING: E-Vina (1, ground ball); Clark (1, ground ball); Edmonds (1, bobble). PB-Marrero. Outfield assists-Lankford (Piazza at 3rd base).

Mets	201	000	021	— 6
St. Louis	010	020	020	— 5

Mets	IP	H	R	ER	BB	SO	HR	ERA
Leiter	7	8	3	3	0	9	0	3.00
Franco (H,2)	2/3	1	2	2	1	0	0	4.91
Wendell (W, 1-0, BS)	1/3	1	0	0	1	1	0	0.00
Benitez (S,1)	1	0	0	0	1	1	0	3.60
St. Louis								
Ankiel	2/3	1	2	2	3	1	0	16.20
Reames	4 1/3	3	1	1	3	6	1	1.17
Morris	2 2/3	3	2	2	2	2	0	3.86
Veres	1/3	1	0	0	0	0	0	0.00
Timlin (L, 0-1)	1	1	1	0	0	0	0	6.75

WP-Ankiel 2, Franco. IBB-Piazza 2 (by Reames, by Morris); McGwire (by Wendell). Pitches-strikes: Ankiel 34-14; Reames 79-45; Morris 51-29; Veres 3-3; Timlin 18-13; Leiter 114-72; Franco 17-9; Wendell 14-6; Benitez 20-11. Ground balls-flyballs: Ankiel 0-1, Reames 3-4, Morris 3-3, Veres 0-0, Timlin 3-0, Leiter 2-10, Franco 2-0, Wendell 0-0, Benitez 0-2. Batters faced: Ankiel 6, Reames 20, Morris 13, Veres 1, Timlin 5, Leiter 29, Franco 4, Wendell 3, Benitez 4.

Umpires: Home-Tschida; First-Rapuano; Second-Scott; Third-Demuth; Left-Rippley; Right-Froemming.

T-3:59. A-52,250.

miscue, Payton made him pay for it. Benitez got his first two hitters in the ninth, walked Edmonds, then struck out Carlos Hernandez on a high fastball for the save.

"You come in here and you'd like to get a split," said Payton, "and they are thinking that they want to leave 2-and-0. No way we thought we'd leave here 2-and-0."

"It's amazing, but we keep coming back," said Leiter. "That has kind of been the way we're playing—very resilient."

"We lost two two-run leads and came away with a victory," said Valentine. "Those guys in the dugout were never fazed. We lost a two-run lead and they came back in ready to score again. That says a lot for the heart of this baseball team."

Mets, Down to Last Out,
Pass Huge Orel Test

1988 NLCS Game 1
October 4, 1988 in Los Angeles

The first eight innings of Game 1 of the 1988 NLCS—like that entire season and post-season—belonged to Orel Hershiser. The Dodger right-hander, riding the career season in a very solid career, completely tamed the Mets, extended his own string of consecutive scoreless innings from the regular season to 67 and made a 2-0 lead feel like the distance separating Los Angeles from New York.

"You wonder if you are ever going to score a run off him," admitted Gary Carter.

However, after the Mets finally clawed their way onto the scoreboard, manager Tommy Lasorda decided that his "Bulldog" was too tired to growl his way to the finish in the ninth. Down to their very last out, the Mets found a way, engineering this save-the-best-for-last great escape at the expense of Jay Howell.

Just as they had done in a ridiculous 10 of 11 regular-season meetings, the Mets beat the Dodgers—this time, 3-2—and the part of the notoriously early-departing Dodger Stadium crowd that hung around for this finish went home sorry they didn't beat the traffic. The Dodgers, already broken by injuries, looked beaten, too, now.

If the Mets—on the verge of wasting a four-hit, 10-strikeout, seven-inning effort from Dwight Gooden—could outlast the unbeatable Hershiser and win Game 1 on the road with a three-run ninth, what could stop them from reaching the World Series?

Pardon the Mets if the reminder of the way they had gotten it done in the 1986 NLCS and World Series made them feel even more bullet-proof and arrogant than usual.

"Looked bad for awhile, didn't it?" said Wally Backman, before indulging in the kind of sadistic laugh that made Davey Johnson's Mets so popular throughout the NL. "We never ever gave up, but we knew that about ourselves two years ago. Is anyone really surprised by this?"

"Unbelievable," said Tim Teufel. "I've seen this somewhere before, haven't I?'

"They lose a game like that, after the way we played them this season, and they've gotta be thinking, 'Damn, how the hell are we going to beat these guys?'" said Backman.

Well, the answer to that question was furnished over seven games.

The Dodgers beat these guys by responding with their bats in Game 2 to derisive comments that appeared under the name of soon-to-be-ex-columnist David Cone. They beat these guys because Mike Scioscia hit the most devastating gopher ball of Gooden's career to create a tie in the ninth inning of Game 4, because Kirk Gibson went deep to break the deadlock in the 12th and because Hershiser got the final out of that game. They beat these guys because Hershiser threw a shutout in the Game 7 clincher.

But, at this particular moment, the Mets loved their chances, which didn't look nearly as promising until the ninth inning rolled around and a nervous Lasorda got out his hook—and the Mets got awfully lucky.

The Dodgers didn't exactly overwhelm the visitors with the offensive business they did do against Gooden. They scored in the first when

Steve Sax singled and stole second and then crossed on a two-out single to right by Mike Marshall and they made it 2-0 in the seventh on a double by Scioscia and a one-out RBI single by Alfredo Griffin over a drawn-in infield.

The Mets' lone real chance to score died a cowardly death when third-base Sam Perlozzo held up Carter at third on Mookie Wilson's two-out single to right in the third.

"Gary is probably the slowest runner we have in the lineup," said Perlozzo. "The ball was hit right at Marshall and he charged it well. It was still early in the game and I didn't think Hershiser was pitching as great as he had been. I thought he would have been out if he had gone. If it had been the sixth or the seventh, maybe I would've gambled."

Hershiser hardly broke a sweat through eight, with a pitch count of only 89 to start the ninth. The rally began immediately, with Gregg Jefferies lining the second pitch to him for a single through the middle. It was the Met rookie's third hit in four at-bats and that represented almost half the total surrendered by Hershiser in his 8⅓ innings. This was the night that the petulant Jefferies—whose September ascent wearing a reputation as the "wonder boy" hitting prospect triggered resentment and jealousy in the clubhouse—made his most memorable contribution to the Mets.

"He is a great pitcher and I didn't try to pull him," said Jefferies. "He was throwing the ball away a lot so I just tried to go with it. I can't say I was expecting to get a hit, but I was one of the guys hitting the ball pretty well, so I was confident."

Then came the play that made the rest of the inning possible: Jefferies was running on Keith Hernandez' ground smash to first and that was the only reason it was not a 3-6-3 double play.

With one out, the hitter was Darryl Strawberry, the epicenter of a storm of his own creation, for a change. Straw, riding a 39-homer, 100-RBI season, had created a furor by telling the *Los Angeles Times* how much he would love to come play for Los Angeles, the city where he sort of grew up, when he became a free agent—*after the 1990 season was over.*

This was 1988.

"Six or seven years in New York is enough for any player," said Strawberry, who promised to play his heart out for the Mets in the meantime and would wind up begging George Steinbrenner for the chance to play in New York again.

Best of all was the timing—on the eve of an NLCS against the team that he hinted would be his future employer.

For someone other than Darryl, the conjecture would have been distracting perhaps, calling into question his focus. Of course, there was never any telling what, if anything, was going on in Strawberry's head. In his first three at-bats, Hershiser "had made me look bad," as he put it. However, in the ninth inning of Game 1, Strawberry appeared unfazed by the fire that he had set and he turned in one of the very best at-bats in a career that featured relatively few disciplined ones.

Hershiser threw him curveball after curveball and he wasted a couple of nasty ones . . . until Orel left one letter high on 2-and-2 and Darryl crushed it to right center for a double, scoring Jefferies and making the score 2-1. It was the first run scored off Hershiser in 35 days, since the Expos had nicked him Aug. 30.

"Darryl's intensity really rose with two strikes," noticed Hernandez. "He really battled."

"Darryl took my best shots and he was still standing. Darryl finally got the pitch out of me that he wanted," admitted Hershiser.

"It's a sign of the maturity I have developed over the years," said Strawberry, who must have meant maturity as a hitter. "I'm more relaxed in situations like that now. I know I am not going to come through every time. But it helps being relaxed . . . It was a great at-bat for me against a great pitcher."

Strawberry's hit was the key because it prompted Lasorda to pull Hershiser in favor of the curveballing Howell, bringing about a celebration in the Met dugout.

"There was some screaming going on on the bench," said Davey Johnson, "like people smelling blood and going in for the kill."

"As soon as we got Orel out of the game, we knew we would beat the Dodgers," wrote Cone.

"I couldn't understand why they took him out," said Kevin McReynolds. "That is why I am not a manager."

"I thought he was getting tired," offered Lasorda after he was left with his regrets.

"It was the right move for sure. I wasn't the guy for the situation. I had no questions, no qualms about coming out," said the diplomat in Hershiser before he answered the question about the state of his gas tank by saying, "You don't throw 59 zeroes if you are tired. If I was tired, I would have been giving up runs."

Hershiser was asked if he attempted to dissuade his manager and he responded, "It's pretty hard to do when they go straight to the umpire for a double switch."

"Everybody was glad to see them go to the bullpen," said Teufel. "It changed the whole attitude on our bench. He had really handled our righties and it didn't look like he was tired."

Howell walked McReynolds and then struck out Howard Johnson, throwing five straight curves to a hitter who handled the breaking ball like Superman handled Kryptonite. Despite Howell's effectiveness in going away from his 95-mph heater, according to the words that appeared under his name in his ghostwritten column, Cone thought the approach was lacking machismo.

"We saw Howell throwing curveball after curveball and we're think-ing *this* is the Dodgers' idea of a stopper. Our idea is Randy [Myers, the winning pitcher for his two shutout innings], who can blow you away with heat," Cone wrote in the column which Lasorda used to fire up his Dodgers for Game 2. "Seeing Howell and his curveball reminded us of a high school pitcher."

Macho aside, there were two out, two on. The hitter was the right-handed Carter, a shade of his formerly dangerous self. The first two pitches were benders, with The Kid watching the first and flailing piti-fully at the second for an 0-and-2 count.

"He made me look silly," said Carter, who said he had faced Howell only once before. "But I figured if he would throw me two curves, then he could throw three. I wanted to make contact . . . I've been in these situations before . . . I just put things into the Lord's hands and, fortunately, I was able to deliver. I still can, you know."

"I had a bad feeling. I'll be honest about it . . . He looked terrible on the first two pitches, but he is a pro and he adjusted," said Hernandez.

Carter adjusted just enough to loft a down-and-away curve 120 feet to center off the end of his bat—a broken-bat fly.

"I had a good curveball," said Howell. "Of course, I was going to throw another one . . . I made a good pitch. The bleeping pitch was on his shoetops. Gary just hit it."

And Dodgers center fielder John Shelby couldn't catch it because he had been positioned too deep for the 1988 version of Carter and then got a late break on top of that. Shelby dove and nearly caught it, any-way, before it broke away from him.

"When I dove, I had a good feeling," said Shelby. "I can live with the decision . . . I wasn't fooled by the hit. I got a very good jump on it. It felt like it hit off my glove and I missed it. I made the best play I could."

"He had to try to catch that ball," said Lasorda.

"I finally got a break," said Carter.

"It was a dork [of a hit], but it was justice, because they scored their two runs on dorks," said Hernandez.

"We were unfortunate in the ninth that Gary didn't hit the ball any better," said Hershiser. "If he had hit the ball better, it would've been an out."

Strawberry scored easily to tie the game and, while Shelby was slow in recovering the ball, McReynolds never broke stride.

Perlozzo was a human windmill, gesticulating wildly from his spot, down the third-base line, toward the plate.

"What I read was that Shelby thought the play was dead, that there was no other play," said the coach. "It looked to me like he was nonchalantly going after the ball. I thought maybe we could catch him off guard."

Indeed, the outfielder was guilty of not releasing the ball immediately.

"When I went back to pick up the ball, I had to pick up home plate," said Shelby. "They say I double-pumped. I don't know. I thought I came up throwing."

McReynolds collided with Scioscia a split second before Shelby's throw arrived to make room and scored the winning run.

"He [McReynolds] was completely under control on the collision," marvelled Davey Johnson. "He is one of the few guys—maybe Straw, too—who can move Scioscia off the plate."

"He [Scioscia] is a pretty good-sized boy [6-foot-2, 219 pounds] and I pretty much zeroed in on him," said McReynolds, whose preferred choice of prey was usually ducks. "A lot of meat flew . . . At least I didn't have a choice to make. He made the choice for me. I just fell right on the plate. Just hard-nosed baseball."

"It's just one game," said Hershiser, who would have the last laugh before this NLCS and World Series were over.

METS	ab	r	h	bl	LOS ANGELES	ab	r	h	bl
Wilson cf	4	0	1	0	Sax 2b	3	1	1	0
Myers p	0	0	0	0	Stubbs 1b	3	0	0	0
Jefferies 3b	4	1	3	0	Woodson ph	1	0	0	0
Hernandez 1b	4	0	1	0	Gibson lf	4	0	0	0
Strawberry rf	4	1	1	1	Howell p	0	0	0	0
McReynolds lf	3	1	0	0	Marshall rf	4	0	1	1
Johnson ss	4	0	0	0	Shelby cf	4	0	0	0
Elster ss	0	0	0	0	Scioscia c	3	1	1	0
Carter c	4	0	2	2	Dempsey ph	1	0	0	0
Backman 2b	3	0	0	0	Hamilton 3b	3	0	0	0
Gooden p	2	0	0	0	Griffin ss	3	0	1	1
Dykstra cf	0	0	0	0	Hershiser p	2	0	0	0
					Gonzalez lf	0	0	0	0
Totals	32	3	8	3	Totals	31	2	4	2

Mets	000	000	003	— 3
Los Angeles	100	000	100	— 2

Game Winning RBI-Carter (1). E-Backman. DP-Los Angeles 2. LOB-Mets 5, Los Angeles 4. 2B-Scioscia, Strawberry, Carter. SB-Sax (1). S-Backman.

Mets	IP	H	R	ER	BB	SO
Gooden	7	4	2	2	1	10
Myers (W, 1-0)	2	0	0	0	0	0
Los Angeles						
Hershiser	8⅓	7	2	2	1	6
Howell (L, 0-1)	⅔	1	1	1	1	1

HBP-Sax (by Gooden).

Umpires: Home-Wendelstedt; First-McSherry; Second-West; Third-Rennert; Left-Davidson; Right-Runge.

T-2:45. A-55,582.

Big Unit Is Bowed
as Fonzie Flexes

1999 NLDS Game 1
October 5, 1999, in Phoenix, Ariz.

Edgardo Alfonzo hardly ever makes an impact with his mouth. It is not his way. Others talk. The Venezuelan-born infielder simply hits.

Lefties. Righties. With two outs. With two strikes. To every field. When the Mets need him most. His hits are his statements.

The night after he had homered in the single-game playoff that brought the Mets to the 1999 Division Series, Fonzie flexed his muscles again and left his handprints all over a stunning, tone-setting 8-4 Game 1 victory at Bank One Ballpark.

While New York fans struggled to stay awake to watch the telecast of a game that ended at nearly 2 a.m. in the East and the underdog Mets pretended they weren't exhausted from the self-imposed ordeal of their wildcard chase, Alfonzo provided the NL West champion Diamondbacks with an eye-opening little message about the postseason being a new season.

Alfonzo exposed Randy Johnson as just another run-of-the-mill, skinny, 6-foot-10 pitcher who can throw 98 miles per hour with a first-inning homer. Later, Alfonzo pinned the defeat on the Diamondbacks' most intimidating force with a tie-breaking, ninth-inning grand slam off Bobby Chouinard.

Suddenly, Arizona's 100 regular-season wins and seven in nine meetings with the Mets amounted to cactus under the bridge.

So what if the Diamondbacks had enjoyed the luxury of setting their rotation for the series so that Johnson could take on the Mets' fifth starter, Masato Yoshii, in Game 1 and be available to pitch again in Game 5?

In the first inning—the same inning that Edgardo had reached the seats against the Reds—Alfonzo found himself in an 0-and-2 hole when Johnson decided there was no need to waste a pitch to the game's second hitter.

"He [Johnson] has got that intimidating factor," said eventual winning pitcher Turk Wendell of the 1999 major league strikeout king with 364. "The guy looks like he is playing darts out there."

Randy threw a belt-high dart and Fonzie laid waste to it, hitting a seed to dead center, 422 feet, to begin a five-RBI night with a hit to the left ventricle that silenced the crowd of 49,584 and gave the Mets a 1-0 lead.

"It was amazing," said Wendell, a pitcher admiring the work of a hitter. "It looked like it was shot out of a gun. Randy was up there at close to 100 [miles per hour]. To see him hit it that square was a sight to see."

It was a sight to see the Mets' first post-season run since the sixth inning of Game 5 of the 1988 NLCS. It was a sight that shouted: Bring it on, big guy. Our bats will be as quick as they have to be, Unit. You may be one scary-looking dude to everyone else with that straight out of *Halloween* look, that Cy Young-winning 17-9 record and 2.48 ERA, but we've danced with death and we have nothing to lose.

The home run was a silent statement, Alfonzo's customary post-game humility notwithstanding.

"I just thought, 'Be patient here. Take a walk or get a pitch to hit.' Randy is one of the best pitchers in the big leagues. You just have to be patient," said Alfonzo.

And you have to be fearless. The next two Met hitters, John Olerud and Mike Piazza, followed with singles. The Mets didn't score any more that inning, but the myth of Johnson's unbeatability had been laid to rest. Olerud, in his next at-bat in the third, became the first left-handed hitter to homer off Johnson since Jim Edmonds hit two against Randy on Sept. 23, 1997.

Olerud's two-run shot to right field made the score 3-0, as it followed a walk and a stolen base by Rickey Henderson, a Hall of Fame pain in the butt to keep off the bases and to manage. Olerud's long ball off Johnson moved the first baseman—0-for-5 for his career vs. The Big Unit coming into the night—to claim he was the benefactor of divine intervention.

"I can't explain it myself," said Olerud, who had only two homers off lefties during the 1999 season. "I don't say this very often, but I definitely got to give the glory to Jesus Christ [who has never actually appeared in a boxscore]. Johnson has such good stuff that you just got to be ready.

"Earlier in that at-bat, I was looking slider and got all fastballs. Then, I got two strikes on me, I'm looking fastball and he throws a slider and I'm out in front. But somehow I got the barrel of the bat on the ball and got enough of it [for it] to go out of the ballpark."

The night would wind up with Johnson victimized for two of Olerud's three hits plus a single and a double by Robin Ventura. Johnson's whipsaw presence gives many lefty hitters attacks of 24-hour leprosy. But this monster—who relied on his nasty slider to hold lefties to a .103 average, just nine hits and only one extra-base hit during the season—wasn't bulletproof after all.

"I just thought they were great at-bats tonight . . . Four hits left-handed," said manager Bobby Valentine. "That is determination. That is reaching down and wanting it."

"Against Randy, you just have to be ready to swing the bat," said Olerud. "You don't have a whole lot of time to read the pitch. You have got to make up your mind if it's a pitch you are going to swing at or not. He throws hard and he has a good breaking ball. He's tough. You definitely have to turn it up a notch."

Johnson, nicked for a fourth run on a Rey Ordoñez squeeze bunt, of all things, in the fourth inning, did settle down and he retired 11 straight Mets before walking Henderson with two out in the seventh. And, sure enough, the Diamondbacks erased their 4-1 deficit. Yoshii coughed up rookie Erubiel Durazo's bases-empty, fourth-inning homer and Luis Gonzalez launched a game-tying, two-run shot into the right-field bleachers—452 feet worth of swimming-pool-clearing bomb in the sixth.

Johnson even had a chance to help get himself a lead after hitting a one-out double in the seventh. But, on Tony Womack's fly to left, Randy left on contact, awarding the Mets with a gift double play. Johnson closed out the eighth with a pair of Ks to bring his total to 11, but the ninth inning showed he was out of octane even though he was still registering 98s on the gun.

Ventura and Ordoñez singled around a popout. As if the Ordoñez hit wasn't telling enough regarding his empty tank, The Big Unit issued a four-pitch walk to Melvin Mora. The bases were loaded with one out and Johnson's count was 138 pitches.

After Alfonzo was done with Chouinard, the fork would really be in Johnson—charged with seven runs, eight hits and three walks in 8⅓ innings and his latest October defeat.

"It's not [about] too much pressure," insisted Johnson concerning being winless in six post-season decisions since his last victory in 1995. "I just tip my hat to the Mets. They played well. And I didn't make my pitches . . . It's not the way I would have wrote the script for tonight."

Arizona manager Buck Showalter had a rested, first-class closer in Matt Mantei (32 saves during the season), but wouldn't bring him into the tie game because, Buck later insisted, there was no base open.

Edgardo Alfonzo (grand) slams Bobby Chouinard to snap a ninth-inning deadlock,
Fonzie's second homer of the night. The silent assassin, bound for the dugout, gets kudos
from John Olerud and is trailed by Rickey Henderson and Melvin Mora.

The implication was, of course, that Mantei couldn't be trusted to
throw strikes.

Neither could Chouinard. He went 2-and-0 on Henderson, who
hit a chopper to third that Matt Williams turned into a brilliant force
play at the plate with a diving stop. Two out.

As the fans chanted "MVP" in recognition of Williams, Alfonzo worked the count to 3-and-1 and then sent a towering shot down the line in left, just to the fair side of the foul pole.

The post-season can leave a manager cruelly exposed.

"Bobby has been one of our best pitchers out of the bullpen," was the best Showalter could offer as a post-game explanation for why his best reliever was a spectator and a pitcher with Triple-A innings on his 1999 resume was on the mound.

Alfonzo's game-deciding blast marked the first time that any player had hit a grand slam in his first post-season game. Ordonez did a full spin as he and his three friends rode a cloud home. Alfonzo's trot was impassive, punctuated only by his usual finger to the sky in honor of his maker.

"That was a pretty good feeling going around the bases," he said.

"He is absolutely even [tempered]. This kid can hit," said Mickey Brantley, with the wisdom of, well, a hitting coach who had nothing to do with it.

"He is learning about himself every day he goes out there and gaining confidence," said Valentine. "And with confidence comes performances like you saw tonight."

Were these the same Mets who had been swept by the Braves and Phillies down the stretch?

Was this the team that had lost eight of nine and faced the prospect of mathematical elimination in four straight games?

Was it the group whose September gag reflex came so close to getting the manager fired that The Little Genius had himself predicted it (presumably to prove that nobody knows more than Valentine, even when it comes to his own ousting)?

"We are playing well and, if we keep playing together, we will be fun to watch," predicted Alfonzo, the five-RBI man.

"I just think they came ready to play," said Arizona's Williams. "Even with the late night they had, they were ready to go. You got a lot of guys over there who have been around the block a couple of times."

Already, one game into the post-season, this had been such a wild ride that Piazza made lots of sense when he said, "From here on out, everything is just icing on the cake . . . We are beyond tired. But I think that is a good thing. We're not thinking. We are just playing ball."

METS

	ab	r	h	rbi	bb	so	lob	avg
Henderson lf	3	2	0	0	2	0	4	.000
Benitez p	0	0	0	0	0	0	0	.000
Alfonzo 2b	5	2	2	5	0	1	2	.400
Olerud 1b	5	1	3	2	0	1	0	.600
Piazza c	5	0	1	0	0	2	1	.200
Agbayani rf	4	0	0	0	0	3	2	.000
Wendell p	0	0	0	0	0	0	0	.000
Hamilton cf	0	0	0	0	0	0	0	.000
Ventura 3b	4	1	2	0	2	2		.500
Dunston cf	3	0	1	0	0	0	0	.333
Cook p	0	0	0	0	0	0	0	.000
Cedeño rf	1	0	0	0	0	0	1	.000
Ordoñez ss	3	1	1	1	0	1	0	.333
Yoshii p	2	0	0	0	0	1	1	.000
Mora cf-lf	1	1	0	0	1	0	0	.000
Totals	**36**	**8**	**10**	**8**	**3**	**11**	**13**	

ARIZONA

	ab	r	h	rbi	bb	so	lob	avg
Womack rf	4	1	1	0	0	1	1	.250
Bell 2b	3	1	1	1	0	0	0	.333
Gonzalez lf	3	1	2	2	1	0	0	.667
Williams 3b	4	0	0	0	0	1	2	.000
Durazo 1b	4	1	1	1	0	0	0	.250
Finley cf	3	0	1	0	1	0	0	.333
Frias ss	4	0	0	0	0	1	2	.000
Stinnett c	3	0	0	0	0	0	1	.000
Johnson p	3	0	1	0	0	1	0	.333
Chouinard p	0	0	0	0	0	0	0	.000
Totals	**31**	**4**	**7**	**4**	**2**	**4**	**6**	

BATTING: 2B-Ventura (1, Johnson). HR-Alfonzo 2 (2, 1st inning off Johnson 0 on, 1 out, 9th inning off Chouinard 3 on, 2 out); Olerud (1, 3rd inning off Johnson 1 on, 1 out). S-Ordoñez. RBI-Alfonzo 5 (5), Olerud 2 (2), Ordoñez (1). 2-out RBI-Alfonzo 4. Runners left in scoring position, 2 out: Ventura 1, Henderson 1, Alfonzo 1. Team LOB-5.

BASERUNNING: SB-Henderson 2 (2, 2nd base off Johnson/Stinnett 2).

FIELDING: Outfield assists: Henderson (Johnson at 2nd base). DP- 2 (Henderson-Alfonzo, Ordoñez-Alfonzo-Olerud).

BATTING: 2B-Gonzalez (1, Yoshii); Johnson (1, Cook). 3B-Womack (1, Yoshii). HR-Durazo 1, 4th inning off Yoshii 0 on, 1 out); Gonzalez (1, 6th inning off Yoshii 1 on, 0 out). SF-Bell. RBI-Bell (1), Durazo (1), Gonzalez 2 (2). Runners left in scoring position, 2 out-Williams. GIDP-Williams. Team LOB-3.

Mets			102	100	004	— 8
Arizona			001	102	000	— 4

Mets	IP	H	R	ER	BB	SO	HR	ERA
Yoshii	5⅓	6	4	4	0	3	2	6.75
Cook	1⅔	1	0	0	1	1	0	0.00
Wendell (W, 1-0)	1	0	0	0	1	0	0	0.00
Benitez	1	0	0	0	0	0	0	0.00
Arizona								
Johnson (L, 0-1)	8⅓	8	7	7	3	11	2	7.56
Chouinard	⅔	2	1	1	0	0	1	13.50

Pitches-strikes: Johnson 138-85; Chouinard 15-8; Yoshii 76-54; Cook 25-13; Wendell 9-4; Benitez 13-9. Ground balls-flyballs: Johnson 6-8; Chouinard 2-0; Yoshii 3-10; Cook 0-3; Wendell 2-1; Benitez 0-3.

Umpires: Home-Gorman; First-Bell; Second-Hirschbeck; Third-DeMuth; Left-Marsh; Right-Schrieber.

T-2:53. A-49,584.

PART 2

Greatest Games in Met History

Leiter Burden: Give Berth

October 4, 1999 in Cincinnati

Nine innings with an entire season riding on their outcome produce memories that will never die: New York Giant Bobby Thomson's game-ending homer off Brooklyn Dodger Ralph Branca in 1951 and Yankee Bucky Dent's three-run shot into the screen at Fenway off Boston's Mike Torrez in 1978, for instance.

When the Mets squared off against the Reds in a single-game special playoff to determine the 1999 NL wild-card winner at Cinergy Field in Cincinnati, that annoying sports cliché finally applied. There really would be no tomorrow for the loser—and 96 wins over 162 yesterdays would be consigned to the meaningless pile by one more defeat.

The 10th one-game playoff in baseball history was the biggest regular-season game in Mets' history.

And, although there was no single moment to rival those of Thomson and Dent, there is just one image that survives from the night of Oct. 4, 1999, when the Mets achieved their first post-season berth in 11 years. It is the sense of almost scary ease with which Al

Leiter, quintessential big-game hunter, stoned the Reds and the pressure in a 5-0 masterpiece.

Millions of spectators found the tension of the stakes stifling, but Leiter was effortless and anxiety-free. The matter was never anything but well-in-hand.

Or maybe in head.

"I've always had somehow, some way, the ability to block a lot of the distractions out," said Leiter, the one-time Yankee who grew up as a fan of the Mets on the Jersey shore. "I forget about all the things that are negative and try to fill myself with a positive mindset. I just think about making pitches."

"When his mind is right, his arm is right," said manager Bobby Valentine.

Leiter came into the game with a mediocre 12-12 record to show for his year, even after beating Greg Maddux and the Braves to end a seven-game losing streak and trigger the Mets' recovery from the brink of self-immolation in his previous start. However, the pitcher who silenced Cincinnati's bats and 54,621 fans had to be the nastiest .500 pitcher anyone has ever seen.

"I'll take a mediocre year any time, if I can get to the playoffs," said Leiter. "Of course, I'd like to be standing here with 20 wins, but I could have fallen apart. I could have crumbled with all the things that happened. But I didn't do that."

He hung around to hang the Reds, instead. Such was Leiter's dominance that the Reds could have been pronounced dead after Edgardo Alfonzo's homer off Steve Parris provided a 2-0 lead just six pitches into the game. Leiter allowed two lousy hits and just a sharp second-inning single to left by Jeffrey Hammonds over the first eight. Leiter retired 13 batters in a row in one immaculate stretch from a two-out walk in the third until a walk in the eighth.

The left-hander, featuring a slider without pity on the hands of those overmatched righty hitters, missed the plate with his first six pitches and then didn't permit a Red to get past first until the ninth.

"Al has pitched a no-hitter [for the Marlins], but I don't know if he has ever pitched a better game than tonight," said Valentine. "He had this look in his eye."

It must have been the eye of a hired killer, because if there ever was a pitching performance as bloodless, inevitable and permanent as a professional hit, this was it.

"I told him, 'You've got great stuff, go after them,'" said Orel Hershiser, "and he gave me a sort of smile that said he understood how good he was throwing, and he was so locked in that nobody had to talk to him for the rest of the night."

"We had a great year," said Cincinnati manager Jack McKeon, whose exhausted team had beaten the Brewers in Milwaukee in a rain-delayed marathon the previous night. "We just ran into a hot pitcher in Leiter. He did the same thing to us here earlier in the year . . . The Mets got the pitching and we didn't."

None of the Reds' hitters had a clue, including 45-homer man Greg Vaughn, who was struck out twice and retired on a popup.

"I picked a bad night to have a bad game," said the left fielder, who could have been speaking for all his friends in the lineup.

"After the third inning, I started to get the feeling that they were a little anxious," said Leiter. "Sean Casey swung at a couple of pitches he normally wouldn't swing at. Vaughn has always been tough on me, but he swung at some balls . . . I knew I had something special going when they started swinging at a lot of my sliders and hitting them way foul."

The Mets made it 3-0 in the third on a walk to Alfonzo (who would later add an RBI double), a double by John Olerud, an intentional walk to Mike Piazza—and a bases-loaded walk to Robin Ventura by Denny Neagle.

In the fifth, the remarkable geriatric Rickey Henderson put his card games on hold long enough to hit a home run that he had promised he would hit, according to Met reliever Pat Mahomes. Combined with Henderson's first-inning single ahead of the Alfonzo blast, the homer reminded everyone the spotlight has always brought out greatness from him and that is the reason Rickey—as he loves to refer to himself—will some day loaf and whine his way into Cooperstown . . . if he ever stops playing.

"Rickey needs a stage. Rickey loves a stage," said Piazza.

In the ninth, Pokey Reese doubled down the left-field line and Vaughn walked, so Leiter was on the ropes, sort of. But Al had one more wish—to finish this one himself. It was granted by Valentine, who had already signalled with his finger to warming reliever Armando Benitez that Leiter would be allowed to face only one more batter in search of out No. 27.

"I wanted to get the last out. I really wanted to experience [the end of] the game on the field, as one of the nine players participating in the celebration," said Leiter, already gone when the 1997 Marlins rallied to win his World Series Game 7 start. "The few times I have experienced it, I was always running from the dugout or someone else. It's a nice thrill."

Finally, Dmitri Young lined out to Alfonzo, who acknowledged in that understated way of his, "When I caught the ball, I was thinking, 'Wow, we did it.' . . . Everybody thought we were out of the wild card, but we always kept the faith."

You have to appreciate both a painful history lesson and a excruciating odyssey to know how good exorcising the demons felt to the Mets.

In 1998, Valentine's Mets lost their last five, including three straight in Atlanta, to blow a lead and leave it to the Cubs to beat the Giants in a one-game playoff for the wild-card spot.

In 1999, the Mets found themselves a game under .500 in early June, when a bunch of coaches were forced to walk the plank for the failures of their charges. Finally, with the Mets one game back of the Braves and four ahead in the wild-card race with 12 left, they did their throat-clutching trick again.

This time, the Mets lost seven straight games—including three in the

After making the Reds hitters his pets with a complete-game shutout in a pressure-filled, loser-goes-home showdown for the wild card, Al Leiter shares the bubbly with Bobby Valentine to celebrate the manager's first trip to the post-season.

circle of Met hell known as Turner Field and three to fairly awful Philadelphia. After winning once, they dropped another extra-inning affair to Atlanta that left them 1½ games out of the wild-card spot with three games left.

So, the 1999 Mets needed to sweep their three-game series against the Pirates at Shea to have a chance to tie for the wild card. When they completed that feat—on a ninth-inning wild pitch, no less, Sunday— the Mets knew they had earned another night of life and there was nothing to celebrate, yet. The champagne and the joy came after Leiter took care of the Reds.

"A lot of people had the dirt thrown on us," said Piazza. "It's great to get the monkey off our back."

"We collapsed at the wrong time, but we responded to that collapse," said Hershiser.

After 1,704 games as a big league manager who until now had never managed a team that reached a post-season, after telling the media he should be fired if the Mets didn't reach in the playoffs in '99, Valentine finally had an invitation to the party.

"I'm drained, I'm excited, I'm elated, I'm thankful. It's a lot of emotions. I don't think I am smart enough to tell you about them," said Valentine, providing either trademark sarcasm or a genuine moment of humility in the face of redemption, because no manager in the game thinks more highly of his IQ than Bobby.

"The last thing I want to do is shed a shadow over what these guys have done over the last week," said Valentine. "I don't know how long I have waited for this, but I am glad to be here . . . This is the first champagne I have tasted."

METS	ab	r	h	bl	CINCINNATI	ab	r	h	bl
Henderson lf	5	2	2	1	Reese 2b	3	0	1	0
Mora lf	0	0	0	0	Larkin ss	3	0	0	0
Alfonzo 2b	4	2	2	3	Casey 1b	4	0	0	0
Olerud 1b	5	0	2	0	GVaughn lf	3	0	0	0
Piazza c	2	0	0	0	DYoung rf	4	0	0	0
Ventura 3b	3	0	1	1	Hammonds cf	3	0	1	0
Hamilton cf	4	0	1	0	Taubensee c	2	0	0	0
Cedeno rf	4	0	1	0	ABoone 3b	3	0	0	0
Ordoñez ss	3	1	0	0	Parris p	0	0	0	0
Leiter p	3	0	0	0	Neagle p	1	0	0	0
					Stynes ph	1	0	0	0
					Graves p	0	0	0	0
					Lewis ph	1	0	0	0
					Reyes p	0	0	0	0
Totals	33	5	9	5	Totals	28	0	2	0

Mets	201	011	000 — 5
Cincinnati	000	000	000 — 0

DP-Mets 1, Cincinnati 2. LOB-Mets 10, Cincinnati 5. 2B-Alfonzo (41), Olerud (39), Reese (37), HR-Henderson (12), Alfonzo (27), S-Leiter.

Mets	IP	H	R	ER	BB	SO
Leiter (W, 13-12)	9	2	0	0	4	7
Cincinnati						
Parris (L, 11-4)	2²/₃	3	3	3	3	1
Neagle	2¹/₃	2	1	1	3	2
Graves	3	2	1	1	2	2
DReyes	1	2	0	0	0	0

Umpires: Home-Froemming; First-Davis; Second-Hirschbeck, M.; Third-Rapuano; Left-Rieker; Right-Nelson.

T-3.03. A-54,621.

Seaver's Imperfect Game

July 9, 1969 in New York

The red eyes and tear tracks were visible on Nancy Seaver's face as she approached Tom, outside the studio from where the Mets' post-game TV show was aired.

"What are you crying for?" he asked. "We won, 4-0."

"I guess a one-hit shutout is better than nothing," said Nancy, smiling at her husband. Then they both laughed, Nancy through her tears, the equivalent of a facial sun shower.

The Mets had won their seventh straight and second in a row from Chicago to cut the Cubs' lead to just three games. However, after the final out, they appeared more deflated than elated, because a special night had failed to become a truly historic one.

Seaver had seen his dalliance with a perfect game—and the first no-hitter in the history of a franchise that is still without one—slip away with one out in the ninth inning.

Jimmy Qualls.

That name carries an association to anyone old enough to remember the 1969 Mets as instant and singular as the name Bill Buckner ignites for followers of the '86 Mets.

Qualls was the Cubs' center fielder on that July night in Flushing, a switch-hitting platoon partner for the right-handed-hitting Don Young, the goat in the Cubs' ninth-inning defeat a day earlier. Qualls was a slap hitter, only 47 at-bats into his first season of a major league career that was over by 1972 (139 at-bats, a .223 batting average, no homers).

But it is Qualls who remains an eternal footnote of regret in the story of what Seaver would call the greatest game that he ever pitched.

The first 25 batters up, 25 retired—most of those outs coming on fastballs from the drop-and-drive master, Seaver. A ballpark full of customers teetered on the brink of delirium. The anticipation of the 11th perfect game in baseball history will do that to a crowd already heated by the promise of a pennant race.

"My heart was beating so much and the feeling was almost out of my arm," said Seaver. "If I just stood there, I felt it might fall off. But I felt I could do it."

From the beginning of the game, when Seaver finally shook off the shoulder stiffness he had experienced during his warmups, something special was in the air. As early as the second inning, pitching coach Rube Walker said to manager Gil Hodges that he thought Seaver had no-hit quality stuff.

"He [Seaver] will probably never be that fast again as long as he lives," said Cubs manager Leo Durocher.

All but a few of the Chicago outs were tame. Randy Hundley hit a liner to left fielder Cleon Jones and Qualls hit a long fly to right fielder Ron Swoboda in the second. Ron Santo managed a long fly to center in the fifth and Don Kessinger lined out to left two innings later. When a pitcher is on this kind of roll, there is pressure on his friends wearing gloves, too.

"You know it's a perfect game and you don't want to be the schlep who fouls it up," said Swoboda.

The biggest challenge that the Cubs figured to pose came in the eighth, when they sent up their 4-5-6 hitters. But Seaver got Santo on a long fly, outlasted Ernie Banks for a strikeout and then blew away Al Spangler, swinging, for his 11th and final K.

"I thought to myself moments like these are reserved for other people—they are for the Sandy Koufaxes and Mickey Mantles and Willie Mayses of the world. Not for the Tom Seavers and the New York Mets," said the pitcher, displaying somewhat uncharacteristic humility.

Seaver received a deafening standing ovation from the club-record Shea crowd of 59,083—including Seaver's father, visiting from California—when the pitcher came up to hit in the bottom of that inning.

Then Tom took a deep breath and went out for the ninth. Hundley, the first Cub hitter and a catcher, shocked everyone by bunting a high pitch to the third-base side of the mound, but the alert Seaver pounced on it in time to get Hundley at first. The strategy—put in motion on a sign from Durocher, who had spotted the Met third baseman playing deep—was booed lustily by the crowd.

"He did me a favor," said Seaver. "He's a tough hitter for me, always has been. It was a relief to come off the mound, use my legs, do something other than pitch."

Now up came Qualls, at 5-foot-10 and 155 pounds, not yet 23 years old, playing in his 18th major league game, amidst a din in which he was the party of the second part.

"I just closed my ears," said Qualls.

And Qualls hit Seaver's first pitch, a fastball that caught too much of the plate—Seaver hadn't thrown a single breaking ball to Qualls the entire game—on a line into short left center. Tommie Agee never had a chance.

Clean hit.

"When they give you a good pitch, you've got to hit it," said Qualls, who had returned to the Cubs from the minors only a week earlier and was something of a mystery to the Mets.

"I didn't know where Tommie was playing, but from the trajectory of the ball, I figured that's got to be a hit," said Seaver.

"When Qualls came up, I said to myself, 'If anybody's gonna break it up, this is the guy who is going to do it, because we don't know where to play him,'" said Agee. "He was pulling the ball early in the game, but I still played him a little to left. If I knew him, I might have played a little more to left, a little shallower. Maybe I could have caught it if I did. But, where I was playing, I had no chance."

"I had never faced Qualls before," Seaver lamented years later. "That was the first time he played against us. So I wasn't sure just how to pitch to him."

After the single, Donn Clendenon, the first baseman, went to the mound to remind Seaver that there were still two more outs to get for his eighth victory in a row, as the crowd's groans became loud we-love-you-anyway cheers.

"He pitched his heart out," said Clendenon. "It was kind of dis-heartening because he deserved the no-hitter. He's a competitor—the best I've ever seen."

Two popups later, Seaver's victory was in the books—a 99-pitch, single-flawed masterpiece.

Bud Harrelson, the Met shortstop and Seaver's roommate, watched the game on television in Watertown, N.Y. while fulfilling an Army reserve commitment, along with some buddies who were also in the majors.

"It was the strangest thing," he said. "I began feeling more and more like a little kid, watching that game and that great performance and I wanted to turn to the others and say, 'I know Tom Seaver. Tom Seaver is a friend of mine.'"

The Terrific One was 14-3 in a remarkable season in which he would finish at 25-7 with a 2.20 ERA and 208 strikeouts. Seaver would go on to strike out a record-tying 19 in a game for the Mets in 1970. He would come within one strike of nine no-hit innings vs. the Cubs in a scoreless game at Wrigley in 1975, before Joe Wallis—as obscure as Jimmy Qualls—spoiled it with a single. Finally, Seaver would pitch a no-hitter for the Cincinnati Reds in 1978, win 311 games and post a 2.86 career ERA on the course to Cooperstown.

"I had great stuff that night, superb control and a mastery of all my pitches. It was better than my no-hitter with Cincinnati," Seaver said years later. "That [the no-hitter] was just a fun game. I really didn't have very good stuff that day. I was lucky. Joe Morgan made a couple of good plays and all the balls were hit at somebody."

How many times do you think Seaver, obsessed with perfecting the art of pitching, has thought about that first-pitch fastball to Qualls on that imperfect night in July 1969?

"Within my grasp was a perfect game," Seaver said. "You just don't get another chance."

"If he pitches like that every night, he will never lose a game," said Durocher, whose Cubs had now lost five straight and held only a one-game edge in the loss column over the Mets.

Chicago was showing signs of withering under the pennant pressure that the Cubs' veterans were predicting would wind up being the young Mets' ruination before summer became fall.

Third baseman Santo, fresh from a pre-game apology to Young for publicly trashing his young teammate as being self-involved a day earlier, made an error in the second. Shortstop Kessinger made one on the following play. The misplays led to two unearned Met runs on RBI hits by Seaver and Agee that made the score 3-0 when combined with a first-inning tally on Agee's triple and Bobby Pfeil's double off loser Ken Holtzman. Later on, second baseman Glenn Beckert committed an error.

"You'll never see the three of us make an error in the same game again," said Santo. "Wait till we get them at Wrigley Field."

CHICAGO					METS				
	ab	r	h	bl		ab	r	h	bl
Kessinger ss	4	0	0	0	Agee cf	5	1	2	1
Beckert 2b	3	0	0	0	Pfeil 2b	4	0	1	1
Williams lf	3	0	0	0	Jones lf	3	1	1	1
Santo 3b	3	0	0	0	Clendenon 1b	4	0	0	0
Banks 1b	3	0	0	0	Charles 3b	4	0	1	0
Spangler rf	3	0	0	0	Garrett 2b	0	0	0	0
Hundley c	3	0	0	0	Swoboda rf	4	0	1	0
Qualls cf	3	0	1	0	Gaspar rf	0	0	0	0
Holtzman p	0	0	0	0	Grote c	4	1	0	0
Abernathy p	2	0	0	0	Weis ss	4	1	1	0
Smith ph	1	0	0	0	Seaver p	2	0	1	1
Totals	28	0	1	0	Totals	34	4	8	4

Chicago	000	000	000	— 0
Mets	120	000	10x	— 4

E-Santo, Kessinger, Beckert. LOB-Chicago 1, Mets 9. 2B-Pfeil, Agee, Charles. 3B-Agee. HR-Jones (10). S-Seaver

	IP	H	R	ER	BB	SO
Chicago						
Holtzman (L, 10-5)	1⅓	4	3	1	0	2
Abernathy	6⅔	4	1	1	2	2
Mets						
Seaver (W, 14-3)	9	1	0	0	0	11

T-2:02. A-59,083.

Seeing it on this night was a comfort to the Mets.

"Seeing them play like that lets us know that if we make a mistake, there is nothing to worry about," said Jones, who contributed his 10th homer in the seventh, off Ted Abernathy. "That is an important thing for a young team to know."

The next day—before the Cubs salvaged the finale of the three-game series and before the graceless Durocher answered the question, "Were those the real Cubs out there today?" by saying, "No, those were the real Mets"—Banks offered a canny reading of the collective blood pressure of the team chasing his team.

"What about those Mets?" he said. "They are pretty calm for so young a team and that is rather odd."

Lifted by Krane

July 8, 1969, in New York

The baseball gods have a sense of history. How else can you explain the last of the first-year Mets winding up as the hitting hero in the first head-to-head pennant-race game in the club's history?

Ed Kranepool, the strapping kid from James Monroe High School in the Bronx, was more suspect than prospect—and he wasn't a kid any more, at 24. On this day, when the Mets showed they weren't kidding about this contending business, the pull-hitting Kranepool delivered an opposite-field, game-winning hit.

"This has got to be the biggest game for us ever, the way we came back," said Kranepool. "It's been all these long years and the club is just starting to mature . . . Damn, I am glad I am here. There is no one left but me since 1962 and I struggled through all that fertilizer and now half the season's gone and no one can say we are not contenders."

It was his most delirious moment in 18 years of wearing a Met uniform. The question posed by a banner sighted five years earlier when he was only 19—"Is Ed Kranepool over the hill?"—had finally been answered.

"It was the first time I heard cheering since I signed," said Kranepool.

The Chicago Cubs came into New York with a five-game lead over the second-place Mets and a sense of incredulity about whether the team chasing them would be for much longer.

Chicago third baseman Ron Santo, with hitters like Billy Williams, Ernie Banks and Randy Hundley supporting him, looked at the pedestrian Met lineup posted on the dugout wall for the opener of a three-game series at Shea and said, "I know Los Angeles won with pitching, but this is ridiculous."

For his part, the Mets' starter Jerry Koosman was accustomed to working without the safety net offered by a team that can score runs in bunches. Koosman came into the game with a record of just 5-5, even though he had permitted a scant nine earned runs over his previous 74 innings. The Mets' ordinary offense and ignominious history—"a seven-year losing streak" as Kranepool put it—meant there were disbelievers everywhere.

Other than a fuming Santo—who said something about the Mets' infield not being good enough to compete for the Cubs' farm in Tacoma afterwards—there were fewer doubters of the young Mets at the end of this statement game. Kranepool certainly was among the believers after he homered—the only hit allowed by Ferguson Jenkins over the first eight innings—and reached the Cubs' ace for that game-ending single to cap a three-run, ninth-inning rally for a 4-3 victory.

"That's what we are out here for," said manager Gil Hodges after the Mets' sixth straight win left them two games behind the Cubs in the loss column. "To make believers out of all you unbelievers. Was there ever any doubt about it?"

With all due respect to Hodges, until the ninth, there was no sign the Mets' offense would come alive. Other than Kranepool's bases-empty homer to right center in the fifth, the Mets offered no resistance whatsoever to Jenkins, who would post his third of six straight 20-win seasons at 21-15.

The 1-0 lead provided by Kranepool's eighth homer of the year and his 59th as a Met was erased almost immediately, when the 38-year-old

Banks victimized Koosman for his 14th homer. Glenn Beckert's RBI hit in the seventh scored Jenkins, who had walked. Then, in a development especially revolting to Met fans who had suffered through too many strikeouts during the non-development of Jim Hickman, the ex-Met crushed a homer into the Cubs' bullpen in left in the eighth to make it 3-1.

To most people, it didn't look like the Mets' day.

"I never felt defeated, but I knew it was going to take a lot of hits for us to win," said Cleon Jones. "Leading, 3-1, they were feeling pretty good. Going out to the outfield, they were patting their pockets. That Banks talks to you all the time. 'That Jenkins can pitch,' he kept saying over and over."

But victory seemed in the offing to Met first-base coach Yogi Berra, who said to Banks as the Cubs left the field in the eighth, "We're gonna get three in the ninth and beat you."

All it took to get the ball rolling was a crucial helping hand from Cubs' rookie center fielder Don Young.

Pinch-hitter Ken Boswell, hitting .245 and suffering from a bruised hand, hit a blooper to short right center that was momentarily lost in the white shirts by Young, who got a poor break. The bloop fell out of reach of second baseman Beckert and shortstop Don Kessinger and in front of Young and Boswell hustled into second when he saw the base was uncovered in the chase for his popup.

Double.

"When I hit it, I knew the ball had a chance. It was just a matter of how deep they were playing me," said Boswell.

"I know what happened to the kid . . . the sun and the stands . . . It's hard to see the ball," said Jones.

"The big thing was Boswell getting on," said Donn Clendenon. "Then, you got the tying run coming to the plate. When Boswell got on, we knew we would get him home."

After Tommie Agee popped out, Clendenon pinch-hit for Bobby Pfeil and pounded a pitch to deep left center. Young got his reputedly reliable glove on it, but it popped out as he hit the wall. Boswell reached third on the Clendenon double.

Cubs' manager Leo Durocher seethed.

"If you can't catch a flyball, you don't deserve to win," said Durocher after the game was over. "We had two chances and didn't catch either . . . The man [Jenkins] pitches his heart out, but the man [Young] can't catch a flyball. It's a disgrace."

Up to the plate walked Jones, in the midst of a .340 campaign.

"I said to myself, 'I gotta get a hit now. If I don't, I'll be teed off at myself driving home in the car,'" said Jones.

Jones avoided the self-flagellation as he lashed a game-tying double into the left-field corner for his 100th hit, on a curve that caught too much of the plate. The Shea crowd of 55,096 continued the wild ride from desultory to ecstatic.

With lefty Hank Aguirre and righty relief ace Phil Regan warm in the bullpen, Durocher opted to stay with Jenkins, who wound up with 23 complete games in 1969. Art Shamsky was intentionally walked to set up an inning-ending double play, but Wayne Garrett's roller to second wasn't brisk enough. It moved runners to second and third with two out. First base was open, but Durocher chose to let Jenkins pitch to Kranepool rather than on-deck hitter J.C. Martin, another lefty batter.

The count went to 1-and-2 on Kranepool after an especially futile swing and a miss on an outside curve. Eddie noticed that Kessinger was playing him toward second base and, expecting Jenkins to work him outside, he reached out and lifted the next pitch just past the reach of the shortstop and into left field. Jones danced home with the game-winning run, setting off a wild hugfest at the plate.

"I knew he wanted me to hit a bad pitch," said Kranepool. "I just made up my mind to go the other way."

"If I value my life, I'll get the hell out of here," said Young as he dressed in the Chicago clubhouse.

And he had reason to feel that way.

"That kid in center field," said Durocher. "Two little flyballs and he just stands there watching one and gives up on the other."

"He [Young] was just thinking about himself, not the team," said Santo. "He had a bad day at the plate so he had his head down. He was thinking about his batting average [.222] and not the team . . . He can keep his head down and keep right on going, out of sight for all I care. We don't need that kind of thing."

Already, you could see the large difference in team chemistry between the nothing-to-lose Mets and the tightly wound Cubs and the foreshadowing of the different ways the teams would react as the pennant pressure mounted.

"We are too young to feel any pressure. We think this is a high school championship," said Boswell.

"We're in command," said Jones. "We beat their big man [Jenkins] and our big man [Tom Seaver, the next day's starter] is coming up. Now we can relax and play our natural game."

Hickman, who had been with the Mets long enough to notice the difference in them, found his current predicament more than a little ironic.

"How do you like that?" he said. "I'm with these guys five years and I never had a chance to win anything, any [post-season] money. Now I am in a position to win some money and these are the guys who might beat me out of it."

CHICAGO					METS				
	ab	r	h	bl		ab	r	h	bl
Kessinger ss	4	0	1	0	Agee cf	4	0	0	0
Beckert 2b	4	0	2	1	Pfeil 3b	3	0	0	0
Williams lf	4	0	1	0	Clendenon ph	1	1	1	0
Santo 3b	3	0	0	0	Jones lf	4	1	1	2
Banks 1b	4	1	1	1	Shamsky rf	3	0	0	0
Hundley c	2	0	0	0	Garrett 2b	4	0	0	0
Hickman rf	4	1	2	1	Kranepool 1b	4	1	2	2
Young cf	4	0	0	0	Martin c	3	0	0	0
Jenkins p	3	1	1	0	Weis ss	3	0	0	0
					Koosman p	2	0	0	0
					Boswell ph	1	1	1	0
Totals	32	3	8	3	Totals	32	4	5	4

Chicago	000	001	110	—3
Mets	000	010	003	—4

E-Jenkins. DP-Mets 1. LOB-Chicago 8, Mets 3. 2B-Boswell, Clendenon, Jones. HR-Kranepool (8), Banks (14), Hickman (4). S-Beckert, Kessinger.

	IP	H	R	ER	BB	SO
Chicago						
Jenkins (L, 11-6)	8²/₃	5	4	4	1	8
Mets						
Koosman (W, 6-5)	9	8	3	3	4	6

Two out when winning run scored.

T-2:09, A-55,096.

Amazin' for the First Time

METS 9, PIRATES 1

April 23, 1962 in Pittsburgh

It is baseball's peculiar charm that even when the schedule brings together the most beatable team of all time and a team that is unbeaten, it remains impossible to predict what will unfold. In 1962, the Pirates began their season with a record-tying 10 straight victories. The Mets, meanwhile, began their inaugural season with a streak that guaranteed their hungry fans wouldn't confuse them with the Dodgers or the Giants.

Their losing streak reached nine straight games, matching the record for the start of a season, with no end in sight.

Manager Casey Stengel understood the nature of the problem for his team, composed of nothing but the wretched rejects of the established teams in the game.

"The trouble is we are in a losing streak at the wrong time," he said. "If we were losing like this in the middle of the season, nobody would notice. But we are losing at the beginning of the season and that sets up the possibility of losing all 162 games."

The possibilities were endless—or at least bottomless—and, to this point, the news had ranged from ominous to depressing. A bunch of Mets got trapped in the Chase Hotel elevator in St. Louis just before their scheduled season opener was rained out. The next night, they fell behind on a run-scoring balk and lost, 11-4. After being welcomed to the city with a ticker-tape parade, the Mets dropped their home opener to the Pirates, 4-3, on Friday the 13th and the Mets were victimized by the team's trademark, the self-inflicted wound, in this case, erratic fielding in the outfield.

Losses in the first two games of the current series vs. the Pirates made it nine straight . . . and counting. The season was 12 days old and the Mets were 9½ games out of first place.

However, on April 23 in Pittsburgh, in the process of being Amazin' for the very first time, the Mets swung the bats, ran the bases and pitched like they just might belong in the National League after all— previous evidence to the contrary be damned.

The Mets celebrated the benching of third baseman Don Zimmer (0-for-24) by mounting a 14-hit attack, paced by three hits each from Zim's replacement, Felix Mantilla, and Mantilla's roommate, Elio Chacon. Shockingly opportunist and no-nonsense in their approach, the Mets advanced on flyballs six times and paddled Pirate knuckle-baller Tom Sturdivant for five runs in just one-plus inning.

Their running fever was so contagious even the venerable Gil Hodges attempted a stolen base in the ninth. The fact Hodges was thrown out by half the length of the distance from Forbes Field to Brooklyn did nothing to dampen the locker room joy and relief generated by this 9-1 victory.

"Break up the Mets," shouted a jubilant Joe Ginsberg, eliciting laughter from teammates after that first W was officially beyond their capacity to blow.

"Where's the champagne?" said Zimmer.

"Nuttin' to it," observed Stengel. "Ninety-nine more and we got the pennant."

Right-hander Jay Hook held the Pirates to just five hits (four of them singles) and one run for a complete-game victory. Just about a month earlier, Hook had been left on a Miami mound to absorb a spring training battering from Baltimore that was so brutal (17 hits, five home runs) it brought tears to his eyes. Now, as the Mets were poised to erase the 1918 Dodgers and the 1919 Braves from the record books with their 10th straight loss to start a season, Hook played the role of stopper.

Clutching the game ball from the franchise's first win, Hook was overcome by the magnitude of the milestone that he and his team-mates had achieved in the face of mounting anxiety. Just 12 credits away from a master's degree in mechanical engineering, Hook temporarily lost his ability to subtract.

"I got through the seventh and I said to myself, 'Well, that's only seven. I got three left,'" said Hook.

Fortunately, Hook's pitching was better than his accounting, not often the case during his 8-19 season in '62. And the fates were with him for a change, too, despite his inability to consistently throw his curve for strikes. Hook admitted he was fortunate that his fastballs became hard outs, instead of hits. And it didn't hurt that the Mets helped ease the burden on him by batting around in a four-run second en route to a 6-0 lead.

Leadoff man Mantilla started the party in the first, with a single, and took second on an outfield bobble. Chacon singled him to third, then took second on a wild pitch. Gus Bell's liner to left scored Mantilla and moved Chacon to third, from where he scored on Frank Thomas' sac fly to left.

Sturdivant got hooked after Charlie Neal doubled and Jim Hickman and Chris Cannizzaro walked with none out in the second. Then Hook, a lefty hitter who finished the game at .333, helped himself with a two-run, line-drive single off 42-year-old, left-handed reliever Diomedes Olivo.

"I drove in two and they only scored one," said Hook, doing the math without a flaw this time.

The bulge became 6-0 on Mantilla's sac fly and Chacon's run-scoring hit.

"That Chacon," said Stengel. "He played like he owned Venezuela."

"I tole you, I tole you," said the Caracas-born Chacon, whose English was often as raw as his talent and whose major league career was over by the end of 1962. "Yesterday, I say we play better today. Tomorrow, we play more better. You watch."

Actually, nobody in New York watched the Mets' first victory. The first nine Met games had been televised, but this one was not. Can they get a witness? Who among the stunned Ladies' Night crowd in Pittsburgh would vouch for what was seen by eyes that they were sure had to be lying?

Of course, Casey viewed his Mets' first step forward in typically unique fashion.

"I don't see how we lost a game," said Stengel, his weathered, 72-year-old face making him look like a grinning basset hound. "That damn streak might cost us the pennant."

This rout was followed by a three-game losing streak. It was no doubt the result of overconfidence.

METS	ab	r	h	bl	PITTSBURGH	ab	r	h	bl
Mantilla 3b	3	2	3	1	Virdon cf	4	0	0	0
Chacon ss	4	2	3	2	Groat ss	4	0	1	0
Bell rf	3	0	1	1	Skinner lf	4	0	1	1
Smith rf	1	0	1	2	Stuart 1b	4	0	0	0
Thomas lf	2	0	1	1	Clemente rf	4	0	0	0
DeMerit lf	1	0	0	0	Burgess c	1	0	0	0
Bouchee 1b	2	0	0	0	McFarlane c	2	0	0	0
Hodges 1b	3	0	2	0	Hoak 3b	2	0	1	0
Neal 2b	5	1	2	0	Mazeroski 2b	3	0	0	0
Hickman cf	4	1	0	0	Sturdivant p	0	0	0	0
Cannizzaro c	3	1	0	0	Olivio p	1	0	1	0
Hook p	4	2	1	2	a-Schofield ph	1	1	1	0
					Lamabe p	0	0	0	0
					b-Logan ph	1	0	0	0
Totals	35	9	14	9	Totals	31	1	5	1

a-Singled for Olivo in 6th; b-Grounded out for Lamabe in 8th.

Mets	240	001	020	— 9
Pittsburgh	000	001	000	— 1

E-Virdon, Groat, Stuart. DP-Chacon, Neal, Bouchee, Burgess, Mazeroski. LOB-Mets 7, Pittsburgh 4. 2B- Neal, Olivo, Thomas, Mantilla. 3B-Smith. Sacrifice-Mantilla. SF-Bell, Thomas, Mantilla.

	IP	H	R	ER	BB	SO
Mets						
Hook (W, 1-0)	9	5	1	1	1	2
Pittsburgh						
*Sturdivant (L, 1-1)	1	3	5	5	2	0
Olivo	5	7	2	1	1	2
Lamabe	2	3	2	1	1	3
Haddix	1	1	0	0	0	2

*Faced 3 batters in 2d.

WP-Sturdivant.

Umpires: Home-Walsh; First-Conlan; Second-Burkhart; Third-Pelekoudas.

Time-2:40. Attendance-16,176.

A 19-K Night Turns Rocky

September 15, 1969 in St. Louis

Steve Carlton decided early on—after his first nine Ks—that he was going after the major league strikeout record for a nine-inning game. He was going to ignore his head cold and two rain delays totalling 81 minutes and blow away the Met hitters. The Cardinals' 24-year-old left-hander, already showing Hall of Fame potential, pounded away with fastballs and sliders.

Before he was finished, Carlton struck out 19 Mets—a major league record—and fanned the side four times to establish it. The Mets' usually reliable infield committed four errors in nonsupport of starter Gary Gentry. It was a listless, shoddy performance, not befitting a first-place team that was riding a 13-game turnaround in the standings over the previous month.

However, winning even when they couldn't get out of their own way was a specialty of the 1969 Mets. By September, the Mets had become so familiar with the miraculous that the magical seemed mundane. Still, coming out with a victory in this one in spite of themselves screamed a message: Whatever it takes.

What it took on this strange night was for Ron Swoboda to hit a pair of two-run homers that erased a one-run deficit each time and powered a 4-3 victory.

"He was on the way to becoming a great pitcher then and he was having the best day of his life," said Swoboda. "He had two strikes on me all four times I came to bat. He got me twice (on strikes) and I got him twice."

"It was the best stuff I've ever had," said Carlton, who wound up 17-11 in his third full major league season.

Talk about stealing a guy's thunder.

On a night that Carlton's stuff was overpowering enough to erase Sandy Koufax, Bob Feller and Don Wilson from the record books, the Mets won anyway, for the 11th time in 12 games and 27th time in 34. Thanks to this latest triumph over reason, with 15 games left, the Mets were sitting pretty with a 4½-game lead over Chicago, a loser in 11 of its last 12.

"It's great to win when you play badly," said manager Gil Hodges.

Hodges understood the youthful spirit that made these Mets so much more than the sum of their parts and sacred in New York baseball annals. But even he couldn't have fathomed how they could look so bad and end up feeling so good.

Carlton struck out the side in the first inning and the second. By the time Swoboda came up in the fourth, the Cardinals had used hits by Curt Flood and Vada Pinson off Gentry to take a 1-0 lead. The margin would have been larger if center fielder Tommie Agee's strong throw home hadn't nailed the comet known as Lou Brock, who had walked before the hits.

After Donn Clendenon drew a leadoff walk in the fourth, Swoboda, a K victim in the first, spotted Carlton two quick strikes. The left-hander then tried to burn another past him rather than waste a pitch and Swoboda turned around the fastball and sent it 400-plus feet, deep into the seats for a 2-1 lead.

"I was throwing 85 percent fastballs and a few breaking pitches to make them look better," said Carlton. "The fastball is still the best pitch in baseball and, if you have it working for you, you stay with it."

Swoboda, who displayed a career-long allergy to breaking balls, had hit a grand slam to beat Pittsburgh three days earlier. However, the Mets' platoon right fielder began this night with just seven homers for the 1969 season—and he didn't think he got all of this one.

"I didn't think I hit it that good," said Swoboda, who had received some pre-game hitting tips from broadcaster and Hall of Fame slugger Ralph Kiner, a free swinger in his day. "I looked at the bat later and there was only a smudge on it."

Carlton was unfazed, striking out the next three Mets and then two more in the fifth. That was the inning in which the Cards scored twice more off Gentry to take a 3-2 lead on consecutive two-out singles by Brock, Flood, Pinson and Joe Torre.

Of course, Swoboda wasn't done, though.

Agee opened the eighth with a single to center, one of nine hits off Carlton. The pitcher then notched Clendenon as his 15th K. By now, the record seemed close enough for Lefty to taste. And Swoboda, prone to not making contact, was next.

"I was trying to strike him out in the eighth," said Carlton. "I'll be honest—I was looking to strike out every man up . . . When I had nine strikeouts, I decided to go all the way [for the record]. But it cost me the game, because I started to challenge every batter."

Swoboda, caught looking his previous time up, jumped on a slider this time, a 2-and-2 pitch that was located poorly by Carlton. It wasn't inside enough and Swoboda relocated it, propelling a line drive over the left-field wall for a 4-3 Met lead.

"He's very quick inside and that is where the pitch was," said Carlton.

"I was going around the bases and all I wanted to do was get back to the bench," said Swoboda. "They [his teammates] live it with you and I wanted to be in there living it, too. Everybody kept hitting me on the top of the helmet and I couldn't hear a thing. I felt like a bongo drum."

The little drummed boy beat Carlton, but somehow Lefty's record-setting beat went on.

Al Weis went down for No. 16, leaving Carlton three short of a new record. Carlton began the ninth with a gimme, victimizing winning pitcher Tug McGraw (three scoreless innings), and then he nailed Bud Harrelson looking for his record-tying 18th.

Carlton ran the count of 2-and-2 on the just-promoted rookie Amos Otis.

"I wanted that last strikeout so bad I put every ounce of energy I had into those last pitches," said Carlton.

Swing and a miss. Cards' catcher Tim McCarver didn't handle the pitch cleanly, but he stopped it and threw out Otis at first. Carlton had made history, at the expense of the Mets' hitters, but winning means never having to acknowledge you were sorry.

So there was no need for long faces in the visiting locker room.

"Hey, Amos, you can send your bat to Cooperstown," said Wayne Garrett.

"Amos always said he would make the record book," said Bobby Pfeil.

Otis, who struck out four times in an 0-for-5 night, had no choice but to take the ribbing in stride, given the outcome of the evening. "Nobody else is No. 19," he said.

Thanks to the unpredictable, undisciplined hitter nicknamed Rocky—"Swoboda is what happens when a team wins a pennant" was the on-target observation of

METS	ab	r	h	bl	ST. LOUIS	ab	r	h	bl
Harrelson ss	4	0	1	0	Brock lf	4	1	2	0
Otis lf	5	0	0	0	Flood cf	5	2	2	1
Agee cf	4	1	1	0	Pinson rf	4	0	3	1
Clendenon 1b	3	1	1	0	Torre 1b	4	0	1	1
Swoboda rf	4	2	2	4	McCarver c	4	0	0	0
Charles 3b	4	0	0	0	Shannon 3b	4	0	0	0
Grote c	4	0	2	0	Javier 2b	4	0	0	0
Weis 2b	4	0	1	0	Maxvill ss	3	0	0	0
Gentry p	2	0	0	0	BBrowne ph	1	0	0	0
Pfeil ph	1	0	1	0	Carlton p	3	0	0	0
Gosger pr	0	0	0	0	Gagliano ph	1	0	0	0
McGraw p	1	0	0	0	Nossek pr	0	0	0	0
Totals	36	4	9	4	Totals	37	3	8	3

Mets	000	200	020 — 4
St. Louis	001	020	000 — 3

E-Javier, Charles 2, Clendenon, Harrelson. DP-Mets 1. LOB-Mets 7, St. Louis 9. HR-Swoboda 2 (9). SB-Pinson, Brock 2.

	IP	H	R	ER	BB	SO
Mets						
Gentry	6	7	3	3	1	2
McGraw (W, 8-3)	3	1	0	0	1	3
St. Louis						
Carlton (L, 16-10)	9	9	4	4	2	19

WP-Carlton.

T-2:23. A-13,806

Detroit manager Mayo Smith—Carlton would always remember his 19 strikeouts didn't add up to one W.

"I'm stiff . . . sore . . . elated," said Carlton. "It's something no other pitcher has ever done. It's quite an experience. It's a lot of things. It's a lot of big words I don't know."

And one four-letter word he knew too well: Loss.

A-Mays-ing Willie
Says Hey to Shea

May 14, 1972 in New York

Only the most special athletes wear the mantle of hero and it's not simply because of numbers, not even solely because of the impact they exert on winning. Heroes never disappoint on the grandest stage, saving their bigger-than-life achievements for the dramatic circumstances that make them unforgettable.

When Willie Mays played in a Mets uniform for the first time, back in New York City, which had loved him up close and then from afar, against the Giants, the team of which he was the soul for 21 years, the moment begged for a show of greatness.

Of course, the Willie Mays whom Mets owner Joan Payson had brought back to New York via trade days earlier was an old man (41) and a shell of his Hall of Fame self. He arrived homeless and a .184 hitter in his 49 at-bats as a Giant in 1972. He came back as a first baseman and leadoff man in his debut for the Mets—no longer the 12-time Gold Glove center fielder (running out from under his cap, making basket catches and making underhanded tosses to the infield) and the No. 3 hitter.

Thing is, he was still Willie Mays.

After walking on five pitches and scoring in his first Met at-bat in the first and striking out against Sam McDowell his next time up, Mays, source of many joyous and indelible moments, produced another for the mental scrapbook. In the fifth inning, with the score tied at 4, Mays savaged a 3-and-2 fastball from the Giants' Don Carrithers and hit a tracer over the left-field fence to give the Mets their edge in a 5-4 victory.

The time-capsule shot capped the Mets' second three-game series sweep of San Francisco in two weeks and left a rain-drenched 35,505 fans saluting a player unlike any other before or since or ever.

"I ain't heard nothing like that in a long, long time," said Mays.

As he rounded third, as Mrs. Payson stood and cheered in her private box, Mays couldn't help but look into the Giants' dugout.

"All I could see was 'Giants' on the shirts and I played for that team 21 years," said Mays. "I don't know what they were thinking. But they traded me and maybe they thought I couldn't play anymore."

Mays was back in New York—which he described after the deal as "paradise"—and it was as much an accommodation to him as anything else. The Mets' plan was Willie would see some time at first base and play a bit in center, spelling Tommie Agee. Still, the divorce from the Giants had stirred his pride and now this homer did the same for his memories.

"My first hit as a Met was a home run and my first as a Giant [in 1951] was a home run," he said. "We lost that game to [Warren] Spahn, 3-1 [in the Polo Grounds], but we won the pennant. Wouldn't it be something if we won a pennant this year? That went through my mind."

Mays' 647th homer in a career that would end with him at 660, in his 10,431st official at-bat, was hit so hard rookie Garry Maddox simply turned and watched it land in the Giants' bullpen. Mays collected his 1,860th RBI, tying another Giant great, Mel Ott, for third place on the all-time NL list.

"He hit the goddamn thing so low I thought it would take the top of the fence off," said Bud Harrelson. "Plus, their outfielder out there [Maddox] is nine feet tall."

In his first start as a Met, a creaky, 41-year-old Willie Mays treats the Shea crowd to a glimpse of how a great player seizes the moment as he victimizes the Giants, his ex-team, with a game-deciding home run.

"Unbelievable," said Ken Boswell. "I am sitting on the bench watching him go around the bases and all I can think is 'That is Willie Mays.'"

Even Willie Mays is prone to a case of the nerves, like the rest of us mortals. The difference lies in the fact that he makes them *work for him*. Mays did not appear immediately following the trade. The night before his eventual debut, Mets fans screamed for Willie to pinch-hit in the eighth inning and booed manager Yogi Berra's choice of John Milner. Before taking the field for this rainy day game, Mays was so tense that he did not talk to reporters or discuss baseball with his teammates.

"I was so nervous," he said, "I didn't think I would hit the baseball."

When Mays took the field, he said to umpire Mel Steiner, "Is that first base?" and pointed to the bag. His first warmup throw, before the game, went over third baseman Jim Fregosi's head.

His first time up, Mays sat on a first-pitch fastball from McDowell but fouled it off, then became the first of three consecutive Mets to walk in front of Rusty Staub. On an 0-and-1 pitch, Rusty exploded out of an 0-for-16 slide that had cost him 57 points in his average by crushing a grand slam off the scoreboard in right-center. The Mets led, 4-0, but Ray Sadecki—who would end up

SAN FRANCISCO	ab	r	h	bl	METS	ab	r	h	bl
Speier ss	5	1	1	1	Mays 1b	2	2	1	1
Fuentes 2b	4	1	4	2	Harrelson ss	3	1	0	0
Bonds rf	5	0	0	0	Agee cf	2	1	0	0
Kingman 1b	4	0	0	0	Staub rf	3	1	1	4
Henderson cf	4	0	0	0	Jones lf	4	0	0	0
Hart 3b	4	0	2	0	Fregosl 3b	3	0	1	0
Maddox lf	4	0	1	0	Martinez 2b	3	0	1	0
Healy c	1	1	0	0	Grote c	2	0	0	0
Rader c	1	0	0	0	Sadecki p	2	0	0	0
McDowell p	1	0	0	0	McAndrew p	1	0	0	0
Williams ph	1	1	1	1					
Carrithers p	0	0	0	0					
Howarth ph	1	0	0	0					
Barr p	0	0	0	0					
Gallagher ph	1	0	0	0					
Totals	36	4	9	4	Totals	25	5	4	5

San Francisco	000	040	000	— 4
Mets	400	010	00x	— 5

DP-San Francisco 2. LOB-San Francisco 8, Mets 3, 2B-Fuentes 2, Fregosl, Speier, Maddox, 3B-Williams. HRs-Staub (3), Fuentes (2), Mays (1). SB-Agee.

	IP	H	R	ER	BB	SO
San Francisco						
McDowell	4	2	4	4	4	7
Carrithers (L, 1-3)	1	1	1	1	2	1
Barr	3	1	0	0	1	5
Mets						
Sadecki (W, 1-0)	5	6	4	4	2	2
McAndrew	4	3	0	0	1	2

Save-McAndrew.

T-2:21. A-35,505.

with his first win of the year, courtesy of Jim McAndrew's scoreless relief work—couldn't hang on to his stake.

In the fifth, Fran Healy—yes, he played, once upon a time—walked, pinch-hitter Bernie Williams tripled to drive in a run, Chris Speier doubled in another and Tito Fuentes clubbed a two-run homer for a 4-4 tie. Then, leading off the bottom half, Mays turned the clock back two decades and caught up with Carrithers.

"Just watching him do it gave me a thrill," said Fregosi, who had precious few thrills and provided even fewer as a Met.

"On a scale of 1-to-10 for drama, I would have to rate that homer about a 12," said Harrelson.

"You couldn't write a script better than that, could you?" said Giant coach and former Mays teammate Joey Amalfitano. "Dammit. I would pay to see that guy play."

Mays walked in the seventh and was thrown out at second when he incorrectly thought he saw a hit-and-run sign.

"He was mad at himself," said Berra.

But there was one more big moment left for Willie.

It came in the eighth inning, when shortstop Harrelson nearly threw away Dave Rader's grounder, toward the inside of first base. Willie, the novice first baseman, gloved it at his considerable peril and made a sweep tag on Rader.

No big deal.

"He made a helluva play," said Harrelson. "It was a bad throw, but he didn't think anything of it. He thought it was routine."

More accurately, he thought it was necessary and he responded.

"That man gets on, it's a bad spot," said Mays, who hit .267 for the Mets with eight homers and 19 RBI that season but had five game-winning hits in 88 games. "It's just a play that had to be made that way."

"I think the kid is going to be all right," said Harrelson.

Eight Crackling Hours, Then Fireworks

METS 16, BRAVES 13

July 4, 1985 in Atlanta

Howard Johnson somehow crammed into a seven-word nutshell six hours, 10 minutes of unforgettable baseball that lasted more than eight hours of actual time and ended at 3:55 a.m.—after 29 runs, 46 hits, 19 innings, 155 official at-bats, 43 players used, 37 left on base, 23 strikeouts and 22 walks.

And, if you were one of the survivors of the saga of Mets 16, Braves 13, you knew HoJo's words were hyperbole-free.

"That was the greatest game ever played," said Johnson. "Ever."

"I saw everything tonight," said 12-year major leaguer Keith Hernandez, whose 12th-inning single made him the fourth Met to hit for a cycle (4-for-10 and three RBI). "I saw things I had never seen in my career before."

During the marathon, Hernandez decided to visit with somebody via Ma Bell, though it is not certain whom. He said to reporters, "There is no way to describe how tired I am. I called my brother [in San Francisco] in the 17th and I said, 'Gary, if I have to be up at 3 in the morning, so do you.'"

In his book, Mex wrote that he called his new girlfriend in New York to wake her. Maybe, he called both of them. Maybe, it was a conference call.

"I got to bat 11 times tonight. Do you know what it's like to play baseball at 3:30 in the morning?" said Lenny Dykstra. "Real strange, man."

The start of the contest was pushed back by an 81-minute rain delay, then there was another of 41 minutes in the third, which ended Dwight Gooden's night after 2⅓ innings. The ace was working on three days' rest to get him three starts before the All-Star break and manager Davey Johnson didn't want Doc to warm up a third time. The fact that Gooden had already walked four, including three consecutively, might have been a factor, too.

The Braves raked a wild Jesse Orosco and Doug Sisk (a three-run double by Dale Murphy) for four runs in the eighth to turn a 7-4 deficit into an 8-7 lead, but the Mets reached Bruce Sutter for the tying run in the ninth on pinch singles by Johnson and Danny Heep and an RBI infield hit by Dysktra.

And the fun was just beginning.

Twice, the Mets handed a lead to Tom Gorman in the extra innings. Twice, the Braves tied the game with two-out home runs. Twice, they came on 0-and-2 counts.

Terry Harper re-tied the game at 10 with his shot, off the foul pole, after HoJo had given the Mets a 10-8 lead with a two-run homer in the top of the 13th, off Terry Forster.

In the 17th, both Darryl Strawberry and his manager were thrown out of the game by home-plate umpire Terry Tata when they disputed a called third strike that wasn't even in the neighborhood of the plate.

"I told him it wasn't even close and all he said was, 'It's 3 a.m. and that makes it a strike,'" said Strawberry.

After Rick Camp's throwing error had led to Dykstra's sac fly and an 11-10 Met lead in the 18th, it was up to Gorman to find the only way to top his 13th-inning failure to nail this game down. With two out, none on, Gorman found himself facing the hapless Camp, an .060 career hitter at the time who wound up at .074. Obviously, Atlanta manager Eddie Haas was out of pinch-hitters.

Hernandez went to the mound and later he said he told Gorman, "I know you've had trouble with pitchers. But that was last year. This is this year. Let's get him."

After getting ahead of Camp with a couple of strikes, Gorman threw a cripple of a pitch. The relief pitcher hit it beyond Heep's reach and over the fence in left field for a game-re-tying homer.

Heep was left with his hands and glove over his head as if he had taken a bullet.

Dykstra fell to his knees.

According to Hernandez, when the Mets returned to the dugout, Gorman said to him, "I didn't know that [Braves' reliever Gene] Garber had that kind of power."

It was the only homer of Camp's 175 at-bat career.

"It's not like pitchers don't hit home runs; they do," said eventual winning pitcher Gorman. "But, in that situation, with two strikes and no balls, and you give the guy a pitch he can hit out, it's embarrassing . . . There is no way to describe the anger and embarrassment I felt."

Camp, raked for five runs in the 19th for his trouble, wasn't giddy about his muscle flexing.

"I couldn't care less about the homer," he said. "That was luck, pure luck. If we have to rely on me to hit a home run to win a game, we're in bad shape."

More accurately, if they have to rely on Camp to hit a home run to re-tie a game, they're in bad shape.

"After Campy hit it, I figured, 'This has got to be our night,'" said Murphy.

But the Mets, on their way to a club-record 28 hits, hung up that five spot and assumed a 16-11 lead in the 19th as Camp pitched like a hitter. Gary Carter started it with his fifth hit. After a sac bunt, Rusty

Staub was intentionally walked. Knight untied it with a run-scoring double. Then came a two-run single by Heep and a single by Wally Backman and an error by Claudell Washington.

Knight had left the bases loaded three times in a game that saw the Mets strand 20 and the Braves 17. He was, well, gratified by his game-winning hit, testifying, "I don't think I've ever been more excited about one base hit in my whole career."

Gorman was done after six innings and starter Ron Darling came on for the bottom of the 19th, his first relief appearance since his freshman year at Yale.

Boolah. Boolah.

"It was a game everyone on this team will remember," said Darling. "I'm just glad I got my name in the boxscore."

Darling was glad he got his name in the boxscore without an L next to it, because, incredibly, there were nervous moments.

With one out, Hernandez misplayed Washington's grounder. With two out, there was a walk to Murphy and a walk to Gerald Perry and a two-run single by Harper. The potential tying run was walking to the plate, with the score 16-13.

The crowd was chanting, "We want Camp. We want Camp."

They got him. After all, Haas hadn't come up with any extra pinch-hitters since the 18th.

"When Camp came to the plate, I jumped into the shower," said Davey Johnson, back in the clubhouse watching on TV thanks to Tata. "There was no way I could watch any more."

Darling threw a 2-and-2 pitch past Camp, who struck out 85 times in those 175 career at-bats.

It was over, over later than any major league game had ended before. Count two hours and five minutes of rain delays and it was eight hours and 15 minutes worth of diamond theater of the absurd. Next came the scheduled 10-minute, post-game holiday fireworks display at 4:01 a.m., to the appreciation of the 800 hearty souls left from a crowd of 44,947 at Fulton County Stadium.

The Mets boarded their bus to the hotel at about 4:30.

Carter caught the entire game. "What a game to catch, what a way to start a road trip," he said. "I love it."

Third-string Met catcher Ronn Reynolds was the only position player not employed. No doubt Reynolds wondered how long it would have to go before he saw daylight, figuratively. Probably longer than it would have taken for him to see daylight, literally.

"I've never pitched before at 3 a.m., but they've never hit before at 3 a.m., either," reasoned Gorman.

Someone reminded Rick Mahler that he had started the game for Atlanta.

"I did?" he said.

METS	ab	r	h	bl	ATLANTA	ab	r	h	bl
Dykstra cf	9	1	3	2	CWashington rf	8	3	3	0
Backman 2b	10	2	4	2	RRamirez ss	9	2	3	2
Hernandez 1b	10	3	4	3	Murphy cf	8	1	1	3
Carter c	9	1	5	2	Horner 1b	4	1	1	0
Strawberry rf	7	0	3	1	Perry 1b	4	0	0	0
Christensen rf	0	0	0	0	Harper lf	10	3	5	4
Foster lf	2	0	0	0	Oberkfell 3b	6	1	3	2
Orosco p	0	0	0	0	Camp p	2	1	1	1
Sisk p	1	0	0	0	Cerone c	4	1	1	1
Chapman ph	1	0	0	0	Hall pr	0	0	0	0
Gorman p	2	0	0	0	Benedict c	2	0	0	0
Staub ph	0	1	0	0	Hubbard 2b	3	0	0	0
Darling p	0	0	0	0	Shields p	0	0	0	0
Knight 3b	10	2	3	1	Komminsk ph	1	0	0	0
Santana ss	4	1	1	0	Sutter p	0	0	0	0
HJohnson ss	5	4	3	2	Chambliss ph	1	0	0	0
Gooden p	1	0	0	0	Forster p	1	0	0	0
McDowell p	0	0	0	0	Garber p	1	0	0	0
Hurdle ph	1	0	0	0	Runge 3b	2	0	0	0
Leach p	2	0	0	0	Mahler p	1	0	0	0
Heep lf	6	1	2	2	Dedmon p	1	0	0	0
					Zuvella 2b	7	0	0	0
Totals	**80**	**16**	**28**	**15**	**Totals**	**75**	**13**	**18**	**13**

Mets	100	401	011	000	200	001	5 — 16
Atlanta	102	010	040	000	200	001	2 — 13

Game Winning RBI-Knight (1) E-RRamirez, HJohnson, Camp, Hernandez, CWashington. DP-Mets 1, Atlanta 3. LOB-Mets 20, Atlanta 17. 2B-Hernandez, Oberkfell, Murphy, THarper, Knight. 3B-CWashington, Hernandez. HR-Hernandez (5), HJohnson (3), THarper (8), Camp (1). SB-Backman (9), Strawberry (8). S-Backman, Christensen. SF-Dykstra.

Mets	IP	H	R	ER	BB	SO
Gooden	2⅓	2	2	2	4	3
McDowell	⅔	2	1	1	0	1
Leach	4	4	1	1	0	3
Orosco	⅔	1	4	4	3	1
Sisk	4⅓	3	0	0	1	0
Gorman (W, 4-3)	6	5	3	3	2	2
Darling	1	1	2	0	2	1
Atlanta						
Mahler	3⅓	6	3	3	4	2
Dedmon	2	5	3	3	0	1
Shields	2⅔	4	1	1	1	1
Sutter	1	3	1	1	0	1
Forster	4	3	2	2	1	3
Garber	3	1	0	0	2	2
Camp (L, 2-4)	3	6	6	5	2	2

PB-Carter.

T- 6:10. A-44,947

Zip through a Straw

October 1, 1985 in St. Louis

It was a bigger-than-life home run by a bigger-than-life talent with bigger-than-life demons.

The most memorable and one of the longest of Darryl Strawberry's 252 regular-season homers as a Met was launched when he still had a chance to be everything that his fans wanted him to become. No, not "the black Ted Williams"—the absurd label given to this unscientific hitter before Straw had even appeared in the majors.

A 500-home run hitter.

Three seasons into the Met portion of a long, sad, winding baseball career held hostage by a death wish, Darryl still wore the look of a Hall of Famer. Although other players played smarter, showed more focus and proved more committed to improving themselves, few had Darryl's gifts. The Straw could stir the Mets like no other.

A special player. A special name. A special homer.

The Mets were three games out with six to go, facing a bitter end in the opener of a three-game showdown that would write the last chapter in a desperate battle for first with St. Louis. The game was still scoreless in the 11th inning when Strawberry hit a homer as majestic

213

as any he had hit and as meaningful as any he would ever hit. It silenced the hostile crowd of 46,026 at Busch Stadium with the suddenness of a bullet to the head.

Ron Darling and John Tudor had staged a brilliant duel amid the numbing tension, but both were gone by the time Straw struck. After Cardinals' reliever Ken Dayley fanned Keith Hernandez and Gary Carter back-to-back to elicit crowd euphoria, the lefty faced Strawberry.

Southpaws were usually an overwhelming obstacle for this free swinger, who never harnessed his power to the opposite field. However, this time, Dayley hung a 1-and-1 curve—an eye-high deuce—and Darryl hung the Cardinals by pulling it.

You could hear it scream as Busch went mute.

"With a power hitter, you can't make the mistake of getting the ball up," said Strawberry.

Darryl's 28th homer took only about 1.5 seconds to come down, crashing into the bottom of the scoreboard in right center, near the digital clock (the time of the Cards' death was 10:44 CDT), beyond the farthest seats. It was a huge shot in the arm for a Met team in need of nothing less than a series sweep to leave behind its respirator.

"I can't remember hitting a home run this important since high school," said Strawberry, evoking his days as a Crenshaw High legend in Los Angeles. "I saw the pitch up in my zone and, I swear, my eyes lit up. It was a mistake pitch.

"You want to be up there in that situation. You want to help. You're happy a guy like Tudor is gone. And then you suddenly see it there."

Hernandez estimated that the homer would have travelled 500 feet if the scoreboard hadn't gotten in the way.

"It was still sailing when it hit the scoreboard," noted the former beloved Cardinal, now a much-booed villain in St. Louis.

Cards outfielder Andy Van Slyke said he had seen longer from Strawberry.

"He hit one in Little Rock [Ark.], when we were playing in the minors, over a fence that was 410 feet away and had a 60- to 70-foot wall. He hit that one onto the highway," said Van Slyke. "This ball was just taking off. I would say it was over 500 feet. It still had some jack. I would say he was probably looking for a breaking ball in that situation."

"Distance doesn't mean anything to me," said Strawberry, with a slugger's poker face.

The man *beat the clock*. Literally.

"Does the clock still work?" asked Darling.

"If the clock is a Timex, we now officially know that they take a licking and keep on ticking," said the Mets' good humor man, Clint Hurdle.

"You cannot hit a ball any harder," noted Mets manager Davey Johnson.

Or hang on any more doggedly than the Mets did to their final contending breaths.

Tudor's ERA against the Mets in 1985 was an astonishing 0.93. He had won 20 coming in, 10 of them in a row, and had been on the happy recap side in 19 of his previous 20 decisions. Tudor also had 10 shutouts under his belt—including a 1-0, 10-inning win at Shea Sept. 11.

The lefty was originally supposed to pitch the middle game of the series Wednesday. However, when Davey Johnson announced 23-game-winner Gooden would be in the slot opposite Tudor Wednesday, St. Louis manager Whitey Herzog said that he would rule the matchups by throwing his ace in the opener if Darling was warming up and throwing Danny Cox, his intended starter for the finale, if Gooden was warming.

"You avoid your best pitcher going against Gooden, especially when you have a three-game lead going in," said Herzog. "I'd hate to send Tudor against Gooden and lose, 1-0. I might lose, 1-0, with him in the opener, but that's a chance I have to take . . . If I was three games back, you'd see Tudor against Gooden . . . As it is, if we win one game, we are in pretty good shape."

Under much heat, Johnson pointed out that while others said going with Darling (16-5) was a gamble, it was an obvious choice to him. Why move Gooden up (he would still have his normal four days' rest) when the Mets needed to take all three games, not just the first? And what would jerking Darling out of his spot say about the manager's confidence level in his No. 2 starter?

"I knew I had to somehow match zeroes with Tudor," said Darling.

So, he did. Darling used a sinking fastball to match Tudor pitch for pitch as the tension built, throwing nine innings of blanks and permitting just four hits compared to Tudor's six-hit work over 10 scoreless innings.

"He [Darling] was the star of the game," said Hernandez. "Ron pitched the game of his life . . . Anyone who said he isn't a tough pitcher can't say it any longer."

"He was at his best," said the Cards' usually clutch-hitting Tommy Herr, who stranded runners in scoring position his first two trips and went 0-for-5.

However, Darling was at his worst when he was asked to lay down a suicide squeeze bunt in the seventh.

With one out, Ray Knight hit a looping single and then Rafael Santana ripped a shot off Tudor's left foot that ricocheted into right field for a double. Howard Johnson pinch-ran for Knight and the hitter was the usually proficient bunter, Darling. On the second pitch, Darling bunted at a low and inside changeup and missed it, hanging out the charging HoJo to dry.

"I felt pretty bad," said Darling. "Thank God, it didn't mean a thing [ultimately]."

"We're going to practice our squeeze plays a little more next spring," said Davey Johnson. "Maybe a lot more."

In the ninth, it was Strawberry's lack of prowess as a situational hitter that cost the Mets, after a leadoff, opposite-field double by Carter. Needing a grounder to the second-base side, Straw lifted a foul popup that was dropped because of a collision between third baseman Terry Pendleton and catcher Darrell Porter. Then Darryl fanned, spectating at a changeup, and Tudor escaped after striking out Johnson and getting Santana on a grounder.

Ron Darling pitched his masterpiece, matching zeroes with the Cards' John Tudor. Darling, in the face of must-win pressure, helped keep the Mets even until Darryl Strawberry literally beat the clock and silenced Busch Stadium.

"Tudor overmatched us the last time and he overmatched us again tonight," said Strawberry. "He didn't make any mistakes."

"You come back to the bench asking yourself, 'Can Tudor really be this good?'" said Wally Backman.

In the 10th, Jesse Orosco replaced Darling on the mound and survived a mini-nightmare. Pinch-hitter Cesar Cedeño walked and stole second. Later, with two out, Orosco intentionally walked Tito Landrum to get to Vince Coleman. Except Coleman didn't hit. Injured St. Louis slugger Jack Clark did.

On the first pitch of his first at-bat since a game-winning homer against Montreal 10 days earlier, Clark ignored his aching ribs and lashed a screaming liner foul down the left-field line. But he wound up flying out to Strawberry in right.

After Strawberry gave the Mets the lead in the 11th, there was a major scare. With one out, Mookie Wilson, playing deep on Herr, overran a flyball to short center and dropped it off his thigh for a two-base error that put the potential tying run a single away from being realized.

"I had a long way to go," said Mookie. "And when I saw Wally, I thought he had a chance."

But Backman never bothered to check Wilson's positioning and therefore the second baseman "really didn't go too hard for it."

Herr went to third on Brian Harper's infield out, but Ivan DeJesus flied out to Wilson to end the game.

"My heart is still up in my throat," said Davey Johnson.

The Mets were two games out with five left and Gooden would oppose 21-game winner Joaquin Andujar the next day.

Who was the pressure on now?

"Who the bleep is in first place?" said Herzog.

"Yeah, but who has to face Doc?" said Strawberry.

"I know one thing: he

METS	ab	r	h	bl	ST. LOUIS	ab	r	h	bl
MWilson cf	5	0	0	0	Coleman lf	3	0	0	0
Backman 2b	5	0	0	0	JClark ph	1	0	0	0
Hernandez 1b	4	0	1	0	Dayley p	0	0	0	0
Carter c	5	0	1	0	McGee cf	5	0	2	0
Strawberry rf	5	1	1	1	Herr 2b	5	0	0	0
Foster lf	4	0	1	0	Porter c	4	0	0	0
Knight 3b	3	0	2	0	BHarper ph	1	0	0	0
HJohnson 3b	2	0	0	0	Van Slyke rf	4	0	1	0
Santana ss	3	0	1	0	DeJesus ph	1	0	0	0
Darling p	3	0	1	0	Pendleton 3b	4	0	1	0
Paciorek ph	1	0	0	0	Jorgensen 1b	1	0	0	0
Orosco p	0	0	0	0	Cedeño 1b	0	0	0	0
					OSmith ss	4	0	0	0
					Tudor p	3	0	0	0
					Landrum lf	0	0	0	0
Totals	40	1	8	1	Totals	36	0	4	0

Mets	000	000	000	01	— 1
St. Louis	000	000	000	00	— 0

Game Winning RBI-Strawberry (8).

E-Pendleton, MWilson. DP-Mets 1. LOB-Mets 9, St. Louis 8. 2B-Santana, Pendleton, Carter. HR-Strawberry (28). SB-McGee (55), Cedeño (13).

	IP	H	R	ER	BB	SO
Mets						
Darling	9	4	0	0	3	5
Orosco (W, 8-6)	2	0	0	0	2	2
St. Louis						
Tudor	10	6	0	0	3	7
Dayley (L, 4-4)	1	2	1	1	0	2

T-3:22. A-46,026.

can't throw any better than the guy did tonight, unless he throws a no-hitter," said Herzog.

Gooden won his 24th game the next night, but the Cardinals beat Rick Aguilera, behind Cox, in the series finale, 4-3, en route to 101 wins. The Mets finished second, at 98-64—but none of the luster was removed from Strawberry's time-stands-still statement.

Take That, Braves: Ten in the Eighth

METS 11, BRAVES 8

June 30, 2000 in New York

Sometimes, a big inning comes along to challenge the imagination without warning—like a torrential late-summer thunderstorm after there had been, with apologies to Bob Murphy, only "wisps of puffy cumulus clouds in the sky." This kind of rally feels like a snowball gaining speed and size going downhill until it produces an avalanche that remains unfathomable even after the winding road to three outs is finally complete.

On Friday night, June 30, 2000, in front of 52,831 at Shea, the Mets set a whole new standard for Amazin' when they climbed out of a canyon the size of Atlanta reliever John Rocker's mouth and wrote a happy ending with a rally that defied belief.

After displaying no signs of life through seven, the Mets matched their all-time most productive inning, turned around a crucial game only four outs from the end and stunned the deep and revered pitching staff of their tormentors, the Braves. Grandfathers will enchant the little ones with the tale of how the Mets scored 10 runs in the eighth inning to overcome an 8-1 deficit and pin an 11-8 shocker on the Braves and the geezers won't have to make up or enhance a thing.

The damage was done on six hits and four consecutive walks—three with the bases loaded.

Nine of the runs scored with two out and 13 hitters got a chance to swing or not swing.

"That was one of the most unlikely innings I have ever seen," said Mets manager Bobby Valentine, who would've liked to have been able to say he planned it exactly that way. "In the minors, I once saw a team score 10 runs with two outs, two strikes and nobody on. And there were no walks and no errors. But that was the minors. This is the majors."

If you harbor doubts that this time-capsule beauty merits its spot at or near the head of the Ripley's Believe It or Not, Flushing Division, consider the following:

1. The Mets had lost 19 of 25 to the Braves after having a seven-game winning streak snapped by Atlanta in the series opener the night before. And those nasty head-to-head numbers didn't even include the Mets' four losses in a six-game NLCS the previous October.

2. The Mets, who had their seven-game winning streak snapped by Atlanta in the series opener the night before, had shown no detectable pulse against Kevin Millwood.

3. The Mets had been let down by ace Mike Hampton (nine hits, six walks, five runs in seven innings) and were buried in that yawning 8-1 hole when Atlanta got three runs off Eric Cammack in the eighth.

How low did the Mets go before bouncing back to the heights? Well, the crowd was actually calling for the much-reviled John Rocker, sociologist/philosopher king/closer, to put the Mets out of their misery or perhaps just to offer some much-needed entertainment.

"We were down there, no doubt," said Valentine. "We were in trouble, but that was erased."

With Jason Marquis having worked two innings in the opener and lefty Mike Remlinger fresh from an MRI on his elbow, Don Wengert took over for Millwood at the start of the eighth. Braves manager

Bobby Cox, being of sound mind, figured his starter was no longer needed to protect a seven-run lead after allowing six hits and one run through 112 pitches.

"Millwood said he was out of gas," said Braves pitching coach Leo Mazzone.

Derek Bell opened the inning with a single and Mike Piazza followed with a one-out single before an error advanced the runners so Bell could score to make it 8-2 on a Robin Ventura groundout. Now the Mets were an out away from being done in the eighth and the heart of the order already had been dispatched.

What better time to kick it into gear?

Todd Zeile and Jay Payton singled to make it 8-3 and finish Wengert. Now the crowd was chanting, again, for the Big Apple-bashing Rocker. But the villain, unbeknownst to the fans, was unavailable because of a callus on the pitching thumb.

So Kerry Ligtenberg, the former closer for the Braves, entered and committed the highest sin a pitcher can commit when his team is swimming in runs. Instead of forcing the Mets to hit the ball, Ligtenberg walked everyone he saw: Benny Agbayani to load the bases, Mark Johnson to make it 8-4 and Melvin Mora to give the Mets their fifth run.

Cox went back out and brought in veteran Terry Mulholland, feeling secure the lefty would restore order in plenty of time.

"You keep thinking when you are sitting there, you're going to get the one pitch to get out of it," said Mazzone.

Mulholland walked Bell on a 3-and-1 pitch to make it 8-6 and leave the bases loaded—that meant the two potential game-tying runs were in position for Alfonzo to plate with a single.

Edgardo took ball one, fouled off a pitch and looked for Mulholland's cutter.

"I told myself if I have to hit it with my knuckles, I'll hit with my knuckles—just put it in play and see what happens," said The Fonz.

Sure enough, the Mets' best two-strike hitter and two-out RBI man hit a grounder through the hole into left. Pandemonium—the

Mike Piazza punches the air in defiant glee after nailing a line-drive, three-run, tie-breaking homer to cap a staggering 10-run eighth inning—enough to turn an 8-1 deficit into a victory that left both the Mets and the shocked Braves shaking their heads.

customary byproduct of a joyful moment so shocking that it feels like a joint hallucination—ensued.

Seven runs in. Tie score at 8-8. Piazza, the hammer, up next.

"Mike gets in certain situations where you feel the pitcher is in trouble," said Zeile.

Mulholland opted for a cut fastball and Piazza hit that first pitch off the blue padding above the wall down the line in left field. Gone in an instant, this line drive stayed fair because he hit it so hard it didn't have the time to hook foul. The celebration had to come after the ball's exit, because it disappeared in a blink.

Three-run homer. No parabola. A tracer. A run of the mill, 10-run-rally-capping bomb on Fireworks Night. A cause for fist-pumping if there ever was one.

"I wasn't sure if it was going to hit the wall or go through the wall," said Zeile.

"He did what any good hitter would do with a bad pitch," said Mulholland. "That is not what you want to have happen. You don't want to walk in runs. You don't want to give up home runs . . . Things happen."

"I really, literally, felt like I let my team down," said Rocker, who tried to throw in the seventh and had his callus split open. "It's one open wound."

He was referring to his thumb, not the Braves' hearts, presumably.

"It's horrible to lose a game like that, in one inning," said Braves catcher Javy Lopez. "It's unbelievable, I have never seen a game like this. It was embarrassing."

The Mets had another adjective in mind: invigorating. Only once in team history had the Mets come back to win from a bigger hole (eight runs down to defeat Houston, 11-8, Sept. 2, 1972).

"I didn't expect to come all the way back . . . Pretty exciting inning," said Alfonzo. "We did the little things it takes to come from behind and win a game. We were patient at the plate. That is a sign, a real good sign."

"People will try to downplay it, especially on the other side. It may not decide the pennant, but it's a big plus for us mentally," said Zeile.

"Hopefully, these are the type of wins that get you into the playoffs," said Piazza. "Hopefully, this will relax us a little bit. People always ask why we can't beat the Braves. It's obvious: they have been playing better. They put pressure on us, take extra bases and pitch better."

The slugger's second hit of the eighth inning and 22nd homer of the year allowed him to tie an NL record for most consecutive games with at least one RBI at 13.

To the Mets, it felt appropriate that a remarkable hitter had provided the finishing touch on this unforgettable night.

"He reminds me of Joe DiMaggio," said Braves GM John Schuerholz of Piazza. "He takes that little step of his and he's behind the ball."

ATLANTA	ab	r	h	bl	METS	ab	r	h	bl
QVeras 2b	4	3	2	0	Mora ss	3	1	1	1
AJones cf	4	2	1	0	DeBell rf	4	2	2	1
BJordan rf	5	2	3	3	Alfonzo 2b	5	1	2	2
Galarraga 1b	3	1	1	0	Piazza c	5	2	2	3
Wengert p	0	0	0	0	Ventura 3b	4	0	0	1
Ligtenberg p	0	0	0	0	Zeile 1b	4	2	2	1
Mulholland p	0	0	0	0	Payton cf	4	1	2	0
JLopez c	3	0	2	3	Agbayani lf	3	1	0	0
Bonilla 3b	3	0	0	0	Benitez p	0	0	0	0
Lockhart pr-3b	2	0	1	1	Hampton p	2	0	0	0
Hubbard lf	5	0	0	0	MFranco ph	1	0	1	1
Furcal ss	2	0	0	0	Cammack p	0	0	0	0
Millwood p	3	0	1	0	MkJohnson ph	0	0	0	1
Joyner ph-1b	1	0	0	0	McEwing pr-lf	0	1	0	0
Totals	**35**	**8**	**11**	**7**	**Totals**	**35**	**11**	**12**	**11**

Atlanta	100	000	130	— 6
Mets	000	100	1(10)x	— 11

E-Furcal (14), Mora (3), Piazza (2). LOB-Atlanta 10, Mets 8. 2B-BJordan (12), DeBell (18). HR-Piazza (22) off Mulholland; BJordan (13) off Cammack. RBI- BJordan 3 (48), JLopez 3 (37) Lockhart (11), Mora (24), DeBell (38), Alfonzo 2 (54), Piazza 3 (88), Ventura (52), Zeile (48), MFranco (5), MkJohnson (6). SB-QVeras (22). GIDP-QVeras, Bonilla, Millwood, DeBell. Runners left in scoring position-Atlanta 5 (AJones, Hubbard 3, Joyner); Mets 4 (Mora, Piazza, Ventura). DP-Atlanta 1 (QVeras, Furcal and Galarraga); Mets 3 (Ventura, Alfonzo and Zeile), (Mora Alfonzo and Zeile), (Ventura, Alfonzo and Zeile).

Atlanta	IP	H	R	ER	BB	SO
Millwood	7	6	1	1	2	6
Wengert	²/₃	4	4	4	0	0
Ligtenberg	0	0	3	3	3	0
Mulholland (L, 6-7)	¹/₃	2	3	3	1	0
Mets						
Hampton	7	9	5	5	6	2
Cammack	1	1	3	3	2	1
Benitez (W, 2-3)	1	1	0	0	1	1

Ligtenberg pitched to 3 batters in the 8th. Inherited runners scored-Ligtenberg 2-2, Mulholland 3-3, IBB-off Hampton (JLopez) 1. HBP-Galarraga (by Hampton). WP-Hampton 3. PB-Piazza.

T-3:25. A-52,831

Truly Terrific
Notches 19 Padres

METS 2, PADRES 1

April 22, 1970 in New York

It stacked up as just another April mid-week afternoon game at Shea between a Mets team one year after its glory and a poor San Diego Padres club in its second season of being awful.

That was until Tom Seaver's remarkable right arm stamped this 2-1 Met victory as unforgettable for the hooky players in attendance.

Seaver, showing the closing kick of Secretariat, kept getting stronger as the game wore on. Nursing that one-run lead, the 25-game winner in 1969—who was presented with his NL Cy Young Award before the game—was overwhelming, even for him. Seaver's knee was smeared with dirt the way it always was when his mechanics were just right.

By the middle innings, he reached a very special zone where the Met fielders behind him served the same purpose as the bats the Padres carried to the plate and back—none.

Seaver had only nine strikeouts with two outs in the sixth. By that time, Seaver's closest buddy Bud Harrelson had scored a run in the first on his infield hit and a hit-and-run RBI double by Ken Boswell. But Al

Ferrara—one of the few dangerous bats in the San Diego lineup—had turned around Seaver's 2-and-1 fastball, hitting it off the top of the left-field bullpen wall and over to tie the score in the second.

"Actually, he wasn't that strong in the early innings," said catcher Jerry Grote, who wound up the day with a record 20 putouts. "He just kept building up as the game went on. The cool weather helped and, by the end of the game, he was stronger than ever."

After Harrelson tripled off loser Mike Corkins to drive in Tommie Agee, who had singled, with the go-ahead run in the third, the rest of the day belonged to Seaver. The only other hit off Seaver other than Ferrara's blast was an infield single by Dave Campbell, off third baseman Joe Foy's glove in the fourth.

Seaver's strikeout march began innocuously, when he claimed the last hitter in the sixth for victim No. 10. It had been a strong effort, certainly, but he wasn't even remotely on a pace to challenge the 19-K, nine-inning, major league-record effort of the Cardinals' Steve Carlton in a loss to the Mets, Sept. 15, 1969.

Then again, Seaver was just kicking it into gear.

He struck out the side in the seventh. Then, in the eighth, he mowed down Bob Barton, Ramon Webster and Ivan Murrell—pinch-hitting for slap hitter Jose Arcia, the only starter whom Seaver did not fan in the game. Now Tom Terrific had seven Ks in a row and 16 in all, breaking the club record of teammate Nolan Ryan that was just a few days old.

"Now, Nolan's a strikeout pitcher," said Seaver after posting his 13th straight regular-season victory.

The suggestion was that blowing people away wasn't how Seaver made his living. So what if, in only his third major league season, he was already the Mets' all-time strikeout leader? Who would argue with The Franchise, even when he would joke, with playful humility, that he was the only Met pitcher ever to lose a World Series game?

When the scoreboard informed the fans that Seaver had matched Ryan's record, Tom said that his total at that point came as "a shock" to him.

"I said to myself, 'My God, I can't have that many.' . . . I knew I had a few. I thought I had 10 or 11," said Seaver, who finished that year with 283 strikeouts, only six fewer than the single-season high for his career, posted in 1971.

In the dugout, Seaver was congratulated by his teammates, but he told them to get more runs.

"All I could think of was that Carlton had struck out 19 of us and still lost," he said.

The Mets didn't score any more. Now, all Seaver needed to do to earn the major league record was get all three ninth-inning outs by knockout.

"I felt sure at least someone would bunt," said Ed Kranepool.

Van Kelly was fed three fastballs. He took one strike, then went down swinging at the next two, the last a nasty one that dipped away from him. Cito Gaston had one strike called, couldn't catch up to a heater on the outside corner and then looked at a third-strike heater, making him the 10th Padre to go down watching. Seaver had nine strikeouts in a row, shattering the modern major league record of eight consecutive held by Max Surkont, Johnny Podres, Jim Maloney and Don Wilson.

One more to go . . . and Ferrara stepping in the box as the tying run.

On a day in which he threw 136 pitches, 96 of them for strikes, Seaver wouldn't desert his hard stuff, even against a good fastball hitter who wouldn't be intimidated.

"Him against me, his best shot against my best shot," said Ferrara. "He was going for the strikeout. I was going for the downs."

"When he first came up, I was just thinking about winning the game," said Seaver. "I was still worried I might make a mistake and Ferrara might hit it out."

Slider on the outside corner as Ferrara took a half swing for strike one.

Slider outside as plate umpire Harry Wendelstedt shook his head no.

"That is when I went for the strikeout," said Seaver. "I figure I may never come this close again, I better go after it."

Fastball, swing and a miss.

Now it was time to go for the kill.

Another fastball. Nineteen. Ten in a row.

"The last one I gave him in the ninth was low—just where I wanted it—and he missed it," said Seaver. "The last two innings, I threw better than I did at any time in the game. The adrenaline really was flowing."

He was so overpowering that Podres, San Diego's minor league pitching director, said, "That one groove he hit, he will never throw that hard again in his life."

Seaver found that amusing.

"That was what Ron Santo said last year after that game [his imperfect game] against the Cubs," he said. "Maybe Podres and Santo ought to get together and have dinner."

SAN DIEGO	ab	r	h	bl	METS	ab	r	h	bl
Arcia ss	4	0	0	0	Agee cf	3	1	1	0
Murrell ph	1	0	0	0	Harrelson ss	3	1	2	1
Roberts p	0	0	0	0	Boswell 2b	4	0	1	1
Kelly 3b	4	0	0	0	Jones lf	4	0	0	0
Gaston cf	4	0	0	0	Shamsky rf	2	0	0	0
Ferrara lf	3	1	1	1	Swoboda rf	1	0	0	0
Colbert 1b	3	0	0	0	Foy 3b	2	0	0	0
Campbell 2b	3	0	1	0	Kranepool 1b	2	0	0	0
Morales rf	3	0	0	0	Grote c	3	0	0	0
Barton c	2	0	0	0	Seaver p	3	0	0	0
Corkins p	2	0	0	0					
Webster ph	1	0	0	0					
Slocum ss	0	0	0	0					
Totals	30	1	2	1	Totals	27	2	4	2

San Diego	010	000	000	— 1
Mets	101	000	00X	— 2

LOB-San Diego 3, Mets 6. 2B-Boswell. 3B-Harrelson. HR-Ferrara (1). SB-Agee.

	IP	H	R	ER	BB	SO
San Diego						
Corkins (L, 0-2)	7	4	2	2	5	5
Roberts	1	0	0	0	0	2
Mets						
Seaver (W, 3-0)	9	2	1	1	2	19

T-2:14. A-14,197.

Agee Hands It to Cubs

September 8, 1969 in New York

No Leo Durocher team is going to go quietly and, with the Mets breathing down the Cubs' necks and running as hot as Chicago was cold, this two-game series at Shea quickly delivered on a potential for ugliness. The Cubs' lead, 9½ games Aug. 13, was down to 2½ and melting like the Wicked Witch of the West.

The extracurricular fun on this September night started almost immediately, when Cubs starter Bill Hands sent Met leadoff man Tommie Agee sprawling to escape his first pitch. A time-honored, testosterone-laced message from one team in a pennant race to another had been delivered: "Would you like a cast or a mouthful of dirt?"

Hands' third pitch to Agee was in a similar place, presumably in case the subtlety of the first had escaped the Mets.

Agee couldn't have appreciated the treatment much. He hadn't forgotten how his 1968 season, his first as a Met, became a .217 disaster after, in his first spring at-bat in their uniform, he was beaned by the Cardinals' nasty Bob Gibson.

"They [the Cubs] were trying to run us out of the ballpark," said Agee, who grounded to third in that at-bat and finished the night in a brown uniform with the patch on his left shoulder torn.

The way it turned out, this particular declaration of baseball war didn't end with the kind of surrender that Durocher and Co. had hoped. In this case, the Mets played as if they were pissed off and the payback was double—coming both from Jerry Koosman's arm and Agee's bat in a 3-2 Met victory that extended the Cubs' losing streak to five.

"I went to the mound," Koosman remembered years later, "and I knew what I had to do . . . Nobody was going to intimidate us . . . We protected each other. We were like family."

Koosman followed the ballplayers' code and, when he came after the Cubs' Ron Santo, he didn't miss. Koosman sent the third baseman to get his wrist X-rayed (eventually) with a perfectly placed fastball on the hands in the second. There were no breaks—just a bad bruise above the wrist bone as a souvenir.

"It's a matter of survival," said Koosman. "Agee doesn't have a chance to get even in center field. His way of getting even is through the pitcher."

"I don't mind getting knocked down. If you are hitting, they are going to knock you down," reasoned Agee. "The only thing I don't like is if we don't retaliate."

"After that [Koosman response], nobody would intimidate us," said coach Joe Pignatano. "And I don't think Santo clicked his heels [his victory-gloat pirouette noted and not appreciated by the Mets earlier in 1969] after that."

Koosman struck out 13 in the game—including five of the first six Cubs he faced—and raised his season record to 13-9 with the masterpiece. However, it was clear exactly which of the left-hander's pitches was the favorite of Agee and manager Gil Hodges. It was the heater that nailed Santo and screamed, "Gentlemen, we are in this thing together."

"Eddie Stanky [who played for Durocher] told me in the minors, 'If they hit your man, hit three of theirs,'" said Koosman.

"I was hoping Kooz would do the job he is capable of doing," said Hodges, who was certain that the Agee knockdown was deliberate.

"Any one of our pitchers knows what should be done, what is required."

Agee, not content to let Koosman do all the messaging, made his own point to Hands in the third. He crushed his 26th homer of the season, with Bud Harrelson aboard on a single and the Mets had a 2-0 lead.

"I hit one [a homer] on the next pitch after [the Phils' Billy] Champion knocked me down Sunday," said Agee. "I guess they came in and said, 'Let's knock him down and see what he can do.' . . . A lot of times when I get knocked down, I get so mad I try to hit the ball too hard. But I'm not as emotional as I used to be.

"A game like this is supposed to bring out the best in a professional. Maybe if you are playing Montreal, you figure you'll win, anyway. But I have been thinking about this game all day long, what I have to do."

Held to one hit through five, the Cubs tied the score in the sixth. Singles by Don Kessinger and Glenn Beckert were followed by Billy Williams' RBI ground single past second baseman Ken Boswell into right on a 2-and-2 curve that was hung by Koosman. Finally, a sac fly to the track in left from Santo—he barely missed a homer statement of his own—made it 2-2.

Now, Agee had to go back to work to get the go-ahead run for the pitcher who had stepped up on his behalf. He slashed a hit past Santo into left leading off the sixth and kept going, stretching it into a double with a belly slide when he correctly concluded that the wet outfield grass would slow Williams' pursuit.

"My roomie plays winning ball," said the injury-idled Cleon Jones of Agee. "He does what he has to do."

When Wayne Garrett pulled the ball through the hole between first and second for a single, ex-Met Jim Hickman charged it in right and fired home to make a play on Agee. The throw was a bit up the third-base line on a bounce. Catcher Randy Hundley, known to a future generation of Met fans as Todd's dad, had to make a lunging tag attempt at the sliding Agee.

Umpire Dave Davidson said safe. Hundley said a few things to Davidson. Way to go wasn't one of them.

"I know I tagged him. I felt the impact," said Hundley. "The ball was in the webbing of my glove. I don't know where I tagged him, but I know I did."

"He wanted me to be out so bad, he thought he touched me," said Agee.

"I couldn't believe they called him safe," said Hundley. "He almost knocked the ball out of my mitt. It was just hanging on the edge."

The 3-2 lead barely survived the eighth, when Beckert singled to right and Williams' high bouncer over the mound went for an infield hit. But Santo bounced into a 6-4-3 double play. Then Koosman struck out Ernie Banks swinging on a fastball with the potential tying run 90 feet away.

"I got Santo on a fastball and I am mighty glad he didn't hit the pitch before that," said Koosman. "It was a bad curve and if he had leaned into it, he would have probably hit it out."

In the bottom of the eighth, it was open season on Koosman. Hands, who was 16-13 after the loss, made his mound opponent dive for cover with an inside pitch.

Not smart. You would think the Cubs would have learned by now.

Koosman struck out the side to strand the tying run in the ninth, a "take that" supplied by a rush of adrenaline in a tired left arm.

By now, even such a noted Met detractor as Santo—who had predicted the Mets

CHICAGO	ab	r	h	bl	METS	ab	r	h	bl
Kessinger ss	4	1	2	0	Agee cf	3	2	2	2
Beckert 2b	4	1	2	0	Garrett 3b	4	0	1	1
Williams lf	4	0	2	1	Clendenon 1b	4	0	0	0
Santo 3b	2	0	0	1	Shamsky lf	2	0	1	0
Banks 1b	3	0	0	0	Gaspar lf	0	0	0	0
Hickman rf	3	0	0	0	Boswell 2b	3	0	0	0
Hundley c	4	0	1	0	Weis 2b	0	0	0	0
Young cf	3	0	0	0	Swoboda rf	3	0	0	0
Rudolph ph	1	0	0	0	Grote c	3	0	0	0
Hands p	3	0	0	0	Harrelson ss	3	1	1	0
Bobb ph	1	0	0	0	Koosman p	3	0	0	0
Totals	32	2	7	2	Totals	28	3	5	3

Chicago	000	002	000 — 2
Mets	002	001	00X — 3

E-Kessinger. DP-Chicago 2, Mets 1. LOB-Chicago 7, Mets 3. 2B-Agee. HR-Agee (26). SF-Santo.

	IP	H	R	ER	BB	SO
Chicago						
Hands (L, 16-13)	8	5	3	3	2	5
Mets						
Koosman (W, 13-9)	9	7	2	2	2	13

HBP-Santo (by Koosman). WP-Koosman.

T-2:09. A-43,274.

would fold during the summer—was convinced the threat they posed was serious. The sliding Cubs' pursuers were 1½ games out, with 19 wins in their last 25 games.

"All right, I eat my words," said Santo. "They have shown me, but I still feel we have the best ballclub. When I said what I did everybody was making a big thing about the Mets and it was too early. I don't think anyone believed it. I'm the first to say they are there because they deserve to be there. They proved it to me by beating the teams they had to beat. I didn't think they could."

Santo's admission probably hurt more than his wrist.

Night of Fists and Firsts

METS 6, REDS 3

July 22, 1986 in Cincinnati

The 1986 Mets had that certain swagger, reflecting the arrogance of their manager Davey Johnson, and were much disliked in dugouts around the NL for their style and their substance, too. Collectively, they wore a chip on their shoulder through a 108-win regular season and weren't bashful about having an occasional fight to keep it there.

On this wild night in Cincinnati, a fight between ex-Red Ray Knight and Eric Davis—the Mets' fourth altercation of the season—became a brawl that cleared the benches (except for George Foster, whose conscientious objector behavior was objectionable to many of his Met teammates). The hostilities, spicy in themselves, turned out to be nothing more than a jumping-off point for the most remarkable aspects of this wild 6-3 Met victory that:

1. was prolonged by a two-run, game-tying, ninth-inning error on a flyball that defied Dave Parker's reach;
2. featured the ejections of five players and one coach;
3. was protested by both teams;
4. was punctuated by catcher Gary Carter's impersonation of Brooks Robinson;

5. took 14 innings to decide, on Howard Johnson's three-run homer off Ted Power and
6. featured the outfield debuts of relievers Roger McDowell and Jesse Orosco.

Truly Amazin' even by Mets' standards.

"Strangest game I have ever been involved with," said Davey Johnson. "Even stranger than Atlanta [the July 4, 1985 19-inning marathon in which Tom Gorman turned Rick Camp into Hank Aaron and which did not end until 3:55 a.m.]."

Bobby Ojeda's bid for his 12th victory was ruined by homers from Parker and Buddy Bell. Reds' rookie starter Scott Terry was ahead, 3-1, and one out away from his first major league win when things got weird.

With Mets on second and third in the ninth inning—Johnson had reached on a called third strike that he then kicked away from catcher Bo Diaz and Tim Teufel doubled off Ron Robinson—Keith Hernandez lofted Cincinnati closer John Franco's pitch to right center.

Parker could be counted on to catch this kind of flyball 99 out of 100 times.

Not this time.

"I was playing in to try to get a play on Teufel," said the Cincinnati right fielder. "I went back and stumbled a little bit, but regained my balance. Then it hit the top of my glove . . . I should have caught the damn ball and then none of the other shit would have happened."

In the 10th inning, Davis—who had been out of the lineup with a bruised hand—entered as a pinch-runner for Pete Rose, who had singled as a pinch-hitter. Eric stole second and then third as Eddie Milner was striking out for the second out. As Davis sprung up from his pop-up slide, Knight and Davis exchanged shoves. A nudge from a Davis elbow earned him a nasty right hand to the side of the face thrown by Sugar Ray.

"He slides so hard, because he is so fast. He made contact and elbowed me coming around," said Knight, a former Golden Gloves boxer. "He jumped up and said, 'You pushed me.' I said that I didn't.

And he said, 'Don't you ever push me again, blah, blah, blah' and started moving forward. I saw in his eyes he was mad and I punched him. It was just reaction. In 10 years, I've never, not one time, played dirty."

"It had to be the best punch of the year," wrote Lenny Dykstra in his book later. "Davis just spun around. He was bleeping clueless, man."

Davis left without talking to reporters after the game, but Parker said, "It was triggered by Knight. He pushed Davis off the base. That is the second time in the series that it has happened."

"I am at peace with myself about it," said Knight. "I don't like to fight with anybody, but I felt threatened . . ."

Knight and Davis were ejected from the game. So were Reds' starting pitcher Mario Soto, the Mets' Kevin Mitchell and Cincinnati coach Billy DeMars. Strawberry already had been tossed by umpire Gerry Davis, for protesting a called third strike in the sixth inning.

Davey Johnson filed an official protest concerning losing two position players to the Reds' one in the fight. Johnson's only remaining available non-pitcher was catcher Ed Hearn, so Carter went from behind the plate to third as Knight's sub.

As if Carter's first appearance at third base since 1975 (when he was an Expo) wasn't bizarre enough, Orosco was sent to right field to be Mitchell's replacement and McDowell entered to retire Wade Rowdon to end the 10th. Johnson rotated Orosco and McDowell, according to individual batting matchups (to get lefty vs. lefty and righty vs. righty), and attempted to hide whichever pitcher was pretending to be an outfielder by putting him in right against righty hitters and left against lefties.

The Reds filed their protest when Orosco was allowed to take warmups again after he switched with McDowell in the 11th—and struck out Max Venable with a runner at second to escape a jam.

Before the night was over, McDowell had played right and left and threw the final two innings to notch the win. Orosco—who had gone from the mound to right, to the mound and to right again—could even tell his future grandchildren that he had made a putout.

Jesse caught Tony Perez' flyball in the 13th.

"When I found out I was going to the outfield after the fight, I was just laughing," said Orosco. "That was a thrill for both of us playing the outfield . . . But I better stay on the mound. I am less nervous out there."

The Reds had runners in scoring position in the ninth, 10th, 11th and 12th. In the 12th, with Reds at first and second and none out, pitcher Carl Willis bunted into a 3-5-4 double play that was turned nicely by the middle man, Carter. Carter also made a fine, charging play on Ron Oester's bunt in the 11th and a great diving stop of Bell's leadoff bouncer in the 12th—although it wound up being an infield hit.

In the 14th, Hearn hit a double and Orosco walked before Johnson launched a 2-and-2 curve from Power for a three-run homer to

METS	ab	r	h	bl	CINCINNATI	ab	r	h	bl
Dykstra cf	7	1	1	1	Venable cf	5	0	1	0
Backman 2b	3	0	0	0	Bell 3b	6	1	3	1
Teufel 2b	3	1	1	0	Parker rf	5	1	2	2
KHernandez 1b	5	0	3	0	BDiaz c	4	0	0	0
Carter c-3b	6	0	0	0	Franco p	0	0	0	0
Strawberry rf	2	0	0	0	Rose ph	1	0	1	0
Mitchell rf	2	0	0	0	EDavis pr	0	0	0	0
Hearn c	2	1	1	0	Browning pr	0	0	0	0
Heep lf	3	0	1	0	Willis p	1	0	0	0
Sisk p	0	0	0	0	Power p	0	0	0	0
Aguilera ph	0	0	0	0	Esasky lf	4	0	0	0
Orosco p-rf	1	1	0	0	Milner cf	2	0	0	0
Knight 3b	5	0	2	0	Rowdon ss	6	0	1	0
McDowell p-lf-rf	2	0	0	0	Perez 1b	5	0	2	0
Santana ss	2	0	1	0	Oester 2b	6	0	1	0
HJohnson ss	4	1	1	3	Terry p	1	1	1	0
Ojeda p	2	1	0	0	Daniels ph	1	0	1	0
Foster ph	1	0	0	0	RMurphy p	0	0	0	0
RAnderson p	0	0	0	0	Stillwell ph	1	0	1	0
Myers p	0	0	0	0	RRobinson p	0	0	0	0
MWilson lf	3	0	1	0	Butera c	3	0	0	0
Totals	53	6	12	4	Totals	51	3	14	3

Mets	000	010 002	000 03 — 6
Cincinnati	002	010 000	000 00 — 3

Game Winning RBI-HJohnson (2). E-Rowdon, Parker. DP-Mets 1, Cincinnati 4. LOB-Mets 16, Cincinnati 11. 2B-KHernandez 2, Teufel, Hearn. 3B-Dykstra. HR-Parker (20), Bell (6), HJohnson (6). SB-Strawberry (21), Rowdon (2), EDavis 2 (47). S-Venable, Oester.

Mets	IP	H	R	ER	BB	SO
Ojeda	5	6	3	3	1	4
RAnderson	1⅓	2	0	0	0	0
Myers	⅔	1	0	0	1	0
Sisk	2	1	0	0	1	0
Orosco	2	3	0	0	0	3
McDowell (W, 8-4)	3	1	0	0	0	0
Cincinnati						
Terry	5	5	1	1	3	2
RMurphy	2	0	0	0	2	1
RRobinson	1⅔	2	2	0	1	1
Franco	1⅓	1	0	0	2	0
Willis (L, 1-1)	3	3	2	2	3	2
Power	1	1	1	1	0	1

Myers pitched to 1 batter in the 8th, Willis pitched to 2 batters in the 14th. WP-Franco. PB-BDiaz.

Umpires: Horne-Davis; First-Harvey; Second-DeMuth; Third-Gregg.

T-5:00. A-23,707.

right. HoJo knew that he had beaten the book, which said he was deathly allergic to breaking balls.

"I'm not supposed to hit those," he said. "If I could bottle that swing and keep it in my back pocket, I could make a million. I just didn't want to get fooled with a curve."

The victory, which gave the Mets a 13½-game lead, said it all about their combativeness and their resourcefulness.

"There is so much pride in this room," said Howard Johnson. "People call us one of the cockiest teams in the league and other people talk about how arrogant we are. They're always looking for a chance to retaliate. But we enjoy fighting and, if that's what it takes, then we will fight. We won't be pushed around."

"We are hard competitors, but we are not malicious," said Davey Johnson. "We don't like people to cuss us and that is what Davis did. That is what caused tempers to flare."

"You remember these kind of games," said Hernandez. "Jesse got a chance in the outfield. Roger and Jesse were in a position to get a win and a save in the same game."

No-No, Then "Oh No" for Maloney

METS 1, REDS 0

June 14, 1965 in Cincinnati

The night belonged to Jim Maloney. The 24-year-old Cincinnati right-hander blew fastball after fastball past the Mets and looked like he could continue impaling them on their bats till morning, if necessary. Met hitters were left testifying to Maloney's dominance . . . as if their utter humiliation wasn't already ample proof. Maloney rang up 18 strikeouts, matching an NL record and setting a new club mark.

And the Mets, losers of 10 straight, were unable to muster a single hit through the first 10 innings.

Still, somehow, after Johnny Lewis led off the 11th inning by hitting a game-winning homer over the center-field fence, Maloney wound up just another losing pitcher and the Mets jubilantly returned to their locker room as giddy 1-0 winners.

You don't get called Amazin' without always doing things the hard way. But this particular ambush was especially memorable for its improbability.

"I told them to strike out," said manager Casey Stengel. "I wanted to make him overconfident."

"I hurt my arm, tipping my hat every inning for those ovations," said Maloney, finding humor in the occasion.

The cheering was well-earned while it lasted. But, thanks to Lewis' blast and eight scoreless innings from starter Frank Lary plus three from reliever Larry Bearnarth, Maloney's 18 strikeouts and 10 no-hit innings were rendered moot by the Mets.

"It's a damn shame," said Maloney, who would pitch no-hitters that counted and that he won later in the '65 season and in '69. "I really wanted it. I thought I had it."

And, at the sight and sound of Maloney's heater, the Mets thought that they had had it.

"No pitcher has ever pitched a baseball faster," said Charlie Smith, who was fanned three times, a distinction he shared with Billy Cowan, Ron Swoboda and Lewis.

Right from the start and almost to the end, Maloney was every bit as in command of the Mets as anyone ever had been—even Sandy Koufax during his no-hitter in 1962 and Jim Bunning during his perfect game at Shea in '64.

Cowan, leading off the first, took two quick strikes, then tried to bunt and fouled it off for the first Maloney K. "I couldn't see the ball," admitted Cowan. "I just wanted to meet it."

There wasn't a fly to the outfield off Maloney until the fifth. The only Met baserunners through the first 10 innings came in the second, when Ed Kranepool walked and Smith struck out and reached when the pitch escaped catcher Don Paveletich. In the seventh, there was a fine, ear-high stab of Chuck Hiller's hard-hit, bad-hop grounder by first baseman Gordy Coleman, who beat Hiller to the bag. But nothing else resembled a hit.

Meanwhile, Lary matched Maloney zero for zero. The closest the Reds came to scoring was in the fourth. Vada Pinson singled and stole second (when shortstop Roy McMillan dropped Chris Cannizzaro's throw on a pitchout) and was tagged out at the plate by Lary as he tried to score from second on Cannizzaro's third-strike passed ball. There was also the eighth inning, when Lary hit Tommy Harper with a pitch and—after a stolen base and wild throw by Cannizzaro had put Harper on third with two out—Pete Rose ran the count to 3-and-1. After being given the take sign much to his chagrin —"I couldn't believe it," he said later—Rose hit the full-count pitch back to Lary.

The Mets went down, quietly, of course, as the tension mounted in the ninth. Pinch-hitter Jesse Gonder lofted a short fly and pinch-hitter Joe Christopher and Cowan fanned. The crowd of 5,989 gave Maloney a standing ovation for what should've been a no-hitter and a done deal. The fans took heart in the notion that the Reds' big boppers Pinson, Frank Robinson and Coleman would find a way to reach Bearnarth in the bottom half, but they didn't.

In the 10th, Bearnarth gave up a single to Edwards and, after a sacrifice and a groundout by Maloney, third baseman Smith fielded a routine bouncer from Harper and made Met hearts race when he fired the ball into the dirt at first. Only a nifty, do-or-die scoop by Kranepool kept the ball from sailing past and pinch-runner Chico Ruiz from scoring.

And in those days before the worship of pitch counts, when starters still sometimes worked even more than nine innings, Maloney was still out there for the 11th. The first hitter was Lewis, a limber, long-armed, left-handed hitter who hit .227 with 22 homers and 194 strikeouts in his 771 career major league at-bats from 1964 through '67. Maloney threw him yet another fastball on a 2-1 count, waist high and on the outside, and the location provided Lewis a chance to catch up to it with his looping swing.

"I have never seen a man throw so hard to me," said Lewis. "I figured on a fastball and he threw it just at medium height."

The blast, Lewis' eighth of the season, struck the wooden portion of the center-field fence, above the yellow line at Crosley Field which marked where the concrete wall ended and home runs began.

"I didn't know it was a homer until I saw the umpire signaling it," said Lewis.

"The pitch from Lewis got away from me," said Maloney. "I was trying to pitch him inside and I got the ball a little too far out over the plate."

It was only the third gopher ball surrendered by Maloney in 85 innings—a small number for a power pitcher. "I've given up three homers and Lewis has two of them," said the pitcher.

Maloney, who overwhelmed Swoboda for his 18th K and gave up a single to McMillan after the homer, joined three other hard-luck pitchers who threw nine no-hit innings and wound up with a defeat over the previous 42 years. The St. Louis Browns' Bobo Newsom threw nine no-hit innings before giving up a hit in the 10th and losing to the Red Sox, 2-1, in 1934. The Pirates' Harvey Haddix threw 12 perfect and famous innings in a 2-0, 13-inning loss to the Milwaukee Braves in 1959. Finally, the Houston Astros' Ken Johnson lost a nine-inning no-hitter vs. Cincinnati on two errors in the ninth, 1-0, in 1964.

"I would have rather given up 10 hits and won the game," said Maloney.

Maloney understandably found little solace in tying the single-game NL record for strikeouts held by Los Angeles' Koufax (18 Ks over nine innings) and Milwaukee's Warren Spahn (18 Ks over 15 innings).

"I haven't a thing to be proud of," said Maloney. "I just lost to the Mets."

METS	ab	r	h	bl	CINCINNATI	ab	r	h	bl
Cowan cf	4	0	0	0	Harper lf	4	0	1	0
Hickman lf	0	0	0	0	Rose 2b	4	0	0	0
Hiller 2b	4	0	0	0	Pinson cf	5	0	1	0
Smith 3b	4	0	0	0	Robinson rf	4	0	1	0
Kranepool 1b	3	0	0	0	Coleman 1b	5	0	1	0
Lewis rf	4	1	1	1	Johnson 3b	4	0	0	0
Swoboda lf	4	0	0	0	Edwards c	4	0	2	0
Klaus 2b	0	0	0	0	Ruiz pr	0	0	0	0
McMillan ss	4	0	1	0	Pavletich c	0	0	0	0
Cannizzaro c	2	0	0	0	Cardenas ss	2	0	1	0
Gonder c	2	0	0	0	Maloney p	4	0	0	0
Lary p	2	0	0	0					
Christopher ph	1	0	0	0					
Totals	34	1	2	1	Totals	36	0	7	0

| Mets | 000 | 000 | 000 | 01 — 1 |
| Cincinnati | 000 | 000 | 000 | 00 — 0 |

E-McMillan, Cannizzaro. DP-Mets 1, Cincinnati 2. LOB-Mets 1, Cincinnati 8. HR-Lewis (8). SB-Harper. S-Cardenas 2.

	IP	H	R	ER	BB	SO
Mets						
Lary	8	5	0	0	1	3
Bearnarth (W, 2-1)	3	2	0	0	1	1
Cincinnati						
Maloney (L, 5-3)	11	2	1	1	1	18

HBP-Harper (by Lary). WP-Maloney. PB-Cannizzaro.
T-2:50. A-5,989

Oh, Doctor

METS 10, CUBS 0

September 7, 1984 in New York

Keith Moreland hit the slow roller down the third-base line. A charging Ray Knight gloved it, but didn't bother to make a throw. An infield hit. Really, nothing worth talking about or remembering in a 10-0 Met victory—if it wasn't the only thing that kept rookie sensation Dwight Gooden from throwing a no-hitter against the Chicago Cubs, at age 19.

"I'm not disappointed," said Gooden. "The hit doesn't matter. I just wanted to win the game."

"Normally, I make adjustments later in the game and play more towards the line," said Knight, who was positioned on the edge of the outfield grass against a line-drive hitter. "But nobody was pulling Doc and Moreland [a right-handed hitter] always goes the other way [to right field] and he doesn't run well . . . Sometimes, you are a victim of being too smart . . ."

"It was a hit," said manager Davey Johnson. "There wasn't any question."

"When the ball came down along the line, I came in at such a sharp angle that I would have had to catch and throw in one motion," said Knight. "I never even got it out of my hand."

Dwight Gooden, who routinely flirted with greatness in 1984 and 1985, came within a scratch hit of the first no-hitter ever pitched by a Met, against the Cubs. The Doctor wound up pitching one for the Yankees, much to every Met fan's enduring chagrin.

There wasn't even a second thought about it at the time, since the play came with none out in the fifth.

"I didn't even know I had a one-hitter until I looked up and saw it on the board in the sixth inning," said Gooden, who pitched his only career no-hitter while wearing the uniform of the Yankees, a checkered baseball lifetime later, in 1996.

Still, it was the right-hander's night as he mixed his fastball and slow curve to record 11 strikeouts. Doc raised his season total to 235 and shattered the NL rookie record of 227 set by Hall of Famer Grover Cleveland Alexander in 1911. Gooden's sixth straight victory and one of three shutouts for him in 1984 was a masterpiece. Gooden tied Tom Seaver's club records with his 13th double-figure strikeout game of the year and third consecutively.

The only flaws in this gem were the hit by Moreland and four walks. The triumph cut the Cubs' lead over the sagging Mets to six games with 21 left.

"Tonight was one of my better games," said Gooden of his 15th win in a Rookie of the Year season that saw him go 17-9 with a 2.60 ERA and 276 strikeouts. "I felt great going into the game and I felt strong at the end."

After he walked Bob Dernier and the leadoff man stole second in the first, Gooden struck out Ryne Sandberg and Gary Matthews and got Leon Durham to ground out to escape unscathed.

"When Dwight is on, you know it right away," said catcher Mike Fitzgerald. "Because when he throws hard in the first inning, he only gets better as he goes along."

Doc fanned Moreland to tie Alexander's record at the start of the second inning. When he got Ron Cey, the next hitter, to break it, Gooden got a standing ovation from the 46,301 fans in attendance and a tip of the cap from the captain, first baseman Keith Hernandez.

After the Mets scored five in the third to take a 6-0

CHICAGO	ab	r	h	bl	METS	ab	r	h	bl
Dernier cf	3	0	0	0	Backman 2b	2	3	1	0
Sandberg 2b	3	0	0	0	MWilson cf	4	1	2	3
Reuschel p	0	0	0	0	Hernandez 1b	5	1	1	1
Lopes ph	0	0	0	0	Strawberry rf	3	2	2	2
Matthews lf	2	0	0	0	Foster lf	3	1	1	3
Cotto lf	1	0	0	0	Heep lf	1	0	0	0
Durham 1b	4	0	0	0	Brooks ss	2	0	0	0
Moreland rf	3	0	1	0	Oquendo ss	2	0	2	0
Veryzer 3b	1	0	0	0	Knight 3b	4	0	0	0
Cey 3b	2	0	0	0	Fitzgerald c	4	1	1	0
Bosley rf	1	0	0	0	Gooden p	3	1	2	0
JDavis c	2	0	0	0					
Hassey c	1	0	0	0					
Bowa ss	2	0	0	0					
Woods 2b	0	0	0	0					
Ruthven p	1	0	0	0					
Brusstar p	0	0	0	0					
Rohn 2b	2	0	0	0					
Totals	28	0	1	0	Totals	33	10	12	9

Chicago	000	000	000	— 0
Mets	105	103	00X	— 10

Game Winning RBI-MWilson (6). E-Sandberg. LOB-Chicago 5, Mets 8. 2B-MWilson, Strawberry. 3B-Backman. HR-Foster (20), Strawberry (21). SB-Dernier (41). S-Gooden. SF-MWilson.

Chicago	IP	H	R	ER	BB	SO
Ruthven (L, 5-10)	2²/₃	4	6	6	3	2
Brusstar	2¹/₂	2	1	1	2	1
Reuschel	3	6	3	3	2	2
Mets						
Gooden (W, 15-8)	9	1	0	0	4	11

T-2:43. A-46,301.

margin and knock out Dick Ruthven, Gooden didn't have to worry about nursing a lead. George Foster unloaded a three-run homer (his 20th of the year keyed the big third, when an error by shortstop Larry Bowa opened the gates) and Darryl Strawberry hit a two-run shot (his 21st in the sixth, off Rick Reuschel).

The Cubs had beaten the Mets seven straight times coming in. And Gooden had endured a poor start Aug. 9 at Wrigley Field, in which he allowed four runs, eight hits in four innings of a 9-3 Met loss that paved the way to Chicago's four-game series sweep—which left the Mets 4½ games behind.

However, this time, Gooden was magnificent, retiring 12 straight Cubbies (seven on Ks) between the walk to Dernier (no other Cub reached second) and the hit by Moreland.

It was the first one-hitter pitched by a Met since Terry Leach had done it, vs. Philadelphia, Oct. 1, 1982.

"He threw a couple of fastballs to Henry Cotto in the ninth that were as hard as the ones he threw in the first inning," said Cubs manager Jim Frey. "He's just an outstanding young pitcher. What can you say? You're going to hear that for the next 15 years."

The Cubs, though overpowered by Gooden, would not be overtaken. Still, if Knight had been just a few steps in and over toward the line . . .

Never mind.

15

The Franchise Comes Home

METS 2, PHILS 0

April 5, 1983 in New York

O pening Day is always special. But, in 1983, when The Franchise came home to Shea, after five-plus seasons in exile in Cincinnati, that was really special.

Naturally, the Tom Seaver who came back to the Mets wasn't the overpowering right-hander who was dumped by them in 1977. He was 38 now, chunkier, coming off the first losing season of his career. And he was brought home, partly for his drawing power, at the paltry price of Charlie Puleo, Lloyd McClendon and Jason Felix.

Ah, but those memories.

The crowd of 51,054—the biggest Opening Day crowd at Shea since 1968—stood and cheered when the PA announcer said simply without speaking a name, "Now pitching for the Mets, No. 41." The fans remained standing and roared from the time that Seaver emerged from the bullpen gate while a visual valentine of highlights filled the Diamond Vision screen. He repeatedly tipped his cap and they continued their homage. Seaver handed the ball from his warmups to a handicapped child in the right-field stands, at catcher Ronn Reynolds' suggestion. The salute was still going on after Seaver reached the dugout and it started all over again when he took the mound with his teammates.

Seaver matched Walter Johnson's major league record for most Opening Day starts with his 14th, but this duel with multiple Cy Young Award winner Steve Carlton of the Phillies was more stirring than any other Seaver curtain riser.

The reverent reception during his stroll in told the pitcher he was back where he always belonged, where it all had started 16 years and 264 wins ago. Usually stoic when it was time to go to work, Seaver was touched.

"It was great, a very emotional moment," said Tom, whose wife Nancy, two daughters, mom and dad and three sisters were on hand. "I didn't think it would be as emotional as it was . . . I have a lot of memories here. It was great to be back . . . After all that happened, you don't want to fall on your face. That would be a big disappointment."

"I have to admit that when he walked in from the bullpen, I had goosebumps," said Met boss Frank Cashen, who was not with the club during the Seaver era.

After all the contract ugliness and character assassination that prevented Seaver from wearing the uniform he had graced from 1968 through the middle of 1977, through two World Series, he was reborn as a Met. He was missing about 10 mph from the 95-mile-an-hour heater that produced two Cy Youngs in a Met uniform and one as a Red. However, the Mets were willing to bet there was still life in that arm—despite a 5-14, 5.50 showing in 1982—and they were certain that Seaver still possessed the mound knowledge and competitiveness that ultimately propelled him to a 311-205 record, a 2.86 career ERA and a presence in Cooperstown.

Seaver struck out Pete Rose (for the first of two times) to open the game, later remembering that he had punched out Rose in the final start of his first Met life. He threw fastballs almost exclusively because, he later explained, "It was so emotional I felt it for two innings . . . I didn't want to try any off-speed pitches until I settled down."

Rose, in his 21st season and with 3,869 hits coming into and going out of this game, said, "I don't remember the last time I struck out twice in a game . . . I only missed two pitches all spring.

"I didn't know he could still throw it that hard. He messed me up. He threw it inside, too, and he established his fastball in the back of my mind. The last three or four years he wasn't the blower he was when he was over here for the first time. But he's still got that good No. 1 [fastball] . . . He made some great pitches—about what you would expect from a Hall of Famer."

Seaver struck out five of the first six hitters and then didn't get anyone else that way.

"To pitch in the big leagues, you have to be able to pitch inside [with the hard stuff]," said Seaver. "You can't let the hitter dive over the plate."

So what if Seaver's fastest pitch of the day was clocked at an ordinary 87 miles per hour? He followed his mother's pre-game advice—don't rush, fall off the mound, swear or spit—to a T. He was a perfect gentleman, leaving the hitters to do the cursing.

"He knew it was Opening Day today and we would all be a little overanxious," said Joe Morgan. "He used that to his advantage."

It still boils down to keeping the bad guys off the scoreboard. Tom threw six shutout innings, allowing only three hits and one walk. While pitching to Carlton in the sixth, he felt a recurrence of some discomfort in the area where he had pulled a left thigh muscle. When Seaver returned to the dugout, he told manager George Bamberger that it was enough—even though the game was still scoreless—and left for pinch-hitter Wally Backman.

"Seven is a good fatigue point for Opening Day," was what Seaver said he told Bamberger.

After Doug Sisk was brought on in the seventh, the Mets finally got to Carlton for their only two runs and beat him for the 32nd time.

Tom Seaver, the prodigal son and the former Franchise, came back to the Mets for a one-season homecoming in 1983 and began it by combining on a shutout of the Phils on Opening Day at Shea.

The game-winning uprising began with a broken-bat single by Dave Kingman off a curve and continued with an opposite-field single by George Foster off a fastball. Then Hubie Brooks laid down an intended sacrifice bunt that hugged the third-base line. It was no sacrifice. Despite Mike Schmidt's best efforts to throw him out, Brooks had a hit.

"I wasn't trying to be cute and beat it out," said Brooks.

"A perfect bunt," said batting coach Jim Frey.

Bases loaded, none out. Mike Howard, Bamberger's right fielder du jour, was the hitter, with 65 major league at-bats and only 11 hits under his belt. His previous two trips against Carlton were a strikeout and a grounder to short. The last big league at-bat of the 25-year-old Howard's career looked to be a mismatch.

"I knew Carlton had to get ahead of me," said Howard. "I knew he was going to throw me a fastball."

Howard poked a grounder through a hole between short and third —courtesy of a drawn-in infield—for a single that scored Kingman and made it 1-0. Brian Giles' sac fly liner to right scored Foster and it was a 2-0 lead.

Now it was the often erratic Sisk's game to win . . . or blow.

"My scenario called for Tom Seaver to pitch seven good innings and then for Neil Allen or Jesse Orosco to come in and finish. I had no idea I would even be used," said the sinkerballer.

Sisk flirted with ruining the day in the ninth, allowing a one-out walk to Morgan and an infield hit to Gary Matthews. But Sisk—who later admitted he had been surprised by Bamberger not summoning the club's closer, Allen—rewarded his manager's show of confidence. Doug retired Schmidt on a fly to center and fanned Tony Perez swinging on a 2-and-2 diver into the dirt.

"I figured if he'd go for a 3-0 pitch [which Perez hit into a double play in his previous at-bat]," said Sisk, "he would go for anything."

With their ninth straight Opening Day win, the Mets tied the St. Louis Browns of 1937-45 for the major league record.

Seaver, who routinely blew away hitters in his youth, showed that fooling them works, too—on Opening Day and in most of his 1983 starts. Tom went a deceptive 9-14 with a 3.55 ERA for a truly awful last-place Mets team that won 68 games.

"I just threw different kinds of fastballs, a slider and the changeup," he said, making it sound as simple as he made it look. "Just good location and a certain movement on the ball. Nothing mysterious, you know."

Seaver, incredibly, was lost by the Mets again that winter, to the Chicago White Sox in the free-agent compensation draft, because Met management foolishly assumed his age would prompt other clubs to pass on him. Even after acknowledging the enormous mistake that was trading him away in the first place, the Mets were still guilty of undervaluing The Franchise.

At least Met fans will always have April 5, 1983 to cherish.

PHILADELPHIA	ab	r	h	bl	METS	ab	r	h	bl
Rose rf	4	0	0	0	Wilson cf	4	0	0	0
Morgan 2b	2	0	1	0	Ballor ss	4	0	0	0
Matthews lf	4	0	1	0	Kingmn 1b	4	1	1	0
Schmidt 3b	3	0	0	0	Jorgensen 1b	0	0	0	0
TPerez 1b	4	0	2	0	Foster lf	3	1	2	0
BDiaz c	3	0	1	0	Brooks 3b	3	0	1	0
DeJesus ss	2	0	0	0	Howard rf	3	0	1	1
Molinaro ph	1	0	0	0	Giles 2b	2	0	1	1
Milbourne ss	0	0	0	0	Hodges c	3	0	0	0
Dernier cf	2	0	0	0	Seaver p	1	0	0	0
Gross cf	1	0	0	0	Backman ph	1	0	0	0
Carlton p	2	0	0	0	Sisk p	1	0	0	0
Matuszek ph	1	0	0	0					
Reed p	0	0	0	0					
Totals	**29**	**0**	**5**	**0**	**Totals**	**29**	**2**	**6**	**2**

Philadelphia		000	000	000	—0
Mets		000	000	20X	—2

Game Winning RBI-Howard. E-Seaver. DP-Mets 2. LOB-Philadelphia 5, Mets 4. SF-Giles

Philadelphia	IP	H	R	ER	BB	SO
Carlton (L, 0-1)	7	6	2	2	0	9
Reed	1	0	0	0	0	2
Mets						
Seaver	6	3	0	0	1	5
Sisk (W, 1-0)	3	2	0	0	2	3

T-2:23. A-51,054.

Mlicking the Yanks

June 16, 1997 in The Bronx, N.Y.

This was no stinkin' spring training game in March in front of a bunch of 70-year-old Florida retirees and a seething George Steinbrenner, whose blood pressure told you he was the only one who didn't get that it was *only* an exhibition.

This was no Mayor's Trophy Game, understandably treated as a mid-season distraction and worthless pain in the ass by both New York teams.

This was the first ever regular-season series between the Mets and the Yankees to actually count.

It was shades of Dodgers and Giants and Yankees in Octobers before the defections. This was an event—the first all-New York baseball game since the New York Giants beat the Brooklyn Dodgers at the Polo Grounds, Sept. 8, 1957—to match the size of its hype. Maybe not totally, but close enough—and the backdrop was a full-fledged fan frenzy fueled by decades of Met fans' hatred for the arrogant pinstripes and Yankee fans' disdain for that inferior other team in town.

Dave Mlicki, a 29-year-old puzzle who was 2-5 with a 4.70 ERA coming in, whose nasty curve always suggested better results than he produced, took a 10-16 career mark as a starter into this series-opening Yankee Stadium assignment. In his crowning moment for the Mets, he wound up with the first complete game and the first shutout of his major league career, a 6-0 win. Mlicki allowed nine hits, struck out eight and held the Yankees to 0-for-11 with runners in scoring position, 2-for-19 with men on base.

After the final strike, catcher Todd Hundley flipped the game ball to Mlicki and told him, "You earned it." Mlicki called this performance "by far, my most memorable game."

Met fans knew they would never forget Mlicki—even if he never put three good starts back to back. He had made their dream come true: they had watched their team humble the Yanks in their Bronx backyard.

"The fans have been waiting for this a long time," said Mlicki. "I'm just amazed at how big it is."

"It was an awesome performance. I am proud of him. This is a statement he had to make," said Met manager Bobby Valentine of the pitcher who rarely kept his focus or stamina late into games.

"He [Mlicki] stayed ahead of us and kept us off balance. We couldn't catch up to him," said former Met manager Joe Torre, whose Yanks were without the injured Bernie Williams. "We expected what we got. But we didn't expect to be shut out."

"He had better stuff than I thought he would," said Yankee first baseman Tino Martinez.

"Mlicki—how do you say his name?—pretty much pitched perfect every time we had runners in scoring position. He has got a great curveball," said Derek Jeter, who struck out twice looking.

Jeter's last strikeout came with two on in the ninth for the final out as the won-over crowd of 56,188 stood and cheered for Mlicki as if the venue had been Shea.

"There was a lot of electricity in here," said Yankee catcher Joe Girardi. "It's just unfortunate there wasn't any on our own side."

"I think there have been a lot of closet Met fans waiting to get out," noted Mets pitching coach Bob Apodaca.

Both teams found themselves at 37-30 for the season at the end of the night. However, the Yanks, after claiming all along this would be "just another game" for them, knew that this was not just another loss.

Before the series, ex-Met and current Yankee David Cone offered candor, as always, pooh-poohing "all the clichés about how it is only three games and we just want to win games and whatever happens, happens" and observing, "This is exciting."

Yankee GM Bob Watson knew the score when he said before the opener, "We are the ones who have the most to lose. If we win, we are supposed to win. If we don't, everyone is going to say how much we messed up."

"Hey, we have to go to restaurants in this town," said Martinez. "We want to win these games."

"It was certainly the most intense big series I've ever played in June," said John Olerud, the Mets' batting star with three RBI.

The Mets jumped on Andy Pettitte. Bernard Gilkey punched a checked-swing double to right with one out in the first and the slumping Olerud chopped a 3-and-1 fastball for an RBI double inside first. After a walk to Hundley, DH Butch Huskey pushed the Met lead to 2-0 with a run-scoring single that left runners at the corners.

Pettitte used his nasty, deceptive, world-class pickoff move to catch Huskey far off first base.

METS	ab	r	h	bl	YANKEES	ab	r	h	bl
LJohnson cf	5	0	0	0	Jeter ss	5	0	1	0
Gilkey lf	3	1	2	1	PKelly 2b	4	0	1	0
Olerud 1b	5	1	2	3	O'Neill rf	3	0	1	0
Hundley c	2	1	0	0	Fielder dh	4	0	1	0
Huskey dh	4	0	2	1	TMartinez 1b	4	0	0	0
Everett rf	4	0	0	0	Hayes 3b	3	0	1	0
Baerga 2b	4	0	0	0	Whiten lf	4	0	1	0
MFranco 3b	4	2	2	0	Curtis cf	4	0	0	0
LLopez ss	2	1	1	0	Girardi c	4	0	3	0
Totals	**33**	**6**	**9**	**5**	**Totals**	**35**	**0**	**9**	**0**

Mets	300	000	201	— 6
Yankees	000	000	000	— 0

E-LJohnson (2), Baerga (2), Lloyd (2). LOB-Mets 6, Yankees 10. 2B-Gilkey (11), Olerud (19), Fielder (12), Girardi (10). RBI-Gilkey (29), Olerud 3 (49), Huskey (35). SB-Hundley (2), Huskey (3). S-LLopez. SF-Gilkey. GIDP-Huskey. Runners left in scoring position-Mets 2: Hundley, Baerga. Yankees 6: Jeter 2, PKelly, Fielder, TMartinez, Hayes. Yankees: 1 (Hayes, PKelly, TMartinez).

Mets	IP	H	R	ER	BB	SO
Mlicki (W, 3-5)	9	9	0	0	2	8
Yankees						
Pettitte (L, 8-4)	7	8	5	5	3	4
Lloyd	2	1	1	0	0	0

HBP-LLopez (by Pettitte).

Umpires: Home-Tshida; First-Denkinger; Second-Shulock; Third-Everett.

T-2:44. A-56,188.

"I forgot what a great move he had," said Huskey. "In the minors, he would walk guys and just pick them off. Over and over."

However, this particular pickoff became a rundown—and eventually a cause to rejoice for the Mets.

Hundley, not a speed merchant by any stretch, broke for home and beat Pettitte's hurried throw by avoiding the tag from Girardi, who was too far out in front of the plate. Todd jumped up, clapping his hands, and the Mets' dugout erupted at the notion of their catcher stealing home for a 3-0 lead.

Good thing the Boss wasn't on hand for this one.

"We are a better ballclub than that," said Torre. "We were too conscious of the man at third base."

"It was one of those games where everything they did went right and everything we did went wrong," said Pettitte.

"I think maybe a couple of people [fans] changed hats after the first inning," said Yankee second baseman Pat Kelly. "The Mets jumped out like that and it really pumped them up."

In the seventh, Pettitte walked the struggling Gilkey before Olerud nailed him again for a two-out, two-run, opposite-field single past the dive of shortstop Jeter that made it 5-0.

"I was trying to make the perfect pitch and, when you do that, your ball doesn't move quite as much as it should," said Pettitte.

The closest thing that Mlicki had to a moment of truth came in the seventh when two Yanks were on base for Cecil Fielder.

"I gave him two sliders and then hung one, which he crushed foul," said Mlicki. "I came back with a curveball and got him [to ground out]."

A little more than an hour after the game had ended and Frank Sinatra's version of "New York, New York" had blared over the speakers, Mlicki snuck back out to the Yankee Stadium mound and scooped some dirt into a plastic cup. It would go next to the ball he used to fan Jeter and close out the Yankees.

"It's just something special, something close to me," he said. "I always wanted to pitch here . . . I've always wanted to come here because of the tradition. And they are the champs."

For exactly one night, the 1997 Mets were the Kings of New York.

"It was magical," said Valentine. "It was special."

"It was a lot of fun out there tonight," said Hundley. "I compare it to the Fourth of July Tournament in American Legion ball."

Kid Opens with Bang

METS 6, CARDS 5

April 9, 1985 in New York

The new guy in town, nicknamed "The Kid," felt like one, one day after his 31st birthday. It was Opening Day 1985 and the perennial All-Star catcher, who had hit 215 homers in 10-plus years in Montreal, was making his Met debut as The Great Crouching Hope.

Gary Carter, imported by the Mets to handle their young pitchers for four players the previous winter, had always welcomed the spotlight. Now, the lights had never seemed brighter.

The first Opening Day sellout crowd in the Mets' 24-year history (46,781) braved 42-degree weather to see Carter and Doc Gooden team up against the Cardinals. And they finished the afternoon standing and chanting Gary's first name, because Carter did not disappoint. In the 10th inning of a 5-5 game, Carter reached out and lifted a nasty bender from ex-Met closer Neil Allen and lined it barely into the left-field bullpen for a game-ending homer.

"Gary Carter is everything he says he is," said Ron Darling.

"Gary Carter is a tough, tough hitter," said Keith Hernandez. "I'm glad he is on my side now."

"He's got the power to take any base hit over the wall," said Wally Backman with envy.

Cardinals manager and longtime Met nemesis Whitey Herzog didn't understand the fuss.

"That is why they pay him [Carter] all that money," said the man known as The White Rat.

"How can I describe it?" said Carter. "Excited. Ecstatic. Enthusiastic. Any adjective you want. I wanted to do well today. I wanted to impress. If I had fantasized about my first game, it couldn't have been any better than this."

Carter punctured the air with his upraised right fist on his tour of the bases and leaped into a huddle of Mets at the plate and this tableau assured that several painful moments—physically and mentally—would be forgotten.

Gary's day didn't start out promisingly as he battled butterflies, the result of "looking forward to this a long time." As a reminder, there was stiffness in Carter's left elbow, which temporarily went numb after absorbing a first-inning fastball from Joaquin Andujar. It was the same spot where Gary had been nailed in 1983.

In the third inning, Carter committed a game-tying passed ball and later got caught looking on a backup slider. Carter gave up a stolen base to the pitcher, Andujar, of all people, and got hit by a pitch a second time.

However, in the end, Carter was able to hold his head up and smile. It was, after all, his homer that relegated the erratic work of Doug Sisk —who spit up the remaining one run of what had been a 5-2 lead by walking St. Louis slugger Jack Clark with the bases loaded in the ninth—to "no harm, no foul" status.

"It was a storybook ending all right," said Met manager Davey Johnson after the three-hour, 42-minute nail-biter. "Losing the lead and then coming back to win is certainly dramatic."

The Mets left 15 runners on, leaving the bases loaded in the first, eighth and ninth innings. They took a gift 2-0 lead in the first on a single and steal by Mookie Wilson, an RBI single by Hernandez, the drilling of Carter, a walk to Darryl Strawberry and a two-out, run-scoring walk to Howard Johnson.

Unfazed by what to do for an encore, fist-pumping Gary Carter marked his first game as a Met with a game-winning, extra-inning shot off ex-Met Neil Allen in the 1985 opener.

However, Gooden—the youngest pitcher to start an opening game in the 20th century, at 20 years, four months and 24 days—couldn't hold it for long. Clark took an 0-an-2 pitch out of the ballpark in the second. Then Carter's passed ball tied it, following Lonnie Smith's single and Tommy Herr's double in the third.

Doc settled down, retiring 10 of 11 batters (four on Ks) until the seventh, and that gave the Mets the chance to take a 5-2 lead. George Foster hit a homer in the third, Gooden singled in the fourth, moved to second on Backman's bunt single and scored on a Hernandez single in the fourth. Then the Mets pushed across their final run off Andujar on a Foster single and Rafael Santana's double in the fifth.

After Gooden gave up no-out singles to Andy Van Slyke and Ozzie Smith in the seventh, Doc was at the 117-pitch mark. And Johnson summoned Sisk.

"It was tough gripping the ball, so I threw more breaking balls than usual," said Gooden. "When Davey took me out, it was a great move."

It didn't look that great. Sisk gave up a two-out, two-run hit to Herr to make the score 5-4. Then, in the ninth, pinch-hitter Willie McGee singled, Lonnie Smith was hit by a pitch and Herr singled to load the bases. Johnson stuck with Sisk, who struck out Terry Pendleton for the second out—and walked Clark to force in the tying run. Jesse Orosco came on to get the out that kept it tied. Tom Gorman threw a scoreless 10th, then Allen struck out Keith Hernandez to start the bottom half.

Allen's first pitch to Carter was a curve, high in the strike zone, that Gary took for a strike. Hitting out of that open stance, Carter reached down and lifted the second pitch, a curve low and away, on a line to deep left.

"It was a nice one, but that was what I was looking for," said Carter. "I thought maybe it had a chance. But, truthfully, I thought it would be off the wall."

In pursuit was left fielder Lonnie Smith, who stands 5-foot-9 when he hasn't lost his footing, a tendency which earned him the nickname Skates. Smith leaped and came down with an empty glove. The ball had landed in the visitors' bullpen.

"I turned the wrong way," said Smith. "If I just turned the other way, I would have caught it. I should have had it."

"If I had a 6-foot-4 outfielder, he would have been out there," said Herzog.

Allen, the ex-Met asked to replace departed 45-save man Bruce

Sutter as the Cards' closer, was left staring down with his hands on his knees.

"I pitched outside to Hernandez and struck him out. I pitched outside to Carter and he hit it out. Give him some credit. It was the best curveball I had thrown all day," said Allen. "That is why they pay Gary Carter $2 million a year—to hit good pitches, bad pitches, all kinds of pitches. I'd feel terrible if I made a mistake. But that was a good pitch."

Allen's ex-teammate Darling could relate.

"Gary did the same thing to me last year in the [home] opener," said the Met pitcher. "Curveball on the outside corner. Good pitch. And he hit a grand slam."

"The game meant a lot more than it meant," Hernandez reflected in Yogi-esque fashion.

The Mets would win their next four games, powered by two more game-winning homers by Carter. The catcher went on to amass 32 homers and 100 RBI in his first season as a Met.

"He has done it his whole career," said Hernandez. "He is an RBI man, a big hit man."

ST. LOUIS	ab	r	h	bl	METS	ab	r	h	bl
LoSmith lf	4	1	1	0	Backman 2b	6	0	1	0
Herr 2b	5	0	3	2	MWilson cf	6	1	2	0
Pendleton 3b	5	0	0	0	Hernandez 1b	5	1	3	2
JClark 1b	3	1	1	2	Carter c	4	1	2	1
Porter c	4	0	0	0	Strawberry rf	3	0	0	0
Landrum ph	1	0	0	0	Heep ph	0	0	0	0
Allen p	0	0	0	0	Christensen rf	1	0	0	0
Braun rf	4	0	1	0	Foster lf	5	2	2	1
BHarper rf	1	0	0	0	HJohnson 3b	4	0	1	1
VanSlyke cf	4	1	1	0	Santana ss	5	0	1	1
OSmith ss	5	1	2	0	Gooden p	3	1	1	0
Andujar p	2	0	1	0	Sisk p	1	0	0	0
Dayley p	0	0	0	0	Orosco p	0	0	0	0
Jorgensen ph	1	0	0	0	Staub ph	0	0	0	0
Campbell p	0	0	0	0	Darling pr	0	0	0	0
Hassler p	0	0	0	0	Gorman p	0	0	0	0
McGee ph	1	0	1	0					
DeJesus pr	0	1	0	0					
Nieto c	1	0	0	0					
Totals	41	5	11	4	Totals	43	6	13	6

St. Louis	011	000	201	0— 5
Mets	201	110	000	1— 6

One out when winning run scored. Game Winning RBI-Carter (1). E-Andujar, Herr. LOB-St. Louis 10, Mets 15. 2B-Herr, Santana, Carter, OSmith. HR-JClark (1), Foster (1), Carter (1). SB-MWilson 2 (2), Andujar (1).

St. Louis	IP	H	R	ER	BB	SO
Andujar	5	8	5	5	2	4
Dayley	1	2	0	0	0	1
Campbell	1⅔	1	0	0	1	3
Hassler	⅓	1	0	0	0	0
Allen (L, 0-1)	1⅓	2	1	1	1	1
Mets						
Gooden	6	6	4	3	2	6
Sisk	2⅔	4	1	1	1	2
Orosco	⅓	0	0	0	0	0
Gorman (W,1-0)	1	1	0	0	0	0

Gooden pitched to two batters in 7th. HBP-Carter (by Andujar), Carter (by Campbell), LoSmith (by Sisk). PB-Carter.

T-3:42. A-46,781.

A Karmic Ricochet

September 20, 1973 in New York

When Ray Sadecki's pitch left Dave Augustine's bat in the 13th inning, the drive looked like it would bounce off the left-field wall. Then, it appeared it might go over. A long double would surely score the first-place Pirates' Richie Zisk—running on anything with two out—from first base with the go-ahead run. A homer would put the Mets two runs behind during the final stages of a desperate divisional race between five teams flirting with .500.

However, in a compelling case for the notion that some things are just meant to be and that the stars were aligned for the Mets to return to the post-season in 1973, the ball somehow landed on the edge of the left-field fence . . . and bounced back on a fly to the waiting glove of Cleon Jones.

Jones threw to cutoff man Wayne Garrett, in for Bud Harrelson at shortstop. Garrett took the ball, turned and threw home and catcher Ron Hodges caught it on a single bounce—with Zisk still five feet from his destination. Umpire John McSherry hesitated to let the dust settle, then closed his fist on the Pirates.

Out. Inning over.

"It was one of the most remarkable plays I ever saw," said Garrett, who was around when strange things happened in 1969.

"What did it miss by—half an inch?" said Pirates' manager Danny Murtaugh.

"The ball hit the corner and it just popped right up to me," said Jones. "I didn't think he hit it high enough to go over. I knew the ball was gonna hit the fence. But it could've gone anywhere . . . I knew we had to win the game after making that play."

"I knew I had to catch the ball and hold onto it," said Hodges. "But I didn't have all that much time. If I had more time, I'd have caught the ball, stepped aside and tagged him . . . I had to block the plate. I'll tell you, I squeezed the baseball as hard as I could squeeze it. I didn't want to drop it."

The Mets won it, 4-3, in the bottom half of the 13th, on Hodges' RBI single to left off Dave Giusti. With nine games left to play, the Mets —who didn't move out of last place for good in 1973 until the final day of August—vaulted into second place, a half-game behind Pittsburgh, a half-game ahead of Montreal, a game ahead of St. Louis and 2½ ahead of Chicago.

The next night, Tom Seaver beat the Bucs and the Mets reached .500 and first place in one swoop.

This couldn't be happening, could it? Did the calendar say 1969?

Jones, for one, recognized an omen when it hit him squarely in his glove hand.

"I am sure we are going to go all the way now," said the left fielder. "Winning the way we have been winning has us all psyched up. We feel we can't lose now."

"This is all so incredible," said Hodges. "I can't believe that it is happening and I am a part of it."

The rookie catcher had also played a vital role two nights earlier in Pittsburgh, when the Mets had erased a 4-1 ninth-inning deficit with a five-run rally for a 6-5 victory—the beginning of a season-high, seven-game winning streak.

Riding the sudden resuscitation of Tug McGraw, these Mets were about to win a division with the lowest winning percentage in history (.512 on 83-79). What a long strange trip this was.

In mid-July, the *New York Post* polled its readers: Whose head should roll? The choices were board chairman M. Donald Grant, GM Bob Scheffing and manager Yogi Berra. Scheffing won, easily. He survived and so did they, against all odds.

"We've struggled," said Ken Boswell. "We have paid the price to be where we are today."

In front of 24,855 fans at Shea, who saw Willie Mays announce his retirement effective at season's end before the game, the Mets came from behind three times. The Pirates scored the first run, off starter Jerry Koosman in the fourth. The Mets got even against Jim Rooker on a two-out RBI single in the sixth by Jones, who had homered twice the night before.

After Richie Hebner went deep to put the Bucs up again, 2-1, in the seventh, the Mets got even again, on a pinch single by Jim Beauchamp, a sacrifice, Felix Millan's single and an error by center fielder Al Oliver. In the ninth, Harry Parker came on for the Mets, in relief of Koosman, walked two and gave up a two-out RBI single to Dave Cash that gave the Pirates a 3-2 lead.

Yet another rally would be necessary. Boswell slapped a broken-bat pinch single in the ninth and was sacrificed to second by Don Hahn. George Theodore took a called third strike from lefty Ramon Hernandez. But pinch-hitter Duffy Dyer prolonged the night with an RBI double to left center to tie the game at 3—his first hit since Aug. 23 and first RBI since July 10.

With Sadecki throwing beautifully in four innings of two-hit, six-strikeout work, the Mets hung in. Augustine's wall ball set the stage for the final, game-winning rally. Luke Walker walked two Mets in the 13th, then Giusti got ahead of Hodges 0-and-2. Hodges saw his third straight fastball, but his one he lofted to left as John Milner headed home.

"I hit the ball good, on the good part of the bat, but at first I thought [left fielder Willie] Stargell might catch it," said Hodges. "It seemed like there were a whole lot of heroes tonight."

And one large omen.

"The incredible thing is that my ball bounced right back to Jones," said Augustine. "If it went a foot to his right or a foot to his left . . ."

PITTSBURGH	ab	r	h	bl	METS	ab	r	h	bl
Stennett 2b	1	0	0	0	Garrett 3b	5	1	1	0
Hebner 3b	4	1	1	1	Millan 2b	5	0	2	0
Cash 2b	6	0	3	1	Staub rf	6	0	1	0
Oliver cf	6	0	0	0	Jones lf	5	0	1	1
Stargell lf	5	1	0	0	Milner 1b	3	1	0	0
Zisk rf	5	0	1	0	Grote c	3	0	0	0
Sanguillen c	6	0	1	0	Boswell 3b	1	1	1	0
Robertson 1b	2	0	0	0	Hahn cf	4	0	0	0
Augustine cf	2	1	1	0	Harrelson ss	3	0	0	0
Maxvill ss	3	0	0	0	Kranepool ph	0	0	0	0
Rooker p	3	0	0	0	Theodore ph	1	0	0	0
DParker ph	1	0	0	0	Hodges c	2	0	1	1
Johnson p	0	0	0	0	Koosman p	1	0	0	0
RHernandez p	0	0	0	0	Beauchamp ph	1	0	1	0
McKee p	1	0	0	0	Martinez pr	0	1	0	0
Walker p	0	0	0	0	HParker p	0	0	0	0
Giusti p	0	0	0	0	Dyer ph	1	0	1	1
					Harts pr	0	0	0	0
					Sadecki p	1	0	0	0
Totals	45	3	7	2	Totals	42	4	9	3

Pittsburgh	000	100	101	000	0— 3	
Mets	000	001	011	000	1— 4	

One out when winning run scored. E-Harrelson, Oliver. DP-Pittsburgh 7. LOB-Pittsburgh 10, Mets 12. 2B-Cash, Dyer, Augustine. HR-Hebner (24). S-Garrett, Maxvill, Hahn, Boswell.

	IP	H	R	ER	BB	SO
Pittsburgh						
Rooker	8	5	2	2	4	4
Johnson	1/3	1	1	1	0	0
RHernandez	2/3	1	0	0	0	2
McKee	1 1/3	0	0	0	1	1
Walker (L, 7-12)	1 2/3	1	1	1	3	1
Giusti	1/3	1	0	0	0	0
Mets						
Koosman	8	4	2	1	4	8
HParker	1	1	1	1	2	1
Sadecki (W, 4-4)	4	2	0	0	0	6

Balk-RHernandez.

T-3:53. A-24,855.

A Breeze for Cool Kooz

April 17, 1968 in New York

There is a single moment in almost every baseball game around which the outcome turns. In the Mets' home opener in 1968, his first full season as a big leaguer, left-hander Jerry Koosman went face to face with his potential Waterloo early—after the first three Giant hitters became the first three Giant baserunners.

The bases were drunk and there was nobody out, with Willie Mays, Jim Ray Hart and Jack Hiatt coming up and a crowd of 52,079 hardly settled into their seats at Shea.

If you were looking for reasons this would turn out well for the Mets in the pitching matchup, the deck sure looked stacked against Koosman. NL Cy Young Award winner Mike McCormick, coming off a 22-win season and with a 4-0 lifetime record vs. the Mets, was Koosman's opponent. McCormick figured to be stingy against a Met team that had managed to play 24 innings without scoring a run two nights earlier.

In 1967, Koosman's ERA against the Giants was a tidy 12.60.

You do the math.

This is what is known in baseball vernacular as deep shit.

During his warmup in the bullpen, Koosman would later remember, there were more reasons to be anything but cheerful.

"I wasn't throwing my good fastball and I wasn't getting my curve over the plate," he said. "I didn't feel right . . . my shoulder was tight."

Koosman had already forgotten to leave a ticket at the pass gate for his wife, forcing her to hunt for traveling secretary Lou Niss to gain admission. This had the makings of a painful afternoon and evening.

Koosman couldn't have felt better when ex-Met Ron Hunt led off with a single, shortstop Al Weis booted Jim Davenport's grounder and Willie McCovey walked. Everyone knew the score, including Mets manager Gil Hodges: the Giants were poised on the brink of an inning the size of McCovey. And Cal Koonce was told to start loosening up in the bullpen.

"Bases loaded, nobody out, Mays up," said Hodges, already feeling like his first year at the Met helm was a tribulation, even though this was only Game No. 6. "If you're ever going to get alarmed, that is the place to do it . . . He better get him out or cold water and hot water will be hitting him before it should."

Mays had collected a triple and a homer against Koosman during the pitcher's 22⅓ inning stay (0-2, 6.04 ERA) with the Mets in 1967.

"I was thinking Mays was a tough hitter," said Koosman. "I wasn't scared though . . . He gave me a terrible time last season. But I did well against him during the exhibition season [when Koosman threw six shutout innings] this spring . . . I found out my own way to pitch to him."

First pitch was a fastball high and Mays, 37 years old with 565 career homers already under his belt in a career that dated back to 1951, swung viciously and missed. The second was a curve that he fouled off. After a fastball for a ball, Koosman fired another heater, low and on the inside corner. And home-plate umpire Lee Weyer actually rang up the legendary Mays—in ninth place on the all-time RBI list as of that day—for watching it.

One out. Now the hitter was Hart, a power threat of a third baseman.

"I thought they would get a runner in from Hart," said Met catcher Jerry Grote. "He doesn't strike out much and he doesn't pop the ball up."

Except this time . . . to Grote, in foul territory. Two outs.

All that remained was Hiatt, a prospect good enough to prompt the Giants to trade Tom Haller to make room for him. Hiatt went down swinging, the second of Koosman's six Ks over the first three innings.

The Mets had escaped without being scored upon, because Koosman did not permit the three Giants to hit a single fair ball.

"We're going to have some fun this year," said Ed Charles to Cleon Jones in the dugout.

Koosman was on the way to becoming the first Met pitcher ever to throw two consecutive shutouts, after throwing a four-hitter at the Dodgers previously.

"I remember him from that [exhibition] game in Arizona," said Giant coach Charlie Fox. "Every hitter, it's strike one. Strike one. Strike one. He is never behind."

And Koosman was never behind in this victory.

Jones sat on a 2-and-0 fastball and took it deep the other way, over the right-field wall, in the second and the Mets had their first run in 26 innings. In the sixth, Ken Boswell led off with a single and eventually scored on Charles' double into the left-field corner. In the seventh, against reliever Bob Bolin, Grote's double, a bunt by Koosman on which he reached when a play was made unsuccessfully by Bolin at third preceded Weis' single for the final run.

Koosman was simply brilliant, allowing just seven hits, walking two and striking out 10 (all over the first seven innings). Only once more after the first did he allow more than one baserunner in the same inning. In the seventh, pinch-hitter Nate Oliver singled and Hunt walked, but Koosman punched out Davenport for a third time.

The pride of Appleton, Minn., discovered by the Mets at least partially because of a tip from Shea Stadium usher John Luchese Sr., had blanked Los Angeles, but that was on the road. Now, after his first-inning Houdini act, Koosman had been discovered by the Flushing faithful.

Koosman ran his consecutive scoreless innings streak to 21, tying Hal Reniff's club record, in his next start and later matched Larry Bearnarth and Bob Shaw for the Met record for consecutive wins when he pushed his record to 4-0. Koosman was headed toward a 19-12 season and what would endure as his career-low 2.08 ERA.

And the left-hander's brilliance was part of a trend. During the span of a week through the home opener, Met pitchers had allowed only two runs in 58 innings and had thrown three shutouts. Through six games, they had allowed an average of 0.81 runs per game. Koosman's shutout was the fifth straight in which the Mets had been involved.

The pitching, the element so vital to all the Mets' future successes, was coming around, at last.

SAN FRANCISCO	ab	r	h	bl	METS	ab	r	h	bl
Hunt 2b	3	0	2	0	Weis ss	4	0	2	1
Davenport 3b	4	0	0	0	Boswell 2b	4	1	2	0
McCovey 1b	3	0	1	0	Agee cf	4	0	0	0
Mays cf	4	0	0	0	Swoboda rf	4	0	1	0
Hart lf	4	0	1	0	Jones lf	3	1	1	1
Hiatt c	4	0	0	0	Charles 3b	4	0	1	1
Alou rf	4	0	0	0	Shamsky 1b	4	0	0	0
Lanier ss	2	0	0	0	Kranepool 1b	0	0	0	0
Oliver ss	2	0	2	0	Grote c	2	1	1	0
McCormick p	2	0	1	0	Koosman p	2	0	0	0
Brown ph	1	0	0	0					
Bolin p	0	0	0	0					
Linzy p	0	0	0	0					
Johnson ph	1	0	0	0					
Totals	34	0	7	0	Totals	31	3	8	3

San Francisco	000	000	000	— 0
Mets	010	001	10X	— 3

E-Weis, Bolin. DP-San Francisco 1, Mets 1. LOB-San Francisco 9, Mets 7. 2B-Charles, Grote. HR-Jones (1). S-Koosman.

	IP	H	R	ER	BB	SO
San Francisco						
McCormick (L, 0-1)	6	5	2	2	2	3
Bolin	0	2	1	0	0	0
Linzy	2	1	0	0	0	0
Mets						
Koosman (W, 2-0)	9	7	0	0	2	10

T-2:22. A-52,079.

20

For Craig, One in a Row

METS 7, CUBS 3

August 10, 1963 in New York

Carolyn Craig was knitting anxiously behind home plate at the Polo Grounds, doing her best Madame Defarge impersonation. Her husband Roger had done his best to pass for a pitcher capable of winning a major league game. After having pitched the Mets to a 3-3 tie and having exited for a pinch-hitter in the bottom of the ninth, Roger now sat huddled in his jacket at the end of the Met dugout—a hit away from the end of months of personal futility.

After pinch-hitter Tim Harkness was walked to load the bases with two outs, Cubs' relief ace Lindy McDaniel ran the count full to Jim Hickman. The crowd stood and roared. The moment was especially suspenseful for the Craig family, what with the summer fading and Roger's personal losing streak at 18 games.

Was Carolyn going to have to knit her beloved a straitjacket?

The ball took off towards left field off Hickman's bat and hung in the air. Billy Williams seemed poised to snatch it.

"I thought it was the third out," said Craig, "and I said to myself, 'At least, I didn't lose this one.'"

However, there was an overhanging scoreboard in left field of the

Polo Grounds and Hickman's lazy flyball nicked it on the way down, just inches above the bottom. Imagine that. What would have been the third out was a home run, instead, and this particular game of inches was over. Hickman had a grand slam and Craig had a 7-3 victory.

It was the win for which he had been waiting forever—or maybe it just seemed like that.

"I turned around to congratulate Craig and he was gone," said Hot Rod Kanehl.

Craig was a blur as he rushed toward the plate to greet Joe Hicks, Al Moran, Harkness and Hickman. As the crowd of 11,566 celebrated with cries of "Break up the Mets," Craig wore a huge smile and waved his cap in the wind in relief. Umpire Al Forman held Craig away long enough for Hickman to touch the plate.

"I just wanted to be sure he touched it," said Craig, who had been pitching well and losing with numbing frequency. "I would have pulled him across or tackled him."

Craig no longer needed to worry about gaining a share of the major league record for consecutive losses in one season, held by John Nabors of the 1916 Athletics, or about leaving behind 1910 Brave Cliff Curtis for undisputed possession of the NL record that Craig had matched in his previous outing. And the right-hander, saddled with a 2-20 mark and winless since a 4-2 victory over the Dodgers April 29, found the perfect way to express the magnitude of his gratitude.

"I think he kissed me," said Hickman, who struck out 120 times that season.

Before the game, Craig, the Mets' player rep, addressed his teammates about two player representative matters. "Then I said 'I want to win one,'" he recalled. Then he shed his usual No. 38 in favor of No. 13, figuring it couldn't hurt, could it?

"I'd like to keep it, if the club will let me," said Craig, who allowed two homers and two triples among eight Cubs hits, struck out eight and walked only one.

Frank Thomas' homer, his 11th, off Cubs starter and new father

Paul Toth, sailed deep into the upper deck in left in the fourth and gave the Mets a 1-0 lead, but that edge was gone in a blink when Andre Rodgers and Lou Brock hit homers off Craig in the fifth.

The pitcher thought what any human being would think after four months of unhappy endings.

"I was up 1-0 and then I gave up two homers," said Craig. "I figured that was it. Here I go again. I get a lead and I can't hold it."

Two unearned runs on Ron Santo's throwing error and singles by the Dukes, Carmel and Snider, gave the Mets a 3-2 lead in the bottom of the fifth. Craig worked his way out of a jam created by Snider's three-base error on a Brock liner to right, getting Ellis Burton on a bad-hop grounder to shortstop Moran to end the seventh inning.

However, in the eighth inning, Craig permitted the tying run as Santo's sac fly scored Williams, who had tripled over Snider's head.

In, the Met ninth, Hicks singled to right with one out and, after Choo Choo Coleman struck out, went to third on the light-hitting Moran's double into the left-field corner. McDaniel was brought in and intentionally walked the lefty-hitting Harkness, who had been inserted for Craig.

"I would have hit for him even if he was my uncle," explained Met manager Casey Stengel.

Now it was up to Hickman, 0-for-4 to this point.

CHICAGO					METS				
	ab	r	h	bl		ab	r	h	bl
Brock rf	5	1	3	1	Hickman 3b	5	2	1	4
Burton cf	4	0	0	0	Carmel 1b	3	0	1	1
Williams lf	4	1	2	0	Hunt 2b	4	0	0	0
Santo 3b	3	0	1	1	Snider rf	4	0	1	1
Ranew 1b	4	0	0	0	Thomas lf	4	1	2	1
Hubbs 2b	3	0	1	0	Hicks cf	4	1	2	0
Bertell c	4	0	0	0	Coleman c	4	0	1	0
Rodgers ss	4	1	1	1	Moran ss	3	2	1	0
Toth p	4	0	0	0	Craig p	2	0	0	0
McDaniel p	0	0	0	0	a-Harkness ph	0	1	0	0
Totals	35	3	8	3	Totals	33	7	9	7

a-Walked for Craig in 9th.

Chicago	000	020	010	—3
Mets	000	120	004	—7

Two out when winning run scored. E-Toth, Santo, Snider. A-Chicago 8, Mets 16. DP-Hickman, Carmel, Brock, Ranew. LOB-Chicago 7, Mets 4. 2B-Moran. 3B-Brock, Williams. HR-Thomas, Rodgers, Brock, Hickman. Sacrifice-Craig. SF-Santo.

	IP	H	R	ER	BB	SO
Chicago						
Toth (L, 3-7)	8⅔	8	5	3	2	6
*McDaniel	0	1	2	2	1	0
Mets						
Craig (W, 3-20)	9	8	3	3	1	8

*Faced two batters in 9th.

HBP-Hubbs (by Craig). PB-Bertell. Umpires: Home-Forman; First-Gorman; Second-Landes; Third-Sudol.

T-2:31. A-11,566.

With his harmless looking fly, Hickman cleared the bases and sent everyone home—including Craig, with a W.

"He places the ball good," said Stengel of Hickman. "Just when we learn how to use that wall, they are taking the ballpark [the Polo Grounds, vacated for Shea in 1964] away from us."

The Mets rode their third straight complete-game effort to their third three-game winning streak of 1963. And Craig—already with the distinction of being the only New York pitcher in the modern era to lose 20 games two years in a row—had a measure of his sanity restored.

"You guys [the media] made it hard for me," said Craig as if no layman knew how to count to 18 without the writers' assistance. "It was a pressure game. Like a World Series."

Weis Crack Shocks Cubs

July 15, 1969 in Chicago

There were so many truly strange, hard-to-fathom victories along the path of the 1969 Mets to their world championship that their ascent was too often attributed to the miraculous (karma or, as Tom Seaver suggested at the time, God living in Manhattan) rather than the mundane (awesome pitching, the great equalizer).

There was a ton of evidence supporting the acts-of-God notion.

However, probably the single most compelling proof of the whatever-it-takes course of that remarkable summer remains the times that Al Weis flexed his muscles.

Twice in two days during the critical July series against the Cubs at Wrigley Field and again in World Series Game 5 against the Orioles, the Mighty Mite went deep.

Considering his skinny frame, his lifetime major league batting average of .219 and his seven homers and 63 extra-base hits in 1,578 lifetime regular-season at-bats, could there have been a more unlikely source of power than Weis?

And could his timing have been any better?

"Let's face it," said Weis, the throw-in with Tommie Agee in the deal the Mets made with the White Sox prior to 1968. "I'm no home-run hitter. I'm not even a hitter. I know my place on this club. I am a fill-in, a substitute."

Weis was a substitute whom manager Gil Hodges left in the lineup on a hunch July 15—even though regular shortstop Bud Harrelson had returned from his service commitment at Camp Drum the previous week.

"Gil is saving me for the World Series," said Harrelson with a smile when he spotted Weis' name on the lineup card.

"Hodges gave me confidence," Weis said years later. "All through the season, he let me hit in situations where other managers would have taken me out . . . He gave a lot of players confidence, especially players like myself, utility men. When I was traded with Agee, Gil told me he wouldn't have made the trade if I hadn't been included."

Weis paid a memorable dividend that July afternoon. The Mets began play trailing the Cubs by 5½ games, after Bill Hands had out-dueled Tom Seaver, 1-0, in the series opener one day earlier. This game now loomed even larger for the visitors and the Bleacher Bums were licking their lips in anticipation of the Second City humbling the one so nice they had to name it twice.

Weis singled and scored the Mets' first run on Agee's RBI triple on a 3-and-0 green light, but the Cubs had gotten even in the bottom of the third against Gary Gentry.

Then, in the fourth, Art Shamsky singled and went to third on a one-out single by Ed Kranepool. J.C. Martin struck out and that brought No. 8 hitter Weis to the plate, against hard-throwing, 25-year-old, ex-Met right-hander Dick Selma.

Selma had been lost by the Mets to the Padres in the expansion draft, then traded to the Cubs. And this product of Fresno (Cal.) High—the same school attended by major league pitchers Dick Ellsworth, Jim Maloney, Seaver and Bobby Jones—went into the game with numbers indicative of his impressive stuff, at long last (9-3, 104 strikeouts in 103 innings).

Selma got two quick strikes against the right-handed-hitting Weis, on breaking pitches, then missed with a fastball, just off of the outside corner. Catcher Randy Hundley signalled for a curve, but Selma shook him off and threw another heater, letter high and over the middle. Ernie Banks, who talked to hitters to distract them or maybe because he couldn't help talking to everybody, shouted that the fastball was coming. This one was letter high over the middle, the wind was blowing out and Weis sent the ball over the left-field wall, over the Bleacher Bums, over the chain fence behind them and out onto Waveland Avenue. The Mets led, 4-1.

"I just wanted to hit it," said Weis, using a 35-ounce bat loaned to him by Kranepool instead of his usual 32-ounce wand. "I just meet the ball now."

Weis admitted that, as he was circling the bases, he was thinking, "Be sure and touch every base." This is what you think when you have hit two homers in 464 games over the previous four seasons. This is what you think when you have given up switch-hitting because you "figured after one home run a season and a .172 average [in 1968 for the Mets] I couldn't do any worse just batting right-handed."

"He hit my best pitch," said Selma. "He hit my fastball. He hit it out of the ballpark. It's that simple."

"You can expect Selma to challenge a hitter, to throw the fastball and Weasel is a good fastball hitter," said Ron Swoboda.

Kranepool couldn't resist sticking the needle into Banks a few innings later, saying to him, "You sure called the pitch on that one, Ernie. You'd make a helluva catcher."

Ken Boswell also homered before Selma left in the fifth, but the Cubs got that run back in the sixth and trailed, 5-2, going into the eighth. Then things got a little hairy for Gentry.

Don Kessinger led off with a single, but Boswell was in the perfect spot to turn Glenn Beckert's grounder into a double play before Billy Williams took Gentry deep, into the center-field stands, for his 10th homer. Instead of the tie game it would have been if Beckert's shot had found the hole, the Mets still led, 5-3.

Then Ron Santo followed Williams' long ball with his 19th homer, on an 0-and-2 curve. That made it a one-run game and signalled the end for Gentry.

"That was a dumb pitch I threw to Santo," said Gentry, who was replaced by Ron Taylor. "I wasn't tired. I just made a mistake. I wanted to waste it inside, but I didn't get it in enough and I didn't have much on it. I should know better by now."

Taylor, with his sinker finely tuned, got the last out of the eighth. In the ninth, Taylor got Willie Smith swinging on a backup slider, then threw his so-so fastball past Hundley for a third strike. The Cubs' last hope was Jimmy Qualls, well-known by Seaver and the Mets by now as a .385 hitter against them. But this time, Qualls grounded to Kranepool, who threw to Taylor covering.

Game over.

Weis, a .220 hitter when his big day was over, got to review his major league homers, one by one, for the media. It didn't take long.

"I hit my first one off Tommy John when he was pitching for Cleveland in 1964," he said. "The next was off Dick Stigman in Minnesota, also in 1964. I hit one off Dave McNally in 1965 and one off Cecil Upshaw last year [1968]. And now this one . . . Why shouldn't I remember them?

METS	ab	r	h	bl	CHICAGO	ab	r	h	bl
Agee cf	4	0	1	1	Kessinger ss	3	0	1	1
Boswell 2b	4	1	2	1	Beckert 2b	4	0	0	0
Jones lf	3	0	0	0	Williams rf	4	1	1	1
Shamsky rf	3	1	1	0	Santo 3b	4	2	2	1
Gaspar rf	0	0	0	0	Banks 1b	4	0	2	0
Garrett 3b	4	0	1	0	Smith lf	3	0	0	0
Kranepool 1b	4	1	1	0	Hundley c	4	0	0	0
Martin 1b	4	0	1	0	Qualls cf	4	1	2	0
Weis ss	4	2	2	3	Selma p	0	0	0	0
Gentry p	2	0	0	0	Nye p	1	0	0	0
Taylor p	1	0	0	0	Spangler ph	1	0	0	0
					Aguirre p	0	0	0	0
Totals	35	5	9	5	Totals	32	4	8	3

Mets			001	310	000	— 5
Chicago			001	001	020	— 4

E-Agee. DP-Mets 1, Chicago 1. LOB-Mets 4, Chicago 4. 3B-Agee. HR-Weis (1), Boswell (3), Williams (10), Santo (19). SB-Qualls. S-Gentry, Selma. SF-Kessinger.

	IP	H	R	ER	BB	SO
Mets						
Gentry (W, 8-7)	7²/₃	8	4	3	1	4
Taylor	1¹/₃	0	0	0	0	2
Chicago						
Selma L(, 9-4)	4¹/₃	8	5	5	1	5
Nye	2²/₃	0	0	0	0	3
Aguirre	2	1	0	0	1	3

Save-Taylor.

T-2:24. A-38,608.

I spread them out."

Weis told the story about how, after one of his long balls, "I came into the dugout and all the guys were all laying on the floor like they were all dead or passed out from shock."

That was pretty much Cubs manager Leo Durocher's reaction to this day's events.

"Weis. Weis. Weis. Don't mention that name," said The Lip. "Selma had to furnish the power. There had to be a tail wind. And he had to swing as hard as he could."

"I'd still like to break up that home run and have four singles for it," said Weis.

Not this one.

Man Bites Dog and ...
Tug Slays Sandy

August 26, 1965 in New York

S andy Koufax, simply brilliant against the entire league, had always been much better than that against the Mets. In his 14 starts against the Mets over four seasons, the 29-year-old Dodger left-hander from Brooklyn had completed 10 games and had gone 13-0 with a 1.15 ERA, including five shutouts and 130 strikeouts in 117 innings.

That included a no-hitter.

Dodger fans reborn as faithful to the Mets, converts with the passion of jilted lovers, lived for the day that justice would prevail over greed and the team that deserted Brooklyn for the left coast, swimming pools and movie stars would get their lumps from the upstart kids in Flushing. But Koufax' dominance over the Mets was echoed by Los Angeles' 58 wins in 68 meetings going into an August 1965 series at Shea Stadium.

The Mets won the middle two games of this four-game set and their stirring prompted a crowd of 45,950 to attend the finale. But this contest mismatched the remarkable Koufax—21-5 for the season with 296 strikeouts coming in—and the first-place Dodgers against a left-hander named Tug McGraw, still a few days shy of his 21st birthday and just a few days removed from his first big league victory.

Even a kid as green as McGraw could not be impervious to fretting about how good he would have to be.

"He was Tug McGraw all day," said his roommate and buddy Ron Swoboda, without elaborating about McGraw's other options. "I think I was scareder about this game than he was."

"All through the game, my stomach kept going wu-wu-wu," said McGraw. "Last night, I couldn't sleep too good, I kept waking up with Koufax on my mind."

"I knew he really wanted to win it," said Swoboda concerning McGraw's demeanor the night before the game. "He stood in front of the mirror, making believe he was pitching and I said, 'For god sakes, Tug, go to bed. You are going to win. You're gonna win.'"

As outfielders go, Swoboda was a helluva prophet.

The Dodgers scored a run in the first on Maury Wills' single, Wes Parker's sac bunt and Lou Johnson's RBI double—the last time Los Angeles would get more than a single hit in an inning until the eighth. Meanwhile, Koufax wasn't his usual high-velocity self and had to resort to a succession of off-speed pitches. And the lead was gone before the first inning was history.

After Ron Hunt walked, Roy McMillan lashed a hit-and-run, game-tying double. No. 3 hitter Joe Christopher sacrificed and then Jim Hickman's two-out bouncer to the shortstop hole was thrown away by Wills. The infield hit made it 2-1, Mets. Though he struck out only five overall, Koufax allowed the Mets only one more hit through the first six innings.

In the seventh, Ed Kranepool sat on a changeup and stroked it into the right-field corner for a double. Dodger manager Walt Alston and Koufax decided to intentionally walk No. 7 hitter Chris Cannizzaro, a .177 hitter at the end of the night. Cannizzaro's shock at the show of respect was such that he said to Los Angeles catcher Jeff Torborg, "You guys are out of your mind."

After pinch-hitter Bobby Klaus became the second out, Dodger third baseman Don LeJohn fielded McGraw's grounder and pulled first baseman Parker off the bag with a high throw as Kranepool crossed the plate to make it 3-1. The run was unearned, but much appreciated.

In the eighth, McGraw issued his only walk, to Dick Tracewski, pinch-hitting for Koufax. Wills lashed a line-drive hit to left center that Hickman, despite being screened by the charging Swoboda, scooped up and fired to Klaus in time to nip the Dodger speedster at second for the second out. The play loomed large when Parker followed with a triple that made it 3-2 and signalled the end for McGraw.

Tug was replaced by Jack Fisher, the veteran right-hander who had been knocked out in three innings the night before and had told manager Wes Westrum he would be happy to work that night.

Fisher even promised better results.

"Usually, I have pretty good stuff when I come back after getting knocked out," explained Fisher.

After walking Jim Gilliam, Fisher got Johnson to bounce into an inning-ending force and worked a 1-2-3 ninth.

By that time, back-to-back homers by Christopher and Swoboda—the latter denting the parked Dodger bus—off aging Dodger reliever Johnny Podres in the bottom of the eighth had given the Mets a 5-2 lead and eased McGraw's nerves.

"I was doing cartwheels and handstands," said the manic McGraw, who jumped up and down when his two-run, eight-hit, five-strikeout performance was officially stamped with the W that attached an L next to Koufax' name.

"Sooner or later, you are going to get beat," said the classy Koufax. "It's over. Fine."

The victory was the Mets' sixth in their last seven games—and this was their first-ever series conquest over the Dodgers.

"Win, win, win," ho-hummed Gary Kolb, pretending to be bored. "It's disgusting . . . This makes us one of the top 10 teams in the league."

Swoboda was moved to find a grounds for comparison between McGraw, the dragon slayer, and Koufax, the dragon—beyond both being left-handed.

"Tug has great stuff and they just made him sit around all year," said Swoboda. "Hell, once he starts getting his curveball going, that will make his other stuff that much more effective. It will make him twice as good as Koufax."

LOS ANGELES	ab	r	h	bl	METS	ab	r	h	bl
Wills ss	4	1	4	0	Hunt 2b	3	1	0	0
Parker 1b	2	0	1	1	McMillan ss	4	1	2	1
Gilliam lf	3	0	0	0	Christopher rf	3	1	1	1
Johnson lf	4	0	1	1	Swoboda lf	4	1	1	1
Lefebvre 2b	4	0	1	0	Hickman cf	4	0	1	1
LeJohn 3b	3	0	0	0	Kranepool 1b	4	1	1	0
Fairly ph	1	0	0	0	Cannizzaro c	2	0	0	0
WDavis cf	4	0	1	0	Hiller 2b	2	0	0	0
Torborg c	3	0	0	0	Klaus 2b	1	0	0	0
Koufax p	2	0	0	0	McGraw p	3	0	0	0
Tracewski ph	0	1	0	0					
Totals	30	2	8	2	Totals	30	5	6	4

Los Angeles	100	000	010 —2
Mets	200	000	12X —5

E-LeJohn. DP-Mets 1. LOB-Los Angeles 5, Mets 4. 2B-Johnson, McMillan, Kranepool. 3B-Parker. HR-Christopher (4), Swoboda (19). S-Parker 2, Christopher.

	IP	H	R	ER	BB	SO
Los Angeles						
Koufax (L, 21-6)	7	4	3	2	2	5
Podres	1	2	2	2	0	0
Mets						
McGraw (W, 2-2)	7⅔	8	2	2	1	5
Fisher	1⅓	0	0	0	1	1

T-2:24. A-45,950.

23

Grand HoJo Beats Heat

September 10, 1985 in New York

The fastball is considered the best pitch in baseball. Every big league hitter needs to be able to hit one but some hit it better or more often than others, of course. Hitters capable of consistently turning around a truly high-octane heater are special.

Howard Johnson was special, displaying wrists quick enough to overpower the fastest fastball with authority.

You might say, in the box, he was a dead-red head.

"He can turn it around as well as anyone," reflected Keith Hernandez.

One of the most memorable proofs of Johnson's prowess at launching zooming fastballs over faraway fences came against the backdrop of the desperate 1985 race in the NL East between the Mets and the Cardinals, who entered the opener of this three-game series tied at the top.

In the first inning, after intentionally walking Darryl Strawberry, Danny Cox lost his cool and punished a dawdling George Foster for stepping out of the box twice by nailing him with a fastball to the butt. The tantrum served to clear the dugouts for a shove fest and it loaded the bases for Johnson.

Slider. Change. Slider.

"In that situation, he had to figure he would get me out easy with breaking balls," said Johnson, a switch-hitter and the lefty half of a third-base platoon with Ray Knight. "I don't see many fastballs with men on base . . . and he got me in St. Louis on breaking balls."

However, with the count 2-and-1, Cox decided he could sneak his cheese past Johnson, an ill-advised conclusion.

The fastball caught most of the plate or would have—if Johnson hadn't pounced on it and sent it off the scoreboard in right center for a truly grand slam. The crowd of 50,195 erupted as Howard was greeted by all of his teammates at the plate. The Mets had a 5-1 lead and were on their way to a 5-4 win, their seventh victory in eight games, which gave them undisputed control of first for the first time since Aug. 22.

You don't spit in the wind, you don't tug on Superman's cape and you don't try to sneak a fastball past Howard Johnson with the bases drunk.

"I'm upset about the pitch to Johnson. It was a fastball down the pipe—the only pitch he can hit," said manager Whitey Herzog, whose Cards lost their fourth straight game. "He can't hit a changeup and he can't hit a breaking ball."

"I blew the game," said Cox.

"It has to be the biggest hit of my career," said Johnson.

The excitement began even before Johnson went deep. The fans warmly cheered Hernandez as he stepped in for his first home at-bat since testifying "the drug was a demon in me" at the cocaine trial in Pittsburgh. He was an admitted former drug user. But now the forgiving faithful chose to see him as their Gold Glove first baseman, team captain and clutch No. 3 hitter. All was forgiven and the fans' ovation touched him.

"They're great fans," said Hernandez. "I just didn't expect that kind of ovation. It got to me. It makes me want to finish my career here."

Hernandez—who said he was too emotional to swing at the first pitch—eventually singled to left center and Mookie Wilson, on first with a leadoff hit of his own, came all the way around to score when Vince Coleman fell down chasing Hernandez' hit. The run tied the game at 1, offsetting a first-inning homer by Tommy Herr off Ron Darling. With two out and first base open, Straw was walked to get to Foster.

The war of nerves began. Foster stepped out. He stepped in and Cox stepped off the rubber. Foster stepped out until home-plate umpire Terry Tata asked if he would mind hitting. And Cox plunked Foster with his first pitch. Foster glared at the pitcher as he ambled toward first, bat still in his hand, as Cox walked toward the Met left fielder.

"You better watch out," said Foster to Cox.

The benches emptied in a blink, though it was a punch-free, typical pick-a-partner-and-dance baseball confrontation that prompted the Mets' Clint Hurdle to quip later, "I was looking for someone with a gold chain I could steal."

Other Mets were aroused.

"He was trying to show Foster up," concluded the always angriest Met Strawberry, who was restrained by Hernandez.

Cox said the pitch just got away from him, even as he expressed annoyance at Foster's dilly-dallying. "It's something he does all the time," said Cox. "He steps out four or five times and you wonder how many more things he can adjust," he said.

"I'm surprised he doesn't get hit more often," said Herr.

Herzog was understandably more pissed off at his starter than any of the Mets were.

"It certainly wasn't the right time to do it," said the Rat. "Cox forgot for a few minutes what he was out there for. He can't let himself get upset about what Foster or anybody else does."

Then Johnson went boom.

"I don't know which was worse, hitting Foster with the pitch or throwing the one that Johnson hit," reflected Herzog.

The Cards got a run in the fifth on a Coleman RBI hit and two more in the seventh that were charged to a weary Darling, who nevertheless boosted his season record to 15-5—thanks to Roger McDowell's 2⅔ scoreless innings of relief.

The night ultimately belonged to Johnson, the former Tiger who had been criticized by his ex-manager Sparky Anderson for choking when the stakes were high and was given only one World Series at-bat in 1984.

"Howard has gotten a lot of clutch hits this year," said Hernandez. "I thought that Sparky said he couldn't play under pressure."

"Maybe it's all part of maturing, growing up as a ballplayer. I didn't come through in Detroit and I have to work through that," said Johnson, whose wrists eventually made him the premier third baseman in Met history.

"It seems like Howard prefers tight situations to normal situations," said manager Davey Johnson. "No shot at Sparky intended, but Howard seems like he would be a good guy to have in a World Series."

ST. LOUIS	ab	r	h	bl	METS	ab	r	h	bl
Coleman lf	5	0	2	2	MWilson cf	4	1	1	0
McGee cf	4	0	0	1	Backman 2b	3	0	0	0
Herr 2b	4	1	1	1	Hernandez 1b	4	1	1	1
Porter c	4	0	0	0	Carter c	4	0	0	0
VanSlyke rf	4	0	1	0	Strawberry rf	2	1	0	0
Pendleton 3b	4	0	0	0	Foster lf	2	1	1	0
Jorgensen 1b	3	1	0	0	HJohnson 3b	3	1	1	4
OSmith ss	3	1	1	0	McDowell p	0	0	0	0
Cox p	1	0	0	0	Santana ss	3	0	1	0
Ford ph	1	0	0	0	Darling p	1	0	0	0
Horton p	0	0	0	0	Knight 3b	1	0	0	0
Braun ph	1	0	0	0					
Landrum pr	0	1	0	0					
Dayley p	0	0	0	0					
Cedeno ph	1	0	0	0					
Totals	35	4	5	4	Totals	27	5	5	5

St. Louis	100	010	200	— 4
Mets	500	000	00X	— 5

Game Winning RBI-HJohnson (8). E-Santana 2, Carter. LOB-St. Louis 7, Mets 2. 2B-OSmith, Coleman. HR-Herr (5), HJohnson (9). SB-Coleman (93). S-Darling.

St. Louis	IP	H	R	ER	BB	SO
Cox (L, 15-0)	4	5	5	5	1	2
Horton	2	0	0	0	1	0
Dayley	2	0	0	0	0	2
Mets						
Darling (W, 15-5)	6⅓	4	4	4	3	7
McDowell S 13	2⅔	1	0	0	0	0

HBP-Foster (by Cox).

T-2:36. A-50,195.

For Piazza, It's Roger and Out

June 9, 2000 in The Bronx, N.Y.

It was a 12-2 June walk through monument park for the Mets, worth savoring mostly for being the most lopsided chapter in the four-year, head-to-head, regular-season history of games against their ring-cluttered Yankee rivals and distressing enough to send George Steinbrenner scurrying home before the final out.

Eventually, though, after all the ugliness that would unfold between Roger Clemens and Mike Piazza on the tracks toward and through a Subway Series in October, this game would be redefined as the one that lit the fuse of the red-necked Rocket named Clemens. This was the prelude to a hideous story without any happy ending or any ending at all, yet—considering the Mets' long memories and strong appetite to settle affairs with Roger Rabid.

Piazza's massive, 425-foot grand slam made the jaws of 55,822 fans fly open, gave Al Leiter a 4-0 third-inning lead and signalled a battering of Clemens typical of the pitcher's checkered history against the Mets to this point (0-3, 13.18 ERA as a Yankee). And no Met hitter had punished Clemens more regularly or more spectacularly than the Pizza Man.

Piazza homered when the Mets and Leiter shattered Clemens' personal 20-game winning streak with a 7-2 victory on June 6, 1999. Piazza took Roger over the wall again, with two on in the sixth inning, for a game-winning homer in a 5-2 triumph on July 9, 1999. Now, the second slam surrendered by Clemens in a career spanning 3,542 innings gave Piazza homers in each of Roger's three starts against the Mets.

"Obviously, he's going to be a Hall of Fame pitcher, but it's tough to pitch when you have guys on," said Piazza, a .385 hitter with four homers and 14 RBI in 10 games against the Yanks overall and a blistering 7-for-12 mark with nine RBI lifetime vs. Clemens when this game was over.

"He [Piazza] seems to get locked in when he comes here, but he is like that every game," said John Franco.

"Mike does things hardly anyone else can do," said Mets manager Bobby Valentine about his All-Star slugger. "And he seems to do them at the right time. That's comforting, reassuring and gives us confidence . . . He is very comfortable being Mike Piazza, the outstanding baseball player playing in New York."

"I know what my role is on this club," said Piazza. "There are situations when I have to give us a lift. I accept that. I don't want to pass it to someone else."

A throwing error on Jason Tyner's bunt by catcher Jorge Posada and a pair of walks loaded the bases for Piazza to clear them. On Piazza's first trip, Clemens had thrown him five fastballs and had struck him out swinging. Strangely, this time, on a 1-and-0 count, came Clemens' third-best pitch—a flat, down and (not far enough) away slider. Piazza swung and his 16th homer of 2000 was a monster, even by his standards.

It surged, screaming into the blackness of the background in dead center. Over a leaping Bernie Williams. Over the fence at the 408-foot sign. Overwhelming.

"There aren't many guys who hit the ball to the farthest point of this ballpark and flip their bat, 'cause they know it's gone," said Yankee manager Joe Torre, admiring both Piazza's 11th career grand slam and the powerful man who gave birth to it. "He's a frightening guy to have on the other side. You make a mistake and it's not a single or double. It's a towering homer. It could be [hit] anywhere."

Piazza (3-for-4 overall) gently laid his bat down at his feet after touching off this bomb and smiled slightly as he began his tour of the bases and Clemens kicked at the rubber. The greatest-hitting catcher of all time is too classy to have felt the need to adorn his domination of the usually intimidating Clemens with taunting or gloating.

Clemens—a tightly wound right-hander nastier than his pitches— wasn't exactly a mystery to Piazza's playmates, either. There were run-scoring singles from Derek Bell (3-for-4 with a double, three-run homer and five RBI) and Todd Zeile. Edgardo Alfonzo crushed a two-run homer, also to center.

Clemens, the five-time Cy Young winner whose season record was now 4-6 after his third straight loss, posted an ugly line: five-plus innings, nine runs, eight earned, 10 hits, three walks. And a balk.

"This ballclub has a way of getting up for big pitchers and big games," noted Piazza. "It's like, 'Fine. Bring on the best and we'll take them on.'"

"I felt I had better stuff than what the final score says," said Roger, originally selected by the Mets in the June 1981 amateur draft. "I just have to keep the ball in the park to give our guys a chance. I gave up too many homers, but there is not a lot you can do about that. They were good pitches."

When Clemens slinked off to his solitary shower to a chorus of boos in the sixth, Torre walked off with his arm around his pitcher's waist and said to him, "We'll get this thing figured out."

Of course, Clemens eventually did figure it out and turned around his season. And Roger figured out something else, too—a cowardly, childish revenge.

Clemens apparently decided he would show Piazza who was boss the next time they met. So, on the night of July 8, when Clemens was pinpoint in his control and the presence of a DH meant Roger wouldn't have to set foot in the batter's box, he drilled Piazza in his head with a 95-mph heater on his first pitch to him.

Even if you didn't notice the complete lack of remorse in Roger, the vicious location of the pitch and Piazza's history of owning Clemens made the pitch's purpose painfully clear to most of the sane world. Piazza, a catcher who can tell the difference between a brushback that slipped and intentional, malicious head hunting, knew that he had been prey.

The toll was just a concussion for Piazza, who was lucky.

Even Yankee fans were struck silent by the sight of Piazza writhing in the dirt and the boldness of Clemens' disregard for the code of the game. Buzzing a hitter or drilling him below the waist is a part of the game. But intentional fastballs to the head show disdain for a fellow player's life and career.

Thanks to stunning inaction by the game's powers, Clemens escaped significant punishment. So, in October, in World Series Game 2, Clemens tried something new to amuse himself and

METS	ab	r	h	bl	YANKEES	ab	r	h	bl
Tyner lf-cf	6	2	2	0	Jeter ss	5	1	3	0
DeBell rf	4	3	3	5	BeWilliams cf	2	0	1	0
Alfonzo 2b	4	2	1	2	O'Neill rf	3	0	0	0
McEwing 2b	0	0	0	0	Jose ph-lf	1	0	0	0
Piazza c	4	2	3	4	Spencer lf	3	0	0	1
Pratt c	1	0	0	0	Posada c	3	0	0	0
Ventura 3b	5	0	0	0	Turner ph-c	1	0	0	0
Wendell p	0	0	0	0	TMartinez 1b	3	1	1	0
RRodriguez p	0	0	0	0	WDelgado ph-2b	1	0	0	0
Zeile 1b	5	0	1	1	Leyritz ph	4	0	1	0
LHarris ph	3	0	0	0	Brosius 3b	3	0	1	1
Franco ph-dh-3b	2	0	1	0	Bellinger 2b-1b	4	0	1	0
Payton cf	4	1	3	0					
Agbayani ph-lf	1	0	0	0					
KAbbott ss	1	0	0	0					
Mora ss	3	2	1	0					
Totals	**43**	**12**	**15**	**12**	**Totals**	**33**	**2**	**3**	**2**

Mets			004	113	300	— 12
Yankees			000	110	000	— 2

E-Posada (4), Clemens (2). LOB-Mets 7, Yankees 3. 2B-Tyner (1), DeBell (15), TMartinez (13). HR-DeBell (8) off Erdos, Alfonzo (12) off Clemens, Piazza (16) off Clemens. RBI-DeBell 5 (31), Alfonzo 2 (47), Piazza 4 (43), Zeile (42), Spencer (25), Brosius (16). SB-Mora (3), BeWilliams (7). SF-Spencer. GIDP-Ventura, Jeter. Runners left in scoring position-Mets 3 (Ventura, KAbbott, Mora), Yankees 3 (Spencer 3, Posada, Bellinger). DP-Mets 1 (RRodriguez, Mora, Zeile), Yankees 1 Bellinger, Jeter, TMartinez.

Mets	IP	H	R	ER	BB	SO
Leiter (W, 7-1)	7	7	2	2	3	4
Wendell	1	0	0	0	0	0
RRodriguez	1	1	0	0	0	0
Yankees						
Clemens (L, 4-6)	5	10	9	8	3	4
Erdos	3	4	3	3	0	2
Watson	1	1	0	0	0	1

Clemens pitched to 3 batters in the 5th. PB-Posada. Balk-Clemens.

T-3:30. A-55,822.

enhance his reputation as a competitor. He heaved the jagged edge of Piazza's broken bat in the catcher's path in the first inning. No ejection under the commissioner's no-homicide, no-foul policy.

But all that was still to come. The dominant pitcher on this June night, Leiter, showed respect for the game and the task ahead of him.

Leiter reprised his role as the other Clemens tormentor, out-pitching him in one of these intracity showdowns for the third time in two seasons. After allowing two runs and seven hits over seven innings, Leiter observed humbly, "When you face a quality pitcher like Roger, you know you might have to throw a shutout to win."

Leiter boosted his season record to 7-1 and moved to 3-0, 2.05 as a Met against the Yankees, the team with which he broke into the majors.

"We have those moments in big moments, when the feeling is just there and you've got to nail it," said Leiter. "We enjoy that."

All the Mets enjoyed a laugher at, of all places, the House That Ruth Built. Tyner, 23, contributed two hits, two runs scored and a diving catch in the outfield. And the kid had a wonderful time once he shook off a gee-whiz moment in the first inning of his fourth major league game.

"I stepped in the box and looked up," said Tyner. "I don't usually look at the pitcher, but for some reason I did this time. I was like, 'Geez, that is Roger Clemens on the mound.'"

Then Tyner doubled.

"Clemens probably thought, 'The bat boy just got a double off me,'" Tyner said later.

The Yankee Stadium tradition and the dulcet tones of Bob Sheppard made the night special for Piazza.

"I think it is awesome," said Piazza. "Just getting your name over the PA is a cool shot of adrenaline. I hope I get an opportunity to play here in a World Series."

In retrospect, perhaps Piazza should have been more careful about what he wished for.

25

Earning Respect From Da Bums

July 16, 1969 in Chicago

On July 16, 1969, the point still needed to be made that the race in the National League was far from over. The Mets needed one more victory to win their series at Wrigley Field, take four-out-of-six contests against the Cubs in a July home-and-home ordeal, cut Chicago's lead to 3½ games and leave the Cubs with serious doubts about which team would be looking down at the other at the finish.

The weather at Wrigley was as hot as the race was becoming, with temperatures in the 90s and the wind blowing out—the kind of Chicago afternoon that makes pitchers queasy.

Certainly, the mound matchup didn't favor the Mets, with 33-year-old Don Cardwell opposing indefatigable Cub ace Ferguson Jenkins. Jenkins was 12-6 with 156 strikeouts in '69 and was coming off a brilliant, albeit ultimately losing effort against the Mets the previous Tuesday.

"That Jenkins doesn't sweat," said Art Shamsky to Ken Boswell before the game. "He wears long sleeves on days like this."

But Shamsky was wrong about the perspiration. The Mets made Jenkins' pores work overtime from the get-go.

Tommie Agee slammed the first pitch of the game past third for a double, matching the Mets' hit output for the first eight innings of their previous tussle with Jenkins. Agee scored on Boswell's bloop hit into right. After Cleon Jones' single and stolen base and a strikeout of Shamsky, Wayne Garrett was intentionally walked.

Once again, Cubs manager Leo Durocher paid the price for his strategy, as the painfully slow Ed Kranepool got an RBI infield single and J.C. Martin—who would finish the day in the hospital with heat prostration—singled in two more for a 4-0 lead.

When Agee led off the second with his 16th homer, into the left-field bleachers, the Mets had their fifth run. The score was 5-0, even though the ball was tossed back onto the field by the Bleacher Bums, according to their custom. Jenkins, yanked in favor of Hank Aguirre at this point, later expressed puzzlement about his outing, saying, "I don't know what was wrong. I wasn't in there long enough to find out."

Aguirre was touched for a run in the second. A 6-0 lead? Even more accustomed to poor run support than most Met starters, Cardwell must have thought that he was hallucinating because of the heat.

Was this going to be easy for a change?

"You never have a comfortable lead in Wrigley Field," says Shamsky. "Not against the kind of lineup the Cubs have and not on a day like this, when the wind is blowing straight out."

Smart right fielder that Shamsky. But not too quick.

In the second, Ernie Banks' double and Randy Hundley's single made it 6-1. And when Shamsky pulled up short on the pitiful-hitting Aguirre's pop to short right, thinking Agee was going to get it, the apparent out became a single. Singles by Don Kessinger and Glenn Beckert cut the margin to 6-3.

Cardwell was relieved—not *relieved* about blowing his chance for a win when he finally got some offensive support—but relieved, as in replaced.

Billy Williams' single off Jim McAndrew made it 6-4. Cal Koonce entered next, following singles by Banks and Willie Smith in the third.

Koonce escaped the inning with three straight outs, but one of them plated Banks and it was a one-run game.

"The momentum was all theirs," noted Tom Seaver.

Not for long. In the fifth, with Rich Nye on for the Cubs, Al Weis stepped into the box.

Nye eschewed the fastball, maybe remembering Dick Selma had challenged the Met shortstop with one of those and lost in the form of that shocking three-run homer the previous day.

The pitcher threw Weis a curve.

A hanger.

"Oh, no," says Cubs' broadcaster Jack Brickhouse. "Not again."

Again.

Into the bleachers this time, not over them completely and onto Waveland Avenue like the day before, but a homer nevertheless.

"Weis has lost a little power," would be the post-game assessment of Gil Hodges, doing his best managing by managing to keep a straight face.

Weis had equalled his home run output for the previous four and a half years in *two days*.

In the eighth, Ted Abernathy, the right-handed side-winder, threw a fastball to Shamsky, who nailed it for a two-run, opposite-field homer, his seventh, and now the score was 9-5.

Before leaving in favor of Ron Taylor in the eighth, Koonce blanked his former team for five innings, retiring Banks and Ron Santo on critical double-play balls.

Durocher had given up on Koonce, a 1962 Cubs draft pick, in 1967 and the right-hander had been a revelation for the Mets with a 2.41 ERA in 1968.

Cal had no love for Leo.

"Durocher would use the same reliever, game after game, until he ran out of gas," said Koonce. "If you were on a hot streak, you knew you were going to be the first one to be called every day . . . During one period, I warmed up in the bullpen 14 days in a row and that takes something out of you."

Taylor pitched a 1-2-3 eighth, but the Cubs threatened in the ninth, putting two runners on for Williams and Santo. But the Cubs' thumpers both went down on popups to second.

As he came out of the dugout to congratulate Taylor, Seaver took a small hop and clicked his heels in the manner that Santo had done in a galling celebration of a victory over the Mets.

As the Mets walked the stairs from the dugout to their clubhouse, one Cub fan said, "You guys are still inferior to the Cubs."

Ron Swoboda's answer was the essence of simplicity.

"Eat your heart out," he said.

"I'll tell you what has happened here—an epidemic," said Hodges. "It's contagious. One guy is picking up the other. You never know who's going to do it next for you."

"The Mets beat us," said Santo. "You have to give them credit for that. Two out of three in our park. I still don't believe it . . . They fooled me. They are much better than I thought they were. They are harder for us to beat than any other club."

Durocher was less impressed.

"Just another ballgame. Don't forget who is in first place," said Durocher.

"I think these boys have made their mark to the Cubs and everyone else," said Hodges. "You don't clinch a

METS	ab	r	h	bl	CHICAGO	ab	r	h	bl
Agee cf	5	2	2	1	Kessinger ss	5	1	2	1
Boswell 2b	5	1	2	1	Beckert 2b	4	0	2	1
CJones lf	5	3	2	0	BWilliams rf	4	0	3	1
Shamsky rf	5	1	3	2	Santo 3b	5	0	1	0
RTaylor p	0	0	0	0	Banks 1b	4	2	2	0
Garrett 3b	3	1	0	1	WSmith lf	4	0	1	0
Kranepool 1b	2	0	1	1	Hundley c	3	0	1	1
Clendenon 1b	3	0	0	0	Qualls cf	3	1	0	1
Martin c	5	0	2	2	Jenkins p	0	0	0	0
Weis ss	5	1	1	1	Aguirre p	1	1	1	0
Cardwell p	1	0	0	0	Spangler ph	1	0	0	0
McAndrew p	0	0	0	0	Nye p	0	0	0	0
Koonce p	2	0	1	0	Heath ph	1	0	0	0
Gaspar rf	1	0	0	0	Abernathy p	0	0	0	0
					Popovich ph	1	0	1	0
Totals	42	9	14	9	Totals	36	5	14	5

Mets	420	010	020	— 9
Chicago	041	000	000	— 5

E-Santo. DP-Mets 3. LOB-Mets 9, Chicago 6. 2B-Agee, Banks. HR-Agee (16), Weis (2), Shamsky (7). SB-CJones, SHundley. SF-Qualls.

	IP	H	R	ER	BB	SO
Mets						
Cardwell	1⅔	6	4	4	0	0
McAndrew	⅓	3	1	1	0	0
Koonce (W, 4-3)	5	4	0	0	0	1
RTaylor	2	1	0	0	1	0
Chicago						
Jenkins (L, 12-7)	1	6	5	4	1	3
Aguirre	2	2	1	1	1	2
Nye	3	4	1	1	1	1
Abernathy	3	2	2	0	0	1

HBP-BWilliams (by Cardwell). WP-Jenkins.

T-3:00. A-36,795.

pennant in July, not with 2½ tough months of baseball to play. But they certainly are a contender now. Ask any of them. They believe."

"Are the nine crucial days [the two series vs. Chicago wrapped around one vs. Montreal] over yet?" asked the sardonic Taylor.

Taylor was told not till midnight.

"Then all that is left is the crucial plane ride to Montreal," he said.

"I have a press release," said Seaver. "Al Weis is only 483 years away from Babe Ruth."

...And One Special Healing Night for New York

METS 3, BRAVES 2

September 21, 2001 in New York

This was a night like no other at Shea Stadium, because it really wasn't about baseball. It was about endurance in the face of shocking tragedy, about patriotism as a response to terror and evil, about real tears shed for real heroes, about baseball being embraced anew as part of the American way. And it was about New York City's resilience following the tragic loss of approximately 3,000 lives in the kamikaze airplane attacks that brought down the World Trade Center's Twin Towers Sept. 11.

It was about a group hug between two baseball rivals and managers who have never cared much for each other and about an appreciation of the fans, from whom the players have become so far removed in the modern era. It was about national unity and nine innings of entertaining diversion. This was a game whose outcome could no longer feel cataclysmic to even the most absorbed baseball fan.

Such is the aftermath of catastrophe.

Against all odds, these September games between the Mets and the

Atlanta Braves actually had significance for both clubs, because of the Mets' out-of-nowhere surge into contention in the final stages of a season that had appeared unsalvageable for months. However, the Mets' stunning 20-5 run from 13½ games back—they had been in fourth place with a record of 14 games under .500 as recently as Aug. 17—to the doorstep of a possible miracle finish was nothing more than a backdrop.

This was the first outdoor sporting event in New York since the tragedy. A divisional race is fun and games when it's placed in the context of a country at war and risk. By just coming out to the event, amid the tightest security and the most natural of fears, fans were making as much of a statement as either team could make on the field.

A ballpark that had served as a staging area for a massive relief effort—where Mets manager Bobby Valentine had pitched in, loading and packing supplies for rescue personnel during the week that baseball went dark—was decorated for this emotional occasion. On the Shea scoreboard, the light blue neon lights representing the miniature New York skyline were lit—except the Twin Towers were darkened and covered with red, white and blue ribbons. "God Bless America" was written on the top of the Mets' dugout and "Welcome to New York City" on the Braves'. There were red, white and blue ribbons painted on the grass. The billboard of a huge flag, 35 feet by 50 feet, replaced the Budweiser sign on the scoreboard in right center.

The Mets players wore the date of the attack, 9-11-01, embroidered on left sleeves of their uniform. They also continued wearing the hats of the city's police department, fire department, emergency service workers and Port Authority police, as they had been during the series in Pittsburgh that preceded this one. "They are going to have to tear the hats off us," said Todd Zeile, referring to major league baseball's wishes the players would return to the Mets' normal headwear because of licensing issues. "I'll keep it in my back pocket if I have to."

As human beings, as Americans, as ultra-visible representatives of the city, the Mets, top to bottom, were able to understand the impact of this tragedy on the families of the dead and missing. Fred Wilpon, the boss, pledged a million dollars and the Met players donated their night's salary, reportedly $446,584.70 in all, to Rusty Staub's New York Police and Fire Widows' and Childrens' Benefit Fund. A day earlier, Al Leiter, Mike Piazza, Zeile, Robin Ventura, John Franco, coach John Stearns and Valentine were among a contingent of team members who went to Ground Zero to encourage the rescue/cleanup workers.

"We talked to persons who had been injured, saw guys still trying to pull some of their buddies out of the wreckage, dead or alive, to get some closure," said Zeile. "For them to take a minute out to tell us we have been at least some slight inspiration has given us something bigger to try for than striving to get to the World Series."

Each of the 41,235 fans was handed an American flag when he or she walked in. At 7 p.m., New York Mayor Rudolph Giuliani was greeted with thunderous cheers and the chanting of his first name as he visited the Braves' dugout and Rudy, the Yankee fan, would receive more cheers, unprecedented for him in Flushing, when he left his front row seat in the fourth. There was a police bagpipe band, the NYPD Pipers, on the field, along with merchant marines and representatives from the police and fire departments and EMS for the pre-game ceremonies. There was an electric rendition of "God Bless America" by Diana Ross and two choirs and Ross concluded by high-fiving an umpire for emphasis.

On the scoreboard appeared a taped request from Valentine, Joe McEwing, Franco and Piazza that fans join them in moment of silence. A commander of the U.S. Marine Corps ended it with a command that triggered a 21-gun salute. There were tears glistening in the players' eyes as they stood on the respective foul lines. Valentine wore an odd-looking, defiant smile on his face and later explained he was determined to not let "them" see him cry. Then Marc Anthony sang the national anthem.

Players from both these two longtime rival organizations embraced and high-fived before returning to their dugouts. Met owners Wilpon and Nelson Doubleday, who don't adore each other, were on the field together and Atlanta manager Bobby Cox and Valentine, another odd couple, shared an embrace. Regardless of past hostilities, they were on the same side in the only fight that truly mattered.

"You just have to keep baseball in perspective," said Piazza. "Obviously, we battle and do everything to win. But it's not like so many thousands of people down there whose sacrifice is life or death. That is what, obviously, baseball is not . . . I feel so sad. I met two kids today who lost their fathers."

"It was very emotional," said Ventura. "You didn't want the game to start, because you didn't want to stop thinking about those who couldn't be here. It was really something—the whole night."

"Nice night for a game—even if it's more than a game sometimes," said Lenny Harris.

The beginning was unforgettable—and so, as it turned out, was the ending of the Mets' fourth straight victory, their 10th in 11 games, their 21st in their last 26. This 3-2 triumph—which carried the third-place Mets within 4½ games of the Braves, with five of the remaining 14 games on New York's schedule head to heads—was fashioned on a moment of baseball lightning from one of the game's most remarkable rainmakers.

The Mets dodged a bullet in the eighth inning on a massive, two-run home run, Piazza's 34th of the season. His 420-foot turnaround of a 96-mile-per-hour fastball from Steve Karsay carried over the center-field fence, onto a television platform. Shea was alive with celebration as the kid with the Pennsylvania roots who became a man in Los Angeles and then a transplanted New Yorker blew a perfect bubble with his gum about a step from third base.

Piazza, who wore an NYPD helmet behind the plate, had used those huge forearms to lift New Yorkers' spirits with old-fashioned, baseball, long-ball dramatics.

"You couldn't make up something that would be that good," said Jay Payton.

"He's Casey," said Zeile. "Everyone on our bench thinks it's going to happen. How more fitting can it be? He swings, makes contact and we know it's gone."

"The sorrow and the pain, the families and the children who lost parents," said Piazza, a resident of the Gramercy Park section in Manhattan, 10 minutes from where the towers had been. "If this helps people get out of the pain, that's great. We are all New Yorkers."

Piazza was careful to not say anything that diminished the impact of the tragedy by remotely suggesting a joyous, liberating, victorious moment in a baseball game could be weighed against the enduring pain of personal loss felt by so many. Still, Piazza was glad to be able to do at least this much to rally his adopted city.

"I was so happy I was able to come through in that situation and give the people something to cheer about. That's what they came out here for, to be diverted a little from their losses and their sorrow," he said. "It was just a surreal sort of energy out there. I'm just so proud to be a part of it tonight."

"We came here and paid tribute to a lot of heroes," said Valentine, "and one of the true New York heroes of the sports world put the icing on the cake."

The night didn't start out so gloriously for Piazza, whose error was responsible for giving the Braves their first run, in the fourth, and furnishing Staten Island product Jason Marquis with the early advantage over Bruce Chen. With two out and Chipper Jones on first, Ken Caminiti sliced a grounder down the first-base line past the lunging reach of Zeile. Chipper would have been a dead duck at the plate if Edgardo Alfonzo's perfect relay on one bounce hadn't gone into and out of Piazza's glove and deflected to his left. Jones was able to score standing.

Piazza's first atonement was a one-out double to right center in the bottom half of the fourth. He then moved to third on Ventura's single and scored on Tsuyoski Shinjo's sac fly. The game stayed tied at 1-1 only because Caminiti made a sensational play at third base to prevent any more runs from scoring. With runners on second and third and two outs, Caminiti backhanded Payton's grounder and made a strong, off-balance throw from foul territory to end the inning.

Chen had been alternately wildly effective and highly fortunate since being acquired by the Mets in a July 27 deal with Philadelphia at the cost of bullpen veterans Turk Wendell and Dennis Cook—the kind of trade a team makes as a concession that its prospects of contention are dead. This game marked the Mets' eighth victory in Chen's nine starts for them.

Clearly, under the circumstances, there had been concerns about the lefty suffering from a case of nerves. After all, the ex-Brave's only previous career start against the team that had nurtured him was a disaster. Atlanta tagged him for seven runs in only two innings July 5—and the Phillies sent him to the minors the next day.

This time, however, Chen was splendid: six hits, one unearned run, one walk, five strikeouts in seven innings.

"It was only a game, but it was a special game," said Chen.

There was no mistaking that. The score was still tied at the seventh-inning stretch, when Liza Minnelli sang a rousing rendition of "New York, New York"—backed by four uniformed police, fire and emergency officers in a chorus line—to the sheer delight of the crowd. The fans chanted "New York, New York" as Minnelli hugged Payton and walked off the field.

Franco, a Staten Islander whose son's Little League coach lost his life in the tragedy, retired his first two hitters, then walked Julio Franco before Chipper Jones singled. Valentine didn't hesitate to go to his best, even though the score was still tied and it was only the eighth inning. Closer Armando Benitez was inserted to face Brian Jordan. Jordan crushed the first pitch for a go-ahead RBI double that scored pinch runner Cory Aldridge and the Mets trailed, 2-1.

Now Franco was entertaining the painful thought that he was destined to be the losing pitcher.

"With the emotion of everything going on the last couple of days, I didn't want to be the losing pitcher tonight," he said. "This was a lot more important to win tonight, emotion-wise than standings-wise."

What Franco couldn't anticipate is that Karsay, a Flushing native and a Christ the King High School graduate, would lose his mind, the game and some pocket money for being ejected in the bottom of the eighth.

After retiring his first hitter, the Braves reliever didn't get the call from home plate umpire Wally Bell on a nasty 1-and-2 fastball that was taken by Alfonzo at the knees and on the outside edge of the plate. Karsay was clearly angered. When ball four was determined to have just missed the inside corner by Bell, completing a nine-pitch walk, Karsay threw up his hands in disgust. Bell came out from behind the plate, took off his mask and jawed at the pitcher.

"It's a situation where you don't want to put a guy on base in front of Piazza. I tried to throw it over the plate and see how far he [Alfonzo] could hit it—and he didn't swing," said Karsay.

"We thought the pitch was right down the middle on Fonzie," said Cox. "[Catcher Javy] Lopez was set up outside, so he had to reach for it."

"I'm a guy who never says anything about balls and strikes," said Karsay. "I don't complain . . . But I was watching the game from the first to the fourth inning. He was calling those balls strikes early in the game. He happened not to call that pitch a strike later in the game."

Karsay got ahead of Piazza with a first-pitch strike before the Met slugger launched a low fastball off the middle tier of a three-tiered camera. After circling the bases, having given the Mets their final 3-2 margin, Piazza took the inevitable curtain call, lifting his helmet with one hand, kissing the fingers on the other hand and pointing to the crowd.

"I cant explain the last at-bat," said Piazza. "I don't think I have faced Karsay but once [it was actually four times, with one hit to show for it], so I didn't know what to expect."

Leiter could explain it. "Mike did what he does best and that is to hit the ball really hard," he said.

Karsay, who hadn't allowed an earned run in his previous 12 outings, said, "I felt it was a pretty good pitch he hit. When you're not getting the close calls, you have to make guys swing the bat to get an out. That's what I was trying to do. It played a factor."

"Mike Piazza is the only guy you really can't let beat you in that situation because has done it too many times," said Chipper Jones.

Still burning, Karsay had a few choice words for Bell as he walked toward the Atlanta dugout at inning's end, but the pitcher didn't charge home plate until after those words had resulted in his ejection.

"I told him the pitch was high. I saw him come running, but they held him back," said Bell.

"When I saw his eyes, I thought he might kill that guy," said Dave Martinez, the first baseman who restrained Karsay and was the last line of security for Bell.

"I've never been thrown out of a game before. But when you are in a pennant race, things get hot," said Karsay. "I felt he didn't give us a chance to win."

Benitez closed it out with a scoreless ninth, sealed thanks to a double play turned by Rey Ordoñez. The final outs were accomplished to chants of "USA, USA" and a standing ovation. The fans didn't want to go home, drinking in a post-game Piazza curtain call, waving their flags, drinking in the sounds of Ray Charles' recording of "America the Beautiful."

"I think a lot of the guys felt the game tonight was more important than any game in the World Series last year," said Zeile.

Even Chipper Jones took a night off from being "Larry, The Brave Whom Met Fans Despise the Most Because John Rocker Is Gone" to appreciate the special quality of the night's proceedings, observing, "We gave the fans a great game . . . Everybody goes away happy tonight, except if you're a member of the Atlanta Braves."

As a hope-generating force against the backdrop of a wounded city's collective nightmare, the Mets could afford to dream.

"Everyone is crossing their fingers and hoping for a miracle, but they are hoping that miracle occurs downtown [with the rescue of additional survivors]," said Mets GM Steve Phillips. "But if it's not going to happen there, it sure would be nice for everyone if it happened here."

"Those naysayers who said we were out of it might have to eat a word or two," said Valentine. "A lot of things didn't go well for five months and we had a lot stored up. I think we have more stored up."

"Just to be back in position to have a chance, I think that is a miracle," said Leiter. "I know the Mets' history, last-to-first [actually next-to-last-to-first] in '69, coming from way back in '73, two runs down and nobody on and one out away from losing the World Series in 1986. But, in light of what has gone on recently, this would beat every one of them."

"Baseball took an absolute back seat tonight," said Zeile. "People came to the park to unite. I think it starts to become about baseball tomorrow. But with us, it's intertwined. And it will be from now on."

The city needed a reason to smile, an occasion to laugh. It got a 420-foot, screaming example of empowerment.

"You can't rebuild a building in a second, but you can rebuild spirits," said Valentine. "You can make people

ATLANTA	ab	r	h	bl	METS	ab	r	h	bl
MGiles 2b	3	0	0	0	Lawton rf	4	0	1	0
JuFranco 1b	3	0	0	0	Alfonzo 2b	3	0	1	0
Aldridge pr	0	1	0	0	Relaford pr-2b	0	1	0	0
Karsay p	0	0	0	0	Piazza c	4	2	3	2
CJones lf	4	1	2	0	Ventura 3b	4	0	1	0
BJordan rf	4	0	1	1	Shinjo lf	3	0	1	1
Caminiti 3b	3	0	2	0	Zeile 1b	3	0	1	0
JGarcia pr	0	0	0	0	Payton cf	3	0	0	0
Helms 3b	0	0	0	0	Ordoñez ss	3	0	0	0
Remlinger p	0	0	0	0	Chen p	2	0	0	0
DMartinez ph-1b	0	0	0	0	McEwing ph	1	0	0	0
AJones cf	4	0	0	0	JoFranco p	0	0	0	0
JLopez c	4	0	3	0	Benitez p	0	0	0	0
DeRosa pr	0	0	0	0					
RSanchez ss	3	0	1	0					
Surhoff ph	1	0	0	0					
Marquis p	2	0	0	0					
SReed p	0	0	0	0					
Gilkey ph	1	0	0	0					
Lockhart 3b	1	0	0	0					
Totals	33	2	9	1	Totals	30	3	8	3

Atlanta	000	100	010—2 9 0
Mets	000	100	02X—3 8 1

E-Piazza (6). LOB- Atlanta 7, Mets 5. 2B-BJordan (28), Caminiti (8), Piazza 2 (24), Zeile (24). HR-Piazza (34) off Karsay. RBI-BJordan (83), Piazza 2 (84), Shinjo (52). SB-JGarcia (6), RSanchez (2). SF-Shinjo. GIDP-RSanchez, Lockhart, Zeile. DP-Atlanta 1 (Marquis, RSanchez, MGiles, JuFranco), Mets 3 (Zeile), (Ordoñez, Alfonzo, Zeile), (Ordoñez, Zeile).

Atlanta	IP	H	R	ER	BB	SO
Marquis	6	7	1	1	0	4
SReed	⅔	0	0	0	0	0
Remlinger	⅓	0	0	0	0	0
Karsay (L, 3-4)	1	1	2	2	1	1
Mets						
BChen	7	6	1	0	1	5
JoFranco	⅔	1	1	1	1	1
Benitez (W, 6-3)	1⅓	2	0	0	1	1

Inherited runners scored-Benitez 2-1.

Umpires: Home-Bell; First-Foster; Second-Hirschbeck; Third-Kulpa.

T-3:07. A-41,236.

feel whole again. That is our job now . . . the fans got what they deserved. Put it in a bottle and whip it out whenever you need to get back into never-never land and get away from things."

"It [the city's united, committed reaction] told the rest of the country and the rest of the world what New York is all about," said Piazza. "It's a tough city and it's a hard city. This is something we'll never forget. It will scar us, but we will move on."

Five More:
Mentioned Honorably,
Remembered Warmly

METS 1, CARDS 0

October 2, 1964 in St. Louis

The Mets went into the final weekend of their third season, in 1964, as virginal spectators to the pennant race going on in their immediate vicinity. They had no clue about what it was like to be good enough to vie for a World Series or tense enough to blow the kind of lead the Phillies had squandered to allow the Cardinals and the Reds new life.

The Mets didn't know what it was like to be contenders.

They didn't even know what it was like to be spoilers.

However, on this Friday night in St. Louis, they found out the next-most fun other than reaching for the stars is coming to town footloose and carefree and ruining some title-chasing team's fun at a time that opponent needs to win the most.

The more unlikely the hill to climb, the sweeter the spoils. In this one, Al Jackson put a champagne celebration of the Cards' first title in

16 years on ice and nearly knocked them out of first place altogether by staring down menacing ace Bob Gibson with a 1-0 victory.

The Mets came in with 41 fewer wins than the Cardinals (who had 92) and they had eight straight losses to their discredit. But Casey Stengel's players were still thinking about baseball—not hunting or fishing or golf. St. Louis, which led Cincinnati by a half-game, seemed primed to take care of business with Gibson, who had won nine of his last 10 and had lost to the Mets only once in his life.

However, Jackson, the fluid left-hander whose performance always seemed better than his record with the Mets, was not to be outdone. Staked to a third-inning run on an opposite-field RBI single by Ed Kranepool that followed George Altman's single and stolen base, Al held the powerful St. Louis lineup to two hits over the first seven.

Then, in the eighth, Jackson was deprived of an apparent jam-escaping third out by umpire Ed Vargo, who inadvertently became an infielder whom the Mets could've lived without. With Cards at first and third on pinch-hitter Ed Spiezio's broken-bat single and Curt Flood's single, Lou Brock nailed a sizzling grounder toward shortstop Roy McMillan that would likely have been the third out. However, it never reached McMillan because it nailed Vargo—working second and stationed at the fringe of the infield grass between short and second—and rolled into short left.

Pinch-runner Dal Maxvill crossed the plate, but was ordered to return to third when the ball was correctly ruled dead. If the ball had struck an umpire beyond the infield, the rules would have deemed it in play and the tying run would have counted. But this one struck Vargo in front of McMillan. With the bags loaded on the Brock "single," Dick Groat slashed a liner to right that Joe Christopher caught on the run for the third out.

Jackson's neat, five-hit, complete-game effort boosted his record to 11-16, lowered his ERA to 4.26 and gave the Mets their club-record 52nd victory. The Mets won the second game of the series, too. Eight St. Louis pitchers, including 20-game winner Ray Sadecki, gave up five homers and 17 hits in a shocking 15-5 romp. Now the Cardinals were really reeling as the Reds pulled into a tie.

Finally, in the season finale, the Mets took a 3-2 lead against Curt Simmons. The margin didn't hold up, but the panicked Cards felt the need to call on Gibson to work four innings in their 11-5 triumph. The Reds lost, 10-0, to the Phillies, so the 93-69 Cardinals finished one game ahead of the Phillies and the Reds.

They could thank the Mets for a weekend of thoroughly unexpected worry.

METS	ab	r	h	bl	ST. LOUIS	ab	r	h	bl
Klaus 2b	5	0	1	0	Flood cf	4	0	2	0
Altman lf	5	1	2	0	Brock lf	4	0	1	0
Christopher rf	4	0	1	0	Groat ss	3	0	0	0
Kranepool 1b	4	0	2	1	Boyer 3b	4	0	0	0
Hickman cf	4	0	0	0	White 1b	4	0	0	0
Gonder c	4	0	1	0	Javier 2b	4	0	0	0
Smith 3b	4	0	1	0	Shannon rf	3	0	1	0
McMillan ss	4	0	0	0	McCarver c	2	0	0	0
Jackson p	4	0	1	0	James ph	1	0	0	0
					Uecker c	0	0	0	0
					Gibson p	2	0	0	0
					Spiezio ph	1	0	1	0
					Maxvill pr	0	0	0	0
Totals	38	1	9	1	Totals	32	0	5	0

Mets	001	000	000	—1
St. Louis	000	000	000	—0

E-White, Boyer, Groat. LOB-Mets 10, St. Louis 6. 2B-Flood. SB-Altman.

	IP	H	R	ER	BB	SO
Mets						
Jackson (W, 11-16)	9	5	0	0	1	2
St. Louis						
Gibson (L, 18-12)	8	8	1	1	0	7
Schultz	1	1	0	0	0	0

T-2:24. A-19,019.

METS 1, GIANTS 0

August 19, 1969 in New York

It was a night dominated by the pitchers—and by the Mets from Mobile.

By the time Tommie Agee crushed Juan Marichal's 151st pitch for a game-ending homer that broke a riveting scoreless tie in the 14th inning, Cleon Jones—Agee's friend and boyhood running mate in Alabama—had done everything else.

Jones collected three of the six Met hits off the Giants' high-kicking right-hander and stole two bases, including third. The Met left fielder also nailed the Giants' Bob Burda attempting to reach second on a hit that went off third base.

Then, in the 12th, as one of four outfielders whom manager Gil Hodges decided to deploy against Willie McCovey, Jones made a miraculous leaping catch to deprive the Giant slugger of his 37th homer. Cleon slammed into the wall, covered his glove with his throwing hand and clung to the final out. The play prompted Agee to say to him, "You hold 'em. I'll think of something."

A few innings later, Agee did and gave the Mets their fifth straight victory.

Marichal was typically brilliant, striking out 13, walking one (and that was intentional) and allowing three singles over the first nine innings. Juan finished '69 at 21-11 with a 2.10 ERA and he had been 21-2 lifetime against the Mets before this start. Marichal was one out into his 28th consecutive scoreless inning when Agee (0-for-5) came up in the 14th.

The first pitch, a breaking ball in the dirt, convinced Agee that the Dominican Dandy finally was finally tiring and was loathe to rely on his fastball as he had done most of the night. Sure enough, Marichal threw a screwball and Agee hit a line drive that cleared the fence above the 371 sign in left center.

Gary Gentry, a 22-year-old rookie, turned in 10 scoreless innings (four hits, four walks) that spanned 157 pitches (back in the days when starters weren't routinely removed when they hit 100 pitches). Winning pitcher Tug McGraw didn't permit the Giants a hit in his four innings.

SAN FRANCISCO   METS

	ab	r	h	bl		ab	r	h	bl
Bonds rf	6	0	0	0	Agee cf	6	1	1	1
Hunt 2b	6	0	0	0	Pfeil 3b	5	0	0	0
Mays cf	6	0	0	0	CJones lf	5	0	3	0
McCovey 1b	5	0	0	0	Shamsky rf	3	0	0	0
Burda lf	4	0	0	0	McGraw p	1	0	1	0
Ethridge 3b	3	0	0	0	Garrett 2b	5	0	0	0
Hiatt c	1	0	0	0	Kranepool 1b	4	0	0	0
Barton c	3	0	1	0	Harrelson ss	5	0	0	0
Marshall ph	0	0	0	0	Dyer c	5	0	1	0
Mason ss	2	0	0	0	Gentry p	3	0	0	0
Lanier ss	3	0	2	0	Gaspar rf	2	0	0	0
Davenport 3b	2	0	0	0					
Marichal p	4	0	1	0					
Totals	**45**	**0**	**4**	**0**	**Totals**	**44**	**1**	**6**	**1**

St. Louis	000	000	000	000	00	— 0
Mets	000	000	001	000	01	—1

One out when winning run scored.

E-Pfeil, Marichal. LOB-San Francisco 10, Mets 5. HR-Agee (21). SB-CJones 2. S-Marichal, Burda, Shamsky.

	IP	H	R	ER	BB	SO
San Francisco						
Marichal (L, 14-9)	13⅓	6	1	1	1	13
Mets						
Gentry	10	4	0	0	4	5
McGraw (W, 6-2)	4	0	0	0	1	0

T-3:44. A-48,968.

METS 5, CARDS 4

April 24, 1986 in St. Louis

The 1986 Mets had a lot to prove after winding up as also-rans to the Cubs in 1984 and the Cardinals in 1985. Baseball is a game of second chances, fortunately. And, on this night, George Foster and Howard Johnson achieved some personal vindication as, two outs from being beaten, the Mets rallied from two runs down to tie and went on to notch a sixth straight win, 5-4, in 10 innings at Busch Stadium.

Johnson, benched in favor of platoon mate Ray Knight at third, singled as a pinch-hitter for Rafael Santana and stayed in the game at shortstop. In the ninth inning, Johnson once again showed that nobody —not even a heat merchant like Todd Worrell—could defy his cat-quick bat. HoJo launched a fastball from the Cards' nasty-as-they-come closer for a two-run, game-tying homer—a 400-plus-foot shot into the mezzanine in right.

"I was disappointed not to start, but I could see the handwriting on the wall," said HoJo. "Ray Knight is hitting good and you have to go with him. But I didn't panic over not starting. And when I got my shot later, I tried to make it count."

In the ninth, Foster nailed a double, setting it up for Worrell against Johnson, who unloaded on a 2-and-2 pitch.

"The deeper I get in the count with a guy, the better hitter I become," said Johnson. "I get a feeling for a pitcher, what he is throwing me, what he has thrown me before. I make an adjustment with each pitch . . . I think this time he wanted to surprise me up and in and he just left it out [over the plate]."

"I thought Worrell had him struck out the pitch before," said Cards manager Whitey Herzog. "The guy is a dead fastball hitter. But give him credit. That was a 93-mile-an-hour fastball he hit."

Foster—who never loomed as the savage RBI man that he had been for Cincinnati—had dropped Jack Clark's wicked line drive in the eighth and the error eventually gave rise to that 4-2 hole which Johnson erased. However, in the 10th, with a man on second and two out, Herzog made the no-brainer choice of intentionally walking Darryl Strawberry to get to Foster.

Foster cranked up the bat speed to slap a two-out, broken-bat single to left for the game-winning RBI. A victory for Foster, a defeat for logic.

"It felt good to be in a situation to win a game," said Foster. "I think it will intensify my confidence and maybe get the word around the league that you can't walk Darryl to get to me."

"It's what you call redemption," said Met manager Davey Johnson.

METS	ab	r	h	bl	ST. LOUIS	ab	r	h	bl
Dykstra cf	5	1	1	0	Coleman lf	4	1	1	0
Backman 2b	4	1	2	0	McGee cf	5	1	2	0
Hernandez 1b	5	0	0	0	Herr 2b	4	2	1	0
Carter c	5	0	2	0	JClark 1b	4	0	0	0
Strawberry rf	4	1	2	1	VanSlyke rf	5	0	1	2
Foster lf	5	1	3	1	Pendleton 3b	4	0	1	0
Knight 3b	5	0	1	0	LaValliere c	2	0	1	0
Santana ss	2	0	0	0	White ph	1	0	0	0
HJohnson ph-ss	2	1	2	2	Heath c	1	0	0	0
Darling p	2	0	0	0	OSmith ss	4	0	0	0
Niemann p	0	0	0	0	Forsch p	2	0	0	0
Corcoran ph	0	0	0	0	Dayley p	1	0	0	0
Mitchell ph	1	0	0	0	Lahti p	0	0	0	0
Leach p	0	0	0	0	Conroy p	0	0	0	0
Heep ph	1	0	0	0	Worrell p	0	0	0	0
McDowell p	0	0	0	0					
Totals	41	5	13	5	Totals	38	4	7	2

Mets	010	000	012 1— 5
St. Louis	000	003	010 0— 4

Game Winning RBI-Foster (1). E-Backman, Santana, Foster. DP-Mets 1, St. Louis 1. LOB-Mets 8, St. Louis 8. 2B-Dykstra, Foster. HR-Strawberry (1), HJohnson (1). SB-Backman (2), Herr (6). S-Herr.

Mets	IP	H	R	ER	BB	SO
Darling	5	6	3	2	1	3
Niemann	1	0	0	0	0	0
Leach	1	1	1	0	0	2
Orosco	1	0	0	0	1	0
McDowell (W, 2-0)	2	0	0	0	1	2
St. Louis						
Forsch	6⅔	8	1	1	0	3
Dayley	1	1	1	1	0	2
Lahti	0	1	0	0	0	0
Conroy	⅓	1	1	1	0	0
Worrell (L, 0-1)	2	2	2	2	2	0

Darling pitched to 5 batters in the 6th, Lahti pitched to 1 batter in the 8th, Leach pitched to 2 batters in the 8th, Conroy pitched to 1 batter in the 9th.

Umpires: Home-Montague; First-Brocklander; Second-Weyer; Third-Rennert.

T-3:35. A-33,597.

METS 7, GIANTS 6

June 14, 1980 in New York

This memory glows more brightly because of the pitch-black hopelessness surrounding this time in Met history, known simply in the Blatt household as the Dark Ages.

The bill was paid by the Mets in the mid-to-late '70s for alienating great talents and giving them away (Nolan Ryan, Amos Otis, Tom Seaver, Rusty Staub, Jeff Reardon). There was no flicker of a pulse until the mid-'80s, when Darryl Strawberry, Keith Hernandez and Gary Carter and a band of young pitchers headed by Dwight Gooden said, "Let there be light."

But this was 1980.

And for Steve Henderson—a mediocre outfield talent stuck with being the poster-boy prospect among the four players whom the Mets received from the Reds for Seaver—this game was something of an exorcism. Having struck out three times already in the game, having gone without a homer for 226 at-bats since the previous July 13, Henderson triumphed in his final at-bat, in the ninth.

One pitch after chin music from Allen Ripley had sent him sprawling in the dirt, Stevie Wonder crushed a drought-ending, five-run-rally-capping, three-run, game-ending home run for a 7-6 victory over the Giants.

"I try to keep my temper," Henderson said. "But when someone does something like that to me, throwing too close, I sort of turn into a monster."

"When Stevie went up to hit, I knew he was a little tight after striking out those three times," said manager Joe Torre, back in his idiot days before his savant days with the Yankees. "So, I just told him to go up and take a swing."

Years of despair meant these Mets—despite winning eight of 10 and 14 of 21, including this down-to-their-last-strike Houdini act—had relatively few witnesses to their resurgence. But those who remained to see the ending among the 22,918 at Shea lingered to prevail upon Henderson for a curtain call.

Could it be? Hope?

"The ones over the Pirates [three of four over the world champs] and Dodgers [a 10th-inning grand slam] were nice," said Doug Flynn. "But this one was unbelievable. You keep busting and busting and then Henderson hits his first home run and it's a three-run game winner."

The Mets didn't manage a hit over the first five innings against John Montefusco en route to a 6-0 hole. Starter Pete Falcone, whose tantalizing stuff made his career a broken promise, got four outs and allowed five runs.

The Mets scored one in the sixth and a second run in the eighth before Flynn sounded the call to arms in the ninth with a one-out single on a bunt wide of first that pitcher Greg Minton couldn't handle. Lee Mazzilli lashed a two-out RBI single to center. Minton walked Frank Taveras and an RBI single by Claudell Washington made it 6-4 before Ripley was summoned.

SAN FRANCISCO	ab	r	h	bl	METS	ab	r	h	bl
Herndon cf	5	0	2	1	Mazzilli cf	5	2	2	1
Evans 3b	3	1	1	0	Taveras ss	4	1	2	0
Clark rf	2	1	0	0	Washington rf	4	1	1	2
Murray 1b	5	1	1	0	Henderson lf	5	1	2	4
Wohlford lf	5	1	2	1	Jorgensen lf	3	0	0	0
Stennett 2b	3	1	1	3	Reardon p	0	0	0	0
LeMaster ss	4	0	0	0	Stearns c	0	0	0	0
Sadek c	4	1	2	1	Maddox 3b	3	0	1	0
Montefusco p	3	0	0	0	Flynn 2b	4	2	2	0
Minton p	0	0	0	0	Falcone p	0	0	0	0
					Bomback p	1	0	0	0
					Hodges ph	1	0	0	0
					Glynn p	0	0	0	0
					Cardenal 1b	2	0	0	0
Totals	34	6	9	6	Totals	36	7	10	7

San Francisco	410	010	000 — 6
Mets	000	001	015 — 7

E-Stennett. DP-Mets 1. LOB-San Francisco 8, Mets 9. 2B-Sadek. HR-Stennett (2), Henderson (1). SB-Taveras. S-Montefusco. SF-Washington.

San Francisco	IP	H	R	ER	BB	SO
Montefusco	7²/₃	6	2	1	2	3
Minton	1	3	4	4	1	1
Ripley (L, 1-1)	0	1	1	1	0	0
Mets						
Falcone	1¹/₃	5	5	5	2	1
Bomback	4²/₃	4	1	1	3	1
Glynn	2	0	0	0	0	3
Reardon (W, 4-2)	1	0	0	0	1	3

Two outs when winning run scored.

Wild pitches-Falcone, Montefusco.

T-2:55. A-22,918.

Henderson lofted his homer into the Met bullpen in right, into the hands of reliever Tom Hausman.

"It's a phenomenal thing," said Torre. "They [his players] don't quit. They didn't even get a hit until the sixth inning. The starting pitching was bad, but the relief men were sensational. What can you say? They believe they can win."

METS 4, CARDS 2

April 6, 1992 in St. Louis

There was a day when Bobby Bonilla was not loathed by Mets fans.

This was before he became a symbol of a player too self-involved to care, too cool to admit weakness and acknowledge failure, too unprofessional to keep himself in playing shape or master a defensive position—and too unproductive to get away with any of the above.

There was one day.

Opening Day 1992, in St. Louis.

Bonilla's first game as a Met saw him hit crack three hits, including two homers, and drive in three runs. His second long ball—a two-run, 10th-inning game winner off Lee Smith, on a hanging slider—gave the Mets a 4-2 victory.

"I believe this is just the beginning," said Bonilla, wearing a smile that would become a smirk in the summer heat and then disappear altogether. "The big boy [Smith] don't give up too many. I can't even say I dreamed of this."

On a night when David Cone struck out nine over eight innings of a no-decision, when the Mets tied the game in the ninth as Mackey Sasser beat a DP relay, Bonilla was simply delighted to be a Met.

"Happiest guy on the planet," little Bo peeped.

Naturally, the homers only served to make the team's fans crazier with anticipation of what their Bronx-born new $29 million free-agent addition might do for their moribund club.

"We haven't had a leader like Bobby since Keith Hernandez," gushed Cone. "I think he showed tonight what he is going to mean for this team."

Wrong. Bobby didn't hit. The Mets didn't win. And he didn't stand up the way New York demands its athletes do.

Not too long after the opener, there would be a game in which the scoreboard showed Bonilla was charged with a first-inning error and the miscue buried the Mets. After the third out, Bo went right to the dugout phone to call the press box and ask why the big 'E' on the board to embarrass him?

That left manager Jeff Torborg to lie about the nature of the phone call to protect the image of his star, the start of Torborg's end.

Met fans would come to give the error to GM Al Harazin for signing the moody player the back pages called "Bobby Boo-Hoo."

"I'm just trying to be myself" was Bonilla's Opening Day promise—and it came to horrific realization.

After being the Opening Day hero and offering the opinion that the win "will take a lot of pressure off the guys," Bonilla assessed his upcoming reception in New York with the trepidation that led to a self-fulfilling prophecy.

"I know people are going to be watching me, saying, 'He ain't worth the money,'" he said. "If you let that get to you, you're in trouble."

For one night at least, Bonilla *was* worth the money. For the rest of two stays in a Met uniform, he was himself.

Unfortunately.

METS					ST. LOUIS				
	ab	r	h	bl		ab	r	h	bl
Coleman lf	4	1	1	0	Lankford cf	4	0	1	0
Randolph 2b	3	0	0	0	OSmith ss	3	1	0	0
Bonilla rf	5	2	3	3	Zeile 3b	4	1	1	0
Johnson cf	5	1	2	0	Galarraga 1b	4	0	1	1
Murray 1b	4	0	1	0	Guerrero lf	3	0	2	1
Gallagher pr	0	0	0	0	Hudler lf	1	0	0	0
Noboa ss	1	0	0	0	MThompson rf	4	0	0	0
Pecota 3b	3	0	1	0	Pagnozzi c	4	0	0	0
Boston ph	1	0	0	0	Oquendo 2b	0	0	0	0
Innis p	0	0	0	0	Jones 2b	3	0	0	0
Franco p	0	0	0	0	Gilkey ph	1	0	0	0
Elster ss	3	0	0	0	Deleon p	2	0	0	0
Sasser 1b	1	0	0	1	Worrell p	0	0	0	0
Hundley c	3	0	1	0	Perry ph	1	0	1	0
Cone p	3	0	0	0	LeSmith p	0	0	0	0
Magadon 3b	1	0	0	0	McClure p	0	0	0	0
Totals	**37**	**4**	**9**	**4**	**Totals**	**34**	**2**	**6**	**2**

Mets	000	100	001	2 — 4	
St. Louis	000	200	000	0 — 2	

LOB-Mets 7, St. Louis 3. 2B-Pecota (1). HR-Bonilla 2 (2). SB-Coleman (1), Johnson (1). CS-Coleman (1), Hudler (1). S-Randolph.

Mets	IP	H	R	ER	BB	SO
Cone	8	5	2	2	1	9
Innis (W, 1-0)	1	1	0	0	0	1
Franco (S,1)	1	0	0	0	0	1
St. Louis						
Deleon	7	4	1	1	2	6
Worrell	1	0	0	0	0	2
LeSmith (L, 0-1)	1⅓	5	3	3	0	1
McClure	⅔	0	0	0	0	1

HBP-Hundley (by Deleon).

Umpires: Home-McSherry; First-Pulli; Second-Davidson; Third-Hohn.

T-3:02. A45,174.

PART 3

Metscellaneous

The All-Time Team

In 40 years, players come and players go. Only a precious few leave a lasting impression on a franchise, in the mind's eye of its fans, in the club's history books. So, Mets fans fondly remember those special players who breathed life into their summers as performers eternally in their prime.

Choosing the creme is rarely easy and usually not done by acclamation, except for a handful of no-brainers. The criteria used in assembling the following team were diverse: players who made the most difference in making the Mets winners, who accumulated the most production over the most time, whose style and performance made them the most popular, whose impact has been the most indelible.

The usual pitfalls that come into play when different eras are reflected in statistics obviously apply in the following breakdowns, but numbers are just a part of the equation. Clearly, being a complete player was a consideration, though not a requirement, as you can tell from Dave Kingman's selection as the No. 2 choice to Cleon Jones in left field.

Say what you want about Kong the man and Kong the fielder and the atrocious Met teams for which he did his muscle flexing in two separate stints. He was a well-travelled, one-trick horse's butt—who else was

FIRST BASE

Keith Hernandez

Born Oct. 20, 1953, San Francisco, CA;
Height 6-0, Weight 205

Year	AB	R	H	HR	RBI	Avg.
1983	325	43	98	9	37	.306
1984	550	83	171	15	94	.311
1985	593	87	183	10	91	.309
1986	551	94	171	13	83	.310
1987	587	87	170	18	89	.290
1988	348	43	96	11	55	.276
1989	215	18	50	4	19	.233
Totals	**3169**	**455**	**939**	**80**	**468**	**.296**

John Olerud

Born Aug. 5, 1968, Seattle, WA;
Height 6-5, Weight 220

Year	AB	R	H	HR	RBI	Avg.
1997	524	90	154	22	102	.294
1998	557	91	197	22	93	.354
1999	581	107	173	19	96	.298
Totals	**1662**	**288**	**524**	**63**	**291**	**.315**

charming enough to gift-wrap a rat for a woman sportswriter?—but Big Dave made 154 baseballs disappear over fences for a franchise that has boasted few legitimate home run hitters.

Going position by position, at first base, it was a choice between mirror images. Keith Hernandez and John Olerud were cut from the same uncommon cloth: textbook No. 3-spot run producers who thrived on game-deciding situations, showed remarkable plate intelligence and bat control and bolstered the overall infield defense with their Gold Glove work. Hernandez rates a slight nod over Olerud because of an intangible that was quite tangible: leadership.

Olerud's run production numbers in his three seasons as a Met were slightly superior, but the Mets became a team to take seriously again at the moment that Mex was imported from the Cardinals in 1983 to become captain of the infield and best friend and crisis-time advisor to unnerved pitchers.

No one has ever played the game within the game more adeptly in setting up a pitcher, has shown more intensity or has been more exacting about making the fundamentally correct play than Hernandez. Whatever fear-strikes-out, paternal head trip fueled the competitive fire in this son of a failed minor leaguer, it burned brightly. Close your eyes and you can see Keith pouncing on a bunt and nailing a lead runner. Or see him taking a lead off second, gesturing with his body to remind the hitter, Darryl Strawberry, to keep his shoulder in against some lefty pitcher whom Hernandez had already solved.

Case closed.

At second base, the quick wrists, the sure hands and the unsurpassed plate coverage that have made Edgardo Alfonzo so vital to the Mets substantiate his selection. The Venezuelan started out as underrated and became famous for it. More outstanding at second than he once was at third, his 2002 destination, Alfonzo is a two-way force not fully appreciated until witnessed on a daily basis. He is simply the most clutch and the most accomplished two-strike hitter on the Mets—including Mike Piazza.

Alfonzo has more ways to punish an opponent than words to discuss them: an acrobatic turn of a double-play pivot, a sat-upon fastball transformed into a crushing homer to left or a fight-it-off, two-strike dunk job to right. The troubling bad back that sentenced Alfonzo to a brutally poor 2001 was the worst

SECOND BASE

Edgardo Alfonzo
Born Nov., 8, 1973, St. Teresa, Venezuela;
Height 5-11, Weight 187

Year	AB	R	H	HR	RBI	Avg.
1995	335	26	93	4	41	.278
1996	368	36	96	4	40	.261
1997	518	84	163	10	72	.315
1998	557	94	155	17	78	.278
1999	628	123	191	27	108	.304
2000	544	109	176	25	94	.324
2001	457	64	111	17	49	.243
Totals	3407	536	985	104	482	.289

Felix Millan
Born Aug. 21, 1943, Yabucoa, Puerto Rico;
Height 5-11, Weight 172

Year	AB	R	H	HR	RBI	Avg.
1973	638	82	185	3	37	.290
1974	518	50	139	1	33	.268
1975	676	81	191	1	56	.283
1976	531	55	150	1	35	.282
1977	314	40	78	2	21	.248
Totals	2677	308	743	8	182	.278

Exhibiting two-way excellence unmatched at second base until the arrival of Edgardo Alfonzo, Felix Millan was a godsend from the Braves for the way he set the table and turned the double play.

thing that could happen in a Met season that featured multiple disappointments.

Felix Millan's steady play in leading the 1973 Mets to a pennant earns him the runner-up nod over Ron Hunt, the human pin cushion and the first-ever Met All-Star starter. Honorable mention is extended to Jeff Kent, who has carried his team even more impressively than Alfonzo in recent seasons. Sadly, however, that team has been the Giants.

Howard Johnson did things that were accomplished by few of the half-billion poor slobs who paraded their sorry stuff at third base for the Mets. Displaying both power and speed, HoJo refused to follow in the damned footsteps of horror shows (Don Zimmer, Joe Foy and Jim Fregosi) and the completely washed up (Ken Boyer, Bob Aspromonte and Joe Torre). Johnson's glove wasn't made out of gold, he was exposed as a lunging patsy by pitches that arrived with a hook in them and his right-handed hitting made you wish he didn't switch, but why quibble?

HoJo hit 36 or more homers three times and drove in 90 or more runs four times—numbers that runner-up Hubie Brooks never approached. The Johnson trademark was the blink-and-

THIRD BASE

Howard Johnson
Born Nov. 29, 1960, Clearwater, FL;
Height 5-10, Weight 195

Year	AB	R	H	HR	RBI	Avg.
1985	389	38	94	11	46	.242
1986	220	30	54	10	39	.245
1987	554	93	147	36	99	.265
1988	495	85	114	24	68	.230
1989	571	104	164	36	101	.287
1990	590	89	144	23	90	.244
1991	564	108	146	38	117	.259
1992	350	48	78	7	43	.223
1993	235	32	56	7	26	.238
Totals	**3968**	**627**	**997**	**192**	**629**	**.251**

Hubie Brooks
Born Sept. 24, 1956, Los Angeles, CA;
Height 6-0, Weight 205

Year	AB	R	H	HR	RBI	Avg.
1980	81	8	25	1	10	.309
1981	358	34	110	4	38	.307
1982	457	40	114	2	40	.249
1983	586	53	147	5	58	.251
1984	561	61	159	16	73	.283
1991	357	48	85	16	50	.238
Totals	**2400**	**244**	**640**	**44**	**269**	**.267**

At a position that had been a black hole for this franchise, third baseman Howard Johnson did it with his bat and his legs, notching 192 homers and 202 steals as a Met.

it's-cleared-for-launching trigger to his swing. Whitey Herzog's cork hunts were futile witch hunts or ineffectual psych jobs. Johnson turned around so many of the fastest late-inning fastballs for game-turning homers against Herzog's Cardinals that the White Rat would've been better off checking his pitchers' heads for rocks.

The two positions at which intangibles and defensive impact were weighed the heaviest were shortstop and catcher—in recognition of the importance of a remarkable glove up the middle and the difference an adept handler of a young pitching staff makes on the bottom line of any club.

At shortstop, the greater offensive diversity and impact exerted by Bud Harrelson gives him the nod over Rey Ordoñez, slightly flashier with the leather but much more clueless with a bat in his hands.

Harrelson made the easy play and the impossible one. His six homers and 242 RBI in 4,390 Met at-bats hardly made him the Alex Rodriguez of his day. But Buddy took a walk and put the ball in play when contact had to be made to produce a run. He could bunt and steal a base and was a fiery, competitive force on the 1969 world champions and the 1973 pennant winners. No Met pitcher complained about a lineup carrying Harrelson's bat in his 13-year stay in Flushing.

"On a team like ours in 1969, when you knew there were a lot of 1-0, 2-1 games you had to win, Buddy was clearly the most irreplaceable player we had," said Tom Seaver.

Ordoñez, Cuba's gift to the Mets, throws more strongly and accurately from one knee than most shortstops can from their feet. He swallows grounders that other shortstops don't even touch. He turns a double play that challenges your eyes' ability to be as quick as his hands.

SHORTSTOP

Bud Harrelson
Born June 6, 1944, Niles, CA;
Height 5-10½, Weight 155

Year	AB	R	H	HR	RBI	Avg.
1965	37	3	4	0	0	.108
1966	99	20	22	0	4	.222
1967	540	59	137	1	28	.254
1968	402	38	88	0	14	.219
1969	395	42	98	0	24	.248
1970	564	72	137	1	42	.243
1971	547	55	138	0	32	.252
1972	418	54	90	1	24	.215
1973	356	35	92	0	20	.258
1974	331	48	75	1	13	.227
1975	73	5	16	0	3	.219
1976	359	34	84	1	26	.234
1977	269	25	48	1	12	.178
Totals	**4390**	**490**	**1029**	**6**	**242**	**.234**

Rey Ordoñez
Born Nov. 11, 1972, Havana, Cuba;
Height 5-9, Weight 159

Year	AB	R	H	HR	RBI	Avg.
1996	502	51	129	1	30	.257
1997	356	35	77	1	33	.216
1998	505	46	124	1	42	.246
1999	520	49	134	1	60	.258
2000	133	10	25	0	9	.188
2001	461	31	114	3	44	.247
Totals	**2477**	**222**	**603**	**7**	**218**	**.243**

Shortstop Rey Ordoñez can whip a team by doing the impossible with his magical leather, but his chronic lack of plate discipline suggests he will never approach the offensive contributions of the speedy, steady Bud Harrelson.

It's clear that Ordoñez won't ever learn the strike zone doesn't begin at his forehead and end at his feet. And he won't accept he's not A-Rod and adjust that wild swing to make line-drive contact on a regular basis. Prior to their makeover, the Mets could ill afford Ordoñez' impotence in the No. 8 spot. But if you think they didn't miss his glove mightily in 2000, you didn't see Melvin Mora or Mike Bordick play in his place.

Catcher is one of the toughest spots to decide, after Mike Piazza is acknowledged as the indisputable No. 1.

Piazza's bat would likely produce about 150 RBI per season if this squatter wasn't such a mule about catching and agreed to move to first base. As it is, he plays through all sorts of pain and always busts his bruised behind. The ball surges off his bat as if it has been struck hard enough to turn from solid into liquid. It's not just the tape-measure jobs on checked swings. It is also the way his topspin grounders and fist jobs elude infielders and become hits, too. No right-handed hitter in the game has more oomph to right field.

Sure, Piazza couldn't throw out godfather Tommy Lasorda stealing.

But the only down side to his game can be easily eradicated. Pray the too-proud-for-his-good Piazza and the people who pay him agree that his crouching is a criminal abuse of a singular slugger and the key reason Mike is never as dangerous in September and October as he is in June. What was good enough for Johnny Bench and what soon will be good enough for state-of-the-art catcher and pro-jected second baseman Pudge Rodriguez should be good enough for Piazza.

Todd Hundley's 40-homer bat and Gary Carter's body of work deserve consideration in the choice of a backup. Injury robbed Hundley of a longer stay in Flushing and, because Carter's knees were shot by the time the Mets acquired him, The Kid enjoyed his prime in Montreal. He was an integral part of the 1986 champions and the 1988 divi-sion winners, but Carter couldn't muster his usual power by the end and couldn't keep base-stealers honest.

So the choice for the slot behind Piazza is Jerry Grote, one prickly Texan whose handling made the very young staff of the 1969 world

CATCHER

Mike Piazza
Born Sept. 4, 1968, Norristown, PA; Height 6-3, Weight 215

Year	AB	R	H	HR	RBI	Avg.
1998	394	67	137	23	76	.348
1999	534	100	162	40	124	.303
2000	482	90	156	38	113	.324
2001	503	81	151	36	94	.300
Totals	1913	338	606	137	407	.317

Jerry Grote
Born Oct. 6, 1942, San Antonio, TX; Height 5-10, Weight 185

Year	AB	R	H	HR	RBI	Avg.
1966	317	26	75	3	31	.237
1967	344	25	67	4	23	.195
1968	404	29	114	3	31	.282
1969	365	38	92	6	40	.252
1970	415	38	106	2	34	.255
1971	403	35	109	2	35	.270
1972	205	15	43	3	21	.210
1973	285	17	73	1	32	.256
1974	319	25	82	5	36	.257
1975	386	28	114	2	39	.295
1976	323	30	88	4	28	.272
1977	115	8	31	0	7	.270
Totals	3881	314	994	35	357	.256

champions even more special. Grote showed off an arm second to none. He didn't drive in many runs, but he had more than his share of big hits. Grote lasted 12 Met seasons and it wasn't because of his por-cupine personality or Met career average of .256. His smarts and toughness simply made him the unsung back-stop of a franchise that, per-haps more than any in his-tory, has lived and died with its pitching.

"Johnny Bench is a hitter who catches and Jerry Grote is a catcher who hits. There is a big difference," said Joe Torre.

The easy choice in left is Cleon Jones. His .340 season in 1969—achieved with lim-ited lineup protection— would be enough to justify his selection, but there are also reparations due here. Once upon a pre-unionized time, Cleon was humiliated by the Mets and forced to deliver a public apology to his wife and America in general for being caught in the back of a van with a woman, not his wife, in spring training. Mets board chairman M. (Massah) Donald Grant's attempt to

LEFT FIELD

Cleon Jones

Born Aug. 4, 1942, Plateau, AL;
Height 6-0, Weight 195

Year	AB	R	H	HR	RBI	Avg.
1963	15	1	2	0	1	.133
1965	74	2	11	1	9	.149
1966	495	74	136	8	57	.275
1967	411	46	101	5	30	.246
1968	509	63	151	14	55	.297
1969	483	92	164	12	75	.340
1970	506	71	140	10	63	.277
1971	505	63	161	14	69	.319
1972	375	39	92	5	52	.245
1973	339	48	88	11	48	.260
1974	461	62	130	13	60	.282
1975	50	2	12	0	2	.240
Totals	**4223**	**563**	**1188**	**93**	**521**	**.281**

Dave Kingman

Born Dec. 21, 1948, Pendleton, OR;
Height 6-6, Weight 215

Year	AB	R	H	HR	RBI	Avg.
1975	502	65	116	36	88	.231
1976	474	70	113	37	86	.238
1977	211	22	44	9	28	.209
1981	353	40	78	22	59	.221
1982	535	80	109	37	99	.204
1983	248	25	49	13	29	.198
Totals	**2323**	**302**	**509**	**154**	**389**	**.219**

preserve the family values of this noble sport smacked of plantation-owner arrogance. Jones' swing was every bit as pure as Grant wished his players would appear to be.

The backup in left is Kingman, who crushed 37 homers in a season twice for the Mets and whose three in a game, vs. the Dodgers, sent Lasorda into a legendary fit of post-game cursing. Kingman nipped Kevin McReynolds, a superb outfielder who had 27 homers and 99 RBI for the 1988 division winners.

K-Mac showed such little passion for his chosen sport that he expressed a longing to go hunting before the Mets had been beaten by the Dodgers in the NLCS that year. Winning players usually have a fire—inside or out. That was not the case with the icy McReynolds, an Arkansas duck out of water.

CENTER FIELD

Mookie Wilson
Born Feb. 9, 1956, Bamberg, SC;
Height 5-10, Weight 170

Year	AB	R	H	HR	RBI	Avg.
1980	105	16	26	0	4	.248
1981	328	49	89	3	14	.271
1982	639	90	178	5	55	.279
1983	638	91	176	7	51	.276
1984	587	88	162	10	54	.276
1985	337	56	93	6	26	.276
1986	381	61	110	9	45	.289
1987	385	58	115	9	34	.299
1988	378	61	112	8	41	.296
1989	249	22	51	3	18	.205
Totals	**4027**	**592**	**1112**	**60**	**342**	**.276**

Tommie Agee
Born Aug. 9, 1942, Magnolia, AL;
Height 5-11, Weight 185

Year	AB	R	H	HR	RBI	Avg.
1968	368	30	80	5	17	.217
1969	565	97	153	26	76	.271
1970	636	107	182	24	75	.286
1971	425	58	121	14	50	.285
1972	422	52	96	13	47	.227
Totals	**2416**	**344**	**632**	**82**	**265**	**.262**

No wonder even the boorish Kingman had a more enthusiastic following among Mets' fans.

In center, there is little doubt: Mookie Wilson, the most popular position player in the club's history as a 10-year Met and a lock to be its future manager. Nobody played harder, circled the bases faster, gave more of himself than Wilson, whose only flaw as a leadoff man was he never saw a pitch he didn't like. Mookie's signature image wasn't the grounder that split Bill Buckner's wickets in 1986 World Series Game 6. It was the way he never broke stride and scored from second on an infield grounder for a Met team that couldn't see .500 with a telescope.

Second, because his impact was really limited to just two lovely seasons, 1969 and 1970, is Tommie Agee. The glove that Agee flashed to ruin the Orioles in the World Series in 1969 wasn't a fluke . . . and neither was his emergence as a power-hitting leadoff man who scored a total of 204 runs in 1969 and '70 for a team that didn't generate many. Honorable mention is awarded to Lenny Dykstra, remembered for his 1986 October heroics and for his eagerness to risk life and limb in pursuit of every fly in front of him.

Finally, in right field, the nod goes to Darryl Strawberry. The only real slugger whom the Mets ever drafted and nurtured, Strawberry faces an

Showing professionalism amid the hopelessness of the early '80s and the guts of a burglar taking the extra base, center fielder Mookie Wilson was an all-time Shea favorite.

unfortunate measuring stick: what he could have been if he had been demon-free, had not abused his body and had not sabotaged his career. He should've stolen 40 bases per season. He should've learned how to position himself against hitters instead of staying in one spot, the Strawberry Patch. He should've thrown runners out with that strong arm. He should've learned to go the other way against left-handers. Indeed, the imagination boggles at the thought of his numbers if he didn't play so many games hung over.

The only thing more striking than Straw's capacity for self-destruction and his lack of interest in mining his full potential was his talent. Not to be overlooked are the numbers it produced: three seasons of 37 or more homers and 100-plus RBI and a total of 252 homers and 733 RBI in eight years as a Met.

RIGHT FIELD

Darryl Strawberry

Born Mar. 12, 1962, Los Angeles, CA;
Height 6-6, Weight 215

Year	AB	R	H	HR	RBI	Avg.
1983	420	63	108	26	74	.257
1984	522	75	131	26	97	.251
1985	393	78	109	29	79	.277
1986	475	76	123	27	93	.259
1987	532	108	151	39	104	.284
1988	543	101	146	39	101	.269
1989	476	69	107	29	77	.225
1990	542	92	150	37	108	.277
Totals	**3903**	**662**	**1025**	**252**	**733**	**.263**

Rusty Staub

Born Apr. 1, 1944, New Orleans, LA;
Height 6-2, Weight 215

Year	AB	R	H	HR	RBI	Avg.
1972	239	32	70	9	38	.293
1973	585	77	163	15	76	.279
1974	561	65	145	19	78	.258
1975	574	93	162	19	105	.282
1981	161	9	51	5	21	.317
1982	219	11	53	3	27	.242
1983	115	5	34	3	28	.296
1984	72	2	19	1	18	.264
1985	45	2	12	1	8	.267
Totals	**2571**	**296**	**709**	**75**	**399**	**.276**

"He has more talent than anyone I've ever seen," said Lee Mazzilli. "There's nobody even close. I'd like to have Darryl's talent just for one year, to see what I could do with it."

Daryl Strawberry, marvelous and maddening, supremely powerful and utterly helpless, unloaded 37 or more homers and drove in 100 or more runs three times in his last four Met seasons.

Runner-up to Straw is Rusty Staub. Staub was underrated as a defensive outfielder because he was more elephant than gazelle; however, he used his smarts to compensate for his lack of speed and had a strong and accurate arm. Staub was beloved for his enormous October 1973 contributions, a 105-RBI season in 1975 and then again for his subsequent turn as a pinch-hitter extraordinaire, from 1981 through '85. Rusty embraced New York and it embraced him, although it was barely able to get its arms around him by the time he was in his twilight. As the players say in simple admiration: The man could hit.

Probably still can.

For utility man, Bob Bailor gets a narrow nod over all-time pinch-hit record holder Lenny Harris, who keeps going and going and going.

As a right-handed pinch hitter, Mark Carreon (.290 on 27-for-93 from 1987 through 1991) rates a small edge over Ron Swoboda (.304 on 28-for-92 from 1965 through 1970).

The title of best lefty pinch-hitter goes to the Steadiest of Eddies, Ed Kranepool, for his 90 pinch-hits from 1962 through 1985. He earned a narrow nod over Staub, who had 77 pinch-hits as a Met and out-hit Krane, .278 to .277, in that capacity.

For the title of top right-handed starter, consider the choice of Tom Seaver to be unanimous. Terrific had a 198-124 record and a 2.57 ERA as a Met and clearly never should have pitched the no-hitter he tossed for Cincinnati or the 300th career victory that he achieved with the White Sox for any team other than the one that he showed how to win in 1969.

For one amazing rookie year, then a magic, 24-4, 1.53 season in 1985, for going 157-85 with a 3.10 ERA for the Mets, Dwight Gooden is the second

RIGHT-HANDED STARTER

Tom Seaver
Born Nov. 17, 1944, Fresno, CA;
Height 6-1, Weight 210

Year	G	IP	W	L	Pct.	ERA
1967	35	251	16	13	.552	2.76
1968	36	278	16	12	.571	2.20
1969	36	273	25	7	.781	2.21
1970	37	291	18	12	.600	2.81
1971	36	286	20	10	.667	1.76
1972	35	262	21	12	.636	2.92
1973	36	290	19	10	.655	2.08
1974	32	236	11	11	.500	3.20
1975	36	280	22	9	.710	2.38
1976	35	271	14	11	.560	2.59
1977	13	96	7	3	.700	3.00
1983	34	231	9	14	.391	3.55
Totals	**401**	**3045**	**198**	**124**	**.615**	**2.57**

Dwight Gooden
Born Nov. 16, 1964, Tampa, FL;
Height 6-3, Weight 210

Year	G	IP	W	L	Pct.	ERA
1984	31	218	17	9	.654	2.60
1985	35	276.2	24	4	.857	1.53
1986	33	250	17	6	.739	2.84
1987	25	179.2	15	7	.682	3.21
1988	34	248.1	18	9	.667	3.19
1989	19	118.1	9	4	.692	2.89
1990	34	232.2	19	7	.731	3.83
1991	27	190	13	7	.650	3.60
1992	31	206	10	13	.435	3.67
1993	29	208.2	12	15	.444	3.45
1994	7	41.1	3	4	.429	6.31
Totals	**305**	**2169.2**	**157**	**85**	**.649**	**3.10**

Rusty Staub, a force behind the 1973 Mets' improbable run to the World Series, was so missed after being given away to Detroit that this clutch RBI man was re-imported to be a pinch-hitter deluxe.

choice, behind Seaver. Gooden wrote his own ticket out with his off-the-field self-destruction. Still, for those Met followers who remember the way Dwight dominated at 19 years old, with a fastball and curve that screamed Hall of Famer, seeing him pitch his no-hitter in pinstripes was bittersweet. In the K corner, Gooden remains, eternally, the Doctor, surgical remover of hitters' self-esteem.

Seaver's sidekick was a brilliant pitcher in his own right, er, left: a knees-buckling, guts-of-a-burglar southpaw named Jerry Koosman. Don't let the underwhelming 140-137 mark he compiled as a Met and his 20-loss season in 1977 fool you. Koosman's 21 victories in 1976 for a Mets team that shouldn't have been allowed out in public, his 2.08 ERA in 1968 and 2.28 mark in 1968 and 1969 and his 48-28 record from 1968

LEFT-HANDED STARTER

Jerry Koosman
Born Dec. 23, 1942, Appleton, MN;
Height 6-2, Weight 220

Year	G	IP	W	L	Pct.	ERA
1967	9	22	0	2	.000	6.14
1968	35	264	19	12	.613	2.08
1969	32	241	17	9	.684	2.28
1970	30	212	12	7	.632	3.14
1971	26	166	6	11	.353	3.04
1972	34	163	11	12	.478	4.14
1973	35	263	14	15	.483	2.84
1974	35	265	15	11	.577	3.36
1975	36	240	14	13	.519	3.41
1976	34	247	21	10	.677	2.70
1977	32	227	8	20	.286	3.49
1978	38	235	3	15	.167	3.75
Totals	**376**	**2545**	**140**	**137**	**.505**	**3.09**

Al Leiter
Born Oct. 23, 1965, Toms River, NJ;
Height 6-3, Weight 220

Year	G	IP	W	L	Pct.	ERA
1998	28	193	17	6	.739	2.47
1999	32	213	13	12	.520	4.23
2000	31	208	16	8	.667	3.20
2001	29	187.1	11	11	.500	3.31
Totals	**120**	**801.1**	**57**	**37**	**.606**	**3.32**

through 1970 with the Mets were the best measures of his skills, savvy and heart. This sweetheart of a guy had an arsenal that was nasty.

Second only to Koosman among Met lefties is Al Leiter, who has secured his spot by being the ultimate big-game tough guy. With a 57-37 mark from 1998 through 2001, with a season-deciding shutout of the Reds in 1999 to his eternal credit, Leiter has talked the talk and

During the months before October, Armando Benitez has been the most automatic closer in Met history—with a blow-away fastball and a game-face scowl to strike fear in the hearts of jelly-legged hitters.

walked the walk by throwing his beast of a slider on the thumbs of right-handed hitters. Al remained the true ace of the staff, even when Mike Hampton cruised through town in 2000. That says something.

Overpowering Armando Benitez (106 saves, 2.74 ERA) gets the nod as the all-time righty reliever, even though the memories of him being overpowered in his 2000 World Series Game 1 failure and his two September 2001 flush jobs against the Braves are still too fresh to bear. Benitez, with the billion-dollar fastball, the nastiest of splitters and the questionable mental makeup,

RIGHT-HANDED RELIEVER

Armando Benitez
Born Nov. 3, 1972, Ramon Santana, DR;
Height 6-4, Weight 229

Year	G	IP	W	L	Pct.	Sv.	ERA
1999	77	78	4	3	.571	22	1.85
2000	76	76	4	4	.500	41	2.61
2001	73	76.1	6	4	.600	43	3.77
Totals	226	230.1	14	11	.560	106	2.74

Roger McDowell
Born Dec. 21, 1960, Cincinnati, OH;
Height 6-1, Weight 197

Year	G	IP	W	L	Pct.	Sv.	ERA
1985	62	127.1	6	5	.545	17	2.83
1986	75	128	14	9	.609	22	3.02
1987	56	88.2	7	5	.583	25	4.16
1988	62	89	5	5	.500	16	2.63
1989	25	35.1	1	5	.167	4	3.31
Totals	280	468.1	33	29	.532	84	3.13

gets the nod ahead of the sinkerballing Roger McDowell, more of a setup man for Jesse Orosco as a 14-game winner in 1986.

Although he's a born-and-bred New Yorker, John Franco, the pride of Staten Island and St. John's and the all-time lefty saves man (274 in 12 years as a Met), has gotten his share of Bronx cheers after flushing victories over the years. But Franco has been special, with that strut and the intestinal fortitude to never throw a strike until he is one more dirt-dipper from destruction. That circle change sticks its tongue out at hitters not disciplined enough to lay off it. Franco never had the gas of Randy Myers, for whom he was acquired, but the key word is moxie. Franco is fearless, an acrobat used to working without a net.

LEFT-HANDED RELIEVER

John Franco

Born Sept. 17, 1960, Brooklyn, NY;
Height 5-10; Weight 185

Year	G	IP	W	L	Pct.	Sv.	ERA
1990	55	67.2	5	3	.625	33	2.53
1991	52	55.1	5	9	.357	30	2.93
1992	31	33	6	2	.750	15	1.64
1993	35	36.1	4	3	.571	10	5.20
1994	47	50	1	4	.200	30	2.70
1995	48	51.2	5	3	.625	29	2.44
1996	51	54	4	3	.571	28	1.83
1997	59	60	5	3	.625	36	2.55
1998	61	64.2	0	8	.000	38	3.62
1999	46	40.2	0	2	.000	19	2.88
2000	62	55.2	5	4	.556	4	3.40
2001	58	53.1	6	2	.750	2	4.05
Totals	**605**	**622.1**	**46**	**46**	**.500**	**274**	**2.96**

Jesse Orosco

Born Apr. 21, 1957, Santa Barbara, CA;
Height 6-2; Weight 205

Year	G	IP	W	L	Pct.	Sv.	ERA
1979	18	35	1	2	.333	0	4.89
1981	8	17	0	1	.000	1	1.59
1982	54	109.1	4	10	.286	4	2.72
1983	62	110	13	7	.650	17	1.47
1984	60	87	10	6	.625	31	2.59
1985	54	79	8	6	.571	17	2.73
1986	58	81	8	6	.571	21	2.33
1987	58	77	3	9	.250	16	4.44
Totals	**372**	**595.1**	**47**	**47**	**.500**	**107**	**2.74**

That is no less true of Orosco, whose slider once made him close to unhittable. What do you call six straight ERAs under 2.74, including two under 2.00, from 1981 through 1986? He had 23 wins and 48 saves in 1983 and 1984. Jesse was on the mound at the end of the 1986 NLCS and the World Series. Then he enjoyed a calendar-defying entire additional career after leaving the Mets.

Orosco assembled a body of work as a Met that narrowly trumps the efforts of the beloved Tug McGraw (a total of 19 wins, 35 saves and back-to-back 1.70 ERAs in 1971 and 1972). The screwball that made McGraw unhittable and the half-sarcastic "Ya Gotta Believe" rallying cry he issued after a clubhouse pep talk from Grant in 1973 are legendary. But McGraw had as much or more success in Philadelphia as he did in Queens, unlike Orosco, who never shone brighter than as a Met.

With that trademark slap of glove against thigh, Tug McGraw bounded off the mound and celebrated each nasty screwball for a strikeout with the joie de vivre of a true "gotta believer."

The All-Time Busts

They bumbled. They fumbled. They failed. They flailed. They fanned. Spectacularly. They disappointed. Hugely. They are more infamous than famous. They were has-beens or never-would-bes. Expected to be answers, they were eyesores.

Picked from a sea of baseball flotsam and submitted for your disapproval, the following team of all-time busts left indelible marks on the Mets' first 40 years.

Of course, the marks happened to be scars.

First Base—Marv Throneberry (1962-63)

He was said to have "Mickey Mantle type" power potential when he was a Yankee minor leaguer, but The Marvelous One showed an affinity for buffoonery, not slugging. For the Mets, Marv Throneberry hit .244 with 16 homers and 49 RBI in 1962, when popups to him were adventures worthy of *National Geographic*.

On one legendary occasion, manager Casey Stengel came out to argue an appeal play that saw Throneberry declared out for missing first base on a triple. Stengel was headed to the umpire when he was intercepted by first-base coach Cookie Lavagetto, who allegedly told him, "Forget it, Casey. He missed second, too."

345

Marv Throneberry became the 1962 Mets' poster boy for futility, thanks to his press agent, Casey Stengel. The Marvelous One's porous fielding at first base, befuddled baserunning and toothless hitting were legendary, insuring he would not be forgotten.

Honorable mention goes to Tim Harkness for hitting .211 in 375 at-bats in 1963. And don't forget Dick Stuart, who came by his classic nickname, Dr. Strangeglove, on merit. Who do you think tied Throneberry for the most errors by an NL first baseman in 1962? And Stuart hit only .215 in 31 games for the Mets in 1966.

Second Base—Carlos Baerga (1996-98)

Once upon a time, Carlos Baerga was part of the Indians' young nucleus, a 100-RBI middle infielder. By the time he came from Cleveland in 1996—in a deal that cost the Mets both Jeff Kent and Jose Vizcaino, two second basemen better than he was—Baerga was labelled a fat cat. Indeed, the extra baggage around this waste showed on every grounder not hit right at him.

Baerga hit .193 for the Mets in '96 and .059 as a right-handed hitter. It's not every day you can import a switch-hitter who is making millions, has misplaced his power stroke and needs both a platoon partner and a defensive replacement.

Before Baerga, the Mets' all-time bust second baseman was Tom Herr. A wonderful clutch player for the Cards in his prime-time years, Herr was a .216 hitter for the Mets from August 1990 until the club mercifully released him in August 1991.

Carlos Baerga was in a free-fall decline before becoming a Met in the deal that sent Jeff Kent to the Indians. Pitifully overmatched from the right side, the switch-hitting second baseman had lost so many steps that he would've lost a race with a Zamboni.

Having misplaced his stroke somewhere in Anaheim, Jim Fregosi found a way to be even more pathetic than Joe Foy as the Mets' reluctant converted third baseman in 1972—and the only thing they had to show for dealing Nolan Ryan.

Third Base—Jim Fregosi (1972-73)

A six-time All-Star with the Angels, Jim Fregosi was craved so deeply by the Mets that they sent Nolan Ryan (and three other decent young talents) to California in the hope Fregosi would stop their eternal third-base revolving door. All the spinning there started with the team's first third baseman, Don Zimmer (.077 on 4-for-52 in 1962), who set a very low standard that was hard but apparently not impossible to bottom.

Fregosi did it.

The Mets didn't let reason dissuade them from pursuing Fregosi. So what if Fregosi was a shortstop, not a third baseman? They decided his horrid season for California in 1971 was a fluke, instead of a bright yellow light.

Fregosi came to camp overweight. That made fielding grounders that were upon him quicker than he had ever experienced before an exotic challenge. He broke his thumb trying to field a spring training shot off the bat of manager Gil Hodges that the manager called "a National League ground ball." When he returned, Fregosi showed he couldn't hit, either. He batted .232 with five homers and 32 RBI and 15 errors in 1972 and .234 with zero homers and 11 RBI and nine errors in 45 games in 1973.

Fregosi followed in the shameful cleatmarks of Joe Foy. A promising, muscular hunk, Foy cost the Mets future Gold Glove center fielder Amos Otis. Foy fought substance abuse issues and they showed: he hit .236 with six homers and 37 RBI and 18 errors in 99 games in 1970. Foy's play left Met fans fighting the urge to self-medicate.

Shortstop—Tony Fernandez (1993)

This free-agent signing was going to be a sure hit. Tony Fernandez was a proven hitter and no slouch with the glove at shortstop. He would love playing in a large-market city with a large Dominican population.

Think again.

The brooding Fernandez hated New York, suffered from various maladies including being misunderstood, and hit .225 in 48 games for the Mets. When they dumped him on the Blue Jays, he instantly re-morphed into the old Tony, a .288 career hitter.

Thanks for the memories.

Despite a respectable glove, Al Moran didn't exactly establish the mold for the slugging shortstop. Cal Ripken didn't grow up wanting to be "Awful Al." But Moran's .195 overall average as a Met in 1963 and 1964 did clear a path for Mario Mendoza.

Garry Templeton—who once snubbed an All-Star Game selection as a reserve by saying, "If I ain't startin', I ain't departin' "—didn't offer a rhyme to explain how a .271 career hitter could find a way to hit .228 in 80 games for the 1991 Mets.

Catcher—Greg Goosen (1965-68)

Greg Goosen was the catching "prodigy" whose potential, at the tender age of 19 as a fledgling Met, unimpressed manager Casey Stengel enough for the old man to observe, "In 10 years, he has an excellent chance of being 29."

Goosen went 6-for-32 in 1966, 11-for-69 in '67 and 22-for-106 in '68 before he disappeared into the black hole of obscurity.

In 1984, the year before the Mets reeled in Gary Carter, John Gibbons was knighted as the team's starting catcher in spring training. He went 2-for-31 as the No. 1 man out of the gate, earning an early demotion for more seasoning. Seasons passed and Gibbons played a total of eight more games in the bigs.

Honorable mention goes to Mackey Sasser, a major league hitter who owes his inclusion here to a mental hangup that saw him struggle with the task of returning the ball to the pitcher accurately.

Outfielders—Vince Coleman (1991-93), Juan Samuel (1989) and Bobby Bonilla (1992-95, 1999)

Vince Coleman, a free-agent import, proved more catastrophe than catalyst. The legs that stole 549 bases in his last six years as a Cardinal managed only 99 steals in three seasons as a Met. One especially unforgettable caught stealing—memorable for the statistics-first selfishness it illustrated—saw Vince thrown out at third for the third out in the ninth inning when he represented the potential tying run at second.

Vince's reaction?

"I'm a base-stealer, man."

Clubhouse legend has it that when Coleman heard about a ceremony honoring Jackie Robinson, Vince—a black baseball player born in the

Free-agent signee Vince Coleman was supposed to make up for the loss of Darryl Strawberry's power with his stolen-base acumen. But the only bang produced by him in his stay as a Met came from the firecracker he tossed at fans.

Bobby Bonilla, left, had a smirk for every occasion as a two-time Met mega-disappoint-ment—and his final moments with the club were reportedly spent playing cards with Rickey Henderson in the locker room while the rest of the Mets were losing Game 6 of the 1999 NCLS.

U.S.—asked, "Who was he?" He told one tabloid reporter that the grass and infield surface at Shea was keeping him out of the Hall of Fame.

Coleman's reign of error as a Met lasted just long enough for him to roll down a limousine window and flip a firecracker toward a youngster in the Dodger Stadium parking lot. What a sense of humor.

Juan Samuel, already failing as a center-field convert from second base in Philadelphia, came at a huge price, costing the Mets the popular and productive Lenny Dykstra and Roger McDowell. Two years removed from 28-homer, 100-RBI production, Juan hit .228 with three homers and 28 RBI as a Met after the June 1989 deal. Sammy was athletic enough to play center, but he played it like a life-long infielder. Despite his speed, he was ill-fit for the leadoff spot, because his slash-at-every-thing-and-burn approach made him a strikeout waiting to happen.

Bobby Bonilla promised New York's fans that he was one of them and that nobody would wipe the smile off his face when he signed a huge free-agent deal prior to 1992.

Instead, he took Jeff Torborg down with him. The manager's decision to ally himself with Mr. Bojangled, despite Bobby's myriad personality problems, contributed to Torborg being dismissed as a joke and in record time.

After averaging over 100 RBI for the Pirates in the four years before becoming a Met, Bonilla managed an average of just 70 in his first, three-plus-season stint in Flushing. Always a liability with his glove, whether at third or in right, he wore earplugs in the field to drown out the booing at Shea.

In interviews, he referred to himself in the third person, an indication of megalomania or schizophrenia. Finally, Bonilla menacingly invited one beat reporter who had written a book unflattering to him to "a tour of the Bronx," where he had (allegedly) grown up.

Bonilla was so productive and so charming that, in a move that defies explanation, the Mets brought him back in 1999. Bonilla made the most of his second chance by reporting to camp looking more fit for the word Goodyear across his side than a uniform. What a surprise it was when knee problems turned him into an absolute glacier in right and he hit .160 in a season spent mostly on the disabled list.

To repay the Mets for activating him for the NLCS, Bonilla spent the final moments of their bitter, season-ending, Game 6, extra-inning loss to Atlanta playing cards with Rickey Henderson inside the clubhouse.

The only hearts evident at the table were in the deck.

The alternate outfield is the all-disappointment group of Don Bosch in center, flanked by Ellis Valentine in right and Mike Vail in left.

Touted as the center fielder for eons to come when he was imported from Pittsburgh, Bosch was generously listed as 5-foot-10 and 160 pounds. He announced to the media that surrounded him that spring, "I don't know if I can play in the big leagues. I don't even know why I am here."

Bosch had a point, if not a clue. He hit an aggregate .157 in 1967 and 1968, making his strong defensive skills a moot point.

Valentine, who cost the Mets Jeff Reardon, hit 95 homers for the Expos and then a total of 13 for New York in 1981 and 1982. All of

Ellis Valentine, unable to get past the trauma of being nailed in the face by a pitch before he left Montreal, wore a face guard at the plate. In honor of the way he handled the bat for the Mets, Shea fans should have been furnished with blindfolds.

baseball, apparently except the Mets, had heard that Ellis was high maintenance and hadn't been, well, treating his body like a temple.

Finally, Vail excited offense-starved Met fans by hitting safely in a rookie-record 31 straight games in 1975 and wound up at .302. Then he broke his foot in a pickup basketball game that winter and hit .246 overall for the Mets in 1976 and 1977 before they unloaded him.

Tease.

Pitchers—Bill Pulsipher (1995, 1998, 2000), Pete Harnisch (1995-97), Hideo Nomo (1998), Tim Leary (1981, 1983-84), Pete Schourek (1991-93), Pete Smith (1994), Anthony Young (1991-93), Craig Anderson (1962-64), Mike Scott (1979-82), Mel Rojas (1997-98), Rich Rodriguez (2000).

The high-strung, easy-to-like Bill Pulsipher—part of GM Joe McIlvaine's ill-fated troika of one-time untouchables, along with Jason Isringhausen and Paul Wilson—was a sad case of never was. This sinkerballer's talent was so tempting the Mets danced with Pulsipher twice—before and after arm problems. He was 5-9 with a 6.91 ERA for them, including a nifty 12.15 ERA in 2000.

Pete Harnisch has been a bull and a workhorse winner almost everywhere he has pitched—before and after he was a Met. But, for them, he went 10-21 in two-plus years, suffered physical problems, sleeplessness from giving up chewing tobacco and depression. Apparently, the only thing more depressing than watching those Mets was pitching for them.

Hideo Nomo, 4-5 with a 4.82 ERA, never found his early career form or even the plate as a Met in 1998 (56 walks in 89⅔ innings). The following spring, Nomo somehow went from a secure rotation spot to an outright release—a stunning development because it essentially amounted to an admission of front-office stupidity.

Tim Leary was going to be another Tom Seaver, they said. Except this legend lasted only the time it takes to get a beer. In his first big league start, poor Tim pitched an April 1981 game at Wrigley Field in the cold, hurt his elbow warming up and left after one scoreless inning.

Leary resurfaced as a Met in 1983 and '84, but went only 4-4 for them before moving on to some decent years with Milwaukee and Los Angeles.

Pete Schourek spent three mostly painful seasons with the Mets, from 1991 through 1993, going 16-24 with a 4.65 ERA. Freed from his spot in Dallas Green's doghouse—the manager was convinced the lefty terminally lacked aggressiveness—Schourek put it together during an 18-win season for Cincinnati.

A lot of good it did the Mets.

Pete Smith allegedly had as much potential as his minor league staff-mates Tom Glavine and John Smoltz and was decent enough as the fifth starter for the Atlanta Braves. When the Mets answered his prayers for more regular work in 1994, Smith went 4-10 with a 5.55 ERA for them, regularly absorbing the kind of poundings that make referees stop fights.

So much for bloodlines.

Anthony Young lost an amazing 19 games in a row as a Met, going 5-35 in the uniform despite a respectable 3.82 overall ERA. Was he snake-bit? Certainly. But losing 19 in a row takes some doing. Even a snake handler doesn't get bitten that often, unless he is doing something very wrong.

It started out badly for Craig Anderson in 1962, when he went 3-17 with a 5.35 ERA for the Originals. He lost two games in a single day. Then it got worse as Anderson posted a 6.85 ERA over the next two seasons.

Mike Scott became a brilliant split-finger genius and a 110-game winner for the Astros and he nearly singlehandedly kept the 1986 Mets from fulfilling their championship destiny in the NLCS. But, before that, he was barely worth a Danny Heep because the righty was 14-27 as a Met from 1979 through 1982. Scott's best chance of getting a hitter out in those days was to put him on and then pick him off with his excellent move.

Mel Rojas blew the first game he entered after the trade that ended his disastrous stint with the Cubs and went on from there. Rojas, who saved a total of 66 games for the Expos in 1995 and 1996, saved a total of four for the Mets in 1997 and 1998 and posted a 5.76 ERA in 73 games. Mel even hurt them after he was gone, because he is the guy they dumped on the Dodgers to bring back Bonilla.

On the topic of contracts too large to eat with an outright release, there was Rich Rodriguez. The lefty was brought in for the Mets' bullpen in 2000, even though they already had lefties galore in Dennis Cook and John Franco and Bobby Jones and Glendon Rusch and Pulsipher.

Rodriguez—in the hollow Met tradition of such unspecial southpaw specialists as Mac Scarce, Tom Gorman and Gene Walter—was nothing like the Rodriguez who had a 26-17, 3.47 mark in 485 career games prior to 2000.

No lead was safe in Rich's hands as he was 0-1 with a 7.78 ERA and gave up 59 hits, 15 walks and seven homers in 37 games—framed around a demotion to Triple A. Barry Bonds hit what was left of Rodriguez' fastball into San Francisco Bay in May.

The only thing launched further and faster should have been Rich.

The 15 All-Time Best Trades

1. Obtained 1B Keith Hernandez from the St. Louis Cardinals for P Neil Allen and P Rick Ownbey, June 15, 1983

Keith Hernandez wanted to vomit when he learned where the Cardinals had sent him at the trade deadline. It was only after he was talked down from the ledge and saw the young arms on the way to being Met aces that Hernandez realized he wasn't going to also-ran hell after all.

The inner demons that drove Keith toward excellence translated into huge dividends for the Mets: leadership, clutch production, contagious preoccupation with playing the game right and an immense clubhouse presence. Acquiring him was the precise moment that contention in the 1980s began.

Neil Allen, blessed with a curve and a fastball each nasty enough to be the out pitch for a big league closer, won 19 games over his first two seasons in St. Louis. But his fragile mental makeup was clear. Legend has it that Allen pleaded guilty to an alcohol abuse problem that he didn't

357

Ex-Cardinal Keith Hernandez—with his head fixed on the ball and his front shoulder tucked in vs. the nastiest left-hander, with his counseling of pitchers, with his ability to pounce on a bunt and nail a lead runner—turned the Mets around with his intensity.

have in an attempt to cover up a marital indiscretion. Allen never regained his early career form that saw him register 69 of his 75 lifetime saves as a Met from 1979 through 1983. Ownbey, a lefty with a nasty curve, never harnessed his terrific stuff, going 3-11 and 4.10 for his career.

Cards' GM Whitey Herzog claimed he made the deal on baseball merits, but anticipation of the 1985 Pittsburgh cocaine trial was already creating suspicion that Hernandez had a problem. He continued to deny that he was a user until his testimony in court, but Herzog wanted him gone. A .296 career hitter lifetime, "Mex" won 11 Gold Gloves.

2. Obtained P Al Leiter and INF Ralph Millard from the Florida Marlins for P Jesus Sanchez, P A.J. Burnett and OF Robert Stratton, Feb. 8, 1998

Al Leiter had just turned the corner from underachieving hard thrower to nasty, fist-pounding magician with a plan when the Mets hijacked him from the world champion Marlins, who were conducting a going-out-of-contention giveaway. Jesus Sanchez and A.J. Burnett have talent, with Burnett looking like a power-pitching force for seasons to come, but how impressive would they have to turn out for the Mets to look back and do anything but smile about this deal?

Leiter has been a big-game, bat-breaking monster of a No. 1 starter from 1998 through 2001. The lefty has shown the guts of a burglar,

Al Leiter, wearing an NYPD hat in 2001, learned command as a Marlin and has hand-cuffed hitters in the uniform of the team that he rooted for as a boy on the Jersey shore.

jamming the living daylights out of right-handed hitters with his slider on the hands, battling well into astronomical pitch count territory and truly craving each win-or-die assignment. Leiter's totally-in-charge, complete-game shutout of the Reds in the single-game playoff that determined the 1999 wildcard winner will never be forgotten by Mets fans or then-Cincinnati manager Jack McKeon. This product of the New Jersey shore came up as a Yankee, but grew up as a pitcher in Flushing. As the Met ace, Leiter has a 57-37 record with a 3.32 ERA. In that span, he has allowed only 714 hits and struck out 678 in 801⅓ innings.

3. Obtained P David Cone and C Chris Jelic from the Kansas City Royals for C Ed Hearn, P Rick Anderson and P Mauro Gozzo, March 27, 1987

Back in 1987, David Cone was an unproven gem whom the Royals were worried wouldn't make it back from a serious knee operation in the minors. Why else would they send a pitcher with an arm like his to the Mets for Ed Hearn (Gary Carter's caddy), Rick Anderson (a journeyman) and Mauro Gozzo (a hard-throwing potential closer who lacked command)? This heist was perhaps Joe McIlvaine's greatest moment and one of the few deals that the razor-sharp John Schuerholz wound up with cause to regret.

Cone went 20-3 with a 2.22 ERA for the Mets in 1988 and won 55 more in their uniform—including a 19-strikeout gem vs. the Phillies—before he was dumped on the Blue Jays in 1992. Cone has been a savvy power pitcher with a flair for creative expression on the mound. Flouting conventional mechanical wisdom, Cone has a million different release points and even names for the pitches he created, like the sidearm slider that he called the "Laredo."

4. Obtained C Mike Piazza from the Florida Marlins for OF Preston Wilson, P Ed Yarnell and P Geoff Goetz, May 22, 1998

Mike Piazza was the catcher whom GM Steve Phillips landed to take the place of the injured Todd Hundley in a deal made possible by the

Dodgers' previous unwillingness to contractually satisfy their star. The Marlins traded for Piazza, then moved him along for three Met prospects. The most significant, power hitter Preston Wilson, has shown superstar potential in Florida if he can just make more regular contact.

However, Piazza is a Hall of Fame-bound hitter, the kind of cleanup force that transforms a lineup. In three-plus seasons as a Met through 2001, he has been a .317 hitter with 137 homers and 407 RBI. Signing him to an extension was the safest investment the Mets have ever made—especially if they prevail upon this stubborn gamer to get out from behind the plate and secure his slugging future.

David Cone, obtained for a song from the Royals, notched the highest-winning percentage (.870) in Met history as a 20-3 force for the 1988 NL East champs.

5. Obtained OF Tommie Agee and SS Al Weis from the Chicago White Sox for OF Tommy Davis, P Jack Fisher, P Billy Wynne and C Dick Booker, Dec. 15, 1967

Tommie Agee and Al Weis are names synonomous with the Mets' World Series heroics in 1969. One-year Met Tommy Davis (.268 with only 50 RBI for the White Sox in '68), old Jack Fisher (8-13 for Chicago in '68), Billy Wynne (8-11 for his career) and radar-screen-blip Dick Booker turned out to be a very small price to pay for the 1969 and 1970 seasons turned in by Agee and for Weis' otherworldly contributions to those Miracle Mets.

After a horrid first year in New York that included an 0-for-34 stretch in 1968, Agee spent the next two years revolutionizing the leadoff position by flashing middle-of-the-order power to go with stolen-base

Tommie Agee, a total flop in 1968 after coming from the White Sox, gave the Mets speed and power in the leadoff spot in '69. But it was his two rally-thwarting catches in center that made all the difference in World Series Game 3.

capacity. He scored 204 runs, drove in 151 and had 50 homers and 53 doubles for a team that desperately needed his punch. His outfield play in center, epitomized by his World Series tour de force, was special.

Weis made all the plays. His only two 1969 homers came on successive days to beat the Cubs in a crucial showdown and Mighty Mite's .455 average and lone post-season blast drove a stake through the Orioles' hearts in the World Series.

6. Obtained P Ron Darling and P Walt Terrell from the Texas Rangers for OF Lee Mazzilli, April 1, 1982

Lee Mazzilli was the poster boy for the Joe Torre era Mets, never delivering on what the club believed his talent had promised. The Brooklyn product was always wildly popular with teen-age girls because of his Italian good looks. But the way Mazzilli filled out those tight double-knits was more impressive than the way he hit and threw—ambidexterity, in his case, simply meant he could throw poorly with both hands—during his first Met stay.

Ron Darling was a baby in the Texas system, as was Walt Terrell. Darling was a thinking man's pitcher who went 72-38 for the Mets from 1984 through 1988 and won 99 games overall as a Met. He was the No. 2 starter to Dwight Gooden for most of his six double-figure-win seasons for the Mets. Terrell, meanwhile, wound up toughing his way to 111 wins over 11 major league seasons, even though only 19 of them came for the Mets. When they moved him to Detroit, Terrell proved even more valuable to the Mets. They received Howard Johnson in return.

7. Obtained 3B Howard Johnson from the Detroit Tigers for P Walt Terrell, Dec. 7, 1984

Howard Johnson developed into one of the Mets' most popular and productive speed-and-power contributors after finally getting the fulltime job at third following the post-1986 World Series departure of platoon partner Ray Knight.

A savage fastball hitter who failed to win the approval of Sparky Anderson in Detroit, Johnson joined Darryl Strawberry in becoming the Mets' first 30-homer/30-steal players in 1987, with 36 homers and 32 steals. It was the first of three such seasons for Johnson, who stole 160 bases and crushed 157 homers from 1987 through 1992, with a high-water mark of 38 homers and 117 RBI in '91. Terrell won 54 games for the Tigers from 1985-88, but HoJo's bat spoke a lot louder than that.

8. Obtained C Jerry Grote from the Houston Astros for P Tom Parsons, Oct. 19, 1965

Jerry Grote, a .181 hitter for Houston in 1964 before losing his job to John Bateman, eventually settled in as the anchor for a young Met pitching staff that thrived thanks to his take-charge professionalism

Former Astro Jerry Grote, the taciturn Texan with the tough-guy swagger, had no trouble communicating with the Mets' young pitchers, and his arm was the envy of every catcher in the game.

behind the plate. It never mattered that this two-time All-Star was a career .252 hitter whose best offensive season among his 13 as a Met was a .295 oddity in 1975. "He gave us that stability, like a Thurman Munson or a Bench," said Mets GM Joe McDonald.

Grote was so good behind the plate that his brilliant catching contemporary Johnny Bench of the Reds once said, "If the Reds had Grote, I would be playing third base" and Lou Brock called Grote "the toughest catcher in the NL to steal against."

The Astros were so sure that Grote, a Texan through and through, wouldn't hit enough that they were willing to take Tom Parsons, who went 1-10 as a Met in 1965 and never pitched in another major league game.

9. Obtained 2B Felix Millan and P George Stone from the Atlanta Braves for P Gary Gentry and P Danny Frisella, Nov. 2, 1972

The Mets so intensely coveted the quiet, professional Felix Millan as a second-base replacement for Ken Boswell that they reluctantly parted with Gary Gentry, who went 41-42 with all kinds of unfulfilled promise as a Met.

While Gentry wound up out of baseball altogether because of arm surgery after going to Atlanta, Millan was all the Mets could have hoped in 1973. He stabilized the Mets up the middle (they turned an NL-leading 179 double plays) and gave them a potent No. 2 hitter (.290). This deal landed the Mets in the 1973 World Series—and it was as much because of the stunning career-season contributions of throw-in George Stone as anything Millan did.

Stone, 6-10 with a 5.63 ERA for Atlanta in 1972, threw softly and accurately enough that you could trust him to pitch in front of your china closet. Somehow, he became a 12-3, 2.80 impact pitcher for the Mets in '73. "We told Felix he was the throw-in in the George Stone deal," joked Bud Harrelson. Stone was ruined by arm problems the following season, but Millan went on to set club records for hits (191) and doubles (37) in 1975.

George Stone, the finesse lefty who was nothing more than an after-thought in the deal that brought Felix Millan from Atlanta, saved his career year (12-3, 2.80 ERA) for the Mets' run in 1973.

10. Obtained 1B Donn Clendenon from the Montreal Expos for P Steve Renko, 3B Kevin Collins, P Bill Cardon and P Dave Colon, June 15, 1969

The addition of Donn Clendenon helped put the 1969 Mets over the top. This right-handed-hitting first baseman was about to retire at age 33 rather than report to Houston when the Expos traded him there prior to the 1969 season. Persuaded to unretire and permitted to return to Montreal by baseball commissioner Bowie Kuhn, "Clink" became Ed Kranepool's platoon partner June 15.

He hit only .252 with 12 homers and 37 RBI, but combined with Kranepool's stats, the Mets got 23 homers and 86 RBI from first base.

Then Clendenon hit .357 with three homers and four RBI in winning the World Series MVP award. He followed that with a 1970 season in which he hit .288 with 22 homers and 97 RBI.

Steve Renko went 68-82 for Montreal and Kevin Collins proved to be a spare part. The other two pitchers the Mets included in the deal didn't make it to the majors.

11. Obtained 1B John Olerud from the Toronto Blue Jays for P Robert Person, Dec. 20, 1996

The Mets owe a large thank you to Cito Gaston for their resurgence in 1997.

John Olerud was rescued off Gaston's Blue Jays reject pile after the manager's failed attempt to get Olerud to hit for more power turned the player into a shadow of his former line-drive-hitting self. Gaston's classless prediction that Olerud would be overwhelmed by playing in New York proved even more wrong-headed than his hitting advice.

Olerud, who had chased .400 with a .363 mark in 1993, re-found himself instantly. As a Met from 1997 through 1999, Olerud drove 63 homers and 177 extra-base hits, knocked in 291 runs and scored 288. He posted a club-record .354 mark in 1998. Defensively, he cleaned up any rare mistakes at first base as the fourth jewel in a world-class defensive infield, with Edgardo Alfonzo, Rey Ordoñez and Robin Ventura in 1999.

Person, bouncing from the rotation to the bullpen, went 8-13 in two-plus seasons for Toronto but eventually matured into a solid starting pitcher for the Phillies in 2001.

12. Obtained the rights to manager Gil Hodges from the Washington Senators for P Bill Denehy, Nov. 27, 1967

That's right: it cost the Mets a player and $100,000 (a lot of money in those days) for the rights to a manager. And it was a worthwhile investment and then some. The Original Met Hodges, through the force of his personality, became the first successful manager in club history.

Hodges hadn't exactly burned up the baseball world in the Senators' dugout but the team had shown a gradual improvement under him, climbing from 56 wins in 1963 to 76 in 1967. Because he was still under contract to Washington, the Mets had to put together a package to pry him loose.

It was no coincidence that after the respected former Brooklyn Dodger legend arrived, the nonsense and the losing habits departed. And there was that famous mid-inning stroll to left field to pull a less-than-hustling Cleon Jones in July 1969.

"We were the big joke in the league when Gil became manager," said Ed Charles. "But Gil instilled a whole different attitude. He made us believe in ourselves. He made us say, 'Hell, we're not going to be patsies, anymore.' He made us respectable."

He made the Mets world champions in 1969 and they won 83 games each of the next two seasons before he succumbed to a spring 1972 heart attack. Denehy, 1-7 for the Mets in 1965, pitched three games for the Senators in 1968.

13. Obtained P Armando Benitez from the Baltimore Orioles and OF Roger Cedeño from the Los Angeles Dodgers in three-team deal that sent C Todd Hundley and P Arnold Gooch to the Dodgers and C Charles Johnson from the Dodgers to the Orioles, Dec. 1, 1998

Trading a catcher who had not proven that he could come back from serious elbow reconstruction is a tricky task, even if he once was a 40-home run man. When the Mets dealt Todd Hundley following the importation of Mike Piazza, they scored big.

Armando Benitez, happy to leave lots of bad memories behind from his brief stint as the Baltimore closer, has become the most dominant fastball-throwing closer in Met history. The big guy's first three Met seasons have been mostly remarkable: 327 strikeouts in 230⅓ innings, an aggregate 2.74 ERA, save totals of 22, 41 and a club-record 43 for 106 overall. Benitez' troubling late-season/post-season history, which followed him from the Orioles to the Mets, is the lone black mark on his work, albeit a truly disturbing one.

Cedeño stayed long enough to hit .313 with 66 steals as a Met in 1999 before the club included him in the package that brought 2000 NLCS MVP Mike Hampton from Houston. The Mets liked Cedeño's leadoff skills enough to re-import him as a free agent prior to 2002.

Meanwhile, Hundley, now with the Chicago Cubs, has struggled mightily with his throwing and has been unable to relocate his power stroke.

14. Obtained P Bobby Ojeda, P John McCarthy, P John Mitchell, and P Chris Bayer from the Boston Red Sox for P Calvin Schiraldi, P Wes Gardner, OF John Christensen and OF LaSchelle Tarver, Nov. 11, 1985

Bobby Ojeda came into his own in 1986 with a career year: 18-5 with a 2.57 ERA. He also led the Mets to a World Series victory with his performance against his old teammates at Fenway Park in Game 3, with the Mets down 0-2 and looking directly into a yawning porcelain resting place. In 1986, the gutsy lefty with the tantalizing changeup must have benefitted from NL hitters' lack of familiarity with him, because Ojeda went a hard-luck 33-35 over the next four years in New York.

The measure of Schiraldi—and the confirmation that his mental makeup didn't suit him to the job of closer—came in Games 6 and 7 of the 1986 World Series. The mention of his name is enough to cause the blood to leave the faces of any Red Sox fan older than 10.

15. Obtained C Gary Carter from the Montreal Expos for 3B Hubie Brooks, OF Herm Winningham, P Floyd Youmans and C Mike Fitzgerald, Dec. 10, 1984

Gary Carter and that smile were made for New York and he did take the city by storm after he arrived from Montreal to fill the Mets' catcher and cleanup spots. Just on the other side of his peak, he made a definite impact as the Mets chased the Cardinals through the summer of 1985 and finally won it all in 1986.

A strong thrower whose banged-up knees robbed him of arm strength and later reduced him at the plate, Carter's best Met years were 1985 and 1986, when he had 32 homers and 100 RBI and then 24 homers and 105 RBI. Until Mike Piazza came along, there was no other Met catcher who exerted Carter's kind of boom, bang presence.

Herm Winningham never established himself as a regular player. Mike Fitzgerald didn't hit much in seven seasons as Carter's replacement behind the plate with the Expos. Talented Floyd Youmans (25-26 for the Expos over three seasons) had too many off-the-field issues to become a big winner. Hubie Brooks drove in 100 runs in the first of his five seasons in Montreal.

But Carter wound up with the ring that he, Ellis Valentine and Andre Dawson couldn't grab north of the border and the Mets wouldn't have won a thing in '86 and '88 without him.

The 15 All-Time Worst Trades

1. Sent P Nolan Ryan, P Don Rose, OF Leroy Stanton and C Francisco Estrada to the California Angels for SS Jim Fregosi, Dec. 10, 1971

Nolan Ryan didn't really hint at a Hall of Fame future as a Texan out of his element in New York—because of recurring blisters that made him go through a deli's supply of pickle brine and the military commitments that jerked him in and out of the rotation. In need of tougher skin on more than just his finger, the shy Ryan was learning to pitch on a major league level.

Yes, Ryan was only 29-38 as a Met from 1966 through 1971, but the fastball was there, rising in the strike zone, and the curve was a work in progress. So it's fair to ask: How do you deal a pitcher with this kind of stuff before his 25th birthday? Well, you don't. But Nolan was history before he became history or even pitched the first of his periodic no-hitters. While Met fans cringed, Ryan spent the next 22 years winning 295 more games and running his strikeout total to 5,714.

*Nolan Ryan, con-
founding the Mets in
Game 3 of the 1986
NLCS as a member of
the Astros here, was
sent, pickle brine and
all, to the Angels before
the no-hitters and most
of the Ks that made
him a Hall of Famer.*

Mets GM Bob Scheffing decided to give up on Nolan when the pitcher lost 10 of his last 12 decisions to finish at 10-14 in 1971.

"We've had him three full years and, although he is a hell of a prospect he hasn't done it for us. How long can you wait? I can't rate him in the same category with Tom Seaver, Jerry Koosman or Gary Gentry (whom California GM Harry Dalton had asked for instead of Ryan)," said Scheffing.

To make matters worse, the Mets agreed to sweeten the pot for shortstop Jim Fregosi, who didn't even play the position they needed to fill—their black hole, third base. They threw in three decent prospects—Leroy Stanton had hit .324 with 23 homers and 101 RBI in Triple-A in 1971 and would hit 27 homers in a season for Seattle in 1977—along with Ryan.

Their return? An overweight Fregosi, coming off a .233, five-homer season. He had averaged about 50 RBI per year over his career and wouldn't come close to that for the Mets. Ryan won 19 games with a 2.28 ERA and an AL-leading 329 Ks in 1972 while the immobile

Fregosi was injured in the spring and hit .232 with 32 RBI in his Met debut. The following year he was unable to win the job from the guy he was supposed to replace, Wayne Garrett, and was sent to Texas in July 1973.

Years later, Mets board chairman M. Donald Grant tried to shift the onus for the deal to the sportswriters who were clamoring for the team to make some move at the time. "I told you to make a deal," responded a writer. "But not that one."

2. Sent OF Amos Otis and P Bob Johnson to the Kansas City Royals for 3B Joe Foy, Dec. 3, 1969

Why take a promising young hitter and athlete with the defensive skills to be an outstanding center fielder and project him as a rookie big league starter at a position he had never played? The Mets did it with Amos Otis in 1969, naming him their third baseman in that spring—as if all the positions were interchangeable and as if hitting major league pitching for the first time wasn't going to be enough of a challenge.

When the bell rang, Otis played like he hated third base and hit like he didn't belong in the majors. He disappeared back into the minors while Wayne Garrett and Ed Charles contributed to the miracle. Otis hit .325 for Tidewater but his major league line was .151 with four RBI in 93 at-bats. Then the 23-year-old—who had been labelled an "untouchable" in trade talks with the Braves a year earlier, at the time Joe Torre was moved to St. Louis for Orlando Cepeda—was deemed touchable. The Mets still needed a third baseman. What else was new?

Otis wound up with a .277 career average with 193 homers, 341 steals and 1,007 RBI, playing 14 of the next 15 seasons in Kansas City. A three-time Gold Glove winner, Famous Amos had a .991 career fielding percentage and 126 outfield assists. Johnson went 8-13 for the weak Royals in 1970, but Otis kept producing like the Energizer Bunny.

Joe Foy's contributions were so meager they served to launch yet another third-base shopping spre—a hunt that resulted in the "How about Jim Fregosi?" stroke of genius. Foy, a 37-steal, 71-RBI man for the Royals in 1969, committed 18 errors and hit .236 for the Mets in 1970, finally losing his spot to—who else?—Garrett.

The Mets came to regret not heeding the 1968 warning sign of Foy's drunkenness arrest, which earned him a fine and suspension from the Red Sox. Besieged by "personal problems," Foy managed six homers, 37 RBI and 22 steals in '70. He was demoted and later was drafted by Washington in December 1970, playing 41 games with the Senators before disappearing from the majors forever.

3. Sent OF Len Dykstra, P Roger McDowell and P Tom Edens to the Philadelphia Phillies for OF-2B Juan Samuel, June 18, 1989

Lenny Dykstra, always a little guy who wanted to be the same size as his heart, let his 1986 World Series homers go to his head and bulked

Juan Samuel, a table-setter prone to making no contact at all, was played out of position, in center, by the Mets. All it cost them to bring him over from the Phillies was Lenny Dykstra, an actual center fielder, and Roger McDowell.

up from weight lifting (and the likely ingestion of steroids instead of Wheaties). The gritty center fielder exhausted manager Davey Johnson's patience with his upper-cut swing while other leadoff men maximized their speed by hitting down on the ball.

Roger McDowell, 1-5 in 1989 at the time of the deal, never seemed to have the same swagger for the Mets after that Terry Pendleton homer broke his back in September 1987.

But why Juan Samuel?

At the time of the deal, Sammy was looking like a second baseman out of water as the Phillies' 1989 experiment in center-field terror. The Mets still had Mookie Wilson, an honest-to-goodness center fielder with as many top-of-the-order skills as the strikeout-prone Samuel. But GM Joe McIlvaine felt certain that Samuel would make a huge impact on the club with his bat.

Juan hit .228 for the Mets with three homers, 28 RBI, 17 extra-base hits and 75 strikeouts in 333 at-bats. His on-base percentage was .299 for them. His three errors in the outfield as a Met didn't tell the whole story of how uncomfortable he looked there. By 1990, Samuel was gone and the Mets, refusing to learn their lesson about infielders becoming center fielders in the majors, tried Howard Johnson and Keith Miller there with cover-your-eyes results. Mantle, Mays and Snider, these guys weren't.

Dykstra hit .325, stole 33 bases, scored 106 runs and drove in 60 runs in 1990. In his last season before his self-destructive streak and injuries reduced him, Lenny carried the 1993 Phillies to a pennant, with 19 homers, 66 RBI, 143 runs, 37 steals and a .305 average. McDowell went 3-3 with 19 saves and a 1.11 ERA after the trade in 1989, then saved 25 more for the Phillies before being dealt to the Dodgers in 1991.

4. Sent 2B Jeff Kent and SS Jose Vizcaino to the Cleveland Indians for 2B Carlos Baerga and SS Alvaro Espinoza, July 29, 1996

After a 39-game pit stop in Cleveland, Jeff Kent gave the Blue Jays, the Mets and the Indians major cause to regret giving up on him.

Jeff Kent, part of the package that inflicted Carlos Baerga on Met fans, became defensively proficient at second base and rang up 138 homers and 581 RBI as the Giants' cleanup hitter from 1997 through 2001.

Quite simply, he became the most productive second baseman in the game in San Francisco.

Kent only hinted at having team-carrying potential when he hit 21 homers and drove in 80 runs for the Mets in 1990. But, for the Giants, in five amazing seasons from 1997 through 2001, Kent has been Superman. He has rung up 138 homers and 581 RBI. He even improved from a liability at second base into a defensive asset and was the 2000 NL MVP after hitting .334 with 350 total bases, an on-base percentage of .424 and a slugging mark of .596.

Meanwhile, in New York, Carlos Baerga's career continued in a free fall so precipitous that it is hard to explain as the result of a few added pounds or too many nights of la vida loca. The two-time Silver Slugger winner grounded into 42 double plays in two-plus seasons as a Met, a measure of both his hitting futility and glacial movement down the line. For the Mets, he had 18 homers and 116 RBI in 1,061 at-bats over two-plus years—after having 21 and 114 for Cleveland in 1993 alone. In 1996, after coming over, Baerga hit .193 with a .301 slugging percentage.

The switch-hitter gave up hitting right-handed altogether after a long run of utter ineptitude. When his woeful hitting made him a candidate for a utility infielder's role, Carlos couldn't do that, either: his only position was second base. After 55 more major league appearances following his last year as a Met, in 1998, he was officially finished.

Alvaro Espinoza was a blip on the Mets' radar screen. But Jose Vizcaino is still around. The Viz reminded everyone what a nice little player he is—still far superior to the postmenopausal Baerga—when he put the Mets to death for the Yankees in Game 1 of the 2000 World Series.

5. Sent P Mike Scott to the Houston Astros for OF Danny Heep, Dec. 10, 1982

In fairness, how could the Mets have guessed that the Mike Scott who had a fastball and a pickoff move and little else going for him while going 14-27 for them from 1979 through 1982 would become the close-to-unhittable split-finger master Mike Scott?

Armed with the new pitch that transformed his career, Scott emerged as the ace of the Astros' staff in the mid-1980s, the 1986 Cy Young Award winner (18-10, 2.22 ERA and 306 strikeouts) and the 1986 NLCS MVP. From 1985 through 1989, Scott went 86-49 for Houston and that included a 20-10 season in '89. His effectiveness in 1986 was so overwhelming that it was considered a near given that the Mets' ninth-inning rally and 16th-inning victory in NLCS Game 6 was the only thing that kept Scott from dominating Game 7 and sending the Mets home to watch the World Series on TV.

Danny Heep was a platoon partner for George Foster, a lefty hitter with some power and no speed to bring off the bench, a nice spare part who contributed 21 homers and 108 RBI from 1983 through 1986.

6. Sent P David Cone to the Toronto Blue Jays for 2B Jeff Kent and OF Ryan Thompson, Aug. 27, 1992

David Cone was too honest, too unbridled, too emotional, too unmarried, too real for the Mets' brass to feel comfortable with him. So the club decided he was no longer worth the trouble after his numbers had fallen from 20-3, 2.22 in 1988 to 13-7, 2.88 in 1992. He was just 29 years old and had gone 75-42 for the Mets from 1988 through 1992. But, with his free agency pending at season's end, Cone (193-123 for his career through 2001) was cast off on a career path that would adorn almost an entire hand with world championship rings in the Bronx. The Blue Jays had him for only one pennant stretch run in his first Toronto stay (4-3, 2.55 in 1992), but were glad they did.

Jeff Kent's thorny personality and his lack of defensive skills at third and second prompted the Mets to make the huge blunder of not holding onto him. Sure enough, Kent became an adequate glove at second and one of the dominant run producers of his era. Ryan Thompson (39 homers and 276 strikeouts in 997 at-bats and no average above .251 as a Met from 1992 through 1995) had a rock-hard body and pectorals that suggested greatness and an ebullient personality, but he played his way into Dallas Green's doghouse and never developed enough bat speed to make it.

7. Sent P Jeff Reardon and OF Dan Norman to the Montreal Expos for OF Ellis Valentine, May 29, 1981

Dan Norman, a Met for a minute and a half, is remembered for being in two of the worst deals the club has made, matching Jeff Kent for that distinction. The outfielder, whose swing was impressive save for the lack of contact, came from Cincinnati as one of four players obtained in the Tom Seaver deal in 1977. Then, when this thickly muscled, raw-boned specimen left the Mets organization, it was as a throw-in with reliever Jeff Reardon in the trade for Ellis Valentine in 1981.

Valentine had been a 25-homer-a-season stud for the Expos twice, with speed and a howitzer for an arm in right field (24 assists in 1978). But the baseball world knew that he was hard to handle and his off-the-field habits suggested, five tools or not, Valentine might not be worth the trouble. In 1980, a fastball from Roy Thomas shattered Ellis' cheekbone and, apparently, his confidence as a hitter. Met GM Frank Cashen fully expected the old Valentine would re-emerge, but wound up fit to be bow-tied.

Reardon, the right-handed sinkerballer who had lost the closer's role to Neil Allen with the Mets, went 3-0 with a 2.19 ERA and eight saves in 1981 to push the Expos to a division title. He managed to overcome career-long back problems to notch 32 wins and 162 saves for Montreal from 1981 through 1986 (including 41 saves in '85) and he concluded his long career with a 3.16 ERA and 367 saves.

Meanwhile, Valentine hit .207 with five homers and 21 RBI the season in which he came to New York, in 1981. Ellis griped about his platoon status and scratched himself from the starting lineup on numerous occasions. On his way out of the door after an 8-homer, 48-RBI encore in 1982, Valentine called the Mets "the worst organization in baseball." Finally, the man had a point.

8. Sent RF-1B Rusty Staub and P Bill Laxton to the Detroit Tigers for P Mickey Lolich and OF Bobby Baldwin, Dec. 12, 1975

Rusty Staub was dumped only two years after being a brave stand-out for the Mets in the 1973 post-season, when he had two homers and five RBI in Game 4 of the World Series, despite being hampered by a separated shoulder. He enjoyed a 105-RBI season in 1975, right before he was dealt.

What prompted this deal? Let's just note it wasn't entire borne of talent-for-talent considerations.

The Mets' front office reportedly had grown tired of Rusty's exacting, idiosyncratic ways. Rusty, whose nickname was Felix after the fussbudget Felix Unger of *Odd Couple* notoriety, insisted on taking a nap and a bowel movement at appointed times before each game. He wanted it written into his contract that the team must use aircrafts of a specified size that landed in an area of specified size and were equipped with specified equipment. When he was told he would have to replace his striped Adidas shoes with the all-black Mets style, he demanded the club provide him with a season supply (13 pairs).

Mets board chairman M. Donald Grant said it was *not the shoes*.

"We felt we couldn't have Ed Kranepool and Staub in the lineup at the same time," said Grant. "They were so slow on the basepaths the other players were bumping into them."

So, the offensively challenged Mets dumped a clutch run producer for Mickey Lolich, a 35-year-old pitcher coming off a 12-18 season, adding him to a staff that already included Tom Seaver, Jerry Koosman and Jon Matlack. The Mets rejected a chance to get Doug DeCinces from Baltimore for Staub and instead begged Lolich, a long way removed from his 1968 World Series heroics, not to use his trade veto power. Oh, yeah, the Mets also liked the potential of Billy Baldwin.

Lolich went 0-4 out of the gate in 1976 and finished at 8-13 with a 3.22 ERA. He was so unhappy in New York, away from his Michigan roots, that he retired after the season—only to come back and pitch again for the San Diego Padres in 1978.

Staub's next three seasons in Detroit were gems: .299 with 15 homers and 96 RBI in 1976, 22 homers and 101 RBI in 1977 and 24 homers and 121 RBI in 1978, when he was named Designated Hitter of the Year. The Mets brought Rusty back in 1980 as a free agent, at 36, but his prime was behind him.

"It was not my idea to leave in the first place," he said.

9. Sent P Tom Seaver to the Cincinnati Reds for P Pat Zachry, 2B Doug Flynn, OF Steve Henderson and OF Dan Norman, June 15, 1977

Tom Seaver's spring 1976 union activism stung the Mets' board chairman M. Donald Grant, with his ballclub-as-dysfunctional-family beliefs, and the trade rumors that ensued disturbed the pitcher. However, just prior to the start of that season, the Mets managed to sign the three-time Cy Young Award winner to a three-year contract that would pay him a maximum of $225,000 annually. But, by 1977, Seaver saw inferior talent commanding vastly superior money and feared the Mets' decline would make his statistical incentives impossible to reach. He was chafing.

The pitcher criticized the club for its passive approach to free agency and sided with Dave Kingman, of all people, in the latter's contract dispute. Columnist Dick Young was doing Grant's public relations work, labelling Seaver as spoiled and selfish for wanting to renegotiate (even though he never made a formal request). The Franchise—who had trade veto power—was asked where he would be willing to go in a deal and his list included Los Angeles, Philadelphia, Pittsburgh and Cincinnati. By this time, Seaver simply wanted to get away from Grant.

Tom Terrific, 189-110 and only 32 years old, with the NL single-game record for strikeouts (19) and nine All-Star selections, was traded to the Reds for a package that didn't include one established regular player. The Pirates had bid hard-hitting Al Oliver and pitcher Jerry Reuss and later Oliver and Bruce Kison. The Dodgers had offered pitcher Rick Rhoden in a three-player package, but the Mets wanted Doug Rau, too.

The Mets got pitcher Pat Zachry, outfielder Steve Henderson, second baseman Doug Flynn and outfielder Dan Norman.

They got who?

"This has got to be one of the biggest steals since the Babe Ruth trade," said Davey Lopes.

Zachry, the NL's co-Rookie of the Year with a 14-7 record as a Red in 1976, was 3-7 at the time of the deal and went 41-46 for the Mets from 1977 through 1982. Henderson hit for average (.297 after the deal, .266, .306, .290), but not with a corner outfielder's power. His 12 homers in 350 at-bats for the Mets in 1977 were the single-season high for his career (68 in 3,484 at-bats) and Stevie Wonder had only eight homers and 58 RBI in 1980, his final Met season.

Flynn was a magician with the glove, could play some mean country western with the guitar and was at a loss what to do with a bat—although he did drive in a miraculous 61 runs from the No. 8 hole in 1979. After he hit .222 in 1981, the Mets grew tired of carrying his pitiful lumber. Norman's Met career lasted for nine homers and 282 at-bats from 1977 through 1980.

Seaver, headed for 311 wins and Cooperstown, closed out a 21-win 1977 season with a 14-3 mark and 2.34 ERA after the deal and then went 61-43 over the next five seasons with three ERAs under 3.14 as a role model for a young Cincinnati staff. He also pitched that elusive first no-hitter, in 1978.

Like Rusty, he was brought back to Flushing, prior to 1983. Like Rusty, he was past his peak and went 9-14. Then, the Mets lost him again, when they figured Seaver was too old to be picked if they left him unprotected in a compensation draft. They tried to give him a final chance at a comeback in 1987, but Seaver decided to call it quits. He should never have worn any other uniform.

10. Sent OF Carl Everett to the Houston Astros for P John Hudek, Dec. 22, 1997

The Mets called it a baseball deal, but that is what teams always say when they get rid of headaches. Dealing Carl Everett is never a baseball decision. The Mets decided they had had enough after Everett's mid-1997 run-in with the authorities regarding abuses in the care of his daughter. The ensuing court struggle determining whether the Everetts would maintain custody had especially ugly potential ramifications for the Mets, because it was the interventionary actions of concerned parties in the players' family lounge at Shea that led to the inquiry.

Everett was clearly on the verge of his long-awaited breakthrough season as the Mets' center fielder in '97, with 14 homers and 57 RBI. After a .296, 15-homer, 76-RBI year for the Astros in 1998, Carl exploded into a superstar: .325 with 25 homers and 108 RBI in just 123 games in 1999. By the time Everett posted 34 homers and 108 RBI for the Red Sox in 2000, it was what was expected of him. So were his tangles with umpires, manager and teammates. Everett is high maintenance.

John Hudek, meanwhile, was no problem at all—not to the Mets nor to the hitters who faced the former closer, coming off a 1997 season that had seen him go 1-3, 5.98 for Houston. In 1998, the right-hander was 1-4 with a 4.00 ERA for the Mets,, who wasted no time reaching for the ejector-seat button on their console.

11. Sent 1B Rico Brogna to the Philadelphia Phillies for P Toby Borland and P Ricardo Jordan, Nov. 27, 1996

The Mets made this deal because they feared that Rico Brogna's back, which was in a degenerative condition that limited him to 55 games in 1996, made him risky business as their first baseman of the future. The Phillies figured for the precious little they were risking that it was worth rolling the dice. The Phillies haven't had the greatest wisdom or fortune with gambles, but this one paid off big. The smooth lefty-hitting, slick-fielding Brogna was healthy enough to rip 20-plus homers in three straight seasons for the Phils (with a career high of 24 in 1999) and drove in 81, 104 and 102 runs respectively from 1997 through 1999.

Brogna, a wonderful line-drive hitter, had been stolen by the Mets from the Tigers before Detroit gave him a full chance and he had hit .351 with 20 RBI in 131 at-bats in 1994, when he arrived in New York. Even allowing that Brogna's effectiveness against lefty pitching was always questionable, the "price" exacted in the Mets' exile of Rico to make room for John Olerud made the trade a clear case of turning something into nothing.

Toby Borland somehow had gone 7-3 for the Phillies in 1996. But, in 1997 as a Met, the scarecrow-thin right-hander looked scared and seemed like he needed a map to find the plate from the rubber, lasting just 13⅓ innings during which he gave up nine runs, 11 hits and 14 walks and unleashed three wild pitches for a 6.08 ERA. Lefty Ricardo Jordan was every bit as big of an asset as Borland, going 1-2 with a 5.33 ERA for the Mets in 1997, surrendering 31 hits and walking 15 and hitting two batters in 27 innings.

That was all the Mets would ever have to show for Rico Brogna.

12. Sent OF Jeromy Burnitz and P Joe Roa to the Cleveland Indians for P Paul Byrd, P Dave Mlicki, P Jerry DiPoto and 2B Jesus Azuaje, Nov. 18, 1994

Jeromy Burnitz' immaturity earned him a spot in Dallas Green's doghouse and the Met organization was too willing to give up on this powerful former first-round draft choice for a package of pitching mediocrities from the Indians. Yes, Burnitz had only 16 homers and 53 RBI and 111 strikeouts in 406 total at-bats as a Met in 1993 and 1994. And it is true that the strong-armed right fielder didn't grow up and blossom until much later, for Milwaukee, in 1997.

However, in the five seasons from 1997 through 2001, Burnitz has hit 163 homers and drove in 511 runs—including a 38-homer, 125-RBI season in 1998. Jeromy was that rare talent for whom it would have been well worth waiting—and the deals in which the Indians sent away Burnitz and Jeff Kent probably belong on that team's 15 worst list, too.

The pitchers ate up innings for the Mets, but none developed into a force. Dave Mlicki blanked the Yanks in the first regular-season game between the teams, but was maddeningly inconsistent. Mlicki's curve was always more impressive than his record (24-30 as a Met from 1995 through 1998)—so something was missing, other than another vowel from his last name.

Jerry DiPoto was 4-6, 3.78 in 1995 and 7-2, 4.19 in 1996 with a total of two saves as a forgettable setup man for the Mets. Then he stepped into a closer's role for Colorado in 1997 and 1998. Paul Byrd went 3-2 for the Mets in 1995 and 1996, but threw only 68⅔ innings for them and didn't come into his own until winning 15 for the Phillies in 1999.

13. Sent P Jason Isringhausen and P Greg McMichael to the Oakland Athletics for P Billy Taylor, July 31, 1999

They were too quick to give up on Amos Otis and Nolan Ryan and Jeromy Burnitz, but the Mets waited forever for Jason Isringhausen. He was one of the organization's ill-fated "big three" pitching prospects, along with Bill Pulsipher and Paul Wilson. Izzy's 9-2, 2.81 debut half-season as a Met in 1995, not to mention his high-velocity fastball and tantalizing knuckle curve, kept the Mets hanging on to him and waiting for more. They held onto him through arm surgery. Through control problems. Through an erosion of confidence. Through tuberculosis.

Finally, embroiled in a race in 1999, the Mets gave Isringhausen a shot at a relief job, then decided they could afford to wait no longer after he went 1-3 with a 6.41 ERA in 39⅓ innings. They sent him and the ubiquitous, lollipop-dispensing Greg McMichael to Oakland.

Considering that the Athletics were in a race of their own when the Mets got Billy Taylor (99 saves from 1996 through 1999), the deal seemed strange. Why would Oakland be willing to spare its closer for a 26-year-old who, despite his overpowering arsenal, had never done that job and would be getting on-the-job training? The Mets found out in a heartbeat and a hail of line drives. Taylor, almost 38, was abruptly finished. He posted an 8.10 ERA in 13⅓ useless innings for the Mets down the stretch.

Meanwhile, predictably, Isringhausen saved eight games and posted a 2.13 ERA for the Athletics in 1999. Then he helped carry them to the playoffs in 2000, going 6-4, 3.78 with 33 saves and 67 strikeouts in 69 innings. Last year, he went 4-3, 2.65 with 34 saves and 74 strikeouts in 71⅓ innings.

14. Sent OF-1B Dave Kingman to the San Diego Padres for INF-OF Bobby Valentine and P Paul Siebert, June 15, 1977

Slugger Dave Kingman, entangled in a nasty contract struggle with the Mets and determined to explore his freedom, was dumped almost without anyone noticing, because Kong was sent packing to the Padres as part of the same midnight massacre that enraged Met fans and made Tom Seaver a Cincinnati Red.

Kingman had hit 36 homers in 1975 and 37 in 1976, despite having no lineup protection on Met teams that lacked punch. He had nine homers at the trade deadline in 1977 and made only an 11-homer, 56-game pit stop in San Diego before being moved to the Angels and then the Yankees in his lame-duck contractual year.

Kingman hit 48 homers and drove in 115 runs for the Cubs in 1979 before returning to the Mets to hit another 72 long balls for them from 1981 through 1983. Kong unloaded 154 of his 442 career blasts wearing a Met uniform—more than he hit for any other team. Of course, he will be spared the decision of which cap to wear to Cooperstown by the personal charm he never displayed in alienating the voting writers and, of course, his lack of aptitude for any part of the game outside of breathtaking parabolas.

Bobby Valentine, whose career was broken as badly as his leg during that collision with a wall as an Angel, hit .133 for the Mets in 1977. All his .269 mark in 1978 did was earn him a release the following spring. Lefty Paul Siebert was 2-1, 3.86 for the Mets in 1977, but only 0-2, 5.14 the following year, the last he spent in the majors.

15. Sent P Tug McGraw, OF Don Hahn and OF Dave Schneck to the Philadelphia Phillies for OF Del Unser, C John Stearns and P Mac Scarce, Dec. 3, 1974

Tug McGraw became a swaggering, wise-cracking, thigh-slapping, fun-loving symbol of the Met franchise when he wrote his own remarkable comeback story and took Yogi Berra's team along for a pennant-winning ride in 1973. The ebullient left-hander posted back-to-back

1.70 ERAs in 1971 and 1972 and had 86 saves as a Met from 1965 through 1974. But, after a disastrous 1974 season during which he went 6-11 with three saves and a 4.16 ERA, McGraw was toast in New York.

"I had this growth on my back. I think they thought I had cancer," said McGraw. "They got rid of me before I died."

The 30-year-old revived his career in Philadelphia, lasting for 10 seasons there, posting three straight sub-3.00 ERAs, 23 wins and 34 saves from 1975 through 1978 and going 5-4, 1.46 with 20 saves for the 1980 Phillies world champions. The screwball was a remarkable pitch for Tug when he had command of it and a fairly good description of his demeanor.

The Mets' return for McGraw wasn't awful, but neither was it close to an even exchange of value.

Center fielder Del Unser had a wonderful .294 season for the Mets in 1975, but batted only .228 for them the following year, which he finished in Montreal. Catching prospect John Stearns emerged as a gritty one-man island of competitiveness in a sea of Met contemporaries who accepted losing like they did another sunrise. Dude, who played baseball like he was still a linebacker at Colorado, was a Met stalwart from 1975 through 1984, but never exceeded 15 homers or 73 RBI in a season. Lefty specialist Mac Scarce, with a name that described his impact, gave up a hit to the only batter he faced as a Met, in 1975. He was gone before it could be determined exactly what his specialty was.

You Can Look It Up

To Marv Throneberry on Marv's birthday: "We was going to get you a birthday cake, but we figured you would drop it."

"Come out and see my Amazin' Mets. I been in the game for a hundred years, but I see new ways to lose I never knew existed before."

"I got one [catcher] that can throw, but can't catch, one that can catch, but can't throw and one who can hit, but can't do either."

On the Mets' choice of Hobie Landrith first in the expansion draft: "If you don't have a catcher, you are gonna have a lot of passed balls."

To the Mets' beat writers after an endless horror show plane trip to Houston in 1962: "If any of the Houston reporters want to see me, tell them that I am being embalmed."

Casey Stengel suffered through 120 losses in the inaugural season, but the Ol' Perfesser was never at a loss for words. In fact, he invented a language—Stengelese.

On John Glenn becoming the first American to orbit the Earth: "He is just what we need—somebody in position to catch a flyball."

"I got this broken arm from watching my team. We are improving magnificently. All they gave me last year was a head cold."

To Ken McKenzie, who once referred to himself as the lowest-paid alumnus in the Yale Class of 1956, when Stengel brought him into a bases-loaded, none-out jam with Willie McCovey, Willie Mays and Orlando Cepeda coming to bat: "Pretend they're the Harvards."

On Lyndon Baines Johnson crossing paths with the Mets in Pittsburgh during his 1964 trip to Appalachia as part of his War on Poverty: "He wanted to see poverty so he came to see my team."

On the Mets releasing the colorful Jimmy Piersall, a .194 hitter: "There is only room for one clown on this team."

"It ain't sex that is troublesome, it's staying up all night looking for it."

"It's great to be back in the Polar Grounds. It's a great honor for me to be joining the Knickerbockers."

"I don't like them fellas who drive in two runs and let in three."

During a spring training drill: "Everyone line up alphabetically, according to your height."

"The secret of managing a club is to keep the five guys who hate you from the five who are undecided."

"It's like I used to tell my barber. Shave and a haircut. But don't cut my throat. I may want to do that myself."

On Ed Kranepool: "He is only 19 and he runs like he is 30, but who else do I have?"

"We are a fraud."

On the Polo Grounds: "Just when my fellows learn to hit in this ballpark, they're gonna tear it down."

After Ron Swoboda's dugout tantrum: "If everybody on this team commenced breaking up the furniture every time we did bad, there'd be no place to sit."

THE EARLY DAYS

"Everybody knows Casey [Stengel] has forgotten more baseball than I will ever know. That's the trouble: he's forgotten it."

—Jimmy Piersall

Warren Spahn, who played for Casey Stengel's Boston Braves in the 40s and then briefly for Casey with the Mets in 1965: "I'm probably the only guy who played for Stengel before and after he was a genius."

"Baseball is a lot like life. The line drives are caught, the squibblers go for base hits. It's an unfair game."   —Rod Kanehl

Charlie Neal after betting teammate Choo Choo Coleman, who called everyone "Bub," that he didn't know Neal's name: "Choo Choo said, 'Sure, I do. You are number four.'"

Unidentified Original Met on noon doubleheader in San Francisco, a town that stays up late: "Noon? I won't be done throwing up by then."

"If I have to be a bench warmer for the Mets, I'll commit suicide."
        —Richie Ashburn upon his retirement after 1962 season

"Most Valuable Player on the worst team ever? Just how did they mean that?"   —Richie Ashburn on being the best of the 1962 Mets

"Hey, Marv [Throneberry], tell them [the reporters] how you are going to throw a party for your fans . . . in a phone booth."
        —Richie Ashburn

"The Mets are a very good thing. They give everybody a job, just like the WPA."   —Billy Loes

"I have a son, and I make him watch the Mets. I want him to know life. It's a history lesson. He'll understand the Depression when they teach it to him in school."   —Toots Shor, restaurant owner, 1962

"People are always saying that one-eighth of an inch is the difference between winning and losing baseball. With the Mets, it's three inches."   —Murray Kempton, *Sport Magazine,* 1962

"The Mets lost an awful lot of games by one run, which is the mark of a bad team. They also lost innumerable games by 14 runs or so. This is the mark of a terrible team."   —Jimmy Breslin

"Having Marv Throneberry play for your team is like having Willie Sutton work for your bank."   —Jimmy Breslin

"Some day I will write a book and call it *How I Got the Nickname Pumpsie* and sell it for one dollar. And if everyone who has ever asked me that question buys the book, I will be a millionaire."
     —Pumpsie Green

Ed Kranepool after that nine-hour, 52-minute Memorial Day 1964 doubleheader vs. Giants, featuring a 23-inning second game that ended at 11:23 p.m.: "I wish it had gone longer. I always wanted to play in a game that started in May and ended in June."

Ron Taylor on the deal that saw Harry Chiti go from Cleveland to the Mets for a player to be named later and back a month later as that player: "I always wondered who got the better of that deal."

"Some people give their bodies to science. I give mine to baseball."
     —Ron Hunt, career record holder for HBPs with 243

Tracy Stallard on the Mets getting six runs in the ninth to take a 19-1 lead over the Cubs at Wrigley, May 26, 1964: "That is when I knew we had them."

Art Shamsky on being Jewish and a Met in 1968: "I told the Mets when I joined them I couldn't play in the World Series on the day of the Yom Kippur game. That always got a big laugh."

BARELY MANAGING

"Well, that was a cliff-dweller."
                    —Manager Wes Westrum after one closer-than-usual loss

"There are only two types of managers: winning managers and ex-managers. I like to work."   —Manager Gil Hodges

"Neil, don't you know, young man, that I've had a bypass? You have to take it easy on me."
                    —Manager George Bamberger to reliever Neil Allen

"Some of the younger guys have me eating the (antacid) tablets and the wrapper."   —Manager Davey Johnson

"I'm not sure I'd rather be managing or testing bulletproof vests."
                    —Manager Joe Torre

"It ain't over till it's over."
                    —Manager Yogi Berra, at nine games back in July 1973

Yogi Berra was often misunderstood and probably said only a small fraction of the memorable malaprops attributed to him, but the man who played for and managed both the Yankees and the Mets was nobody's fool when it came to baseball.

THE MIRACLES

"We are here to prove there is no Santa Claus."
> —Brooks Robinson before the 1969 World Series

"I remember the Mets. When I was with the Dodgers, I remember they never used to hit a cutoff man."
> —Pete Richert before 1969 World Series

"Some people still might not believe in us . . . but then some people think the world is flat."   —Cleon Jones after the 1969 World Series

"There is nothing miraculous about us."

—Gil Hodges on 1969 Mets

Tug McGraw on Donn Clendenon: "He was our pressure exorcist. He scared the demons right out of the clubhouse."

"By 1969, they had earned the right to call themselves fans . . . In 1965, I mean, they should have put a disclaimer on the ticket saying that any resemblance to major league baseball was purely coinciden- tal. But they came."   —Jerry Grote on Mets' fans

Cardinals' Mike Shannon on Jerry Koosman: "When I first saw him, I wanted to throw up."

Unidentified Met after Art Shamsky "ran" through a stop sign and was thrown out at the plate: "It's all right to carry that piano on your back, but don't stop to play it."

Cleon Jones on his football skills at Mobile Training High in Mobile, Ala.: "When I was playing, I could throw a football sixty yards in the air and then run down field and catch it."

"Fifteen minutes after the [1969] Mets had clinched their champi- onship, their followers had torn up the Shea Stadium surface . . . And being true Mets fans, with their roots in 1962, they missed first base."   —Leonard Koppett

"I enjoy Shea Stadium. But the fans there are something else. I look at each game there as an experience. I get to go to a zoo and I don't have to pay an admission."

—Pete Rose after his 1973 NLCS fight with Bud Harrelson

THE TUGGER

"I was like a carpenter with a whole new set of tools. It's like you have all these power tools with no electricity. Well, the screwball provided me the electricity."   —Tug McGraw

"Ninety percent of my World Series share I'll spend on whiskey and women and other good times. The other 10 percent I will probably waste."   —Tug McGraw

Tug McGraw on back-to-back series sweeps of the Giants and Dodgers in 1969: "From the fans' standpoint, the idea was to take this little baby of a team, feed it, stroke it, change its diapers and forgive it when it messed up. And some day this baby was going to grow up and when those Dodger bullies and those Giant bullies came to town, it was going to kick their ass so high they would have to shit through their ribs."

Tug McGraw on the difference between grass and artificial turf: "I don't know. I never smoked Astroturf."

"Tug McGraw has about 48 cards in his deck."   —Tom Seaver

MR. HODGES' NEIGHBORHOOD

Tug McGraw on Gil Hodges: "I loved him more than any man I have ever loved in my life. He understood me, he helped me, he guided me. I was a kid when he came to the Mets. He made me a man."

Ron Swoboda on Gil Hodges, when his judgment was questioned: "I could see his muscles tighten. He didn't say another word. The next thing I knew I was standing against the urinal and I couldn't pee. When Gil wanted to intimidate somebody, he could make all your body come to a stop."

"He managed like the Marine he was. He understood that was the best way for him. He was the platoon leader. We were the privates. This is the way we do it. Nobody argued with him."   —Tom Seaver

Ed Kranepool on Gil Hodges giving him only 47 at-bats: "He has about as much confidence in me as I have in him."

TOM TERRIFIC

"There was an aura of defeatism and I refused to accept it. Maybe some of the others started to feel like I felt because I noticed the team started to play better behind me than it did for any other pitcher."
—Tom Seaver

"Only three or four outs directly affect the outcome of any given game . . . You can train yourself to identify the outs you must get and . . . and to go about getting them. You must be like a prize-fighter going after his opponent. Once you have him cornered or hurt, you must keep the pressure on. Make the batter go after the pitch you throw, not wait for the pitch he wants."
—Tom Seaver, in *The Art of Pitching*

Tom Seaver on the World Series: "It's like the Fourth of July, New Year's Eve and your birthday all wrapped up into one."

"There are only two places in the league. First place and no place."
—Tom Seaver

Don Sutton when asked what he would do with his new $114,000 contract in 1973: "Invest in Seaver."

"Hey, son, would you get me a beer."
                        —Lou Brock, mistaking Tom Seaver in street clothes
                        for a batboy hours before the 1967 All-Star Game.

"He's always trying to throw the perfect pitch."
                        —Danny Frisella on Tom Seaver

Merv Rettenmund, when asked if he would rather face Jim Palmer or Tom Seaver: "That is like asking if I would rather be hung or go to the electric chair."

"Blind people come to the park just to listen to him pitch."
                        —Reggie Jackson on Tom Seaver

SAY HEY, WILLIE

Willie Mays in response to TV show director's question about how he planned to play himself: "I don't know. Just turn the cameras on and if it ain't me, let me know."

"I look at the kids over there and the way they are playing and the way they're fighting for themselves and that says one thing to me: 'Willie, say goodbye to America.'"
                        —Willie Mays announcing his impending retirement at Shea

"I can't very well tell my batters, 'Don't hit it to him.' Wherever they hit it, he's there anyway."   —Gil Hodges on Willie Mays

"I'm not sure what charisma is, but I get the feeling it's Willie Mays."
                        —Ted Kluszewski

THE ONE AND ONLY ROCKY

"When you strike out five times [in a doubleheader], they should line up alongside the road and boo you all the way home. If we had lost, I would be eating my heart out. But since we won [once], I'll only eat one ventricle."

—Ron Swoboda

Ron Swoboda on the long-in-the-tooth Windsor Hotel in Montreal, which was frequented by the Mets because it was an M. Donald Grant favorite: "You know what the valet just brought to my room? Babe Ruth's suits."

"Why am I wasting so much dedication on a mediocre career?"

—Ron Swoboda

Casey Stengel on a young Ron Swoboda's outfield skills in right: "He's a little weak on balls in the air. He leaps after them when they ain't there."

Yogi Berra to Ron Swoboda, who was attempting to emulate Frank Robinson's crowd-the-plate stance: "If you can't imitate him, don't copy him."

THE BLEAK YEARS

"Bill Buckner had a 19-game hitting streak going and always wore the same underwear. Of course, he didn't have any friends."

—Lenny Randle

George Foster responding to ex-teammate Pete Rose's remark that he only got his uniform dirty once per three weeks: "I'll slide when I have to. But I'm going to be trotting a lot more than he will."

George Theodore on his winter profession: "Philosopher" and his marital status: "Agnostic"

"Dave Kingman has the personality of a tree trunk."   —John Stearns

Tim Burke on whether his religious beliefs affected his attitude on the diamond: "If Jesus was on the field, he would be pitching inside and breaking up double plays."

"It's gotten to the point now where I am scared to pitch."
                                                    —Neil Allen in 1983

"The only thing running and exercising can do for you is make you healthy."   —Mickey Lolich

"I'm like an old tin can in an alley. Anyone who walks by can't resist kicking it." —M. Donald Grant, former Mets Chairman of the Board

"The Mets always said I couldn't win the big games. I'd like to know the last time the Mets had a big game."
                        —Pete Falcone after being traded to the Braves

THE MODERN ERA

"Sometimes, I like a good crash. You know, bodies flying around when you come into a bag."   —Lenny Dykstra

"Superstitious people don't discuss their superstitions."
                                                         —Rusty Staub

"If he was throwing the ball any better, we'd have to start a new league for him."   —Umpire John Kibler on Dwight Gooden
                                                                    during his 1984 rookie season

"The DH is a 10th player. Softball is 10 players. Baseball is nine."
                                                                    —Dwight Gooden

"Todd Hundley walked intensely his last time up."
                                —Mets' malaproprietor and broadcaster Ralph Kiner

"I used to love the way we treated other teams. We didn't care at all what they thought of us. We liked it more if they hated us. We'd sit in the dugout and just curse them . . . We were a little crazy. If we lost four straight, we wanted to fight. Now we're gentlemen. It takes the fun out of it."   —Darryl Strawberry in 1990

Bibliography

Allen, Maury, *After the Miracle: The Amazin' Mets Twenty Years Later.* Franklin Watts, 1989.

Angell, Roger, *Once More Around the Park: A Baseball Reader.* Ballantine, 1991.

Bock, Duncan and Jordan, John, *The Complete Year-by-Year N.Y. Mets' Fans Almanac.* Crown, 1992.

Breslin, Jimmy, *Can't Anybody Here Play This Game?: The Improbable Saga of the New York Mets' First Year.* Viking, 1963.

Carter, Gary and Hough Jr., John, *A Dream Season.* Harcourt Brace Jovanovich, 1987.

Cohen, Stanley, *A Magic Summer: The '69 Mets.* Harcourt Brace Jovanovich, 1988.

D'Agostino, Dennis, *This Date in New York History: 20 Amazin' Years . . . From Marvelous Marv to Lee Mazzilli.* A Scarborough Book, Stein and Day, 1981.

Durso, Joe. *Amazing: The Miracle of the Mets.* Houghton Mifflin, 1970.

Dykstra, Lenny with Noble, Marty, *Nails: The Inside Story of an Amazing Season.* Doubleday and Co., 1987.

Fox, Larry, *Last to First: The Story of the Mets.* Harper and Row, 1970.

Hernandez, Keith and Bryan, Mike, *If At First . . . A Season with the Mets*. McGraw-Hill, 1986.

Honig, Donald, *The New York Mets: The First Quarter-Century*. Crown, 1987.

Jacobson, Steve, *The Pitching Staff: A Classic Portrait of Baseball's Most Unique Fraternity*. Thomas Y. Crowell, 1975

Koppett, Leonard, *The New York Mets: The Whole Story*. The Macmillan Company, 1970.

McGraw, Tug and Durso, Joe, *Screwball*. Houghton Mifflin Co, 1974.

Nelson, Kevin, ed., *Baseball's Greatest Quotes: The Wit, Wisdom and Wisecracks of America's National Pastime*. Fireside, 1982.

Rubin, Lewis D., ed., *The Quotable Baseball Fanatic*. Lyons, 2000.

Vecsey, George, *Joy in Mudville: Being A Complete Account of the Unparalled History of the New York Mets from Their Most Perturbed Beginnings to Their Amazing Rise to Glory and Renown*. McCall, 1970.

Wallace, Joseph, *The Autobiography of Baseball: The Inside Story from the Stars Who Played the Game*. Harry N. Abrams, 1998.

Zimmerman, Paul and Schaap, Dick. *The Year the Mets Lost Last Place: The Most Amazing Year in the History of Baseball*. Signet, 1969.